Studies in Cognitive Corpus Linguistics

ŁÓDŹ
STUDIES IN LANGUAGE

Edited by
Barbara Lewandowska-Tomaszczyk

Vol. 18

PETER LANG
Frankfurt am Main · Berlin · Bern · Bruxelles · New York · Oxford · Wien

Barbara Lewandowska-Tomaszczyk
Katarzyna Dziwirek
(eds.)

Studies in Cognitive Corpus Linguistics

PETER LANG
Internationaler Verlag der Wissenschaften

Bibliographic Information published by the Deutsche Nationalbibliothek
The Deutsche Nationalbibliothek lists this publication in the Deutsche Nationalbibliografie; detailed bibliographic data is available in the internet at <http://www.d-nb.de>.

ISSN 1437-5281
ISBN 978-3-631-59399-8

www.peterlang.de

TABLE OF CONTENTS

EMERGENCE OF COGNITIVE CORPUS LINGUISTICS

The last few years have been an interesting period in language studies. The rapid development of a cognitive perspective in different forms has been proceeding parallel to new advances in computer science and computational linguistics. The former emphasises the status of meaning in linguistic theory and description. The latter is instrumental in the identification of meaning structures, their context, and their quantitative characteristics in language. Corpus linguistics with concordancing programs as well as new tools offers a possibility of systematically accessing larger context. This is essential for numerous applications of corpus data. A good translation professional must, obviously, be familiar with conventional uses, but, at the same time, s/he also has to be aware of probabilities of other, less frequent, options. Corpus data, provided the corpus is sufficiently large, can provide both. Moreover, the information on the frequencies of such items, keywords, collocations and clusters, available in most software now, as well as access to multimodal corpora with the spoken and visual modes can help a translator and a foreign language teacher in selecting a target language equivalent of similar currency or visualising a problem area in a second language.

On the other hand, corpus data cannot be properly interpreted without accessing a language researcher's intuitive judgments about language. This is where the cognitive linguistic paradigm is of assistance. A cognitive semantic inquiry can benefit considerably from looking at a broad range of authentic linguistic material contained in language corpora. Examples of interesting areas at this interface are *semantic prosody* (cf. Sinclair 1992), *polysemy* (cf. Lewandowska-Tomaszczyk 2007), or an analysis of register-diversified corpora Biber (1993) with differences across different registers in the *frequency of use* of similar lexical items.

The present volume presents studies on a range of issues concerning cognitive approaches to language in a broad sense on the one hand and language corpora and corpus tools on the other. The topics presented are thus of both theoretical and applicational relevance and many contributions are of an interdisciplinary character. This, we believe, can stimulate an exchange of thoughts, ideas, and methodology between linguists, particularly cognitive linguists, and computer and corpus researchers. The topics of the papers include prototypical meanings, image-schematic representations, identification of categories in corpus data, polysemy and corpus methodology, figurative meanings (analysis and acquisition), and emotion concepts. The studies utilize traditional and multimodal corpus data, focus on context and the semantics-pragmatics interface, and offer synchronic and diachronic perspectives.

The volume includes eighteen papers presented in five parts. Part 1 on *Theory and Tools* contains three papers. Piotr Pezik proposes a methodology for extracting highly idiomatic multiword nominal collocations from samples of American political discourse by introducing a quantitative approach to find similarities and differences between the discourses of American communists and Republicans. Galina I. Kustova, Olga N. Lashevskaja, Elena V. Paducheva and Ekaterina V. Rakhilina present a verb taxonomy as drawn from the Russian National Corpus. The authors look at the combination of semantic and morphological tagging, which makes it possible to answer multiple queries. These concern not only separate words and word forms but also semantically characterized classes of words, as well as constructions with components presented as morphologically and/or semantically described classes. Karen Sullivan uses a corpus of metaphoric sentences to assess a claim put forward by William Croft (2003), that conceptually dependent elements in metaphoric constructions tend to involve metaphorically used words, while autonomous elements typically include non-metaphoric words.

Part 2 of the volume includes two papers dealing with *Multimodal Corpora*. Hanna Pułaczewska analyses the phenomenon of syntactic reduplication in the spoken language based on the results of a contrastive corpus study of directives in Polish, English and German. The paper shows cross-linguistic differences in the application of reduplication as well as the implementation of the universal iconic principles in the? individual languages. Monika Kopytowska presents a corpus study of television? news with reference to the mechanism of framing to maximize the validity of a cognitive approach and corpus methodology in the domain of news discourse. The study combines quantitative and qualitative methods in this new approach to the mechanism of framing.

Part 3 *Monolingual Studies* contains seven contributions, presenting corpus-based cognitive analyses of materials drawn from one language. This part begins with a theoretical analysis presented by Kamila Turewicz, who addresses issues that emerge at the interface of corpus findings and theoretical positions of Jennifer Coates's work on the semantics of English modals. Turewicz identifies correspondences between Coates's findings and relevant aspects of Ronald Langacker's Cognitive Grammar (1987, 1991). Eliza Kitis concentrates on emotion predicates, particularly, *fear* psych-verbs and traces back their original meanings to the domain of action (motion). The author shows how the predicates developed into syntactic constructions expressing a variety of other cognitive functions and particular speech acts. Agnieszka Kaleta looks at English aspectual verbs and their complements – gerunds and infinitives in particular – especially with reference to the verb *begin*, and considers Langacker's (1987, 2002) distinction between *perfective* and *imperfective processes* and the notion of conceptual *boundedness* vis a vis data drawn from the British National Corpus. Lily I-wen Su and Louis Wei-lun Lu compare a corpus-based approach and a traditional introspection-based approach to distinguish synonyms, or what the authors call analogous words exemplified by the English words *worry* and *bother*. Using the Sketch Engine the authors examine statistics underlying the lexical properties and syntactic behaviour of the analysed words. The results show how introspection complements a corpus-based methodology, predominantly as a starting point of linguistic research. Giuliana Fiorentino uses corpus data of written and spoken Italian in her paper, where she argues in favour of a different ordering distribution of adverbial and main clauses with reference to cognitive restrictions on written and spoken Italian. Jerzy Gaszewski analyses a polysemy of the Polish response particles: *tak* 'yes' and *nie* 'no' in terms of radial categories and radial networks of meaning. The analyzed material is retrieved from the spoken-conversational section of the PELCRA Reference Corpus of Polish (University of Lodz). Martine Delorge takes up a diachronic perspective on the constructional behaviour of verbs of reception in Dutch. She focuses on the constructional evolution of four verbs of reception drawing her materials from a diachronic corpus of Dutch.

Part 4, *Cognitive Contrastive Studies* includes two papers. The first contribution, by Dagmar Divjak and Stefan Th. Gries is a corpus-based contrastive study of phasal verbs in English and Russian and in particular, five verbs that express 'begin' in both languages, i.e. *begin*, *start*, *načinat'/načat'*. *načinat'sja/načat'sja* and *stat'*. The authors conduct a quantitative analysis of data extracted from the ICE-GB and the Uppsala Corpus and identify the set of characteristics and the prototype for each The authors present *The Behavioral Profiling* approach they developed. Katarzyna Dziwirek and Barbara Lewandowska-Tomaszczyk analyse transitive verbs in the LIKE/LOVE and DISLIKE/HATE fields in Polish and English and identify similar referent *prototypes*, even though frequencies of their occurrence in corpus data and categorization patterns are different.

Part 5 *Applications and Implications* includes studies which present applications of Cognitive Corpus Linguistics in translation and foreign language teaching. Mikołaj Deckert investigates redundancy in language and pays particular attention to the phenomenon of *pleonasm*. The author uses the Relevance approach (Sperber and Wilson 1986) argues for *processing effort-contextual/cognitive effects* dichotomy in his corpus data. Hu Ying-Huseh and Ho Yi-Chen investigate implications of polysemy networks in teaching English as a foreign language, particularly with reference to a system of spatial prepositions. The authors present results of a statistical analysis which demonstrates positive effects of the introduction of cognitive-based semantic networks in foreign language teaching. Anna Turula focuses on implicit learning of foreign language grammar using a technique of an extensive study of a film corpus with the aim to reduce differences between native and non-native use of language by learners at the advanced proficency level. The author proposes an *organic approach deductivised.* The paper by Irena Czwenar, who analyses spoken language of adult learners of English concludes the volume. The author relates her findings of the longitudinal study of oral proficiency to the assumptions of the usage-based approach to language acquisition.

The editors of the volume wish to acknowledge a support of two EU projects, FP6 *IntUne* project and COST A31 *Classifiers* project, as well as the corresponding support of the Polish Ministry of Education, granted to the Department of English Language and Applied Linguistics of the University of Łodź. The projects and the financial support made it possible for the first of the editors to implement the idea of a Cognitive Corpus Linguistics in the format of the present volume, and for both the editors, to identify its scope and overall methodology of the field of Cognitive Corpus Linguistics.

We hope that the present volume, as a contribution to language studies introducing a new sub-field, can reach a wide linguistic community and stimulate an interesting debate as well as serve as an incentive to start new cognitive corpus linguistic projects.

Barbara Lewandowska-Tomaszczyk
Lodz University

Katarzyna Dziwirek
University of Washington

REFERENCES

Biber, D. (2003). "Variation among university spoken and written registers: A new multi-dimensional analysis". In: Ch. Meyer & P. Leistyna (eds.). *Corpus Analysis: Language Structure and Language Use.* Amsterdam: Rodopi: 47–70.

Croft, W. (2003). "The role of domains in the interpretation of metaphors and metonymies". In: R. Dirven & R. Pörings (eds.). *Metaphor and Metonymy in Comparison and Contrast.* Berlin/New York: Mouton de Gruyter: 161–206.

Lakoff, G. (1987). Women, Fire, and Dangerous Things: What *Categories Reveal about the Mind.* Chicago: Chicago University Press.

Langacker, R. W. (1987/1991). *Foundations of Cognitive Grammar.* Vols. 1 and 2. Stanford.

Langacker, R. W. (1988). "A usage-based model". In: B. Rudzka-Ostyn (ed.). *Topics Cognitive Linguistics.* Amsterdam: Benjamins: 127–161.

Lewandowska-Tomaszczyk, B. (2007). "Polysemy, prototypes, and radial categories". *Oxford Handbook of Cognitive Linguistics.* Oxford: Oxford University Press: 139–169.

Sinclair, J. M. (1992). "Trust the Text". In: M. Davies & L. Ravelli (eds.). *Advances in Systemic Linguistics: Recent Theory and Practice.* London: Pinter: 5–19.

Part One

THEORY AND TOOLS

Piotr Pęzik

University of Łódź

EXTRACTION OF MULTIWORD EXPRESSIONS FOR CORPUS-BASED DISCOURSE ANALYSIS

Abstract: In recent years, a number of corpus techniques have been applied to the study of different registers of discourse (Baker 2006), including political discourse (Partington and Morley 2004). Although corpus techniques are generally effective in explicating the lexico-semantic level of discourse, some of them leave much to be desired. As an example, corpus linguists often attempt to extract the key lexical features of a corpus by generating lists of frequent keywords, which may lead to the simplex word fallacy.

In this paper I first address this problem by introducing a quantitative approach to extracting highly idiomatic nominal collocations from samples of American political discourse. In the course of this analysis it becomes clear that key terms of discourse often reflect the predominant ideology represented by a given corpus. In particular, I demonstrate how a term identification procedure may reveal the encoding of ideology-specific metaphors in the collocations of *free* and *freedom* found in the discourses of American communists and Republicans respectively.

Keywords: corpus-driven discourse analysis, metaphors of freedom, political discourse, term extraction.

In recent years, a number of corpus techniques have been applied to the study of different registers of discourse (Baker 2006), including political discourse (Partington and Morley 2004). Although corpus methodologies are generally effective in explicating the lexico-semantic level of discourse, some of the commonly used high-throughput techniques leave much to be desired. For example, corpus linguists often attempt to extract the key lexical features of a corpus by generating lists of frequent keywords. In many cases this may lead to the simplex word fallacy, which can be defined as the decomposition of highly lexicalized collocations into constituent words. Since multiword expressions (MWEs) constitute a huge portion of the lexicon (Sag 2002), the decomposition of their meaning into simplex words calls into question the usefulness of frequency and keyness lists.

In this study I describe the results of using a quantitative approach to extracting highly idiomatic nominal collocations from samples of American political discourse. In the process of extracting key terms from political discourse, it becomes clear how they reflect the predominant ideology represented in a given corpus by conveying discourse-specific concepts. Thus, the MWE identification procedure used in this study is not only necessary to avoid the simplex word fallacy, but it also reveals the formation of ideology-specific metaphors in some collocations.

In the first part of the present study I consider both the unique theoretical advantages and limitations of using quantitative approaches to analyze discoursal phenomena. The second section of the chapter outlines the main corpus techniques currently used for discourse analysis. Next, I briefly characterize the two corpora used in this study, which were compiled to represent American political discourse. Finally, using a quantitative approach to extract multiword nominal expressions from the two corpora, I demonstrate that many MWEs found in distinct registers of political discourse convey ideologically charged metaphorical meanings.

1. Quantitative approaches to studying discourse

Hardt-Mautner (1995) examines the analytical procedures of Discourse Analysis and Critical Discourse Analysis – a framework expounded by authors such as Fairclough (1989), van Dijk (1997) and Wodak (1990), and compares them with the methodological paradigm of corpus-assisted discourse analysis. Hardt-Mautner generally recognizes the validity of using quantitative corpus linguistics routines in discourse analysis, but at the same time identifies several possible objections to such an approach. These objections are summarized below:

a) "There is no constant relationship between linguistic structure and its semiotic significance" (Fowler 1991: 90 quoted in Hardt-Mautner 1995). Hardt-Mautner refers to Simpson's criticism of "interpretative positivism" – a rather extreme approach where one ascribes an invariable meaning to a given linguistic feature (Simpson 1993). This observation apparently undermines the validity of those corpus techniques which rely on generating concordances of words and phrases (explicit linguistic forms) and categorizing them as the main, if not the only, accessible realizations of a range of discursive meanings.
b) Quantitative analysis is largely limited to "surface indicators", providing a 'superficial content analysis' – a term used by van Dijk (1988), who

nevertheless suggested that the quantitative approach is complementary to the qualitative one (Hardt-Mautner 1995: 4). Similar concerns are expressed by Widdowson (2000), who claims that corpus linguistics provides a limited analysis of real language.

c) Hardt-Mautner also points out that the "semiotic impoverishment" of the original format of discourse typically affects corpus studies more than many discourse analysts would be ready to accept. As an example, in written discourse pictures, layout and formatting are sometimes important elements of the semiotic dimension, which get lost permanently in the preprocessing stage of many corpus studies.

d) The neatness of the presentation format in corpus studies may be conducive to the *l'art pour l'art* fallacy. In other words, despite having an esthetic effect neat data presentation formats may reveal little substance.

The first objection is a fairly general one. To avoid throwing the baby out with the bath water, however, one would have to observe that "no constant relationship between linguistic structure and it semiotic significance" does not at all mean "no relationship" or even "little relationship". In fact, most of the time, linguists tend to depend heavily on such a relationship and corpus linguistics provides a methodology which makes the identification of regular meaning-form dependencies lucid and consistent.

The second observation is more specific, and van Dijk certainly does have a point when he suggests that some discourse structures "elude quantification" to use Hardt-Mautner's phrase (Hardt-Mautner 1995). In the present study I am mainly interested in the identification of ideologically-loaded lexis. Admittedly, in order to fully account for the discursive significance of the results obtained, one has to turn to more traditional methods of verification and I provide examples of such validation with concordances. I argue that quantitative methods do constitute a complementary approach to critical discourse analysis in that they bring interesting insights which human analysts are unable to make due to the sheer volume of naturally occurring corpus data.

The next objection is largely valid, although it has to be noted that many analyses of discourse focus on the linguistic component at the expense of the non-linguistic semiotic aspects for purely practical reasons. As long as this methodological choice is clearly stated, such studies may still produce interesting results. Interestingly, it is technically possible to partly avoid the effect of semiotic-impoverishment in multimedia corpora, where the original sound, footage or page layout can be accessed independently of the standard tabularized result sets such as the *keywords in context* alignment (the most popular format of corpus concordances). To minimize the risk of semantic impoverishment, in the online version of the results presented in this study I provide instantly accessible electronic references to the original sources used to compile the respective corpora.

The last one of the four remarks made by Hardt-Mautner, is directed mainly to inexperienced users of corpus tools and techniques, who may draw far-fetched conclusions lacking empirical basis due to their initial fascination with the neatness of corpus data presentation. However, such pitfalls can be easily avoided if proper consideration is given to a few basic verification criteria which have to be considered in any statistically valid study.

In order to get a balanced view on the matter it is useful to consider the areas where qualitative discourse analysis is best complemented by corpus methods.

a) Representativeness. Implicit, vague statistical assertions are often made in linguistic descriptions without ever being formalized. Linguists and discourse analysts, repeatedly make use of adverbials or modals denoting frequency or degree of typicality in their descriptions of linguistic features, which they classify as "common", "usual", "rare", "typical", "unusual", etc. If not used carefully, many such descriptors may turn out to be appeals to folk statistics or anecdotal evidence. As an example, Sinclair (2001, 2004: 115) shows how Fairlclough (1992) refers to corpus evidence to verify his intuitions about the phrase "killer riot", and how this verification could be improved by consulting a more representative body of language data.
b) Objectivity and verifiability suffer directly from a loose approach to representativeness. Sinclair suggests that "the huge assimilation of usage that is lodged in the corpora" can add objectivity to intuitional discourse analysis, and that corpus methodology ensures the replicability of research experiments, thus making them verifiable by other analysts. Having fully acknowledged the danger of committing "interpretative positivism", one needs to avoid committing "interpretative nihilism". This can be achieved only by using verifiable criteria of presenting naturally-occurring language data as evidence. After all, both more qualitative Discourse Analysis and corpus-assisted Discourse Analysis depend, although to different degrees, on the "quotation of used language" (Sinclair 2004). Van Dijk mentions this requirement as one of the fundamental principles of Discourse Analysis:

> Perhaps the most pervasive in the study of discourse is the virtually exclusive focus on actually or naturally occurring talk and text. Unlike much work in formal linguistics and philosophy, invented or constructed examples [...] are avoided in favor of examples and corpora of 'real data', Data are in principle not edited or otherwise 'sanitized', but studied 'as is', that is, close to their actual appearance or use in their original contexts. (van Dijk 1997: 29)

Sinclair suggests that whenever possible such an appeal to 'real data' should be governed by reasonably objective rules of data selection:

> [...] citation of 'used language' proves nothing in itself about language unless the process of selectivity that is inevitable in such circumstances is controlled. The way in which massed corpus evidence can show the ideological trappings of a word or phrase is very good news for those students of discourse who are prepared to accept a moderate discipline for objectivity. (Sinclair 2004: 117)

Using corpus evidence to show "the ideological trappings of a word or phrase" is the focus of this study. The results obtained with the computational techniques implemented to that effect are treated with full awareness of their limited conclusiveness in describing discursive phenomena, especially in view of the emphasis of many qualitative analysts on the holistic methodology of studying discourse as a "sociocultural" process (van Dijk 1997: 17). Having said that, it is impossible to ignore consistent patterns and distributions of lexical units and their "ideological trappings" as one dimension of political discourse. Once identified, such findings may then be used to extend the analysis to other planes of discourse.

It seems clear that discourse-specific lexical phenomena can be reliably studied only with the aid of representative corpora. Using quantitative methods for discourse analysis on levels of linguistic analysis other than lexicality requires a balanced view. Such a view is sometimes expressed as the "triangulation approach" where an eclectic methodology making use of both quantitative and qualitative techniques is applied to the study of discourse (McNeill 1990, Baker 2006).

2. Overview of corpus techniques for discourse analysis

Baker (2006) provides an overview of corpus techniques currently used for discourse analysis with special emphasis on analyzing lexicality as well as on identifying discourses in corpora. Below I discuss the main characteristics of each of those techniques with their limitations, before introducing a complementary approach in the next section.

Concordances

Concordances will long remain the basic research technique of corpus linguists. Perhaps the biggest advantage of concordances is that while giving some quantitative indications, they also leave much room for qualitative judgments, since word usage fetched by means of concordances is provided with extensible context of occurrence.

One problem with concordances however, is that, while giving a detailed level of insight into the usage of lexical forms in their original context, they can be overwhelmingly difficult to summarize or generalize upon when working with large corpora. Some commonly used solutions used to alleviate the reading of concordances include multi-stage and zig-zag sorting, keyword highlighting, or – more recently – the permuted alignment of keyword contexts based on query term syntax and query expansion support (Pęzik *et al.* 2007). With the size of corpora rapidly growing, however, more automated techniques have been applied to obtain quick overviews of lexis found in corpus data.

Frequency, dispersion and keyness lists and the simplex word fallacy

Frequency lists generated from a corpus may be useful in "determining the focus of a text" and thus to identify discourses in a corpus (Baker 2006: 71). Although frequency lists are usually computed for words, other quantifiable units or features can be indexed as well:

> Frequency counts give an exact, quantitative characterization of a text, so that different texts can be compared in very precise terms. By themselves, however, frequency counts cannot identify linguistic dimensions. Rather, a linguistic dimension is determined on the basis of consistent co-occurrence patterns among features. That is, when a group of features consistently co-occur in texts, those features define a linguistic dimension (Biber 1988: 13).

Apart from simple frequency counts, it is also common to apply tests of statistical significance, such as log-likelihood or chi-square to compute how distinctive a given word or phrase is for a given corpus. Also, dispersion statistics are used to measure how evenly distributed (and thus how representative) a given word or phrase is in a corpus.

If, however, we focus on frequency values computed for a lexical item to mean:

> a formal item (at least one morpheme long) whose pattern of occurrence can be described in terms of a uniquely ordered series of other items occurring in its environment (Sinclair 1966: 412),

then one fundamental problem with the interpretation of frequency lists or any other frequency-based statistical values computed for lexical units lies in the identification of the lexical unit itself. The most commonly applied definition of a lexical unit for the purposes of frequency statistics is purely orthographic, where any space- or punctuation-separated string counts as a separate lexeme. This often renders frequency lists largely useless if concordances are not generated and analyzed for each item in the list. I refer to this situation as the simplex word fallacy.

Let us consider the following possibility. *Times*, *city*, *new* and *york* (case-normalized) come up as some of the most significant items in a frequency or keyness list. Of course, such words hardly ever simply occur next to each other in the list; rather, they tend to be strewn across the list in a way that makes it very difficult to interpret them. The following are frequencies of these four words and their ranks in a corpus of American political discourse:

Table 1. Frequencies and ranks of some single word tokens (case-normalised)

Rank	Word	Frequency
46	new	4699
260	times	866
272	city	833
286	york	784

The frequencies of the simplex words *times*, *city*, *new* and *York* are rather difficult to interpret here because of a potentially large number of collocational relations these single word units may come into. So, although they could make convenient headwords in a dictionary generated for the corpus in question, the entries placed under such headwords would have to provide separate descriptions for at least the following collocations and terms (and their homonyms):

Table 2. Possible lexemes composed of the simplex words New, York, Time and City

New
York
times
City
New York
New York Times
New York City
...

In fact there are many more collocations characteristic of the corpus in question, which involve at least one of the words listed above, e.g. *new generation*, *new jobs*, *new markets*, etc. In other words, those simplex words are phraseologically productive and it makes little sense to analyze their frequencies as simplex words. Therefore it seems crucial to consider lexeme identification methods which result in more reliable frequency statistics. Such an improvement could give more validity to lexicographic statements about frequency lists obtained from corpora.

N-grams/lexical bundles

Word n-grams are basically sequences of n words found in a given corpus. The most recurrent n-grams are often referred to as clusters or lexical bundles:

Lexical bundles are simply the most frequent recurrent sequences in a corpus of text (Biber 2004: 165).

Because of the method of their extraction, n-grams often span syntactic and lexical units. Interestingly however, frequent n-grams or lexical bundles are also very often found to bridge units of grammatical structure:

Because lexical bundles are identified on the basis of frequency, they are not necessarily complete structural units or fixed expressions. For example, the 4-word sequences 'do you want to' and 'I don't know what' are common lexical bundles in conversation.

Most lexical bundles do not represent a complete structural unit. Instead most lexical bundles bridge two structural units: they begin at a clause or phrase boundary, but the last two words are the first elements of a second structural unit, e.g. I want to know..., well, that's what I... (Biber 2004: 165)

The extraction of frequent n-grams seems to be a particularly revealing approach especially when analyzing spoken discourse, where seemingly incomplete structural units play a very important role in structuring the flow of conversations.

However, extracting n-grams from written discourse presents certain difficulties.

First of all, written discourse tends to contain more structurally complete lexical units which are often difficult to capture with the rather crude definition of n-grams. Besides, because n-grams are extracted in a context-free fashion, there are problems with marking their boundaries. As an example, how can one know exactly when to treat a bigram as complete, rather than a subsequence of a longer lexical unit? If we consider one of the lexemes from Table 2, e.g. *New*

York then the frequency obtained for this string of words by itself is difficult to interpret, unless we know how many of its occurrences are contributed by its frequencies in other phrases, such as *New York Times* or *New York City*. Of course, one could decide to select the longest reasonable n-grams first and manually make sure which of them subsume shorter ones, but this would be a rather daunting task for large corpus data volumes. Additionally, traditional n-gram analysis does not allow for any normalization techniques such as lemmatization or word-order variations, which do seem justified in the case of syntactically flexible MWEs.

Collocation and term extraction techniques

In discussing the possibility of identifying discourses by looking at typical collocations, Baker notes:

> A collocation analysis is useful for two reasons. First it provides a focus for our analysis which is particularly helpful when a large number of concordance lines needs to be sorted multiple times in order to reveal lexical patterns. Secondly, it gives us the most salient and obvious lexical patterns surrounding a subject, from which a number of discourses can be obtained. When two words frequently collocate, there is evidence that the discourses surrounding them are particularly powerful – the strength of collocation implies that these are two concepts which have been linked in the minds of people and have been used again and again – perhaps to the point where even one half of the pair is likely to prime someone who hears or reads that word to think of the other half (Baker 2006: 114).

Such collocations are typically extracted on the basis of the relative frequency of their constituents. While being right in pointing out that discursive features are manifested in collocations, Baker only focuses on the notion of a collocation as an arbitrarily salient association of two orthographically defined words. This in turn means that longer word groupings, such as many multi word nominal terms, which happen to be institutionalized in a given strand of discourse are often overlooked in the task of collocation extraction. Below I briefly introduce a method of extracting multiword nominal terms and collocations which is complementary to the corpus techniques discussed above mainly in that it addresses the simplex word fallacy.

Multiword expressions

There exist surprisingly many definitions of multiword expressions and collocations, which is partly due to the gradable nature of lexical processes, and partly to the variety of factors that contribute to the fossilization of a sequence of orthographic words. Some collocations are highly institutionalized, while others exhibit a considerable level of syntactic and semantic flexibility. Although a comprehensive discussion of the different types and defining criteria of multiword expressions is outside the scope of the current study, it is useful to keep in mind a number of different types of MWEs, such as:

a) collocations – lexically acceptable combinations of words,
b) idioms – fixed expressions whose meaning may but does not have to transcend the meaning of the constituent simplex words (non-compositional vs. compositional idioms),
c) technical terms – MWEs situated in a distinct domain of discourse (most multiword terms are nominal compounds),
d) lexical bundles (discussed above),
e) skip-grams (Guthrie *et al.* 2006)
f) other MWEs.

Some definitions of MWEs are based on distributional criteria, while others are derived from the compositional semantics of multiword lexical units. The criteria of syntactic malformedness, conventionality and lexical substitution have also been applied in an attempt to define complex lexical units (Sag 2002). In the present study I focus on left- and right-headed nominal multiword terms which are found to be highly institutionalized (as reflected by their statistical significance) in the analysed samples of discourse.

3. Corpus material

Before discussing the methods used to identify ideological markedness and the results obtained, it is useful to describe the general characteristics of the two corpora of American political discourse analyzed in this study.

The Communist Party of the USA corpus

Representing the discourse of American communists is a corpus comprising roughly 1100 texts including news articles, manifestoes, transcripts of speeches as well as political pamphlets published on the websites of the Communist Party of America (CPUSA – http://www.cpusa.org) and the People's Weekly World newspaper (PWW – http://www.pww.org). These two sources are very closely related in terms of their ideological outlook. In fact, many articles featured on the CPUSA website were originally published by the PWW, and the PWW is sometimes described as the newspaper of the CPUSA. The total size of this corpus at the moment of writing is 1,017,006 word tokens. This figure includes punctuation and non-alphanumeric strings, but words containing a hyphen are always treated as a single word unit. The corpora cover roughly the same period of mid-2003 through mid-2006, and since both of them focus on current affairs, this time span is indicative of the range of topics they contain.

The Grand Old Party corpus

The second corpus is a compilation of 818 texts (1,020,309 words) published on the website of the Republican National Committee (http://www.rnc.org/). This corpus is henceforth referred to as the GOP (Grand Old Party) corpus, and it contains news articles, promotional materials, speech transcripts and official memos. In contrast to the CPUSA corpus, this collection features a greater proportion of transcripts of speeches typically delivered by top-rank representatives of the Republicans such as party leaders, government officials or the then president of the United States.

The motivation behind such a compilation of sample corpora is rather straightforward. Since they represent two very different ends of the American political spectrum, it is very likely that they can illustrate differences in the ideological bias on a range of controversial topics. Many of the systematic differences between the ideologies are reflected in the distribution of lexis and they are possible to identify using quantitative methods.

4. Identifying terms of discourse

Regular associations between two or more seemingly independent words may reveal ideologically motivated prosodic bias at the phraseological level of lexical analysis. Using a special technique called *Cascaded Term Extraction* I have extracted a dictionary of nominal collocations from the two corpora of political discourse introduced above. The entire dictionary is available in the form of a web-based interface (Pęzik 2008). This section demonstrates how this dictionary can be used to study the formation and use of nominal collocations involving the nodes *free* and *freedom* as one example of automatically extracted terms of political discourse.

Automatic extraction of collocations

There are numerous methods of MWE extraction, each of which addresses a different aspect of the above-mentioned typology. (Evert 2005) uses the notions of *relational* and *positional* collocations to underline an important distinction between two general frameworks of identifying collocations. The more traditional terms used for the same distinction in lexical acquisition models based on word co-occurrence are *window-based*, and *syntactic* respectively (e.g. Greffenstette 1996). Window-based models are typically classified as knowledge-poor approaches since they do not make use of the morphological and syntactic information incorporated in knowledge-rich relational models. Positional collocations depend more on the definition of the collocation span as the physical distance of *n* orthographic words to both sides of the node word. On the other hand, relational frameworks put more restrictions on the possible context of a potential collocation, by specifying its span not in terms of orthographic distance measured in words but in terms of syntactic boundaries. As an example, an adjective may only be tested for its collocability with a noun if both of these words occur within the boundaries of the same noun phrase. Hybrid approaches are also used, where fixed-length positional windows are restricted to the boundaries of a syntactically complete sentence.

Cascaded Term Extraction

The CTE model used in the present study to identify nominal collocations and other MWEs in samples of political discourse could be described as relational in that it is based on variable-length predefined sequences of grammatical categories, although it uses morphological (part-of-speech) rather than syntactic information to define potential collocation patterns. Similar approaches to defining collocational or terminological patterns have been used in the past for extracting technical terms from special language corpora e.g. (Daille 1995), although few of them have dealt with identifying the boundaries of nested terms composed of more than two simplex words which is a specialty of the CTE approach. In CTE a corpus representing a distinctive strand of discourse is first part-of-speech tagged. Next, twenty-five part-of-speech (POS) patterns are tested for statistically significant collocability. To illustrate, the following two rules can be used to measure the collocability of potentially nested noun compounds:

1. IF [N+N==PASS] THEN [N+N=NN]
2. IF [NN+N==PASS] THEN [NN+N==NNN],

where PASS stands for passing the statistical test of significant co-occurrence.

Rule 1 conflates two adjacent nouns into a single lexical unit if the association strength between the two nouns meets the minimum criteria.[1] Rule 2 appends a third noun to the sequence if it frequently co-occurs with the previously conflated combination of two nouns.

In addition to measuring association strength between the simplex constituent words of a potential term with standard test such as Mutual Information, the eveness of a pattern's distribution is measured with Juilland's dispersion (Juilland *et al.* 1970). Details of the CTE implementation can be found in Pęzik (2008). For the purposes of the present study it suffices to say that it achieves up to 85% precision in the identification of nested nominal MWEs. This level of accuracy does some justice to the phraseology of the lexis found in the two corpora of American political discourse and it helps avoid the simplex word fallacy inherent in some corpus techniques discussed above. The following table illustrates the result of processing a corpus with the CTE algorithm.

Table 3. Statistically significant MWEs are treated as atomic lexical units

#	POS	Lemmatized	Unlemmatized
1	C_NIN[2]	war_in_Iraq_	War in Iraq
2	VVZ[3]	Take	Takes
3	ADJ[4]	Horrifying	Horrifying
4	N[5]	Toll	Toll
5	...	...	...

The example sentence contains the noun-preposition-noun sequence of *War in Iraq* which has been annotated as a potentially institutionalized phrase based on the distributional salience of this phrase in the discourse represented by the corpus used. Thus, the simplex word fallacy is at least partly avoided in this case

[1] It could be paraphrased to mean: "if two nouns co-occur next to each other with a frequency much higher than random, then they should be treated as multiword expression".

[2] **C_NIN** – Collocation consisting of a noun (N), preposition (I) and another noun (N).

[3] **VVZ** – Third person, singular noun.

[4] **ADJ** – adjective.

[5] **N** – noun.

by recognizing *war in Iraq* as a term of the Communist Party of the USA discourse. The identification of potentially nested nominal collocations is carried out for the entire corpus and the results are stored in a relational dictionary which can be browsed online. Table 4 shows the number of statistically significant nominal MWEs extracted from the two corpora analyzed. The prefix C_ indicates that the following sequence of nouns (**N**), prepositions (**I**), and adjectives (**J**) forms a salient collocation in a given corpus.

Table 4. Frequency of statistically significant nominal MWEs

TYPE	GOP	CPUSA
C_NIJN	28	9
C_NIN	470	307
C_NINN	40	19
C_NN	1873	1907
C_NNIJN	4	0
C_NNIN	26	16
C_NNINN	12	5
C_NNN	517	352
C_NNNN	120	90
C_NNNNN	43	16

It is worth emphasizing that the significance of these MWEs as potentially typical terms of discourse would be obfuscated in a traditional decomposed frequency or n-gram list.

Results

One of the defining features of many collocations and other multiword expressions is the institutionalisation of their composite meaning. Such institutionalisation is often dependent on the discourse in which a given collocation is found more frequently than elsewhere. By extracting such collocations it is possible to identify some of the concepts and ideas typical of a given sample of discourse. To illustrate the process of conserving concepts in collocations, let us consider the set of nominal collocations of the noun *freedom* and the adjective *free* extracted with the CTE algorithm from the two corpora at hand. By comparing two ideologically polarized corpora we can find collocations whose distribution is unique for a given sample of discourse.

Freedom in the CPUSA corpus

Twenty nominal collocations involving the simplex words *free* and *freedom* found in the CPUSA corpus have been tagged as statistically significant with log-likelihood scores sufficiently high to refute the null hypothesis of random co-occurrence with $p < 0.01$ (Dunning 1993).

The part-of-speech type of a collocation, its particular instance, basic frequency, Juilland's dispersion as well ad Mutual Information and Dunning's log-likelihood association scores are presented in the respective columns of the table below. Results are presented in the order of descending dispersion, with the most regularly occurring terms and collocations at the top of the list.

Table 5. The nodes *free* and *freedom* in the CPUSA corpus

#	Type	N-gram	A	JD	MI3	G2
1	C_NN	free trade	39	77.671	18.188	369.539
2	C_JN	free trade	32	76.449	17.34	289.036
3	C_NNNN	Employee Free Choice Act	17	74.732	14.417	180.845
4	C_JN	free market	16	72.181	15.17	137.467
5	C_JN	Free Speech	27	71.595	17.081	255.251
6	C_NN	Freedom ride	58	71.563	21.079	795.169
7	C_NNNN	Immigrant Workers Freedom Ride	18	70.986	14.007	154.638
8	C_NNN	Free Trade Area	14	70.856	14.791	134.631
9	C_NN	freedom fighters	6	65.757	14.88	73.022
10	C_NNN	Free Trade Agreement	21	65.299	16.241	231.153
11	C_NNNNN	North American Free Trade Agreement	9	64.184	10.014	51.381
12	C_JN	free elections	7	63.192	10.286	32.726
13	C_NNNNN	Central American Free Trade Agreement	8	57.451	9.674	44.981
14	C_JN	free education	5	55.978	7.871	13.695
15	C_NIN	Freedom of Information	4	50.521	15.769	68.162
16	C_NIN	freedom of assembly	5	47.518	12.092	44.221
17	C_JN	reproductive freedom	5	47.518	12.219	44.237
18	C_JN	toll-free numbers	4	38.977	13.542	53.157
19	C_NIN	Freedom of the press	4	37.919	13.962	51.432
20	C_NNNN	Immigrants Rights Freedom Ride	5	33.764	10.388	40.904

The second column of the table specifies the part-of-speech type of the collocation. It is interesting to see that the part-of-speech tagger used to pre-process the corpus data produced inconsistent annotations of the phrase *free trade* as a noun-noun or adjective-noun sequences (item 1 and 2 in the list respectively). This did not affect the quality of the results, since both of these part-of-speech patterns were found to be highly significant. The third column lists phrases extracted for a given part-of-speech pattern in a case-insensitive manner. The fourth column contains the basic frequency of a given collocation. The last three columns indicate the eveness of distribution and two measures of the strength of association between the collocates forming a given phrase.

The list presented in Table 5 brings interesting insights into the phraseological potential of the words *free* and *freedom* in American communist discourse. As an example, it reveals that abortion rights seem to be described as part of *reproductive freedom* (17), a term which is not found in the corresponding list of results for Republican data discussed below for. Perhaps the term *free education* (14) may also reflect communist ideology. The analysis of the frequencies of the decomposed constituents of these phrases as in a traditional frequency list may not reveal these collocations for two major reasons. First of all the frequencies of the single word tokens *free* and *freedom* are difficult to interpret when separated from their collocates. Secondly, it is difficult to predict the collocations of any given word, so that they can be evaluated individually in separate queries. Finally, the size of a concordance generated for a frequent keyword may be too overwhelming for manual analysis.

Even more interesting is the analysis of the terms extracted for the same collocational nodes from the GOP corpus.

The radial nature of freedom in GOP

The collocations extracted from the GOP corpus form a different picture (Table 6 and Table 7). First of all, the two collocational nodes in question are much more phraseologically productive in the GOP corpus with as many as 56 statistically significant terms and collocations extracted. *Free society* and *the cause of freedom* (2,17) crop up as highly institutionalized phrases, which occur with a high regularity over the whole corpus as indicated by the dispersion value of 80. *Nations* (3), *societies* (1), *peoples* (14), *countries* (20) and *humans* (16) are modified by the adjective *free*. There are obvious differences between the typical collocates of *free* and *freedom* found in GOP and the ones extracted from the CPUSA corpus covering a similar time period (see Table 5). The highly salient phrase *free Iraq* (6) is only found in the GOP data.

Furthermore, there is a surprisingly high variety of ways of expressing the idea of the gradual spread of *freedom*:

a) advance of freedom (15)
b) freedom around the world (5)
c) hope of freedom (22)
d) circle of freedom (29)
e) freedom spread (39)
f) freer world (7)
g) freedom progress (47)
h) expansion of freedom (48)

It is worth noting at this point that the basic frequency of all the statistically significant collocations of the collocations involving the words *free* and *freedom* in the GOP corpus amounts to 705. It would be extremely time-consuming to manually summarize the concordances of these occurrences, especially if we further add a number of phraseologically insignificant usages of the two words. Spotting the subtle and variously worded metaphor of the gradually extending circle of freedom would also require a stroke of luck. Therefore, the use of the high-throughput method described in this chapter seems to be the only reasonable alternative for the corpus-oriented discourse analyst.

Incidentally, at least two erroneously extracted collocations can be observed in this list: *struggle because freedom* (41) and *belief that freedom* (43). These have resulted from the performance of the automatic part-of-speech tagger used (the conjunctions were mistaken for prepositions). Such a trade-off of using automated methods of discourse analysis seems to be acceptable in view of the benefits gained. *Freedom cause* (17) is actually a lemmatised version of the correctly identified form freedom's cause. Interestingly, *free Iraq* (6) occurs both as an independent phrase and as part of longer phrases as in *security forces of a free Iraq* (28), which again show the importance of identifying the exact boundaries of potentially nested collocations.

Clearly, a discourse analyst faced with such a summary may want to investigate to what extent this variety of phrases of describing the *spread of freedom* in places like the *Middle East* (40) could serve to justify the *war on terror*, given that the *enemies of freedom* (42) are likely to be identified as terrorists. The radial nature of freedom as it is depicted in Republican discourse emerges from the subtle variations of the conceptually similar metaphor found in discourse-specific collocations. This only becomes apparent when a set of collocations is extracted from an ideologically coherent corpus.

Table 6. The nodes *free* and *freedom* in the GOP corpus (part 1)

#	Type	N-gram	A	JD	MI3	G2
1	C_JN	free society	57	81.229	18.47	546.869
2	C_NIN	cause of freedom	26	79.141	14.934	164.459
3	C_JN	free nations	69	78.537	17.737	438.491
4	C_JN	free elections	35	77.159	15.094	179.501
5	C_NIN	freedom around the world	20	75.276	12.249	67.509
6	C_JN	free Iraq	56	73.714	17.193	359.436
7	C_JN	freer world	17	73.371	12.285	68.026
8	C_NN	Free trade	24	73.114	17.6	255.239
9	C_NNN	Free Trade Agreement	21	72.341	17.055	261.858
10	C_NIN	power of freedom	18	72.192	13.003	87.605
11	C_JN	Iraqi Freedom	19	72.192	13.969	144.512
12	C_JN	freer trade	17	72.077	13.394	96.801
13	C_JN	religious freedom	17	70.839	16.873	208.066
14	C_JN	free peoples	24	69.594	10.494	16.019
15	C_NIN	advance of freedom	19	68.387	14.822	149.426
16	C_JN	human freedom	12	67.894	12.515	68.386
17	C_NN	freedom cause	9	67.894	16.084	122.956
18	C_JN	free markets	16	66.942	14.412	128.652
19	C_JN	own freedom	13	65.868	11.2	46.814
20	C_JN	free country	9	64.184	9.532	24.584
21	C_NNNNN	Central American Free Trade Agreement	10	63.591	11.122	67.618
22	C_NIN	hope of freedom	10	63.591	10.941	42.781
23	C_JN	free government	7	63.192	9.368	24.337
24	C_JN	economic freedom	6	60.028	8.053	14.06
25	C_NN	Free societies	7	57.913	14.49	77.07
26	C_NIN	Freedom in Iraq	8	57.73	11.347	53.099
27	C_NIN	Freedom of speech	8	57.451	13.333	81.84
28	C_NNIJN	security forces of a free Iraq	5	55.978	8.731	37.994

Table 7. The nodes *free* and *freedom* in the GOP corpus (part 2)

#	Type	N-gram	A	JD	MI3	G2
29	C_NIN	circle of freedom	5	55.978	11.214	42.117
30	C_NIN	freedom of religion	5	55.978	10.714	34.819
31	C_NNNNN	Dominican Republic Free Trade Agreement	6	53.473	9.648	39.057
32	C_JN	Free Speech	6	53.473	9.652	27.093
33	C_NIN	freedom of assembly	7	53.225	12.948	71.548
34	C_NIN	foundations of freedom	4	50.521	9.833	26.961
35	C_NIJN	success of a free Iraq	4	50.521	8.225	19.939
36	C_NNNNN	North American Free Trade Agreement	4	50.521	8.478	25.594
37	C_NN	Free nations	4	50.521	11.39	34.038
38	C_NN	freedom power	4	50.521	9.115	21.004
39	C_NN	freedom spread	4	50.521	13.16	46.67
40	C_NINN	freedom in the Middle East	4	50.521	8.594	25.809
41	C_NIN	struggle because freedom	4	50.521	11.012	35.804
42	C_NIN	enemies of freedom	4	50.521	8.441	17.825
43	C_NIN	belief that freedom	4	50.521	8.579	18.421
44	C_JJN	other free nations	7	48.967	9.646	39.671
45	C_JN	free enterprise	6	47.735	10.859	38.871
46	C_NIJN	enemies of a free Iraq	5	47.518	9.453	34.576
47	C_NN	freedom progress	5	47.518	12.462	46.095
48	C_NIN	expansion of freedom	4	47.518	8.585	18.684
49	C_JN	free men	8	44.448	9.036	20.223
50	C_JN	great freedom	4	42.566	7.803	13.943
51	C_JJN	first free elections	3	42.566	9.406	26.442
52	C_NNN	USA Freedom Corps	18	402	16.719	223.903
53	C_NNNN	The USA Freedom Corps	4	29.293	8.145	17.722
54	C_NNIN	America ideal of freedom	5	27.864	11.474	57.262
55	C_JJN	free national elections	3	25.391	11.576	38.163
56	C_NN	Freedom House	5	–0.509	8.396	17.387

Let us now see if the working hypothesis formulated to explain the use of the metaphor of freedom as a gradually expanding circle can be further verified with concordances extracted for some of the lexically conserved collocations of *freedom* presented above. The following below provide a broader context of the use selected of *freedom* in the Republican data.

The first excerpt is taken from the RNC Chairman's speech delivered at a National Association for the Advancement of Coloured People (NAACP) convention. In the course of his speech, Ken Melhman attempts to present the expansion of the circle of freedom as an ongoing process which can be related to the ideas of Martin Luther King. Interestingly, in contrast to the other excerpts discussed below, the emphasis of Melhman's speech is domestic rather than international. This in turn indicates that the concept of the expanding circle of freedom is also used to describe domestic political initiatives taken by the Republicans.

1	***RNC Chairman Ken Mehlman's Remarks Today At The NAACP National Convention*** Today, the work to uphold the dream continues. Dr. King said the "goal of America is freedom." Have we reached that goal? Have we achieved the dream? Like the Old Testament prophets, Dr. King didn't live to see it...but I believe we will eventually **expand the circle of freedom** to reach every American...in every corner of America...at every stage of life...with every means available.

Most of the remaining excerpts relate the idea of spreading freedom, more or less explicitly, to the war on terror. Paradoxically, the *advance of freedom*, which in fact involves military efforts in the Middle East, is supposed to lead to the enhancement of peace (Quote 2). Thus, through rhetorical entailment war is justified as an effort to expand freedom and ultimately ensure peace.

2	***Excerpts from the President's State of the Union Address*** The United States has no right, no desire, and no intention to impose our form of government on anyone else. That is one of the main differences between us and our enemies. They seek to impose and expand an empire of oppression, in which a tiny group of brutal, self-appointed rulers control every aspect of every life. Our aim is to build and preserve a community of free and independent nations, with governments that answer to their citizens, and reflect their own cultures. And because democracies respect their own people and their neighbors, **the advance of freedom will lead to peace.**

	Our generational commitment to the **advance of freedom, especially in the Middle East**, is now being tested and honored in Iraq. That country is a vital front in the War on Terror, which is why the terrorists have chosen to make a stand there. Our men and women in uniform are fighting terrorists in Iraq, so we do not have to face them here at home.

Freedom's progress is opposed by terrorists, who stay in the way of advancing liberty (Quote 3). In Quote 3 below President Bush also likens Iraq reconstruction efforts to the sound of the new *Liberty Bell echoing across the broader Middle East.* This is yet another metaphor used to picture the radial nature of freedom and justify the war on terror operations including the ousting of Saddam Hussein (Quote 4).

3	***Monday, December 12, 2005, Remarks By The President On The War On Terror, Park Hyatt Philadelphia*** Today in the Middle East, freedom is once again contending with a totalitarian ideology that seeks to sow anger and hatred and despair. And like fascism and communism before, the hateful ideologies that use terror will be defeated by the unstoppable power of freedom. (...) And **the advance of freedom in the Middle East requires freedom in Iraq.** By helping Iraqis build a lasting democracy, we will **spread the hope of liberty** across a troubled region, and we'll gain new allies in the cause of freedom. By helping Iraqis build a strong democracy, we're adding to our own security, and, like a generation before us, we're laying the foundation of peace for generations to come. (...) **The terrorists know that democracy is their enemy, and they will continue fighting freedom's progress with** all the hateful determination they can muster. Yet the Iraqi people are stepping forward to claim their liberty, and they will have it. When the new Iraqi government takes office next year, Iraqis will have the only constitutional democracy in the Arab world, and Americans will have a partner for peace and moderation in the Middle East. (...) Not far from here where we gather today is a symbol of freedom familiar to all Americans -- the Liberty Bell. When the Declaration of Independence was first read in public, the Liberty Bell was sounded in celebration, and a witness said: "It rang as if it meant something." Today, **the call of liberty is being heard in Baghdad and Basra**, and other Iraqi cities, and its sound is **echoing across the broader Middle East**. From Damascus to Tehran, people hear it, and they know it means something. It means that the days of tyranny and terror are ending, and a new day of hope and freedom is dawning.

4	***President Bush Requests Additional FY 2005 Funding for the War on Terror*** When President Bush made the decision to respond to the attacks of 9/11 by dealing with al-Qaida and its Taliban sponsors, and protect America from a gathering threat by removing Saddam Hussein from power, he committed: to provide our troops with whatever they need to protect themselves and successfully complete their mission; and to stand with the Afghan and Iraqi people against the terrorists trying desperately to derail democracy and **the advance of freedom.**

The perpetual advance of freedom is claimed to be deeply rooted in American history. When addressing coast guard graduates, president Bush describes the global war on terror as an operation similar to the Marshall Plan, the Berlin Airlift, or the liberation of concentration camps, which is worth every *effort and sacrifice.*

5	**President Bush Speaks to Coast Guard Graduates** America will not relent in the war against global terror. (Applause.) We will hunt the terrorists in every dark corner of the earth. And we're making good progress. Nearly one-half of al Qaeda's senior operatives have been captured or killed. (Applause.) We will deny the terrorists the sanctuary and bases they need to plan and strike -- as we have done in the battle of Afghanistan. We will not permit terror networks or terror states to threaten or blackmail the world with weapons of mass destruction -- as we have shown in the battle of Iraq. (Applause.) Our country has been attacked by treachery in our own cities -- and that treachery continues in places like Riyadh and Casablanca. We have seen the ruthless intentions of our enemies. And they are seeing our intentions: we will press on until this danger to our country and to the world is ended. (Applause.) Yet, the national interest of America involves more than eliminating aggressive threats to our safety. We also stand for the values that defeat violence, and the hope that overcomes hatred. **We find our greatest security in the advance of human freedom.** Free societies look to the possibilities of the future, instead of feeding old resentments and bitterness. Free countries build wealth and prosperity for their people in an atmosphere of stability and order, instead of seeking weapons of mass murder and attacking their neighbors. Because **America loves peace, America will always work and sacrifice for the expansion of freedom.** (Applause.) (...)

	The advance of freedom is more than an interest we pursue. It is a calling we follow. Our country was created in the name and cause of freedom. And if the self-evident truths of our founding are true for us, they are true for all. As a people dedicated to civil rights, we are driven to defend the human rights of others. We are the nation that liberated continents and concentration camps. **We are the nation of the Marshall Plan, the Berlin Airlift and the Peace Corps. We are the nation that ended the oppression of Afghan women, and we are the nation that closed the torture chambers of Iraq.** (Applause.) **(...)** **The advance of freedom** and hope in the world is also challenged by an ancient enemy: famine.

Al Qaeda terrorists are again named as the chief enemies of the triumphal progress of freedom are again named in Quote 6.

6	**Tuesday, January 10, 2006, Remarks By The President On The War On Terror, Omni Shoreham Hotel** And as democracy takes hold in Iraq, the terrorists like Zarqawi and his al Qaeda associates are suffering major defeats. Zarqawi tried to stop the elections throughout the year 2005, and he failed. He tried to stop the writing and ratification of a new constitution, and he failed. **The advance of freedom is destroying his and al Qaeda's greatest myth**: These terrorists are not fighting on behalf of the Iraqi people against a foreign occupation -- they are fighting the will of the Iraqi people expressed in free elections.

The progress of freedom should be nurtured not only in America (as in Quote 1), but in *the broader Middle East* (Quote 7) and in *the entire world* as well (Quote 8).

7	**President Addresses United Nations High-Level Plenary Meeting,** United Nations Headquarters, New York (…) This is a moment of great opportunity in the cause of freedom. Across the world, hearts and minds are opening to the message of human liberty as never before. In the last two years alone, tens of millions have voted in free elections in Afghanistan and Iraq, in Lebanon and the Palestinian territories, in Kyrgyzstan, in Ukraine, and Georgia. And as they claim their freedom, they are inspiring millions more across ***the broader Middle East.*** We must encourage their aspirations. We must **nurture freedom's progress**. And the United Nations has a vital role to play. (…)

8	***Celebrating Freedom, Honoring Service*** THROUGHOUT HISTORY, Americans have come together on Inauguration Day to celebrate American traditions, and the principles and ideals of a democratic nation. As President Bush said at the Celebration of Freedom concert on Jan. 19, "An inauguration is a time of unity for our country. On Jan. 20, 2005, the nation celebrated the 55th inaugural ceremonies and President George W. Bush was sworn-in to his second term as president of all Americans. The President's inaugural speech aptly reflected this year's theme, Celebrating Freedom, Honoring Service. In his address, President Bush recognized the bravery and sacrifice of the men and women of the Armed Services, reaffirmed his commitment to America's freedom and security, and said, ultimately, America's goal is to end tyranny. **"The best hope for peace in our world is the expansion of freedom in all the world."**

Some reflection on the possible different interpretations of the war on terror is shown in Quote 9 only to be refuted as unfair and unjustified.

9	***Bush, Sharon Plan for Peace*** While President Bush's meeting with PM Sharon received extensive coverage, ***the story of the expansion of freedom in Iraq*** continues to get overlooked or glossed over. "When it comes to reporting on the Iraq War, the Old Media might as well be an appendage of the anti-war wing of the Democratic Party. It is astonishing how little coverage we've seen of the positive trend there over the last few months," writes columnist David Limbaugh for townhall.com. Why would such significant signs of progress go virtually ignored?

The examples presented above show how the idea of the gradual spread of freedom is used to indirectly justify the war on terror in Republican discourse. We can conclude that describing freedom as an ever-expanding circle or as the echoing sound of the Liberty Bell serves an ideologically-specific rhetorical purpose. Interestingly, this metaphor is institutionalised in a number of discourse-specific collocations, thus proving that the lexical analysis of corpora can be revealing for cognitive and discourse linguists as well.

Summary

Corpus linguistics has contributed to the analysis of discourse by revealing the linguistic evidence lodged in representative corpora. Despite the theoretical misgivings of traditional discourse analysts, corpus techniques do play an important role in focusing and validating the researcher's intuitions about the distributional characteristics of linguistic forms. In this study I have outlined a number of corpus techniques used to support discourse analysis. While concordance analysis has an indisputable qualitative value, it may prove impractical in the face of overwhelming data sets. On the other hand, data summarisation techniques such as frequency and keyword lists may be prone to the simplex word fallacy. I have introduced Cascaded Term Extraction as a method of extracting nominal collocations which recognizes the non-compositionality of multiword expressions. By identifying a number of nominal terms whose distributional features indicate a discourse-specific institutionalisation I show that the cognitive power of the metaphor is exploited in political discourse and it is manifested at the phraseological level. I argue that the idea of the continuous spread of freedom used in Republican discourse to justify the efforts invested in the war on terrorism could be overlooked if only traditional methods of corpus-driven discourse analysis were applied. New, scalable corpus techniques are needed to deal with the increasing volumes of corpus data representing different registers of discourse and the MWE extraction method presented in this study is a step in this direction.

REFERENCES

Baker, P. (2006). *Using Corpora in Discourse Analysis.* Continuum: London, New York.

Biber, D. (1988). *Variations across speech and writing.* Cambridge University Press.

Biber, D. (2004). *Lexical Bundles in Academic Speech and Writing.* PALC 2003 Proceedings Łódź Studies in Language, PETER LANG.

Daille, B. (1995). *Combined Approach for Terminology Extraction: Lexical Statistics and Linguistic Filtering.* UCREL Technical Papers. Vol. 5. Department of Linguistics. University of Lancaster.

Dunning, T. (1993). *Accurate Methods for the Statistics of Surprise and Coincidence.* Association for Computational Linguistics.

Evert, S. (2005). *The Statistics of Word Co-occurrences Word Pairs and Collocations.* Dissertationsschrift zur Erlangung der Würde eines Doktors der Philosophie (Dr. phil.), eingereicht bei der Philosophisch-Historischen Fakultät der Universität Stuttgart.

Fairclough, N. (1989). *Language and Power.* London and New York: Longman.

Fairclough, N. (1992. *Linguistic and intertextual analysis within discourse analysis.* Discourse and Society, 3, 2: 193–217.

Fowler, R. (1991). *Language in the News*: Discourse and Ideology in the Press. London and New York: Routledge.

Greffenstette, G. (1996). "Evaluation Techniques for Automatic Semantic Extraction: Comparing Syntactic and Window Based Approaches". In: Boguraev, B., Pustejovsky, J. (eds.). *Issues in Text-based Lexicon Acquisition*. Corpus Processing for Lexical Acquisition. Massachusetts Institute of Technology.

Guthrie, D., Allison, B., Liu, W., Guthrie, L. and Y. Wilks (2006). "A Closer Look at Skip-Gram Modelling". *Proceedings LREC'2006*. Genoa, Italy.

Hardt-Mautner, G. (1995). *Only Connect. Critical Discourse Analysis and Corpus Linguistics*. Institut für Englische Sprache. Wirtschaftsuniversitat Wien.

Juilland, A. G., Brodin, D., Davidovitch, C. (1970). *Frequency dictionary of French words*. The Hague: Mouton de Gruyter.

McNeill, P. (1990). *Research Methods*. Second Edition. London, Routledge.

Partington, A., Morley, J. (2004). *At the heart of ideology: Word and cluster/bundle frequency in political debate*. PALC 2003 Proceedings, Łódź Studies in Language, PETER LANG.

Pęzik, P., Kim, J., Rebholz-Schuhmann, D. (2007). *MedEvi – a permuted concordancer for the biomedical domain*. Proceedings of PALC 2007. PETER LANG Publishing.

Pęzik, P. (2008). *Computer-assisted identification of ideological markedness in American political discourse*. PhD thesis defended at the University of Łódź. Available at http://pelcra.ia.uni.lodz.pl/pezik.

Sag, I. A., Baldwin, T., Bond, F., Copestake A., Flickinger, D. (2002). *Multiword expressions: A pain in the neck for NLP*. Proc. of the 3rd International Conference on Intelligent Text Processing and Computational Linguistics (CICLing-2002): 1–15. Mexico City, Mexico.

Sinclair, J. (1966). *Beginning the study of lexis*. In memory of J R Firth. Longman's Linguistics Library. Longman's, Green & Co. Ltd.

Simpson, P. (1993). *Language, Ideology and Point of View*. London and New York: Routledge.

Sinclair, J. (2004). *Trust the Text*. Ed. with Ronald Carter. Routledge.

Van Dijk, T. A. (1988). *News Analysis*. Case Studies of International and National News in the Press. Hillsdale, NJ: Lawrence Erlbaum Associates.

Van Dijk, T. A. (1997). *The Study of Discourse*. In: Discourse as Structure and Process. Ed. Teun A. van Dijk. SAGE Publications.

Widdowson, H. G. (2000). *On the Limitations of Linguistics Applied*. Applied Linguistics 21.

Galina I. Kustova, Olga N. Lashevskaja,
Elena V. Paducheva, Ekaterina V. Rakhilina

Russian Academy of Sciences, Moscow

VERB TAXONOMY: FROM THEORETICAL LEXICAL SEMANTICS TO PRACTICE OF CORPUS TAGGING

Abstract: One of the main advantages of the Russian National Corpus is its semantic tagging based on an extensive semantic classification of the lexicon – separate for nouns, verbs, adjectives, adverbs and numerals (see Kustova *et al.* 2005). Semantic annotations, combined with morphological tagging, make it possible to answer queries that concern not only separate words and word forms but also semantically characterized classes of words, as well as constructions with components presented as morphologically and/or semantically described classes.

Keywords: ontological classification, Russian, semantic filters, semantic tagging, taxonomy, verb, word-sense disambiguation.

1. Introduction

Semantic tagging of the Russian National Corpus (RNC, www.ruscorpora.ru) is being carried out with the help of the database, where every dictionary meaning of a word is assigned a set of characteristics along the following parameters:

- taxonomic class: 'persons', 'spaces', 'texts', etc. (for nouns); 'motion', 'location', 'emotion' etc. (for verbs); 'speed', 'duration', 'place' etc. (for adjectives and adverbs);
- mereological class (for nouns): names of 'parts', 'sets' etc.;
- topological class (for nouns): names of 'containers', 'horizontal surfaces', etc.;
- causative/non-causative (for verbs);
- positive and negative evaluation (for all parts of speech);

- derivational class: diminutives (for nouns), prefixal (for verbs), derived from nouns (for adjectives), etc.

At present our database consists of 375000 entries, of which 33000 are entries for verbs.

The classification in the database follows the multi-facet principle: each parameter constitutes a separate principle of division. In other words, we have several classifications (some of them hierarchical) independent of one another. In this paper we deal only with verbs. In Section 1 we present the taxonomic classification of verbs in the database. In Section 2 we describe the application of this classification to semantic tagging of the Corpus, paying attention to ambiguity that arises and to disambiguation devices used to overcome it.

2. Taxonomic classification of verbs

2.1. General

Modern semantics distinguishes two main taxonomic classifications of verbs: one may be called **ontological** (or **thematic**), the other is **actional** (it is also called **aspectological**).

Among ontological classifications of verbs, the most developed one is that suggested by Beth Levin (1993) for English verbs. This classification, though having indisputable merits, was carried out in the ideology of transformational grammar: every class is substantiated by its participation in transformations of different kinds, such as diathesis alternations, locative shift, morphological derivations and so on. This feature of Levin's classification is discussed in Baker & Rupperhofer (2000), where it is compared with the classification in FrameNet. Their conclusion is that concentration on formal procedures sometimes leads to classes irrelevant from purely semantic point of view.

In our ontological classification, we appeal directly to the meaning of a word. It goes without saying that we wanted to get classes that would be linguistically relevant, i.e. classes of words that would be similar in their linguistic behavior. But we relied upon semantics, starting from the assumption that semantically identifiable classes might be a reliable basis for grammatical predictions. Also, other things being equal, semantic classes tend to be more universal.

The actional classification is a ramification of the famous Vendler's classification according to which verbs are divided into four classes – actions, activities, processes and states. Actional class determines different details of linguistic behavior of a verb (aspect, voice, co-occurrence with modifiers of time and purpose, combinability with aspectual verbs etc.) and is one of the central notions in modern theoretical grammar studies.

Thematic and actional classifications are independent of one another (Paducheva 2004b). On the one hand, there are mental, perceptive, emotional, volitional, physical, physiological, social actions and states; on the other hand, mental verbs may belong to the class of states (*znat'* 'know', *pomnit'* 'remember'), actions (*rešat'* – *rešit'* 'to solve') and activities (*razmyšljat'* 'reflect').

In this paper we discuss only thematic, i.e. ontological classification. Actional classes won't be in the focus of our attention. Thus, verb taxonomy is understood, in this paper, as a thematic classification of verbs.

Let us begin with some general remarks about thematic classes.

Thematic classification, according to its very nature, is such that a word, even a non-ambiguous word, may belong to several different classes. Class attribution of a word (more precisely, a word taken in one of its meanings, a **lexeme**), is determined by the corresponding **semantic component** in its meaning. For instance, *videt'* 'see', *slyšat'* 'hear', *podgljadyvat'* 'watch furtively' have a common semantic component 'perception', and, thus, belong to the class of PERCEPTION; *bit'* 'beat', *rezat'* 'cut' have a common semantic component 'impact' and belong to the class of IMPACT. (Presumably, these components predict some feature(s) of behavior of the lexeme). But the meaning of a lexeme may include several equally conspicuous semantic components, and thus it may be identified as belonging to several different classes. For example, *ubedit'* 'convince' is a verb of SPEECH and, at the same time, of influencing volitional and mental states; *ogljanut'sja* 'look back' is a verb of CHANGE OF POSITION and PERCEPTION; *zastat'*, *zastič* 'take unawares' – MOVEMENT and PERCEPTION. The verb *skryt'sja* 'escape' has the same two components, though in a different configuration. The verb *oblokotit'sja* 'lean one's elbows on a surface' belongs to the class of SPATIAL CONFIGURATION and CONTACT & SUPPORT. A widespread conjunction of semantic components (and, therefore, thematic classes) characterizes the verb *napolnit'* 'load': PUTTING and CHANGE OF STATE OR PROPERTY; the verb *zabit'* <*gvozd'*> 'drive <a nail>' – PUTTING and IMPACT. The verb *plakat'* 'weep, cry' belongs to two classes – SOUND and PHYSIOLOGY.

The fact that a non-ambiguous word (or a lexeme) belongs to two different thematic classes characterizes its meaning and is not a drawback of the classification. In fact, *napolnit'* 'load', which is assigned to the classes PUTTING and CHANGE OF STATE OR PROPERTY, has a more sophisticated semantics than *položit'* 'lay', which expresses only 'putting', and *namoknut'* 'get wet', which expresses only 'change of state'.

On the other hand, a verb can be **ambiguous**, and then its multiple class attribution reflects its multiple meanings.

Example 1: *zametit'* =

(i) 'notice', verb of PERCEPTION;
(ii) 'make a remark', verb of SPEECH.

Example 2: *videt'* =

(i) 'see', verb of PERCEPTION;
(ii) 'believe', verb of MENTAL SPHERE (*On vidit vo mne sopernika* 'He considers me to be a rival').

Ambiguity is a characteristic feature of the lexicon of any language. At the same time, used in context an ambiguous word normally (i.e. if we exclude pun) has only one meaning. Therefore, the semantic annotation of corpus texts presupposes disambiguation. This task is discussed in section 2.

What information is deduced from the verb's ontological class?

1. First of all, thematic class influences the argument structure of the verb – the set of its participants (theta roles). The fact is that verbs of the same thematic class usually refer to the same typical situation. Verbs of creation must have the participant Result, verbs of (bounded) movement must have Initial point (cf. *ujti* 'leave') and Final point (cf. *prijti* 'arrive'). Verbs of speech imply Addressee and Text; verbs of selling and buying presuppose Agent, Counteragent, Goods, Money; verbs of sound imply Sound Emitter, Observer (off stage) and Sound (as an incorporated participant, see Jackendoff 1990: 61; Paducheva 2004a: 57–58).

Thematic classes "are at the heart of the area of linguistics called argument structure: the study of the possible syntactic expressions of the arguments of a verb" (Levin & Rappaport Hovav 2005: 1). The issue is illustrated with the classic example from Fillmore 1977:

(1) a. The boy *broke* the window with a ball;
b. The boy *hit* the window with a ball.
(2) a. The window *broke*;
b. *The window *hit*.

Though (1a) and (1b) may describe the same situation, (1a) has a lexico-syntactic correlate (2a), while (1b) does not. And, what is important, this is not an isolated pair of verbs: *hit* and *break* are representatives of their thematic classes: *break* belongs to verbs of PHYSICAL IMPACT and *hit* is a verb of CONTACT. Contact does not necessarily imply effect (and change of state): it is possible that the ball hit the window but the window did not break.

Analogous differences are found in many languages, so it is reasonable to assume that different languages have similar thematic classes.

2. Thematic class predicts, to a reasonable degree, the **derivational potential** of a word – a set of its possible derived meanings. For example, mental derivatives of perception verbs (*Videl v nej tol'ko sopernika* 'He saw in her only a rival'); existential meaning of verbs of non-directed movement (*V prudu plavali utki* 'There were ducks swimming in the pond'); speech meaning of verbs of emotion (*Gosti vosxiščalis' vidom iz okna* 'The guests admired the view out the window'). A paradigm of derived meanings of sound emission verbs is presented in Atkins *et al.* (1988). A semantic derivation paradigm for verbs of *spray-load* class is given in Paducheva & Rozina (1993).

3. Thematic class may predict **referential status** of a participant. For example, the object of a CREATION verb is, normally, an indefinite NP: *postroit'* <*dom*> 'build <a house>', *napisat'* <*poemy*> 'write a poem'. (Hence the genitive object of creation verbs in negative sentences in Russian.)

Before we go down to the list of thematic classes, the notion of a **constructional component** must be introduced (Paducheva 2004a: 45). Constructional components should be delineated in order to substantiate thematic classifications: two words that are differentiated solely by a constructional component may belong to one and the same thematic class. Cf. such constructional components as **causation** (*videt'* 'see' – *pokazat'* 'show'; *prijti* 'come' – *prislat'* 'send' belong to the same thematic class), **modality** (*vpustit'* 'allow to enter' belongs to the same class as *vojti* 'enter'), **negation** (*otkazat'sja* 'refuse' belongs to the same class as *soglasit'sja* 'agree'), **inception** (cf. *zacvesti* 'start to flower' and *cvesti* 'flower').

2.2. Ontological (= thematic) classes of verbs

Thematic classes of verbs now searchable in the RNC are shown in Fig. 1. Below we discuss thematic classes of verbs one by one, providing each class with its linguistic substantiation.

1. MOVEMENT (*bežat'* 'run', *djorgat'sja* 'twitch', *brosit'* 'throw', *nesti* 'carry'). This is one of the largest classes (more than 2000 words). There are different subclasses inside this class. Some subclasses can be identified (for the sake of information retrieval) by means of prefixes (*vy-*, *iz-*, *s-*, *ot-* for elative verbs; prefixes *v-*, *do-*, *pri-*, *za-* for lative verbs). Some subclasses of movement

verbs are traditionally used in the Russian grammar because they are of direct relevance to morphology (such as verbs of non-directed movement, *xodit'* 'walk', *begat'* 'run', *ezdit'* 'ride', *letat'* 'fly' etc.).

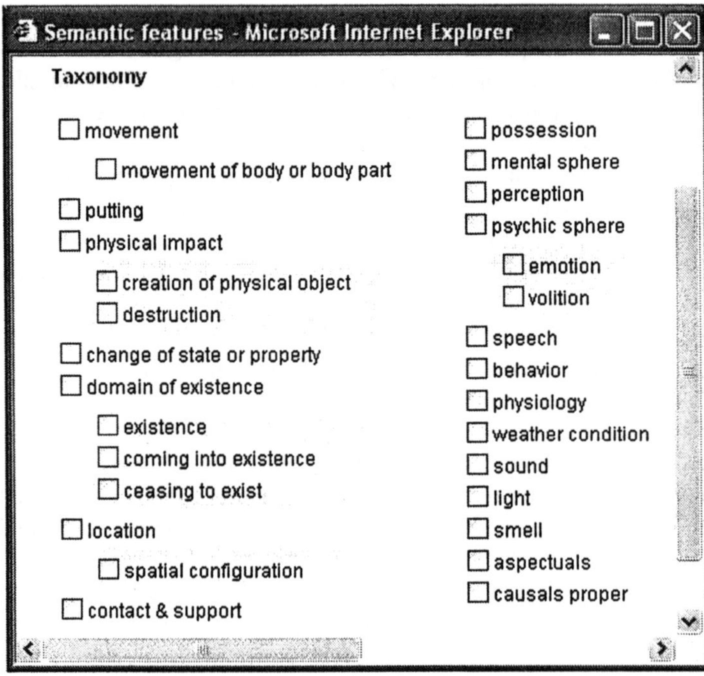

Fig. 1. Thematic classes of verbs

1.1. MOVEMENT OF BODY OR BODY PART (*leč* 'lie down', *vstat'* 'stand up', *nagnut'sja* 'bend down'; *sognut'* < *ruku v lokte*> 'bend < one's arm at the elbow>'). This is the only subclass inside MOVEMENT verbs that is distinguished as a separate class in the RNC. Moving your own body part is something different from moving external physical objects: *sognut' ruku* <*v lokte*> 'bend one's arm' is not the same as *sognut' kočergu* 'to bend a poker'. Movement of body parts presupposes inner causation (according to Wierzbicka 1980), or psychological causation according to Podlesskaya & Rakhilina (1999).

Class 1.1 is restricted as to taxonomic class of its object: not only must it be a body part – it must be a body part of the Agent – *položit'* in *položit' kurinye nožki na skovorodku* 'to put the chicken legs into a frying-pan' is not a verb of MOVEMENT OF BODY OR BODY PART.

It is important to compare class 1.1 with class 6.1 SPATIAL CONFIGURATION (containing verbs *stojat'* 'stand', *sidet'* 'sit', *ležat'* 'lie', *viset'* 'hang', their synonyms: *vossedat'* 'sit (as) on the throne', and derivates: *posidet'* 'sit for a bit'). Class 6.1 contains only non-causative verbs, while class 1.1 includes both non-causatives and causatives (*nagnut' golovu* 'bend one's head'). This means that in class 1.1 causation is treated as a constructional component. Note that in Wierzbicka 1980 intransitive verbs of class 1.1, such as *vstat'* 'stand up', are treated as causatives; in fact, the meaning of *vstat'* implies an incorporated participant Body: *vstat'* means 'cause your body to be in a vertical position'. Class 1.1 differs from 6.1 also in that verbs in 1.1 constitute aspectual pairs (*leč – ložit'sja* 'lie down'), which is normal for verbs of movement, while verbs in 6.1 are imperfectiva tantum.

2. PUTTING (or PLACEMENT OF OBJECT according to Levin 1993). This class consists mostly of transitive verbs (*položit'* 'put', *vložit'* 'put in', *sprjatat'* 'hide'). Not all transitive verbs of movement belong to the PUTTING class. The semantics of verbs *nesti* 'carry', *vezti* 'drive', for instance, don't correspond to that of PUTTING class verbs: *nesti* and *vezti* imply movement of the subject, not only of the object. Another example: the verb *brosit'* 'throw' doesn't belong to PUTTING class because 'to throw' doesn't necessarily imply 'to put'.

Verbs of PUTTING are semantically close to verbs of PHYSICAL IMPACT, class 3. For example, *zasunut'* 'slip into' is a verb of putting; it has two participants different from the Agent: "What?" and "Where?", while the verb *zabit'* (in the context *zabit' gvozd' v stenu* 'drive a nail into the wall') belongs to two classes: PUTTING and PHYSICAL IMPACT. The verb *zaplombirovat'* 'stop a tooth', which has the same two participants (one of them incorporated, namely, a stopping) is included in the class PHYSICAL IMPACT, the tooth being treated, in the first place, as the object of impact, not as the place for a stopping (cf. the verb *zaminirovat'* <*gavan'*> 'mine <the harbour>').

3. PHYSICAL IMPACT (*bit'* 'beat', *kolot'* 'prick', *vytirat'* 'wipe'). According to several linguistic sources, this class contains many different subclasses. Thematic classification of the RNC brings forward two subclasses inside the class of physical impact:

3.1. – CREATION (*vykovat'* 'forge', *sšit'* 'sew');

3.2. – DESTRUCTION (*vzorvat'* 'explode', *sžeč* 'burn down', *zarezat'* 'slaughter', *ubit'* 'kill').

There is an important subclass of CREATION verbs – verbs OF IMAGE CREATION, such as *narisovat'* 'draw', *vyšit'* 'embroider', *nadpisat'* 'inscribe' (see Levin 1993). These verbs are mentioned in Fillmore (1977), because of the double semantic role of their syntactic object. In (3) *Maša* denotes either Maša herself or her portrait:

(3) I painted Maša.

Class 4 CHANGE OF STATE OR PROPERTY verbs will be discussed later – for the reasons that will become clear in a while.

5. EXISTENCE. Three subclasses are distinguished in class 5:

5.1. EXISTENCE (*žit'* 'live', *proisxodit'* 'happen', *vodit'sja* 'be found', *suščestvovat'* 'exist')

5.2. COMING INTO EXISTENCE (*vozniknut'* 'arise', *rodit'sja* 'be born', *sformirovat'* 'form', *sozdat'* 'create')

5.3. CEASING TO EXIST (*likvidirovat'* 'liquidate', *iskorenit'* 'root out', *vymeret'* 'die out', *issjaknut'* 'run dry' <about moisture>, *izgladit'sja* 'to be blotted out' <of one's memory>).

The class of COMING INTO EXISTENCE verbs includes such verbs as *zaroždat'* 'generate', *roždat'* 'give rise to', *plodit'* 'produce', *razžigat'* 'inflame', *sozdavat'* 'set up', i.e. verbs of causing existence of a situation, not a physical object.

There is a close affinity between CREATION verbs, class 3.1, and the subclass 5.2 of verbs of EXISTENCE. A problem arises in connection with the borderline between verbs of class 5.2 with the meaning 'cause to come into existence' (*sformirovat'* 'form', *sozdat'* 'create'), and class 3.1. In its prototypical manifestations creation is not reducible to 'begin' and 'exist'. In fact, semantics of a verb of creation presupposes an activity of a specific kind which leads to the object's coming into existence, (see Wierzbicka's (1980) and Fodor's (1970) arguments about why *to kill* does not mean 'cause to die'). In other words, CREATION verbs are mostly actions. Which is not the case with 'cause to begin to exist' verbs. Here again aspectological considerations interfere with purely semantic divisions. Such verbs as *žit'* 'live' and *rodit'sja* 'be born' belong not only to verbs of EXISTENTCE, but to the class PHYSIOLOGY as well. Still, in their derived use (as in *rodilas' ideja* 'an idea was born') they denote pure COMING INTO EXISTENCE. Note that in the class of COMING INTO EXISTENCE verbs the component INCEPTION cannot be treated as constructional.

6. LOCATION is a class of primary importance ontologically (see, for example Levin & Rappaport Hovav (2005: 79) on centrality of localization component in the theory of semantic roles). In fact, for a material object it is natural to be localized somewhere.This is an axiom that occupies an important place in the sphere of entailment rules of lexical semantics. Still, lexically

LOCATION is not a clear cut class; it is represented by a stylistically deficient *naxodit'sja* 'be situated', highly ambiguous *byt'* 'be' and by secondary uses of verbs of other classes, e.g. by SPATIAL CONFIGURATION verbs in their bleached meanings, as in *Dom stoit na gore* 'The house stands on a hill'.

The LOCATION class is sufficiently numerous – some two dozens of verbs; among them verbs with an incorporated participant Time interval: *nočevat'* 'pass the night', *zimovat'* 'pass the winter'.

In the LOCATION class 'causation' is not a constructional component: the causative of a location verb doesn't belong to the same class as the verb itself; so *položit'* 'put', a causative of *ležat'* 'lie', is not a verb of location, it is a verb of PUTTING, class 2.

6.1. SPATIAL CONFIGURATION; verbs of this class are also called STANCE verbs; in Rakhilina (2000) they are called verbs of POSITION: *stojat'* 'stand', *ležat'* 'lie', *sidet'* 'sit', *viset'* 'hang'. Note that *prislonit'sja* 'lean against', *oblokotit'sja* 'lean one's elbows on a surface' also belong here. Verbs of this class have a common set of semantic valencies (on valencies of SPATIAL CONFIGURATION verbs see Apresjan 2006): Agent (*Ivan sidit* 'Ivan is sitting'), Location (*stojat' na uglu* 'stand on the corner')', Supporting Body Part (*stojat' na odnoj noge* 'stand on one leg'), and Direction (*sidet' licom k stene* 'sit with one's face to the wall').

A verb of SPATIAL CONFIGURATION class may have the meaning of LOCATION; in which case the participant Location becomes obligatory:

(4) a. *Počemu ty stoiš? Sjad'* 'Why are you standing? Sit down' [non-obligatory participant Location];
b. *Cerkov' stoit na gore* 'The church stands on the hill' [obligatory participant Location].

7. CONTACT & SUPPORT (*kasat'sja* 'touch', *obnimat'* 'embrace', *oblokotit'sja* 'lean one's elbows on a surface', *opirat'sja* 'lean against smth').

This is a big class, more than one hundred words. It is linguistically important, because here a thematic component implies stativity, an actional feature (Vendler's STATE). The borders of this class are not quite clear: contact is a prerequisite and at the same time a consequence of many different and heterogeneous situations. In the RNC only the verbs for which "contact" is an assertive component are included in this class.

Classes 8. POSSESSION, 9. MENTAL SPHERE, 10. PERCEPTION, 11.1. EMOTION, 11.2. VOLITION, 12. SPEECH, 14. PHYSIOLOGY (*est'*, *pit'*, among others) are commonly accepted and need no comments.

In thematically clear-cut classes causativity and inceptivity function as true constructional components; for example, *pokazat'* 'show', a causative verb, belongs to the same class (PERCEPTION) as *uvidet'* 'see'; *zabolet'* 'fall ill', an inceptive verb, belongs to the same class (PHYSIOLOGY) as *bolet'* 'be ill'.

Class 13. BEHAVIOR contains such verbs as *šalit'* 'be naughty', *priveredničat'* 'be fastidious', *potvorstvovat'* 'connive'. This is a new class; it is only recently that it was deemed linguistically relevant. Some verbs of this class are conceived as "verbs of interpretation" in Apresjan (2004b).

Class 15. WEATHER, contains verbs with natural forces as a subject (as in *buševala burja* 'the storm raged', *dul veter* 'the wind blew').

Classes 16. SOUND, 17. LIGHT, 18. SMELL are represented in Levin (1993) as subclasses of EMISSION verbs (also including such verbs as *dymit'sja* 'smoke', *krovotočit'* 'bleed', *puzyrit'sja* 'bubble', *penit'sja* 'foam').

The last two small classes of the thematic classification – 19. ASPECTUALS (e.g. *nachat'* 'start', *prodolzhat'* 'continue', *prekratit'* 'stop') and 20. CAUSALS PROPER (*vyzvat'* 'cause', *privesti k* 'bring to') are unproblematic.

Let us now return to class 4, CHANGE OF STATE OR PROPERTY (*povzroslet'* 'become adult', *razbogatet'* 'become rich', *rasširit'* 'widen', *ispachkat'* 'dirty up'). Emotional, mental and physiological states (e.g. *zabolet'* 'fall ill') are provided with thematic classes of their own, so that CHANGE OF STATE OR PROPERTY is a kind of default class: verbs formed from adjectives belong to this class; but verbs that denote a change of a certain specific state belong to more specific classes, such as MOVEMENT, EMOTION, POSSESSION, MENTAL SPHERE, CONFIGURATION and are not included here. There are many different states and properties denoted by adjectives that may change: color (*poželtet'* 'turn yellow'), form (*vytjanut'sja* 'lengthen'), weight (*oblegčit'* 'lighten'), temperature (*oxladit'sja* 'chill'), attribute of a person (*poglupet'* 'grow stupid'), see the taxonomy of adjectives in the RNC.

The class of CHANGE OF STATE OR PROPERTY VERBS is not to be confused with the class of **change of state** verbs, see, e.g., Levin & Rappaport Hovav (2005: 89). The latter term is widely used by linguists of different theoretic orientations. Change of state verbs do not constitute a thematic class in the sense in which verbs of movement or verbs of perception do; the class of CHANGE OF STATE OR PROPERTY VERBS includes only a small part of change of state verbs. Change of state verbs seem to occupy an intermediate position, being neither purely thematic nor purely actional.

The causatives of a CHANGE OF STATE OR PROPERTY verb belong to the same class as the initial verb; for example, *oxladit'* 'chill something.' belongs to the same class as *oxladit'sja* 'chill'.

There is a subclass of CHANGE OF STATE OR PROPERTY verbs derived, formally or semantically, from the comparative form of an adjective and denoting a change of a parameter, such as size, length, velocity, price, etc. (on their aspectual relevance see Glovinskaja 1982: 86). These verbs are called GRADUALS, examples: *uveličit'sja* 'increase', *sokratit'sja* 'decrease', *uskorit'* 'quicken', *podorožat'* 'rise in prise'.

Some verbs of CHANGE OF STATE OR PROPERTY class have a derived meaning of manifestation (of a property); for example, *belet'* = 'to be seen as white'. These are verbs implying the presence of the observer.

2.3. Evaluation

Though our major topic is ontology, a few words should be said about another facet of the verb classification in the RNC database, namely, **positive and negative evaluation**. Semantics of verbs of BEHAVIOR include, more often than not, the component "negative evaluation", as in *vytvorjat'* 'be up to no good', *natvorit'* 'make balls of something', *podsidet'* 'intrigue against', *pilit'* 'pester, lit. saw'. There are many verbs with negative evaluation in the class of verbs of speech (*komkat'* 'crumple up <one's speech>', *mjamlit'* 'mumble', *nyt'* 'whimper', xamit' 'be rude'), verbs of possessive sphere (*obsčitat'* 'cheat', *pičkat'* 'stuff with', *navjazat'* 'thrust <one's opinion>'), and even verbs of perception (*ustavit'sja* 'stare stupidly'). The verb *prozevat'* 'miss, lit. yawn' (as in *prozevat' rasprodažu* 'miss the sale') differs from *propustit'* 'miss' only in its negative evaluation component.

Many verbs acquire the negative evaluation component when used in their derived meaning: *mazat'* 'lit. oil' in the meaning 'paint badly'; *komkat'* 'lit. crumple a piece of paper' in the meaning 'crumple one's speech', *zavodit'sja* 'get wound up' in the meaning of a psychological state.

The class of interpretation verbs (see Apresjan 2004b; Kustova 2004: 232–241) is not present among RNC ontological classes. It could have been localized in the facet 'evaluation'.

In fact, verbs of interpretation may belong to different thematic classes: *narušit'* 'violate', *oblegčit'* 'alleviate', *pomoč* 'help', *pomešat'* 'hinder', *spasti* 'save' interpret physical actions; *opozorit'* 'dishonour' interprets a psychological state; *preuveličivat'* 'exaggerate' refers to speech. The verb *ošibat'sja* 'be wrong' is thematically (and actionally) ambiguous (see Mel'čuk 2004: 45): in the imperfective it means 'to have a wrong opinion', while in the perfective it can be used in the meaning 'to perform a wrong action'.

The same can be said about the class of manifestation verbs – both such as *belet'* 'be seen white', *zvučat'* 'sound', *paxnut'* 'smell', *gorčit'* 'taste bitter', *žečsja* 'sting' (all characterized by the presence of an observer-experiencer), and *plakat'* 'cry', *okamenet'* 'turn into stone' (which are emotion manifestations, Iordanskaja 1972, Apresjan 2004a).

3. Semantic annotation and word sense disambiguation

A semantically tagged corpus makes it possible to verify various linguistic hypotheses concerning semantic and syntactic compatibility of words and forms in texts. Every query addressed to a corpus is a potential **construction** in the sense of Fillmore (Fillmore & Kay 2005, Fried & Östman 2004), i.e. a hypothesis of admissible configuration of words with certain characteristics. Below we deal with configurations of words and word classes defined by a combination of morphological and semantic tags. We intend to demonstrate how the notion of construction contributes to the semantic disambiguation of a verb in a given context. Special attention is paid to the role of taxonomy (of verbs and nouns).

Up till now much research was devoted to the role of the **syntactic context** in verb disambiguation. For example, Levin & Rappaport Hovav (2005) relies upon **taxonomy** of the words constituting the context and its interplay with the taxonomy of a verb itself. In other words,

1) we pay attention to ambiguity expressible in terms of ontological classes of verbs;

2) we consider the taxonomic class (of nouns, adverbs etc.) to be one of the main disambiguating factors – a factor that up till now has remained unnoticed.

Every verb class has semantic prerequisites concerning the thematic class of each argument. A change of the thematic class of the argument may change the thematic class of the verb. This is demonstrated below with verbs which in their primary meaning have a participant necessarily belonging to the thematic class HUMAN.

Example 1 concerns verbs of BEHAVIOR. The subject of such verbs necessarily belongs to the thematic class HUMAN. Some verbs of behavior are non-ambiguous (such as *besčinstvovat'* 'commit outranges', *bujanit'* 'kick up a row', *važničat'* 'put on airs', Paducheva 1996: 149ff); but there are verbs which may mean not only behavior. For these verbs a filter is provided that cancels the tag BEHAVIOR in the context of the non-HUMAN subject. See (5a, 6a) where the verbs belong to the class BEHAVIOR and (5b, 6b) where this is not the case:

(5) a. Petja lomaetsja 'Petja behaves as a poseur';
b. Pribory lomalis' 'The instruments were being broken down'.
(6) a. Petja sovershenno raspustilsja 'Petja got out of hand',
b. Akacija raspustilas' 'The acacia has flowered'.

Example 2 concerns MENTAL verbs, whose subjects belong to the class HUMAN. If the subject doesn't belong to this class the meaning of the verb changes. This can be shown on the example of the verb *znat'* 'know'. *Znat'* 'know' in the negative form, when used in the context of a non-HUMAN subject changes its meaning and has a very general meaning of CONTACT:

(7) Ee iznežennye pal'cy ne *znali* igl (A. Pushkin) 'Her delicate fingers didn't know needles'
= 'never were in contact with needles'.

In (8) the thematic class of *znat'* 'know' can be identified as EXISTENCE; (8a) = 'there are no titles and ranks in art'; (8b) = 'successes like this don't exist in the world practice':

(8) a. Iskusstvo ne *znaet* titulov i rangov (RNC) 'The art doesn't know titles or ranks';
b. Mirovaja praktika ne *znaet* podobnyx uspexov (RNC) 'lit. World practice doesn't know such success'.

Example 3: Verbs of speech change their meaning in the context of a non-HUMAN subject. Such shifts are possible for great many verbs (Paducheva 2004: 371): *dokazat'* 'prove', *podtverdit'* 'confirm', *podčerkivat'* 'underline', *izvinjat'* 'excuse', *obeščat'* 'promise', *trebovat'* 'demand' etc.:

(9) a. Komposicija *podčerkivaet* glavnuju mysl' proizvedenija (RNC) 'The composition stresses the main idea of the piece';
b. Večer *obeščaet* byt' interesnym 'lit. The party promises to be interesting'.

Transferring tags from the semantic database to the the corpus is done in the following way: an ambiguous word in the database has several semantic tagsets which are differentiated by thematic class markers. The **Primary program** assigns tags to words in the texts automatically; it assigns every occurrence of the word in question all the tags that this verb has in the database. Roughly speaking, this program doesn't know the meaning of a word in a particular context. The second half of the program is called **Semantic filters**. The function of a filter is to isolate the tags of an ambiguous word which correspond to this context and erase all the unwanted tags.

A filter is a combination of lexical, morphological and semantic characteristics determining the context which substantiates (or gives rise to) a particular meaning of the word. All the other tags of a word in the set of examples responding to the filter are then erased. In this way disambiguation is carried out up to the thematic class. The user has the opportunity to formulate queries and receive answers, say, not about the verb *idti* 'go', but about *idti* in the meaning 'motion' (as in *poezd idet* 'the train goes'); or in the meaning 'take place' (as in *idjot urok* 'the lesson takes place'), etc.

Verb ambiguity is, more often than not, **regular ambiguity**, i.e. polysemy. For example, many verbs of physical impact have a derived meaning in the thematic class SPEECH: *pilit' brevno* 'to saw the log' vs. *pilit' muža* 'to nag one's husband', *rezat' xleb* 'to cut the bread' vs. *rezat' pravdu-matku* 'to cut the truth', *molot' muku* 'to grind the flour' vs. *molot' čuš'* 'to talk nonsense'. Every occurrence of such a verb in the course of automatic tagging, receives two tags, 'impact' and 'speech'. Filters are responsible for the disambiguation.

Several examples of filters are given below. The left part of a filter consists of an ambiguous verb (its meanings, identified by their thematic class, are given in brackets) and a noun with morphological and semantic characteristics. Nouns, according to the semantic classification of the RNC, are subdivided into three major classes: CONCRETE nouns, i.e. names of physical objects, ABSTRACT nouns and PROPER nouns. On the next level of hierarchy concrete nouns are divided into classes HUMAN, ANIMAL, TRANSPORT, STUFF, SPACE, TEXT, FOOD, etc.; abstract nouns are divided into classes MOVEMENT, PHYSICAL IMPACT, ..., SPEECH (basically, all verb classes are relevant also for deverbal nouns), as well as TIME, PARAMETER, COLOUR, etc. Here are three filters disambiguating verbs *pilit'*, *molot'* and *s"est'*:

F1. a. ***pilit'*** (impact, speech) + Noun: Acc: CONCRETE (*pilit' brevno* 'to saw the log') → *pilit'* (impact)
b. ***pilit'*** (impact, speech) + Noun: Acc: HUMAN (*pilit' muža* 'to nag one's husband') → *pilit'* (speech)

F2. a. ***molot'*** (impact, speech) + Noun: Acc: STUFF (*molot' muku* 'to grind the flour') → *molot'* (impact)
b. ***molot'*** (impact, speech) + Noun: Acc: SPEECH (*molot' čuš'* 'to talk nonsense') → *molot'* (speech)

F3. a. ***s"est'*** (physiology; ceasing to exist) + Noun: Acc: FOOD (*s"est' jabloko* 'to eat an apple') → *s"est'* (physiology)
b. ***s"est'*** (physiology; ceasing to exist) + Noun: Nom: STUFF (*ržavchina s"ela mašinu* 'rust ate the car') → *s"est'* (ceasing to exist)

It is not always possible to assign the derived meaning to any of the existing thematic classes. In some cases the tags "metaphor" or "metonymy" are used in order to differentiate meanings, cf. the use of the verb *idti* 'go' in *vremja idet* 'time goes' or *urok idet*, lit. 'the lesson goes'.

Thus, the hierarchy of thematic classes may fulfill the role of a co-ordinate system in the intricate network of a word's meanings: the thematic class serves as a reasonable objective of disambiguation.

In the RNC word classification semantics is in the foreground. Linguistic relevance of the classes, we hope, should emerge as a consequence of the semantic contiguity between words of the same class – due to the hypothesis of close relationship between combinability of linguistic entities (on the different levels of structure) – and their semantics. The use of the Russian National Corpus in ongoing linguistic research seems to confirm this hypothesis.

REFERENCES

Apresjan, Ju. D. (2004a). "Sinonimičeskij rjad *zameret'* 1.1, *zastyt'* 2.1, *ostolbenet'*, *ocepenet'* 1, *okamenet'* 2". In: Apresjan, V. Ju. e. a., *Novyj ob"jasnitel'nyj slovar' sinonimov russkogo jazyka.* Izd. 2. Moskva-Vena: Jazyki slavjanskoj kul'tury: 348–354.

Apresjan, Ju. D. (2004b). "Interpretacionnye glagoly: semantičeskaja struktura i svojstva". *Russkij jazyk v naučnom osveščenii*, 1 (7): 5–22.

Apresjan, Ju. D. (2006). "Fundamental'naja klasifikacija predikatov". In: Apresjan, Ju. D. (otv. red.). *Jazykovaja kartina mira i sistemnaja leksikografija.* Moskva: Jazyki slavjanskoj kul'tury: 75–109.

Atkins, B. T., J. Kegl & B. Levin (1988). "Anatomy of a verb entry: from linguistic theory to lexicographic practice". *International Journal of Lexicography*, 1 (2): 84–126.

Baker, C. F. & J. Ruppenhofer (2002). "FrameNet's frames vs. Levin's verb classes". In: J. Larson & M. Paster (eds.). *Proceedings of the 28th Annual Meeting of the Berkeley Linguistics Society*: 27–38.

Fillmore, Ch. J. & P. Kay (2005). *Construction grammar.* Stanford, CA: CSLI.

Fillmore, Ch. J. (1977). "The case for case reopened". In: P. Cole & J. M. Sadock (eds.). *Syntax and Semantics 8: Grammatical Relations*. N. Y. etc.: Acad. Press: 59–81.

Fodor, J. A. (1970). "Three reasons for not deriving 'kill' from 'cause to die' ". *Linguistic Inquiry* 1: 429–438.

Fried, M. & J.-O. Östman (2004). *Construction Grammar in a Cross-Language Perspective*. Amsterdam: John Benjamins.

Glovinskaja, M. Ja. (1982). *Semantičeskie tipy vidovyx protivoposavlenij russkogo glagola*. Moskva: Nauka.

Iordanskaja, L. N. (1972). "Leksikografičeskoe opisanie russkix vyrazhenij, oboznačajuščix fizičeskie simptomy čuvstv". *Mašinnyj perevod i prikladnaja lingvistika*, vyp. 16. Moskva.

Jackendoff, R. S. (1990). *Semantic Structures*. Cambridge etc.: MIT Press.

Kustova, G. I., O. N. Lashevskaja, E. V. Paducheva & E. V. Rakhilina (2005). "Semantičeskaja razmetka leksiki v nacional'nom korpuse russkogo jazyka: principy, problemy, perspektivy". *Nacional'nyj korpus russkogo jazyka: 2003–2005*. Moskva: Indrik: 155–174.

Kustova, G. I. (2004). *Tipy proizvodnyx značenij i mexanizmy jazykovogo rasširenija*. Moskva: Jazyki slavjanskoj kul'tury.

Levin, B. & M. Rappaport Hovav (2005). *Argument Realization*. Cambridge UP.

Levin, B. (1993). *English Verb Classes and Alternations: A Preliminary Investigation*. Chicago UP.

Mel'čuk, I. (2004). "Actants in semantics and syntax I: actants in syntax". *Linguistics* 42–1: 1–66.

Paducheva, E. V & R. I. Rozina (1993). "Semantičeskij klass glagolov polnogo oxvata: tolkovanie i leksiko-sintaksičeskie svojstva". *Voprosy jazykoznanija*, 6: 5–16.

Paducheva, E. V. (1996). *Semaničeskie issledovanija*. Moskva: Jazyki russskoj kul'tury.

Paducheva, E. V. (2004a). *Dinamičeskie modeli v semantike leksiki*. Moskva: Jazyki slavjanskoj kultury.

Paducheva, E. V. (2004b). "O parametrax leksičeskogo značenija glagola: ontologičeskaja kategorija i tematičeskij klass". *Russkij jazyk segodnja*, t. 3, Problemy russkoj leksikografii, red. L. P. Krysin. Moskva: 213–238.

Podlesskaya, V. I. & E. V. Rakhilina (1999). "External possession, reflexivization and body parts in Russian". In: D. L. Payne & I. Barshi (eds.). *External Possession*. Amsterdam etc.: John Benjamins: 505–521.

Rakhilina, E. V. (2000). *Kognitivnyj analiz predmetnyx imen: semantika i sočetaemost'*. Moskva: Russkie slovari.

Wierzbicka, A. (1980). *Lingua Mentalis*. Sydney etc.: Acad. Press.

Karen Sullivan

University of California, Berkeley
Universitat Autònoma de Barcelona

GRAMMATICAL CONSTRUCTIONS IN METAPHORIC LANGUAGE

Abstract: Croft (2003) argues that the use of grammatical constructions in metaphoric language tends to follow certain predictable patterns. Croft attributes these regularities to grammatical constructions' semantics, which he represents in terms of conceptual autonomy and conceptual dependence (cf. Langacker 2002). Specifically, Croft observes that "...domain mapping (metaphor) occurs with dependent predications" (2003: 192). Conceptually dependent elements, then, tend to involve "metaphorically" used words, while autonomous elements more typically include "non-metaphoric" words.

In this paper, I test the generality of Croft's observation by examining metaphoric language in a corpus of 1570 metaphoric sentences, involving 2415 metaphorically used constructions. Over 98 percent of the 2415 constructions belonged to one of the following six types: predicating modifier constructions (such as *bright student*), domain constructions (*mental exercise*), compounds (*rumor mill*), predicate-argument constructions (*the cinema beckoned*), copula constructions (*time is money*), or preposition phrase constructions (*the foundation of an argument*). Each of these constructional types involves a particular pattern of autonomy and dependence (Langacker 1987). The metaphorically used examples of these constructions in the corpus supported Croft's generalization, in that conceptually dependent elements evoked the source domain of the metaphor (were used "metaphorically"), while conceptually autonomous elements expressed the target domain of a metaphor (typically with a "non-metaphoric" meaning). This paper examines how Croft's predictions are borne out in each of the six common constructional types. The paper also discusses the combinations of constructions found in the corpus, including the combination dubbed the "*xyz* construction" (Turner 1991).

Keywords: conceptual dependence, conceptual autonomy, elaboration, source domain, target domain, mapping, domain adjectives, domain adverbs, relational nouns, *xyz* construction.

1. What is metaphoric language?

Many metaphoric phrases are comprehensible even when considered out of context. For example, the context-free noun phrase *a bright student* can be understood metaphorically to mean "an intelligent student" by any competent speaker of English.

There is evidence that *a bright student* is comprehensible partly because the items *bright* and *student* are used in a particular grammatical construction. In *a bright student*, the predicating adjective *bright* is "metaphoric," in that it evokes the concept of LIGHT-EMISSION in the source domain of SEEING, while *student* evokes the concept of INTELLIGENCE in the target domain of KNOWING. Together, these items evoke the metaphor KNOWING IS SEEING and its mapping INTELLIGENCE IS LIGHT-EMISSION (emission of light, which makes objects more visible, maps onto intelligence, which makes concepts easier to understand). It is not possible to instead attach a target-domain ("non-metaphoric") predicating modifier to a source-domain ("metaphoric") head. For example, the noun phrase *an intelligent light* cannot evoke KNOWING IS SEEING, and cannot refer to an intelligent student. Apparently, the predicating modifier construction itself allows the two domains in *a bright student* to be put together correctly to retrieve the metaphor KNOWING IS SEEING and the mapping INTELLIGENCE IS LIGHT-EMISSION.

The current study examines the metaphoric uses of constructions such as the predicating modifier construction, using a database of metaphoric sentences drawn from the British National Corpus (BNC).

2. Methodology

The corpus that forms the basis of this study consists of 1570 metaphoric sentences involving 1697 instances of conceptual metaphor. Within these sentences, I identified 2415 metaphoric constructions involving at least two open-class items, which I classified according to their constructional type. These metaphoric phrases were collected from the BNC as a by-product of the Berkeley FrameNet project.[1] I modified this corpus in that I discarded a small number of sentences that did not involve metaphor, but instead involved only metonymy or non-metaphoric idioms; and I annotated the remainder of the corpus according to

---

[1] FrameNet data is available at: http://framenet.icsi.berkeley.edu

the constructions involved. In this paper, I use this corpus to analyze the frequency of these constructions, their possible combinations in metaphoric language, and the manner in which they can and cannot be used to communicate metaphor.

This project has a narrower focus than other corpus-based studies of metaphor, such as the Pragglejaz metaphor identification project at the Vrije Universiteit Amsterdam (cf. Pragglejaz Group 2007, Steen 2007). Since the study reported here examines only metaphoric phrases that are comprehensible out of context, it bypasses complications arising from considerations of speaker/writer intent and contextually available information. Phrases that required further context in order to be interpreted metaphorically were not included in the corpus. The corpus was also limited in that it contained only metaphoric phrases with analyzable mappings or mapped image-metaphoric gestalts. Examples of "figurative" language that did not involve metaphor as defined in Conceptual Metaphor Theory (Lakoff and Johnson 1980, 1999) were discarded. These simplifications allowed me to focus on the role of grammatical constructions in metaphoric language without considering other factors in metaphor communication, and without analyzing figurative language other than conceptual metaphor.

3. Conceptual autonomy and conceptual dependence

The goal of the current study is to test the prevalence of the patterns William Croft (2003) observes in metaphorically used grammatical constructions. Croft attributes these regularities to the semantic asymmetry between elements that are conceptually autonomous and conceptually dependent in a construction. A brief overview of conceptual autonomy and conceptual dependence (Langacker 1987, 1991, 2002) is therefore necessary in order to evaluate Croft's hypothesis. As Langacker describes, "when two component structures combine (via a grammatical construction), normally an asymmetry exists between them ... One structure is said to be dependent on another to the extent that it presupposes it as part of its own internal structure" (2002: 122). In the phrase *tall man,* the element *man* is autonomous, because it is perfectly possible to conceptualize a man without considering his height; whereas the element *tall* is dependent, because the meaning of *tall* depends on the conceptualization of a person, animal or object that demonstrates the quality of tallness. This is shown in Figure (1).

In the lower left-hand rectangle in Figure (1), we can see that part of the structure of *tall* (the large oval) corresponds to the entire structure evoked by *man* (shown in the lower rectangle on the right). The meaning of *tall* is "dependent" on an autonomous element, such as the meaning of *man* or *mountain*, which can fill in this part of its semantic structure.

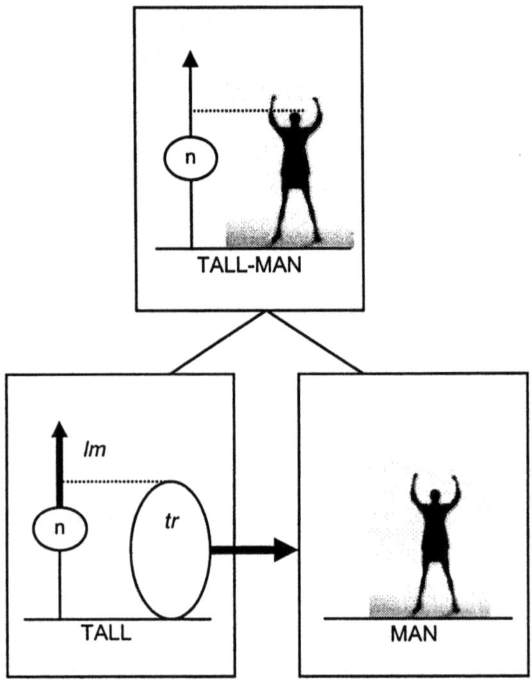

Fig. 1. In *tall man, tall* is dependent and *man* is autonomous

The large oval in Figure (1) is labeled "tr" because it represents the trajector of the structure evoked by *tall.* A *trajector* (TR) is a substructure which is understood relative to a *landmark* (LM) substructure. For example, *tall* involves a relation between a thing, such as a *man,* and a range above a certain norm (the oval labeled "n") on an abstract scale of comparison (Langacker 2002: 175–6). The thing is the TR, while the range on the scale (against which it is understood) is the LM. The TR and LM can be "filled in," or *elaborated*, by other structures. In *tall man,* the TR is elaborated by *man.* When one element in a construction (here, *man*) elaborates another element (here, *tall*), the elaborating element is conceptually autonomous relative to the elaborated element. In *tall man*, the element *man* is therefore autonomous and *tall* is dependent.[2]

William Croft (2003) argues that metaphoric language occurs when autonomous and dependent elements representing different conceptual domains are grammatically combined, which forces at least one element to be interpreted metaphorically. Croft also observes that "...domain mapping (metaphor) occurs with dependent predications" (2003: 192). In other words, dependent elements tend to involve lexical items that evoke the source domain of a metaphor. This generalization predicts, for example, that when predicating modifier constructions (such as *tall man*) are used metaphorically, the (dependent) predicating modifier will generally evoke the source domain of a metaphor, while the (autonomous) head will tend to evoke the metaphor's target domain.

The results of the study in this paper suggest that the correlation between autonomous/dependent elements and target-domain/source-domain items is widespread and regular. The analysis of these results also illustrates how Croft's generalizations surface in a variety of real-world examples.

4. Autonomy/dependence relations in the corpus

Most of the metaphoric constructions in the corpus could be categorized into six classes, which I refer to as *predicating modifier constructions*, *domain constructions*, *compounds*, *predicate-argument constructions*, *copula constructions*, and *preposition phrase constructions*. Rarer constructions, such as resultatives and idioms, also play a role in the evocation of metaphor. However, the six types listed above account for the bulk of metaphoric language (over 98% of the 2415 constructions in the corpus) and are therefore the focus of the current study.

Table (1) summarizes the patterns of autonomy and dependence in the corpus. In the rightmost column, target-domain items are in boldface and source-domain items are in italics.

Each of the six most common constructions, as listed above, demonstrates a clear pattern of conceptual autonomy and dependence according to Langacker's

[2] Conceptual dependence differs crucially from the syntactic "dependency" found in dependency and generative grammars. Phrases that are syntactic "heads," in a dependency grammar, are often found to be conceptually dependent, and likewise, syntactic "dependents" can often be shown to be conceptually autonomous.

analysis.[3] In all non-idiomatic metaphoric uses of these constructions in the corpus, dependent elements evoked metaphoric source domains (i.e., were "metaphoric") and autonomous elements represented metaphoric target domains (typically with a "non-metaphoric" meaning).[4] These trends appear to corroborate Croft's (2003) hypothesis about the role of autonomy and dependence in metaphoric language. In the following sections, I will examine each of the classes listed in Table (1).

Table 1. The constructions most commonly used in metaphor

Construction type	Percent of total	Source-domain (dependent) slot	Target-domain (autonomous) slot	Examples from corpus
Predicating modifier constructions	7.8	predicating modifier	head	*bitter* **thoughts** **perform** *brilliantly*
Domain constructions	3.1	head	domain Adj/ Adv	**political** *game* **verbally** *attack*
Compounds	1.8	head	modifier N	**heroin** *tsar*
Predicate-argument constructions	47.3	head	argument NP(s)	**the cinema** *beckoned* **fire** *gutted* **the embassy**
Copula constructions	3.7	copula-linked NP, PP, AP	head	**trade unionism** was a *difficult road*
PP/possessive constructions	34.2	head N	nominal in PP/ possessor	*the foundation of* **an argument**
Other constructions	1.4	-	-	They say he's *gone soft*

Most of the constructional classes listed in Table (1) can be broken down into a range of subtypes, as shown in Table (2).

---

[3] Domain constructions are not analyzed by Langacker, so my interpretation of these is based on studies such as Levi (1978), and on Langacker's analysis of semantically similar constructions, such as compounds.

[4] Idioms, which demonstrate unique patterns of metaphor evocation (Sullivan 2007a, 2007b), were classified as "other constructions".

Table 2. The constructions most commonly used in metaphor

Construction type	Construction subtype	Count in corpus	Percent of total	Example from corpus
Predicating modifier constructions	Adj-N Adv-V Adv-Adj	165 24 3	6.7% 1.0% 0.1%	a *juicy* **story; campaigned** *vigorously*; *largely* **rehabilitated**
Domain constructions	Domain Adj. Domain Adv.	69 7	2.8% 0.3%	the **academic** *world*; **verbally** *scampered*
Compounds	Noun-noun compound	45	1.8%	**heroin** *tsar*
Predicate-argument constructions	Intransitive Transitive Ditransitive	515 648 2	20.9% 26.3% 0.1%	your **morals** *reek;* my **faculty of speech** was *deserting* me; Meredith *flung* him **an eager glance**
Copula constructions	Equations NP BE AP NP BE PP	64 23 5	2.6% 0.9% 0.2%	**international trade unionism** was *a difficult road;* **he** was utterly *allergic to* **the suggestion; Jones** was now *in the twilight* of a ... **career**
PP/ possessive constructions	Head-PP Possessor- NP	829 16	33.6% 0.6%	*a taste of* **his temper; her mind's** *eye*

An investigation of these subtypes will be part of the examination of each constructional class.

5. Predicating modifier constructions

Predicating modifier constructions are easily analyzed in terms of autonomy and dependence. We saw one example, *tall man*, in Figure (1). Another non-metaphoric example is diagrammed in Figure (2).

Here, *bright* evokes the relation shown in the lower left-hand rectangle, in which a light-emitting TR is compared to a LM range on a brightness scale. The noun *light* evokes the structure shown on the lower right. The TR in the structure evoked by *bright* is elaborated by *light* (as indicated by the arrow), resulting in the complex structure shown in the upper part of the diagram. Clearly, the predicating modifier *bright* is conceptually dependent, since part of its structure (the TR) is elaborated by *light.*

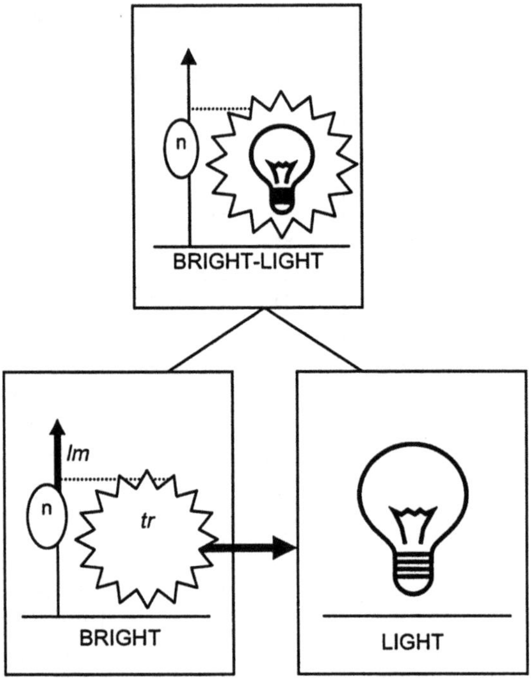

Fig. 2. In *bright light, bright* is dependent and *light* is autonomous

As predicted by Croft (2003), metaphoric uses of predicating modifier constructions are shaped by the pattern of autonomy and dependence apparent in non-metaphoric examples like *bright light.* This is apparent in all three subtypes of metaphoric predicating modifier constructions, as listed in Table (3). Again, source-domain items are italicized and target-domain items are in boldface.

All non-idiomatic metaphoric uses of predicating modifier constructions in the corpus involved a source-domain adjective/adverb and a target-domain head. For example, we've seen that in *bright student*, the head *student* evokes the domain of KNOWING, whereas the predicating modifier *bright* evokes the domain of SEEING, together evoking the metaphor KNOWING IS SEEING. Since predicating adjectives and adverbs are conceptually dependent, as shown in Figure (2), this type of construction bears out Croft's prediction that conceptually dependent elements tend to evoke source domains.

Table 3. Types of predicating modifier constructions

Construction type	Count in corpus	Percent of total constructions	Examples from corpus
Adj-N	165	6.7%	*black* **humour; a** *dirty* **look;** *stony* **faces; a** *soft* **giggle; a** *juicy* **story;** *top* **players**
Adv-V	24	1.0%	**campaigned** *vigorously*; **said** *tautly*; **bubbling** *furiously*
Adv-Adj	3	0.1%	*largely* **rehabilitated;** *obliquely* **modernist**

It is especially clear that the predicating modifier in a metaphoric predicating modifier construction is the conceptually dependent element if we compare non-metaphoric *bright light*, as in Figure (2), with metaphoric *bright student*, shown in Figure (3).

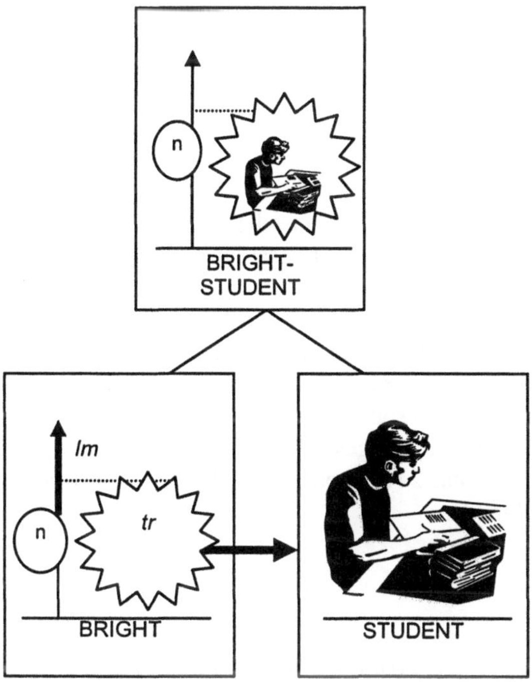

Fig. 3. In *bright student, bright* is dependent and *student* is autonomous

In *bright student*, as in *bright light*, the predicating modifier *bright* evokes a relational structure in which a TR is compared to a LM region on a scale of brightness. Interpretation of the metaphoric phrase *bright student* then involves an additional step: since a student cannot literally emit light (as would otherwise be suggested by the completed structure in the upper part of Figure 3), the phrase *bright student* must be understood metaphorically. The meaning of *bright* is already influenced (elaborated) by the meaning of its head, whether this head is *light, student,* or something else. On the other hand, the meaning of *light* or *student* is not substantially affected by its role in elaborating the TR of the *bright* structure. Given this asymmetry, it seems logical that we would adapt the domain of *bright* in *bright student* to be compatible with the meaning of *student*, rather than choosing to adapt the meaning of *student* itself.

In fact, predicating modifier constructions following the pattern of *bright student* appear to be frequent in metaphoric language. Predicating modifier constructions with this pattern accounted for 7.8% of the constructions in my corpus, making these the third most common type in the corpus (after the predicate-argument and preposition phrase constructions).

6. Domain constructions

The metaphoric uses of domain adjectives/adverbs are strikingly different from those of predicating adjectives/adverbs.[5] As we've seen, predicating modifiers evoke the source domain of a metaphor, while their heads evoke the target, as in *bright student*. Domain adjectives and adverbs appear to follow the opposite pattern. For example, in *mental exercise*, the domain adjective *mental* evokes MIND, the target domain of the metaphor THE MIND IS A BODY, whereas *exercise* evokes BODY, the source domain.

The totals and percentages of domain constructions demonstrating this pattern (out of the total 2415 metaphorically used constructions in the corpus) are shown in Table (4).

[5] A "predicating" adjective can appear in the post-copula position, whereas a domain adjective cannot; for example, *a beautiful princess* has the corresponding construction *a princess who is beautiful*; but *a rural policeman* does not have a counterpart construction **a policeman who is rural* (Levi 1978: 3). Non-predicating adjectives like *rural* are called "domain adjectives" (cf. Sweetser 1997); the constructions in which they occur are called "domain constructions".

Table 4. Types of domain constructions

Construction Type	Count in corpus	Percent of total constructions	Examples from corpus
Domain adjective	69	2.8%	my **inner** *cheerleader*; a **psychological** *jungle*; the **academic** *world*
Domain adverb	7	0.3%	**financially** *sound*; **emotionally** *damaged*; **verbally** *scampered*; **environmentally** *conscious*

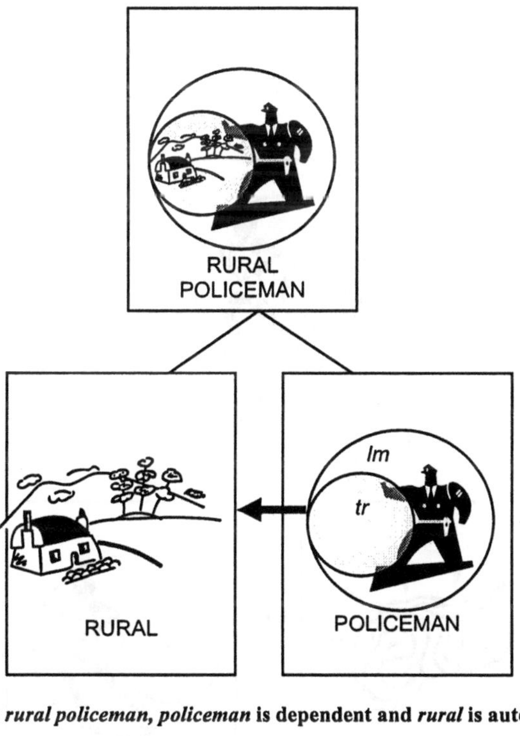

Fig. 4. In *rural policeman, policeman* is dependent and *rural* is autonomous

Phrases involving domain adjectives/adverbs, and those with predicating adjectives/adverbs, superficially appear to have a similar (modifier-head) structure, so it may seem counterintuitive that their uses in metaphor are diametrically opposed. The explanation for this difference has its basis in the constructions' patterns of autonomy and dependence. In predicating modifier constructions, we've seen that the head is the conceptually autonomous element.

In domain constructions, this pattern of autonomy and dependence is reversed, and the head is the conceptually dependent element. For example, in the non-metaphoric phrase *rural policeman*, the domain adjective *rural* refers to a subtype of policemen, as shown in Figure (4).[6]

In the phrase *rural policeman*, the head noun refers to a category, or type, rather than an instance of that type (Langacker 1991, section 2.2.1 explains how nouns can refer to types vs. instances). As such, the TR is a subtype within the category as a whole (the LM). Here, the domain adjective *rural* elaborates the TR. The domain adjective *rural* is therefore the autonomous element in this relation, and *policeman* is conceptually dependent.

In a metaphoric domain construction, the pattern of autonomy and dependence is the same. Compare non-metaphoric *rural policeman* with metaphoric *mental exercise*, in Figure (5).

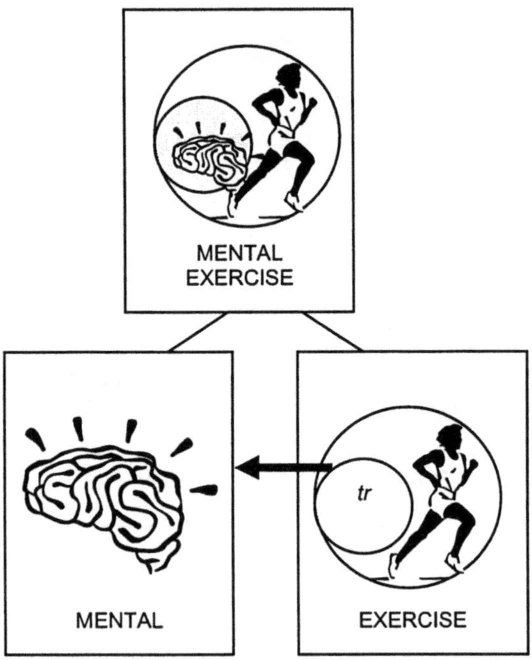

Fig. 5. In *mental exercise, exercise* is dependent and *mental* is autonomous

[6] The internal structure of *rural* is omitted in this diagram to emphasize the relation between *rural* and the head noun.

In the phrase *mental exercise*, the (autonomous) domain adjective *mental* evokes the target domain MIND, and the (dependent) head noun *exercise* evokes the source domain BODY. The construction as a whole reconstructs the metaphor THE MIND IS A BODY and its mapping MENTAL EXERCISE IS PHYSICAL EXERCISE. Metaphoric domain constructions' behavior in the corpus therefore follows Croft's prediction, in that the conceptually dependent element, the head, evokes the source domain, while the autonomous domain adjective or adverb evokes the target domain.

7. Compounds

Metaphoric compounds appear to be rare, as only 45 examples appeared in the corpus:

Table 5. Compounds in the corpus

Construction Type	Count in corpus	Percent of total constructions	Examples from corpus
N-N compound	45	1.8%	heroin *tsar*; bargain *hunting*

The corpus did not include A-N compounds, or compounds in which one element was a phrase, as in *over-the-fence gossip* (cf. Benczes 2006: 7). I will therefore limit my analysis here to N-N compounds, which appear to be the most common compounds in metaphoric language.

The autonomy/dependence pattern found in N-N compounds looks most like the pattern in domain constructions, as can by seen by comparing Figure (5) with Figure (6). As Langacker (1991) notes, the first element of a N-N compound is conceptually autonomous, and the second is dependent. This is similar to the pattern found in domain constructions, in which the domain adjective or adverb is autonomous and is followed by a conceptually dependent head noun.

Mark Turner (1991: 204–5) offers a compatible analysis of metaphoric compounds such as *rumor mill*. He analyzes N-N compounds as involving an element from the target domain (the first noun) and one from the source domain (the second noun). He then asserts that the compound involves the replacement of a source domain element with the target domain referent of the first noun. In *rumor mill*, the mill's PRODUCT, probably grain, is "replaced" with RUMORS; that is, the PRODUCT maps onto RUMORS. This analysis is consistent with Langacker's in that Turner refers to the "replacement" of part of the meaning of *mill*, which Langacker would describe as the *elaboration* of part of its meaning.

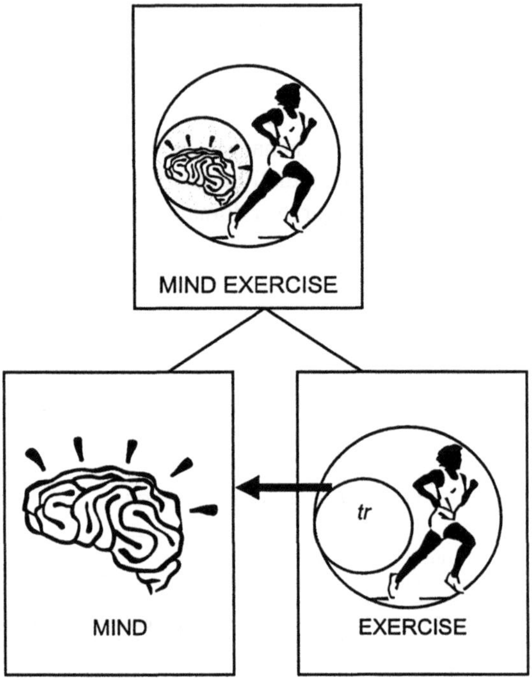

Fig. 6. In *mind exercise, exercise* is dependent and *mind* is autonomous

Turner's analysis of metaphoric N-N compounds is supported by the corpus examples, all of which shared the target domain-source domain pattern. Turner's analysis is also consistent with Croft's generalization about metaphoric phrases in general, in that the dependent element in N-N compounds evokes the source domain in these constructions' metaphoric uses.

8. Predicate-argument constructions

Predicate-argument constructions appear to be the most common means of communicating a metaphor using language. These accounted for 47.3% of the metaphoric constructions in the corpus, and included intransitive, transitive and ditransitive constructions, as shown in Table (6).

Table 6. Types of predicate-argument constructions

Construction type	Count in corpus	Percent of total constructions	Examples from corpus
Intransitive	515	20.9%	your **morals** *reek*; the **cinema** *beckoned*; the **riots** *blazed*
Transitive	648	26.3%	he *built* **power**; two people…are *chasing* the same **world title**; my **faculty of speech** was *deserting* me
Ditransitive	2	0.1%	Meredith *flung* him **an eager glance**

In all 1165 non-idiomatic metaphoric predicate-argument constructions in the corpus, the predicate evoked the source domain of the metaphor, while at least one argument noun evoked the target domain. This conforms to Croft's prediction, because the predicate in a predicate-argument construction is always conceptually dependent relative to its arguments.

The pattern is easiest to see in intransitive constructions, in which the autonomous subject evokes the target domain and the conceptually dependent verb evokes the source domain, as in *the cinema beckons* in Figure (7). Here, the conceptually dependent head *beckons* evokes the source domain of a personification metaphor, and *cinema* evokes the target domain.

Metaphoric transitive constructions are more varied than intransitives, and may follow one of three patterns. In the first type, the subject evokes the target domain and the object is *domain-neutral*, meaning that it evokes neither domain because its meaning is compatible with both. For example, the pronoun *it* always falls into this category. In a second type of transitive construction, the object evokes the target domain, and the subject is domain-neutral. The third pattern occurs when both subject and object help evoke the target domain. These three possibilities and their frequencies in the corpus are given in Table (7).

These three patterns are possible because transitive constructions involve two autonomy/dependence relations that are relevant in metaphoric language. The first relation appears when the verb and its direct object combine to form a constituent, as described by Langacker (1991: 172–3). Within this constituent, the direct object supplies the autonomous element and the verb supplies the dependent element. For example, in the phrase *the criticism hurt his ego*, the constituent *hurt his ego* combines the autonomous element *his ego* (which evokes the MIND domain) with the dependent element *hurt* (which evokes the BODY domain), thereby communicating the metaphor THE MIND IS A BODY. The second relevant autonomy/dependence relation comes into play when we consider the full phrase *the criticism hurt his ego*. The subject, *the criticism*, now elaborates the structure evoked by the VP constituent *hurt his ego*. Both *his ego* and *the criticism* elaborate the structure of *hurt*, so both help communicate the target domain in the metaphoric phrase *the criticism hurt his ego*.

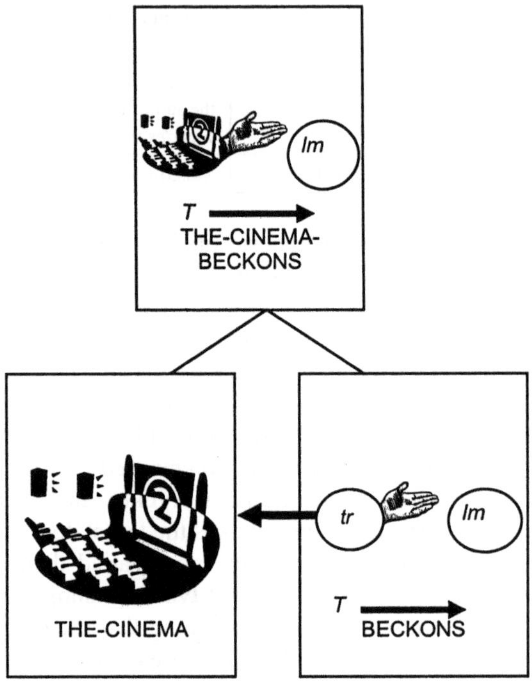

Fig. 7. In *the cinema beckons, beckons* is dependent and *cinema* is autonomous

Table 7. Types of transitive constructions

Transitive Construction Type	**Count in corpus**	**Percent of total constructions**	**Examples from corpus**
Target-domain Subj.	51	2.1%	my **faculty of speech** was *deserting* me; the **criticism** *stung* him
Target-domain Obj.	407	16.9%	two people… *are chasing* the same **world title**; He built **power**; Miller *piles on* the **earnestness**; Clinton *wooed* the **Irish vote**
Target-domain Subj. and Obj.	190	7.9%	**surprise** *hammered* **her heart**; **the remark** *soothed* **Yussuf's pride**

In a metaphoric predicate-argument construction, then, any or all of the verb's arguments may help evoke the metaphoric target domain. This results in a variety of metaphoric uses of the constructions, which contributes to their usefulness in communicating metaphor and helps explain their preponderance in the corpus.

9. Copula constructions

Copula constructions include equations, such as *time is money*, along with phrases with copula-linked adjectives and PPs. Equations enjoy a certain prominence in the notation of modern conceptual metaphor theory, where they have been adopted as the standard format for naming conceptual metaphors (as in TIME IS A RESOURCE, THE MIND IS A BODY, etc.). However, metaphoric uses of copula constructions are relatively rare, as shown below.

Table 8. Types of copula constructions

Construction type	Count in corpus	Percent of total constructions	Examples from corpus
NP BE NP/ Equations	64	2.6%	**last night** had been *a glorious voyage of discovery*, **international trade unionism** was *a difficult road*, **places** have become *commodities*
NP BE AP	23	0.9%	**he** was utterly *allergic* to the suggestion, **everything** is *gilded* with the last glow of the sunset
NP BE PP	5	0.2%	**Jones** was now *in the twilight* of a complex and often controversial career, ever since she had met him **she** had been *on a roller-coaster*

The standard pattern found in these phrases is for the copula-linked element to evoke the target domain, while the head noun evokes the source domain. The vast majority of copula constructions follow the pattern found in *time is money* (shown in Figure 8) in which the target-domain item precedes the copular phrase.

The internal structure of *is money* has been omitted in the above diagram; this structure is explored for non-metaphoric equations in Langacker 2002. Figure (8) shows, however, that the subject *time* elaborates the TR role within the structure evoked by *is money*. It follows that *money* is the autonomous element in the relation and that it will evoke the target domain in a metaphoric use of an equation. Ninety-two of the ninety-four copula constructions in the corpus followed this pattern.

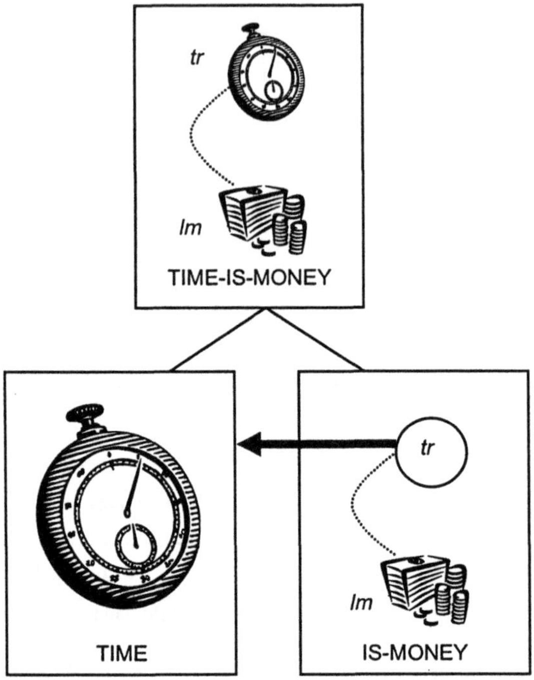

Fig. 8. In *time is money, is money* is dependent and *time* is autonomous

The two exceptions involved the head noun *key*, as in *The key is to keep the fish just warm to avoid overheating...* The item *key* is an example of what Turner (1991: 144–7) calls "extremely basic" source-domain nouns, which, when used in metaphoric equations, follow a source-target pattern instead of the usual target-source one (Turner 1991: 145; Turner's examples are *root*, *key* and *fountain*). These exceptions were considered idiomatic, and were therefore counted in the "other constructions" category rather than grouped with the copula constructions.

10. Preposition phrase constructions

Metaphoric preposition phrase constructions are less straightforward in their autonomy-dependence relations than the other constructions we've seen, and as a result, their use in metaphor is somewhat more complex. Nevertheless, these constructions are extremely common, and accounted for over a third of the metaphoric constructions in the corpus, as shown below.[7]

Table 9. Types of preposition phrase constructions

Construction type	Count in corpus	Percent of total constructions	Examples from corpus
Head-PP	829	33.6%	*a taste* of **his temper**, *the barons* of **beer**, *the divisions in* **the nation**, *barriers* between **religions**
Possessor-NP	16	0.6%	**her mind's** *eye*, a **child's** *links* to a **birth parent**

There is no question that preposition phrase constructions' metaphoric uses are highly regular. In all of the instances included in the above totals, the head evoked the source domain and the NP within the PP evoked the target. The question of how to analyze this regularity, however, is somewhat more problematic. Prepositions themselves have schematic, relational meanings, and are always conceptually dependent. This does not explain why the NP within a PP would evoke a target domain, while the NP modified by the PP would evoke a source domain. Both NPs are autonomous relative to the preposition itself, but the relation between the two NPs is less obvious.

Croft (2003) makes an argument for the relative dependence of NPs within metaphoric PPs, as compared to the NP modified by the PP. His argument is based on the prevalence of *relational nouns* in metaphoric preposition phrase constructions. For example, in the phrase *mouth of the river*, the head noun *mouth* is relational, because it refers to a part of a whole (in the source domain, this whole is typically an animal or an animal's head). In the target domain, the whole that *mouth* is part of is elaborated by *river* (via an image metaphor that maps the shape of a mouth to the shape of a river's outlet). Since *river* elaborates the whole of which *mouth* is a part, *river* is autonomous relative to *mouth* in *mouth of the river*.

A similar example from my corpus is *the foundation of an argument*, which reflects the conceptual metaphor THEORIES ARE BUILDINGS. *Foundation* is a relational noun, designating a part of a whole (in the source domain, a foundation is part of a building). This phrase is diagrammed in Figure (9).

[7] I am classifying possessive constructions as preposition phrase constructions for two reasons: first, due to their similarity to preposition phrase constructions with *of*; and second, because languages with more cases and fewer prepositions than English, such as Finnish, assign a metaphor evocation function to case endings which resembles that of English prepositions (Sullivan 2007b).

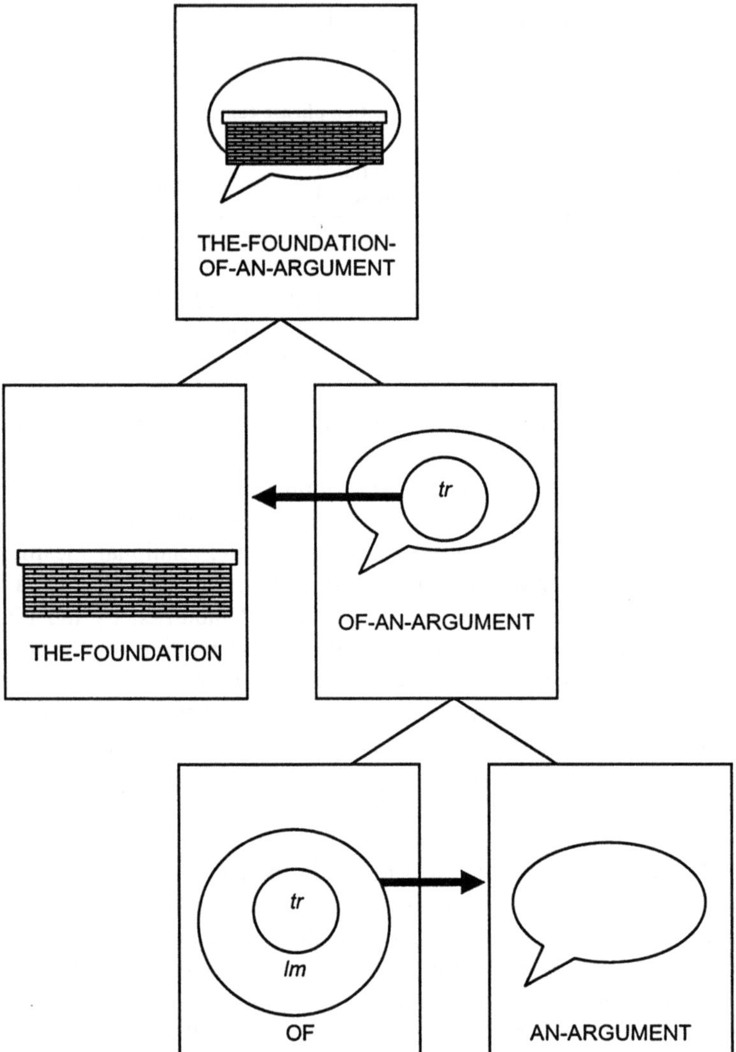

Fig. 9. In *the foundation of an argument, foundation* and *argument* are autonomous relative to *of*, but *argument* is autonomous relative to *foundation*

The gray arrows show that both *argument* and *foundation* elaborate the structure of the preposition *of*. The relative autonomy and dependence of *argument* and *foundation* are not directly shown in the diagram. However, the structure in the uppermost rectangle, in which the TR *foundation* is shown within the LM *argument*, suggests how *foundation* is conceptualized as "part" of an argument in the target domain, thereby following the autonomy-dependence pattern suggested by Croft (2003).

Another common class of metaphoric preposition phrase constructions can be shown to follow the trend noted by Croft. When a verb is nominalized, the verb's arguments often correspond to PPs, as Langacker (1991: 37) describes. For example, the phrase *good and evil struggled* evokes the same metaphor as the NP-PP *the struggle* ***between*** *good and evil*; the phrase *European ideas emigrated* evokes the same metaphor as *the emigration* ***of*** *European ideas*; and *it steals the self/the self was stolen* evokes the same metaphor as *the stealing* ***of*** *the self* (these are NP-PPs from the corpus).

Based on these trends, it seems reasonable to hypothesize that in all preposition phrases, the noun within the PP is conceptually autonomous relative to the head modified by the preposition phrase. This hypothesis is supported by the non-idiomatic metaphoric preposition phrase constructions in the corpus, which involved a source-domain head and a target-domain NP within the PP.

11. Constructional combinations

It only takes one construction to evoke a conceptual metaphor. But in most metaphoric sentences, either the target or the source domain is evoked by multiple items. In the corpus I analyzed, the 2415 constructions evoked 1697 instances of conceptual metaphor, involving 2456 target-domain items and 1935 source-domain items. There were more source- and target-domain items than there were instances of metaphor, because in many cases, several items were used to evoke a single conceptual metaphor. In fact, sixty-seven percent of the analyzed constructions took part in constructional combinations expressing a single conceptual metaphor. A smaller number of items evoked the source or target of one metaphor, and additionally evoked the source or target of a different metaphor. These items were counted twice, once for each use as either a source- or a target-domain item.

Example (1) is a typical phrase from the corpus:

(1) Many countries are already proceeding towards democracy.

Here two constructions are relevant: the predicate-argument construction which relates the (autonomous) target-domain term *countries* with the (dependent) source-domain element *proceeding*; and the preposition phrase construction which connects the (autonomous) target-domain element *democracy* with the element *proceeding*. Both relevant constructions evoke the Location Event-Structure Metaphor (also called ACHIEVING A GOAL IS REACHING A DESTINATION).

The "*xyz* construction," found in phrases such as *necessity is the mother of invention*, was made famous by Mark Turner (cf. 1991). The analysis presented here suggests that the *xyz* construction follows the compositional rules that are shared by all metaphoric phrases. The examples of *xyz* constructions in the corpus evoked metaphor following a pattern similar to the one in *many countries are proceeding towards democracy*, in (1). Example (1) differs from the *xyz* constructions only in that it involves a predicate-argument construction and a preposition phrase construction, whereas *xyz* constructions combine an equation and a preposition phrase construction. The head noun in an *xyz* construction (Turner's "X") and the noun within the PP (the "Z") are target-domain; the post-copular noun, which is also the head of the NP-PP ("Y") evokes the source domain. A typical instance of a metaphoric *xyz* construction is given below.

(2) ...inflation is a remedy for unemployment.

Here, the preposition phrase construction *a remedy for unemployment* evokes THE ECONOMY IS A BODY by relating the dependent element *remedy* to the autonomous element *unemployment*. As predicted by the analysis of preposition phrase constructions in section (10), the element *unemployment* evokes the target domain (ECONOMY), while the dependent element *remedy* evokes the source domain (BODY; "remedies" are typically applied to bodily ailments). The unit *a remedy for unemployment* is then related to the item *inflation* via an equation (see section 9). As expected, the head *inflation* refers to the target domain (ECONOMY) rather than the source domain (BODY). The post-copular element *a remedy for unemployment* fulfills its constructional responsibility of evoking the source domain, via the item *remedy*. The phrase additionally evokes the target domain, via *unemployment*; but the corpus results indicate that repeated evocation of a domain is apparently preferred, rather than avoided, in metaphoric language.

It seems, then, that metaphoric *xyz* constructions result from the compositional combination of autonomy/dependence relations.

12. Summary

The study reported in this paper supports Croft's (2003) hypothesis that conceptually dependent elements tend to be "metaphoric". In non-idiomatic uses of the six most common types of metaphoric phrases in the corpus, the dependent element evoked the metaphoric source domain and the autonomous element evoked the target domain. This pattern is a logical use of the communicative resources of autonomy and dependence. Speakers recognize that a dependent element presupposes the existence of an autonomous element, and that the meaning of the dependent element varies depending on the choice of an autonomous element. Speakers therefore tend to use the dependent element to evoke a metaphoric source domain, with the assurance that this element's meaning will be understood differently – and even understood within a different domain – based on the meaning of the autonomous element.

REFERENCES

Benczes, R. (2006). *Creative Compounding in English.* Amsterdam: John Benjamins.

Croft, W. (2003). "The role of domains in the interpretation of metaphors and metonymies". In: R. Dirven & R. Pörings (eds.). *Metaphor and Metonymy in Comparison and Contrast.* Berlin/New York: Mouton de Gruyter: 161–206.

Lakoff, G. & M. Johnson (1980). *Metaphors We Live By.* Chicago: University of Chicago Press.

Lakoff, G. & M. Johnson (1999). *Philosophy in the Flesh.* New York: Basic Books.

Langacker, R. W. (1987). *Foundations of Cognitive Grammar.* Vol. I. Stanford: Stanford University Press.

Langacker, R. W. (1991). *Foundations of Cognitive Grammar.* Vol. II. Stanford: Stanford University Press.

Langacker, R. W. (2002). *Concept, Image and Symbol: The Cognitive Basis of Grammar.* New York: Mouton de Gruyter.

Levi, J. N. (1978). *The Syntax and Semantics of Complex Nominals.* New York: Academic Press.

Pragglejaz Group (2007). "MIP: A method for identifying metaphorically used words in discourse". *Metaphor and Symbol* 22 (1): 1–39.

Steen, G. J. (2007). *Finding metaphor in grammar and usage: A methodological analysis.* Amsterdam: John Benjamins.

Sullivan, K. (2007a). "Lexical Filledness and Metaphor in Idioms". In: M. Nenonen, S. Niemi and J. Niemi (eds). *Collocations and Idioms.* Joensuu, Finland: Joensuu University Press: 330–341.

Sullivan, K. (2007b). *Grammar in Metaphor: A Construction Grammar Account of Metaphoric Language*. Ph.D. Dissertation. University of California, Berkeley.

Sweetser, E. (1997). "Compositionality and blending: semantic composition in a cognitively realistic framework". *Fifth International Cognitive Linguistics Conference*. Amsterdam: 129–162.

Turner, M. (1991). *Reading Minds: The Study of English in the Age of Cognitive Science*. Princeton, NJ: Princeton University Press.

Part Two

MULTIMODAL CORPORA

Monika Kopytowska

University of Łódź

CORPUS LINGUISTICS AND AN ECLECTIC APPROACH TO THE STUDY OF NEWS – THE MECHANISM OF FRAMING

Abstract: The objective behind this study is to maximize the validity of a cognitive approach and corpus methodology in the domain of news discourse along with the processes within this discourse and the practices behind it. Based on the premise that providing frames of reference – highly stereotyped representations of specific situations, media influence the frames we use when interproting information about events, it is an attempt to investigate some stereotypical framing techniques and the interaction between linguistic and visual means employed by the news media to define problems, diagnose causes, make moral judgments, and suggest remedies when reporting on the Third World-related issues, in particular on the two most frequent Africa-focused stories, namely famine and ethnic conflict. It also examines the motives behind and the possible implications of imposing a humanitarian frame, a heroic frame, an attribution of responsibility frame and a security frame, and discusses the techniques of increasing the degree to which the audience can empathize with the news actors. To this end, the study combines quantitative and qualitative methods, thereby showing that in this new eclectic approach to the mechanism of framing, keyword analysis, conducted with the tools provided by corpus linguistics, constitutes an important initial step in the investigation of the frame-building and frame-setting process.

Keywords: Africa, corpus, discourse, frame, framing, keywords, key-images, news, representation, stereotype.

1. Introduction

Owing to its social, political and cultural importance, the news genre has inspired critical studies in such disciplines as semiotics and discourse analysis. Yet, what can be observed despite a multiplicity of approaches and methods of analysis is the absence of integrated accounts of television news discourse and the dominance of the ideology-oriented research, not supported with the analysis of the local instantiation of discourse in specific contexts. Early critiques by Verschueren (1985: vii) describing the linguistic research on media discourse as being either insufficiently contextualized and ignorant of "structural and functional properties of news gathering and reporting process", or excessively ideology-oriented and prone to draw obvious conclusions apparently still hold true. So do the comments of Bell (1991: 215), who argued that content-analytic approaches to media discourse display a "lack of sound, basic linguistic analysis," and erroneously presume "a clearly definable relation between any given linguistic choice and a specific ideology", and Fowler (1996: 8), arguing that qualitative analyses "tend to be fragmentary [and] exemplificatory".

Responding to the need for a cognitive pluralism in analysis, and steering a course between a vacuous linguistic hyper-analysis with little bearing on socio-cultural reality and the exaggerated relativism of what Lakoff and Johnson (1980: 224) call "café phenomenology", this study proposes an eclectic approach to television news, which combines a cognitivist perspective with insights from communication studies and semiotics, and draws on the merits of corpus linguistics. The objective behind it is to show that Cognitive Linguistics along with corpus tools can be effectively applied to the analysis of such dynamic, culturally embedded and politically determined texts as television news, in order to investigate how values, stereotypes and multifarious ideological meanings are conveyed through language, and how the audience is made to empathize with particular news actors and accept a certain point of view.

2. Cognitive Linguistics, "pictures in our heads" and framing

The core of Lippmann's (1922: 29) claim that the news media are the primary source of the "pictures in our heads", generating impressions concerning the vast external world of public affairs that is "out of reach, out of sight, out of mind", was that the elements prominent in the media picture become prominent in the audience's picture. Given that viewers not only acquire factual information about public affairs, but also learn how much importance to attach to a topic on the basis of the emphasis placed on it in the news, the media can influence what issues people pay attention to, and determine the audience's judgments about political and social problems and their remedies. In the words of Berelson (1949: 117) "some kinds of issues, brought to the attention of some kinds of people, under some kinds of conditions, have some kinds of effects".

Such observations are compatible with the Cognitive Linguistics notion of a *conceptualization*, defined by Langacker (1990: 18) as "the cognitive activity constituting our apprehension of the world," which truly emphasizes the dynamic nature of our concepts, and the process of constructing them. Hence, the same situation in the world can be conceptualized in multiple ways. Another claim of particular relevance to this analysis is that we cannot study the meaning of linguistic expressions without situating them in a specific conceptual environment, a suitable conceptual domain that will let us access stored knowledge and experience, as "[m]ost concepts presuppose other concepts and cannot be adequately defined except by reference to them, be it implicit or explicit (Langacker 1987: 147)."

While Langacker (2001) himself acknowledges that Cognitive Linguistics can be applied in the investigation of the discursive dimension of language, attempts to find points of convergence between cognitive grammar and discourse analysis are a relatively recent phenomenon. Cap (2003: 104ff) examines the analogies between mainstream discourse theories and Langacker's cognitive grammar apparatus in their approach to the analysis of a given discourse type, and points to "the pre-existence of some common ground between cognitive grammar and mainstream discourse theories" (ibid. 127). Lennon (2004) tries to combine the approaches of pragmatics and Cognitive Linguistics in his analysis of news discourse.

This study focuses on framing, one of the basic cognitive mechanisms, which is both used and affected by the media. The nature of this mechanism explains why the mass media, a major source of definitions and images, have such a powerful effect on the audiences' reception of events in the world, especially those of which the public has little first-hand knowledge. As pointed out by Schramm (1949: 259) news "exists in the minds of men", and this mental image of the event not experienced directly is likely to determine people's judgment and emotional attitude.

Although Entman (1993) notices the lack of a precise theoretical definition of frames and their influence on thinking, the common perception among those who have used this concept in linguistics (cf. Fillmore 1975, Lakoff 1987, 1996, 2004, Lakoff & Ferguson 2004, Tannen 1993), cognitive psychology (cf. Fodor 1983, 2000, Minsky 1975), communication science (cf. Gitlin 1980, Entman 1991, 1993, 2003, 2004), anthropology (cf. Bateson 1972), and sociology (cf. Goffman 1974), is that the function of a frame is to help people to organize the complexity of the world into meaningful categories. While some researchers believe that frames are to be found in media coverage (cf. Entman 1991, 2003,

2004, Pan & Kosicki 1993, Schaefer 2003), others claim they are in the recipient's mind (cf. McLeod & Detenber 1999, Scheufele 2004), or both in the sender and recipient (cf. Scheufele 1999). Entman (1993: 52) argues that "frames have at least four locations in the communication process: the communicator, the text, the receiver and the culture". Still, a distinction has to be made between media frames, constructed by the journalist to make the event more accessible to the public, and audience frames, or "information-processing schemata" (Entman 1991: 7), composed of interpretations enabling a person to understand the incoming information, or in the words of Goffman (1974: 22) to "locate, perceive, identify, and label".

In Cognitive Linguistics frames have been mostly defined as cognitive structures, based on prior knowledge and used to facilitate the thinking process, while framing has been referred to as a process of selectively using frames to evoke a particular image or idea. Since every word evokes a frame with certain background knowledge and a set of presuppositions, each framing implies something different. Even this general description shows two dimensions of a frame: the "internal" one, corresponding to individual frames and involved in the process of schema formation, and the "external" one, which is related to media frames, "persistent patterns" of presentation used by journalists to change the degree of salience of the issues described. Increased salience means greater probability that viewers will focus their attention on a given piece of information and then store it in their memory. This is achieved, among other ways, by providing and repeating certain words and visual images, and putting them in a particular context, which results in drawing attention to some aspects of reality while obscuring other elements. In this way, news frames contribute to the process of schema formation, termed frame setting (cf. De Vreese 2005: 51–53). The public is thus stimulated to adopt the frames constructed by the newsmakers and to view reality from the same perspective as they do.

3. Corpus linguistics and keywords

Corpus linguistics, in particular when used in combination with qualitative approaches, can become a valuable tool for discourse analysis as it allows for the quantification of recurring linguistic features necessary to substantiate qualitative insights and for reliable generalizations concerning the effects of various linguistic choices (cf. Stubbs 1997: 107, 111; O'Keeffe 2006: 51). As a method it has been used by a growing number of media researchers, mostly in corpus-based analyses of the press language. Among others, Caldas-Coulthard (1993) applied it to investigate the representation of women in the news, Galasinski and Marley (1998) to compare the agency in British and Polish newspapers, and Jeffries (2003) to investigate local newspaper reporting of the 1995 water crisis in Yorkshire. It has also been applied in research concerning the Internet and broadcasting media, namely in Coperias Aguilar and Beso's (1999) analysis of Northern Ireland Republican and Unionist party websites, Carter and McCarthy's (2002) study on broadcast political interviews, Chang's (2002) analysis of pronouns in an American phone-in radio programme, O'Keeffe's (2002, 2003, 2005) investigation of socio-cultural indices of identity, vague language, and questioning in radio phone-ins, and O'Keeffe's (2006) extensive study of spoken interactions in the media. The tools provided by corpus linguistics which all these studies rely on are word frequency list generation, cluster analysis, and concordancing.

Although, according O'Keeffe (2006: 158), corpus linguistics can "give statistical support to qualitative findings", a statistical investigation has rarely, if at all, been used as a starting point in the analysis of such a powerful and opinion-forming media mechanism as framing. Given the nature of the mechanism in question, and the fact that news texts tend to render a particular meaning system through key words combined in a specific form, a careful examination of word choices, the extent of their use in news coverage as well as their semantic associations should reveal a lot about the decisions on framing. The frequency of certain lexical items can thus justifiably be considered a starting point for identifying and describing news frames (cf. Scott 1998, 2000, Stubbs 1996).

4. Background to this study and data

The fact that the news media are responsible for "making pictures in our heads" seems to be of particular significance in the case of issues, events and cultures relatively unfamiliar to the audience, best exemplified by Africa, which receives extensive, though highly selective, coverage only when crises or conflicts occur on that continent. What the Western public is continually presented with is Africa plagued with political and socio-economic upheavals, prone to violent conflicts and suffering from natural disasters (cf. Alozie 2005, Fair 1993, 1996, Hawk 1992, Livingston and Eachus 2000, Sorenson 1991). Additionally, the news media, which often fail to contextualize the stories covered, tend to present the events in terms of irrational tribalism, portray the

African people as irrational, primitive, and inhumane, and place excessive emphasis on the benevolence of the West (cf. Benthall 1993, Ebo 1992, Fair 1992, Philo 1990, Sorenson 1991).

The present study investigates how frames are constructed in TV reporting on Africa and what linguistic and visual means are employed to define problems, diagnose causes, make moral judgments, and suggest remedies in the case of two most frequent Africa-focused narratives, namely famine stories and reports on an ethnic conflict. The data included the CNN news reports on the famine in Niger (June–August 2005) and on the conflict in Darfur, the region in western Sudan (May 2004–December 2006), referred to as "Rwanda in slow motion", and acknowledged in early 2006 to be a humanitarian and human rights tragedy of the first order. The transcripts were downloaded from the CNN website, and printscreens were made from online broadcasts. The Niger corpus and the Sudan corpus consist of 30111 and 143148 words, respectively.

Given that the news texts render a particular meaning system through the keywords they employ, the first step in the process of identifying and describing news frames is to examine such words and their semantic import. Keyword analysis serves as a starting point for the discussion of the motivation behind and the possible implications of imposing a humanitarian frame, a heroic frame, an attribution of responsibility frame and a security frame, and the techniques of increasing the audience's empathy with the news actors. WordSmith Tools 3.00 (1999) was used to generate wordlists on the basis of the text files in the Niger corpus and the Sudan corpus. The lists were then used as an input to the KeyWord programme, which compares frequencies with a reference corpus (British National Corpus) to produce lists of keywords. To assign the keyness value to each item, WordSmith computes the frequency of this item in a given corpus and in the reference corpus, and the number of running words in both corpora, and cross-tabulates these, using the chi-square test of significance or Ted Dunning's Log Likelihood test (cf. Scott 1999: Help Menu). The lists compiled in this way, consisting of words that are unusually frequent in comparison with "what one would expect on the basis of the larger wordlist" (Scott 1999: Help Menu), give a measure of saliency, i.e. the importance of the word in the corpus, manifested in the keyness value assigned to each word. The higher the score, the stronger the keyness of the word, indicating how statistically unusual, and thus significant the word is in a particular text.

Since the analyzed corpora are of different sizes, the percentage columns rather than the raw frequency columns were compared. Where there is no figure at all, it is because the percentage is so small as to be negligible. After filtering out words reflecting the CNN news discourse in general, such as *CNN*, *videotape*, *camera*, *unidentified*, etc, and most proper names of places and public figures, the following lists were obtained:

Table 1. Niger Keywords

WORD	NIGER.TX%	BNC.LST %	KEYNESS
FOOD	0,40	0,02	489,0
FAMINE	0,17		447,1
CHILDREN	0,46	0,04	412,8
DOCTORS	0,22		386,2
STARVING	0,14		378,1
AID	0,25		354,0
RELIEF	0,20		285,1
DROUGHT	0,11		262,2
STARVATION	0,10		254,7
CRISIS	0,17		241,3
PEOPLE	0,50	0,11	226,0
HUNGRY	0,12		224,8
MOTHERS	0,12		176,1
MALNOURISHED	0,05		171,0
HUNGER	0,09		129,8
WORST	0,11		128,6
CROPS	0,08		128,1
MILK	0,10		118,0
RAINS	0,05		113,0
HELP	0,21		112,6
THOUSANDS	0,10	0,04	109,7
LOCUSTS	0,03		104,3
EDEMA	0,03		103,4
CATTLE	0,07		100,7
MALNUTRITION	0,04		100,5
NOMADS	0,04		99,1
ALIVE	0,08		98,9
DIE	0,09		96,9

Table 2. Sudan Keywords

N WORD	SUDAN.TXT %	BNC.LST%	KEYNESS
JANJAWEED	0,15		1 607,9
GOVERNMENT	0,49		934,4
GENOCIDE	0,08		621,6
MILITIAS	0,08		592,1
HUMANITARIAN	0,09		560,5
ARAB	0,13		519,7
PEOPLE	0,50		493,1
REBELS	0,08	0,12	381,3
TROOPS	0,11		354,2
INTERNATIONAL	0,18		309,7
PEACE	0,02		309,3
MILITIA	0,05	0,02	295,5
REBEL	0,07		286,2
REFUGEES	0,07		282,7
AID	0,12		277,7
DISPLACED	0,05		271,4
CONFLICT	0,10		271,0
PRESIDENT	0,15		269,3
REGION	0,11		254,2
SECURITY	0,13	0,02	252,3
CRISIS	0,09		247,2
CAMPS	0,06	0,01	236,8
RWANDA	0,03		233,7
PEACEKEEPERS	0,03		210,2
DISARM	0,03		175,3
RESOLUTION	0,06		167,9
SITUATION	0,11		165,8
SANCTIONS	0,04		163,3
AFRICANS	0,03	0,02	160,8
PEACEKEEPING	0,03		160,4
WORLD	0,20		152,0
MILLION	0,12		145,7
REFUGEE	0,04	0,06	143,9
UNION	0,10	0,02	139,0
CIVILIANS	0,03		138,9
HUMAN	0,10	0,02	126,9
MALE	0,08		123,4
THOUSANDS	0,06	0,02	122,7
OIL	0,07		112,5
VIOLENCE	0,06		110,2
FORCE	0,09		109,9
FOOD	0,09		108,3
ATROCITIES	0,02	0,02	103,4
UNICEF	0,02	0,02	101,7
CAMP	0,04		101,3
KILLED	0,06		98,5
RAPING	0,02		98,3
RIGHTS	0,07		92,7
AGREEMENT	0,07		87,9
ETHNIC	0,03	0,01	85,8

5. The heroic frame and the humanitarian frame

In Niger corpus, the humanitarian frame often used in the coverage of disasters in the Third World, intertwines with the heroic frame, which is not surprising as the two are perfectly compatible. The latter allows journalists to produce compelling narratives and pictures full of drama and conflict, as well as heroes, villains and innocent victims, while the former provides news actors to fit into these roles. A high keyness of *children*, *doctors* and *mothers* in Niger corpus indicates that these categories of people appear most frequently in the news reports, implying that mostly, if not only, these groups are affected by famine. This observation is compatible with earlier research on media coverage of disasters in Africa showing two tendencies, namely the focus on children and women as victims, and the excessive emphasis placed on the role of doctors among those involved in offering relief.

Women and children, seen as helpless and vulnerable, are perfectly suited to the role of a victim, and thus often used as famine icons (cf. Christie 1996, Moeller 1999). A certain correspondence can be seen between the keywords and key images, i.e. iconic images that reappear in the news and that are intended to involve the viewer emotionally. The reports on Niger abound in the images of individual children being fed, or doctors and aid workers tending to the sick and hungry. Having one suffering child staring directly at the camera, the audience is encouraged to empathize with all the young victims in Niger. Apart from children, close-ups feature the hands of the humanitarian workers and containers with food. The former stand metonymically for the aid-givers and their actions, while the latter make use of the CONTAINER FOR CONTENT metonymy.

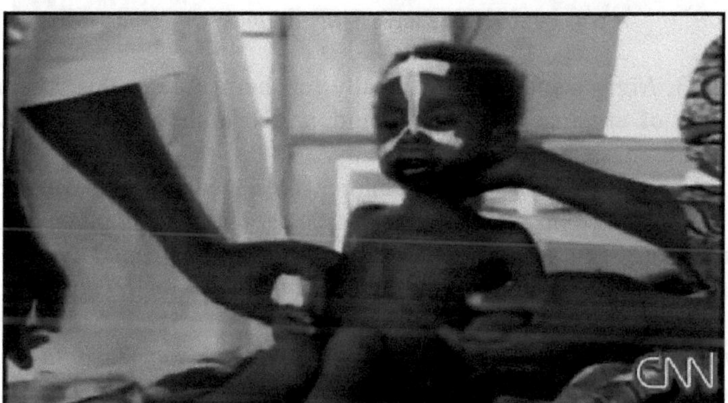

Fig. 1. Source: CNN 2/8/2005

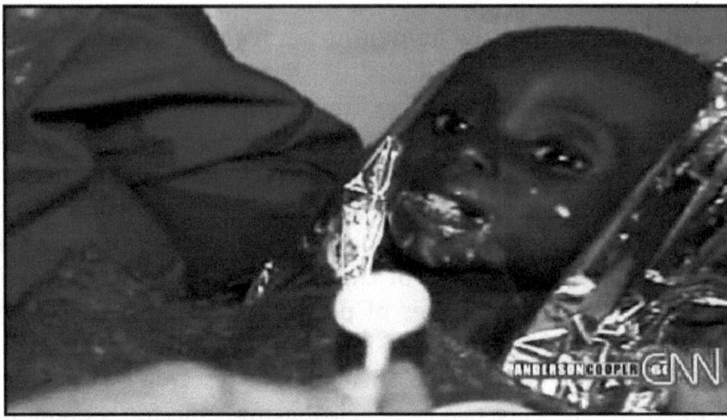

Fig. 2. Source: CNN 2/8/2005

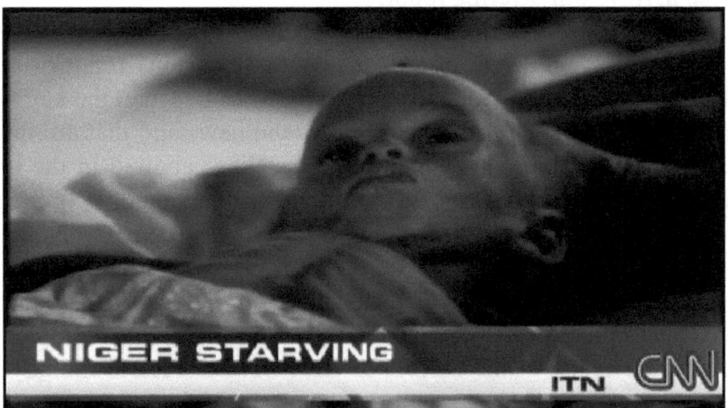

Fig. 3. Source: CNN 2/8/2005

In Fig. 3, *Niger* stands metonymically for the people in this country, while the condition of an emaciated dying child, which is the result of starvation, is meant to represent the whole event visually.

Despite this iconic role of the children presented in the news reports, the audience is encouraged to identify with a particular child, being given his/her name and other details. Such personalization of the story, accompanied by repetitions, is likely to appeal to the emotions of the audience, thereby eliciting empathy:

1. *Amino is OK and his mom is pretty confident, but Rashido is in septic shock and* ***Habu*** *– well,* ***Habu*** *died several hours ago. He was just 10 months old. (CNN 2/8/2005)*

2. *And just a few hours ago we found out that **Amino**, that little boy you met in that piece, whose skin was peeling off, **Amino** died [...] last we checked, **Rashido**, that little child who we found – who was admitted while we were videotaping that piece, **Rashido** is still alive, being watched over right now by his mother back there in that tent. (CNN 2/8/2005)*

In order to increase the empathy of the audience, whenever children are concerned, the adjectives *tiny* and *little* are used, implying greater vulnerability:

3. *With **tiny Barahatzu** strapped firmly in place, she loads her millet and starts her long trek back. (CNN 5/8/2005)*

4. *...**little Aminu**, who seemed to be doing better, **little Aminu**, died. (CNN 5/8/2005)*

5. *...**a little boy who captured all of our hearts, a little boy** named Aminu, who was fighting for his life. (CNN 5/8/2005)*

The same goal is achieved visually by filming children from a high camera angle, and thus slightly from above, making them look even smaller and more vulnerable. To emphasize how week and sick the children are, they are often presented as lying down or having to be supported by their mothers or humanitarian workers.

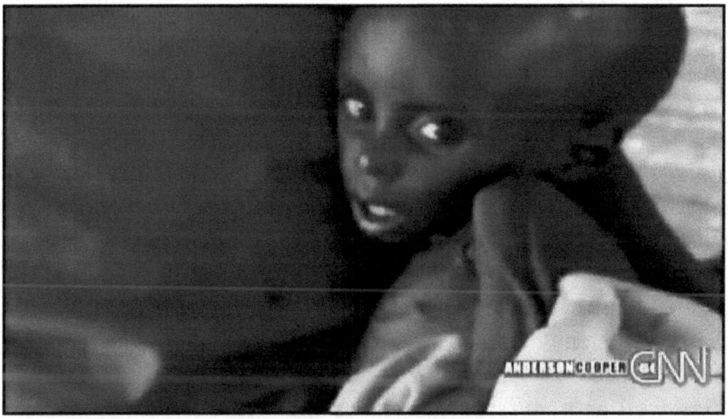

Fig. 4. Source: CNN 2/8/2005

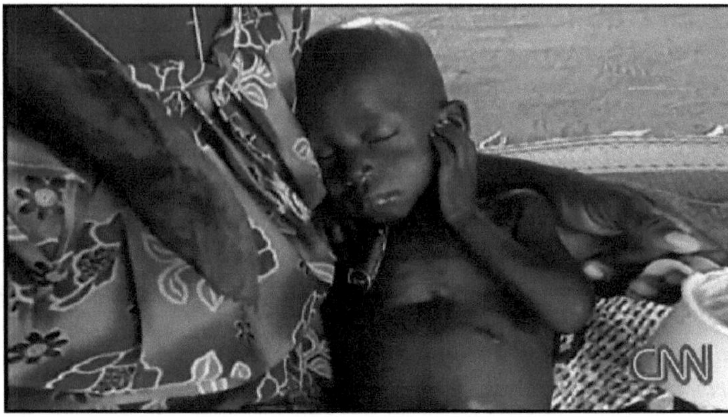

Fig. 5. Source: CNN 2/82005

The extremity of the starvation is also expressed lexically by means of qualifying adjectives: *sick*, *starving*, *hungry*, *desperate*, *exhausted*, *emaciated*, *teary-eyed*, *miserable*, and *downtrodden*. Another technique used to emphasize the seriousness of the victims' condition, is the frequent use of the comparative constructions with the adverb *too*. Since all these constructions include verbs connected with either movement or speaking, the image of the sick as passive, motionless and voiceless is strengthened yet again:

6. *In the countryside and in the villages, we are told, there are more deaths, with* ***people too weak to walk and too sick to cry out for help.*** *(CNN 27/7/2005)*

7. *They know there are many more* ***too sick to make it to the hospital.*** *(CNN 5/8/2005)*

8. *Tens of thousands of other Nigerians met the same fate, many of them in the desolated countryside –* ***too weak, too poor to venture into bigger towns for aid and medical help.*** *(CNN 28/8/2005)*

What contributes to the formation of the humanitarian frame in Niger corpus, is the frequency of such lexical items as *relief*, *aid*, and *help*. *Relief* entails the existence of an *affliction* and an *afflicted party* harmed by that affliction, as well as a *reliever* who takes that affliction away and is therefore a *hero* (cf. Lakoff 2004). The concept of *relief* and *aid* divides the news actors into those who need help and those who offer it: *relief workers*, *relief centers*, *relief agencies*, and *relief organizations*. While the Nigerians are the passive recipients of aid, the latter, central heroes of the famine world, *bring, give, offer* relief or aid, *try to help*, and are struggling against all difficulties. Their work is referred to as *tough, heroic, extraordinary,* while they are described as *dedicated, caring,* and possessing almost miraculous powers of life-givers. The images show them at work, emphasizing either the immense need for their efforts or the benevolence of their work. Temporal expressions and the metaphor AID WORKERS AND TIME ARE COMPETING IN A RACE, are frequently used to show the seriousness of the situation and the time pressure that these humanitarian workers are facing:

9. *Aid agencies **are racing against time** to save lives. (CNN 7/8/2005)*

10. *International aid agencies **are racing against the clock** to deliver food and shelter. (CNN 10/8/2005)*

Just as there are heroes in this heroic frame, there are also several villains, the chief one among them being the famine. It is conceptualized as a kind of animated entity possessing beast-like characteristics, namely being *vicious, ferocious, merciless*, etc. These features make it seem violent, uncontrollable, unpredictable, and fit for the role of a villain. Animated in this way, the famine is also capable of acting intentionally, its actions ranging from *threatening* to *killing* its victims. Such animation, in turn, makes it possible to portray the efforts made to cope with famine as a fight against an enemy:

11. *Niger **struggles to win the fight with famine**. (CNN1/8/2005)*

12. *The country is forced to **fight another battle with famine**. (CNN 31/7/2005)*

13. *Niger **wrestles with famine**. (CNN 2/8/2005)*

14. *Emergency measures to **combat famine**. (CNN 5/8/2005)*

Yet, as the crisis continues, attempts are made to identify other villains. Hence, it is implied that the Nigerian authorities are not able to manage the country properly, and the crisis is stereotypically put down to *corruption* and *ethnic* divisions.

It can be seen that the keyness value of *starving* and *starvation* is higher than that of their synonyms *hungry* and *hunger*, which confirms other research findings showing that famine, as represented by the media, is almost always presented in its extreme version and equated with starvation unto death (cf. de Waal 1989, Moeller 1999):

15. Children ***are starving to death.*** *(CNN 5/8/2005)*

16. We're seeing ***children dying here every day from starvation.*** *(CNN 5/8/2005)*

The concept of hunger is made more negative by the fact that it is often used attributively in a phrase *hunger crisis*, or premodified by adjectives describing its scale and seriousness:

17. And ***a hunger crisis*** *with more than 3 million on the brink. (CNN 5/8/2005)*

*18. The World Food Program's country director for Niger, Giancarlo Cirri, called the situation "****some of the worst hunger I have ever witnessed.****" (CNN 7/8/2005)*

19. ***Acute and widespread hunger*** *in Niger. (CNN 13/8/2005)*

20. ***Mass hunger*** *in Niger. (CNN 8/8/2005)*

The high keyness value of *thousands* is not surprising either, as famine has to be multiplied by the hundreds, thousands and millions who are suffering. Such statistics are supported visually by wide shots of motionless crowds waiting for humanitarian aid. The shot of people treated in a hospital (Fig. 6), taken with a wide lens, slightly exaggerating depth, and thus creating the impression of a higher number of beds with patients, was accompanied by the commentary*...but they [doctors] fear* ***this is just the tip of the iceberg***, where the metaphor implies the scale of the problem and the numbers of the sick involved.

Fig. 6. Source: CNN 31/7/2005

6. The conflict frame and the attribution of responsibility frame

The conflict frame, dominant in the coverage of Sudan, and frequent during the Bosnian War and the genocide in Rwanda, presents violent conflicts as a result of primordial, long-standing, irrational, and irresolvable ethnic divisions between peoples. Such an emphasis on conflict is nothing new in the case of Africa, as anarchy and violence on this torn-apart continent have always been foregrounded in the media.

The first group of words in the Sudan corpus includes agents responsible for the conflict, namely the *government*, *Janjaweed*, *militia*, *Arab* and the other side, i.e. *rebels*, *Africans*. Interestingly, whenever the *militia* is mentioned, the noun is always accompanied by the attribute *Arab*, and is usually linked with the noun *government*, by means of pre- or postmodification. In this way, both the government and militia are lumped into one category of agents responsible for what is happening; whenever the atrocities of the latter are mentioned, the implication is that that they are fully approved by the former.

21. *Darfur's indigenous Africans, they have become victims of ethnic cleansing by* ***a government-backed Arab militia*** *called the Janjaweed. (CNN 17/5/2004)*

22. *Sudan pledged to disarm and prosecute* ***pro-government Arab militias*** *(CNN 31/7/2004)*

23. *...**a government-sponsored Arab militia known as the Janjaweed** continues to rape, pillage and burn everything in sight. (CNN 30/5/2005)*

24. *This is the work of **an Arab militia sponsored by the government in Khartoum.** (CNN 30/6/2004)*

Animal metaphors are used to imply the inhumanity of militia's acts; Janjaweed are like dogs that have been *unleashed*, got out of control and have to be *muzzled*. What they do is referred to as *butchery*, *slaughter*, *horror*, while such generalizing indeterminate pronouns as *anybody*, *everything*, and determiners *any*, *every* imply certain indiscriminateness of their brutality:

25. *They **don't distinguish** between men, women, old men. They **just kill everybody. Anybody they see, they will kill.** (CNN 14/5/2004)*

26. *Janjaweed **murder every man** and **gang-rape every** woman in towns. (CNN 20/5/2004)*

27. *...government-sponsored Arab militia known as the Janjaweed continues to **rape, pillage and burn everything in sight.** (CNN 30/5/2005)*

28. *They come to people's houses to take things, if you resist then they **take everything**, if you don't resist then they **take everything.** (CNN 10/4/2004)*

29. *The Janjaweed then enter the village, **killing any boys** or men who have not managed to flee, loot and pillage, burn the huts, and **rape any women** they can. (CNN 25/7/2005)*

30. *Since then, government-backed Arab militias, **have gone on a rampage,** destroying villages, killing and raping. (CNN 11/8/2004)*

31. *Darfur refugees tell of **Janjaweed killing spree**. (CNN 4/3/2005)*

Similarly, expressions such as *spree* or *rampage* imply wild, uncontrolled behaviour or a frenzy, while *systematically* adds an element of intentionality to it:

32. *Janjaweed, have **carried out a systematic campaign of destruction**. (CNN 13/5/2005)*

33. *The Janjaweed are **systematically raping** hundreds of African girls and women. (CNN 1/7/2004)*

34. *The Sudanese Government and the Janjaweed are* ***systematically killing*** *civilians. (CNN 23/8/2005)*

All this is complemented by graphic, detailed descriptions of the militia's acts with verbs denoting violent actions:

35. *The Janjaweed* ***broke the limbs of girls and women to prevent them from escaping****. (CNN 19/7/2004)*

36. *They* ***even tossed babies into the fire.*** *(CNN 19/7/2004)*

37. *The Janjaweed* ***grabbed the baby*** *from her* ***back, threw it to the ground and beat it to death*** *in front of her. (CNN 29/11/2005)*

The second group of keywords includes lexical items related to the concept of violence and lack of security, namely *killing*, *raping*, *violence*, *atrocities*, as well as to the measures necessary to both stop the violence and restore order, e.g. *peacekeeping, peacekeepers, resolution, sanctions, agreement, security*. While in the case of Niger it was the notion of *relief* that divided the news world and news actors, here it is done by *violence* and *security*.

The third group comprises keywords related to another important category of people appearing in the Sudan corpus, i.e. *refugees*, who either figure as numbers or are portrayed with water metaphors as something unstoppable that cannot be prevented and is beyond human control:

38. *...a new* ***flood of refugees*** *moves into Chad. (CNN 2/7/2004)*

39. *...* ***a seemingly endless stream of refugees*** *fleeing brutal attacks in Darfur, Sudan. (CNN 15/7/2004)*

40. *...****a massive new wave of refugees.*** *(CNN 29/5/2004)*

41. *...* ***the deluge of Sudanese refugees into camps*** *along Chad's border with Darfur. (CNN 30/6/2004)*

42. *Hundreds of thousands of* ***refugees are spilling*** *over the border. (CNN 20/8/2004)*

The coverage not only refers to the refugees as a flow, but also makes use of specific visual strategies to portray them in this way, namely panoramic wide shots of refugees, tracking shots showing them from behind, or close-ups panning across refugees' faces. Alternatively, they are presented both visually and linguistically as confined to particular spaces (cf. Girardet 1996). Most frequently, they are *holed up* or *stuck in the refugee camps.* This spatial "incarceration of the native" (Appadurai 1988: 36–49) is represented metonymically by fences, ropes, barbed wire, or soldiers shown as an integral element of the camps, which are shown from the distance, sometimes with a wide camera lens, in such a way as to show masses of people squeezed in there.

Fig. 7. Source: CNN 22/12/2004

Fig. 8. Source: CNN 14/5/2004

Sudan emerges as a *center of death*, of primitivism, of savagery and of barbarity, where *warlords* and their rag-tag militias abuse the weak and helpless, and where political disorder is the rule. *Warlord*, the word coined by the British press to describe the Somali faction leader General Farrah Aidid, and since then widely applied to describe rebel leaders in Africa, is used here to express the potential for even greater violence and anarchy:

43. *...the whole area could evolve into sort of a* ***warlord situation, the type of which we saw in Somalia.*** *(CNN 4/11/2004)*

44. *UN Warns That Darfur Could* ***Descend into Anarchy with Warlords.*** *(CNN 25/11/2004)*

The reference to Somalia leads the audience to believe that violence and tribal power struggles are an integral part of African reality. Likewise, the comparison of the conflict to the one in Rwanda is an exercise in moral equivalence, signaling to the viewers the nature of the conflict, the scale of deaths as well as the intent of the murderers:

45. *Darfur is tasting, smelling, looking in every way, shape (and) form like* ***a repetition on a similar scale of what happened in Rwanda 12 years ago****. (CNN 17/9/2006)*

46. *Up until now, few journalists have managed to get into Sudan's Darfur region to reveal the truths about* ***what some are calling the next Rwanda****. (CNN 24/7/2004)*

47. *U.S. officials continue to say the Bush administration has no intention of allowing* ***another Rwandan-type genocide in Darfur****. (CNN 16/9/2006)*

The visual images, though not as horrific as in the case of Rwanda, are reminiscent of the previous conflict; burnt villages, dead bodies, people praying over mass graves – all these images stand metonymically for similar scenarios, evoke similar frames and, as a consequence, similar inferences concerning the causes, solutions, and moral judgements. Since "even when we negate a frame, we evoke a frame" (Lakoff 2004: 4), in all the instances where it is suggested that the scale of what is happening in Sudan is not to be compared with Rwanda, associations with what happened there and possible implications are still awoken.

As in the case of other conflicts in Africa, here too the conflict is reduced to a struggle between eternally opposed ethnic groups, and associated with tribal violence and hatred. The word *tribe* evokes a certain sub-frame, and connotations with primitive savagery, leading to the portrayal of violence and conflict in Sudan as primordial, irrational and unchanging, and suggesting that irrational violence is inherent and natural to Africans.

48. *Violence has continued to rage in Darfur in recent weeks, with* ***tribal clashes*** *flaring. (CNN 24/4/2006)*

49. *African Union says 62 killed in Darfur* ***tribal fighting****. (CNN 19/4/2006)*

50. ***Tribal violence*** *has raised new concerns about security that is hindering aid work in Darfur. (CNN 1/3/2006)*

What is more, the words habitually used by journalists to describe extreme violence – *brutal*, *savage*, *barbaric*, and *inhuman* – tend to take the violence away from the sphere of the human or the comprehensible and to re-label it as something animal, demonic or "other". The audience is thus presented with an oversimplified portrayal of the conflict as a good-versus-evil contest between rampaging Arab herdsmen armed by Khartoum, and African farmers. This is where another frame intertwines with the conflict frame, namely the attribution of responsibility frame. The government of Sudan emerges as doubly responsible for the conflict; it does not comply with UN's demands, and as it is allegedly supporting the Janjaweed militia, it is to blame for its brutal acts. The accusations levelled against it can be seen in the interview with the Sudanese foreign minister who ends his turn with a rhetorical question implying that the government should not be blamed for the rapes and killing – a question meant to be left unanswered. However, as the camera zooms in on a swollen belly of a child (Fig. 9) and then tilts to show its face (Fig. 10), the answer is given. It is the belly and the phrase *has done plenty* that are supposed to evoke a connotative chain of meanings:

51. *SUDANESE FOREIGN MINISTER: [...] But the question is did the government do anything? VOICE-OVER:* ***The government has done plenty. Complicit in mass killings and the worst humanitarian crisis it stands in the world's dock.*** *(CNN 18/7/2006)*

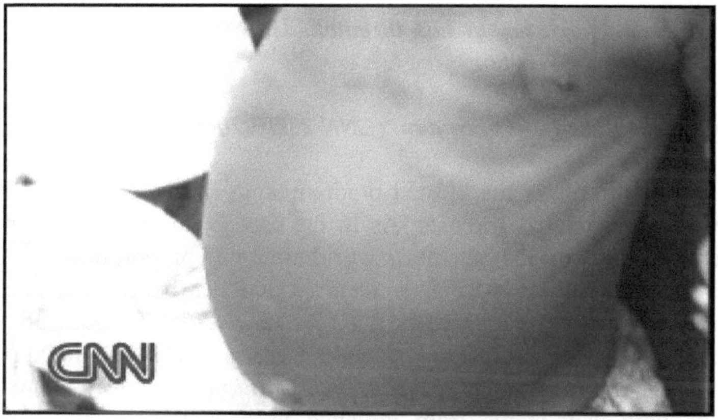

Fig. 9. Source: CNN 18/7/2006

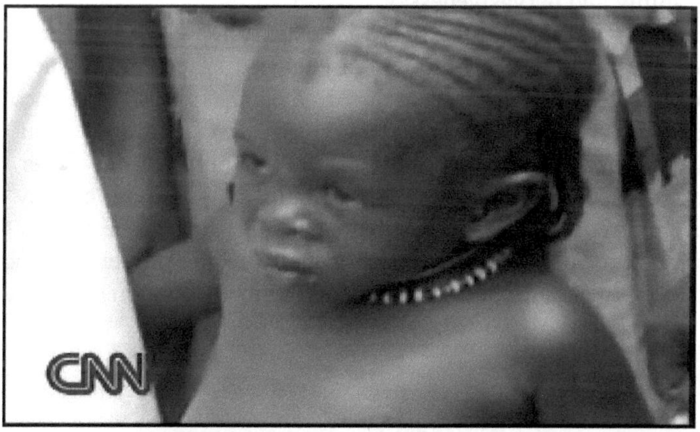

Fig. 10. Source: CNN 18/7/2006

It can be seen from the very beginning which side of the conflict the CNN identifies with. The black residents of Darfur, though sometimes referred to as rebels, are a passive, victimized side of the conflict, depicted as *indigenous African* people, who used to lead a peaceful life of *farmers*, until an *Arab-dominated* government come to power. At the same time, even apparently non-violent actions performed by the government are described with verbs implying physical force:

52. *...the Sudan government has* ***threatened to kick out*** *the African Union forces. (CNN 17/9/2006)*

53. *Jan Pronk* ***kicked out of Sudan.*** *(CNN 23/10/2006)*

The security frame is manifested predominantly in the frequent use of the word *security*, and related lexemes. As in the case of the humanitarian frame, where the word *relief* divided the news world assigning proper, pre-defined roles to groups and individuals, here it is *security* that lies behind the sticking of labels. *Security* implies that there is a *threat*, and a *threatened*, and that the *threatened* needs *protection* (cf. Lakoff and Ferguson 2004). The threat posed by the *lack of security*, *absence of security*, *deterioration of security*, or *worsening of security*, obviously stems from violence in its various forms, frequently depicted with water metaphors, implying massive scale, wildness, unmanageability and pervasiveness:

The act of "containing" the threat is visually represented by fences, walls, ropes, etc. The images of people within enclosed spaces intertwine with other images characteristic of the security frame, the shots of armed soldiers juxtaposed with women and children, which take on a somewhat symbolic meaning, emphasizing and exposing the vulnerability of the latter. Yet, the impression of security that these images are supposed to convey becomes somewhat blurred when the inadequacy and helplessness of the local peacekeeping forces is pointed out, also visually, as the soldiers, through careful cropping, are shown individually or in small numbers, often in open spaces.

Fig. 11. Source: CNN 7/10/2006

When the reports do portray people taking positive steps to deal with the violence in Sudan, they are almost always Westerners, preferably Americans. The idea that these are the people capable of dealing with the conflict is reinforced by relying on them for quotes and portraying them as actively helping to solve the problem. The attention of the viewer is drawn to the verbal actions performed by the U.S. While chief among these are the acts of *labelling* or *terming* the crisis a genocide, as this is what will determine further actions, other verbs describing the actions of the West are *accusing*, *warning*, *pressing* and *urging*. The emphasis on portraying the U.S. as well as the UN as exerting pressure on the Sudanese government is not surprising in view of the fact that they were criticized for neither imposing sanctions nor sending troops to Sudan; at least "doing things with words" could be considered a form of action.

7. Conclusions

As already pointed out by several researchers, both poverty and conflicts in Africa are exaggerated, simplified and often misunderstood. Although the specific details of events change over time – the famine in Niger is not the same as the famine in Somalia or Ethiopia, the genocide in Sudan is not a "re-play" of Rwanda – journalistic portrayal of these occurrences has been shaped by how similar events were covered in the past. Conventional frames have provided contextual cues, simplifying complex problems, actions and events, by slotting the new into familiar storyline categories. Framed as a humanitarian issue, Africa encourages compassion, approached as a security issue, it may evoke fear and anxiety. In both cases, the stories with their imagery of powerlessness, passivity, and lack of agency of the Africans emphasize the responsibility of the West to fix Africa's problems. The study was an attempt to explain how this image of Africa is construed by the news media in order to be incorporated into the audience's mental schemata.

Fauconnier (2004: 657), elaborating on the contribution that Cognitive Linguistics can make to the analysis of meaning, mentions framing among other "[d]istinctive and powerful cognitive capacities" which "lie at the heart of perception, conception and action, and suffuse our lives with rich meaning – sometimes unbearably rich meaning." The news media, with the plethora of visual and linguistic stimuli that they offer, undoubtedly have their say in the generation of this meaning and the formation of our mental schemata. Hence, I have argued in this paper that though media content and audience interpretation have different thought structures and purposes, they do have the potential to connect. Although the audience tends to assess the news in line with their previous knowledge, interpersonal resources, and direct experiences, media frames do shape individual frames by rendering particular concepts more accessible than other concepts, and thus constraining the range of options that the members of the audience have in making sense of the world. In this way, frames serve several functions, both cognitive by linking together disparate facts, events and people, and evaluative, by naming perpetrators, identifying victims, and attributing blame.

Manifesting themselves in the coverage in many ways, frames always involve selection at various levels and in several discursive dimensions. The choice and frequency of lexical items, images, as well as sources are behind the creation of particular frames. I have tried to demonstrate that looking at the keywords as well as concordances in which they appear has considerable explanatory value and should constitute the first step in the process of frame analysis, which should subsequently focus on the examination of the relationship between keywords and key images, and on the semantic associations that both of them generate. Cognitive Linguistics, fully committed to the analysis of meaning in all its various facets, can be used as a prism through which to look at the interplay of the word and image in the news discourse as well as the possible implications of this interplay for the audience. Nevertheless, due to the fact that television news discourse is ideologically determined, culturally embedded and shaped by various journalistic routines and practices, it should be complemented with insights from semiotics and communication science, and used in tandem with corpus methodology allowing for the analysis of large amounts of the transcribed data and providing the basis for and the validation of qualitative findings.

REFERENCES

Alozie, E. C. (2005). "Sudan and South Africa – a Framing Analysis of *Mail* and *Guardian Online*'s Coverage of Darfur". *Ecquid Novi* 26(1): 63–84.

Appadurai, A. (1988). "Putting Hierarchy in Its Place". *Cultural Anthropology* 3 (1): 36–49.

Bateson, G. (1972). *Steps to an Ecology of Mind: Collected Essays in Anthropology, Psychiatry, Evolution, and Epistemology.* Chicago: University of Chicago Press.

Bell, A. (1991). *The Language of the News Media.* Oxford and Cambridge, MA: Blackwell.

Benthall, J. (1993). *Disasters, Relief, and the Media.* London: I. B. Tauris.

Berelson, B. (1949). "What 'missing the newspaper' means". In: P. F. Lazarsfeld and F. N. Stanton (eds.). *Communications Research, 1948–1949.* NewYork: Harper & Brothers: 111–128.

Caldas-Coulthard, C. R. (1993). "From discourse analysis to Critical Discourse Analysis: The differential representation of women and men speaking in written news". In: J. M. Sinclair, M. Hoey and G. Fox (eds.). *Techniques of Description: Spoken and Written Discourse.* London: Routledge: 196–208.

Cap, P. (2003). *Analytic Determinism of the Study of Persuasive Discourse: Inductive and Deductive Processes.* Łódź: Wydawnictwo Uniwersytetu Łódzkiego.

Carter, R. A. and McCarthy, M. J. (2002). "From conversation to corpus: a dual analysis of a broadcast political interview". In: A. Sanches Macarro (ed.). *Windows on the World. Media Discourse in English.* Valencia: University of Valencia Press: 15–39.

Chang, P. (2002). "Who's behind the personal pronouns in talk radio? Cartalk: a case study". In: A. Sanches Macarro (ed.). *Windows on the World. Media Discourse in English.* Valencia: University of Valencia Press: 115–152.

Christie, N. (1996). "The Ideal Victim". In: E. A. Fattah (ed.). *From Crime Policy to Victim Policy.* London: MacMillan Press: 17–30.

Coperias Aguliar, M. J. and Andreu Beso, J. V. (1999). "The battle of words: a political and linguistic analysis of the Northern Irish conflict". *Studies in English Language and Linguistics*, 1: 41–56.

De Vreese, C. H. (2005). "News framing: Theory and typology". *Information Design Journal + Document Design*, 13 (1): 48–59.

De Waal, J. (1989). *Famine that Kills: Darfur, Sudan, 1984–1985.* New York: Clarendon Press.

Ebo, B. (1992). "American Media and African Culture". In: B. Hawk (ed.). *Africa's Media Image.* Westport, Praeger Publishers.

Entman, R. M. (1991). "Framing U.S. coverage of international news: Contrasts in narratives of KAL and Iran Air incidents". *Journal of Communication* 41: 6–27.

Entman, R. M. (1993). "Framing: Toward Clarification of a Fractured Paradigm". *Journal of Communication* 43(4): 51–58.

Entman, R. M. (2003). "Cascading Activation: Contesting the White House's Frame after 9/11". *Political Communication* 20: 415–32.

Entman, R. M. (2004). *Projections of Power: Framing News, Public Opinion, and U.S. Foreign Policy.* Chicago: University of Chicago Press.

Fair, J. E. (1993). "War, Famine and Poverty: Race in the Construction of Africa's Media Image". *Journal of Communication Inquiry* 17(2): 5–23.

Fair, J. E. (1996). "The Body Politic, the Bodies of Women, and the Politics of Famine in U.S. Television Coverage of Famine in the Horn of Africa". *Journalism and Mass Communication Monographs*: 158.

Fauconnier, G. (2004). "Pragmatics and Cognitive Linguistics". In: Horn, L. and G. Ward (eds.). *The Handbook of Pragmatics.* Oxford: Blackwell: 657–674.

Fillmore, Ch. (1975). "An alternative to checklist theories of meaning", First annual meeting of the Berkeley linguistic Society. University of California, Berkeley.

Fodor, J. (1983). *The modularity of mind.* MIT Press, Cambridge, MA.

Fodor, J. A. (2000). *The mind doesn't work that way: the scope and limits of computational psychology.* Cambridge, Mass.: MIT Press.

Fowler, N. (1996). "On critical linguistics". In: C. R. Caldas-Coulthard and M. Coulthard (eds.). *Texts and Practices: Readings in Critical Discourse Analysis.*London: Routledge: 3–14.
Galasinski, D. and Marley, C. (1998). "Agency in foreign news: A linguistic complement of a content analytical study". *Journal of Pragmatics*, 30: 565–587.
Girardet, E. R. (1996). "Reporting Humanitarianism: Are the New Electronic Media Making a Difference?" In: R. Rothberg and T. Weiss (eds.). *From Massacres to Genocide. Washington.* D.C.: Brookings Institute: 45–67.
Gitlin, T. (1980). *The Whole World Is Watching. Mass Media in the Making and Unmaking of the New Left.* Los Angeles: University of California Press.
Goffman, E. (1974). *Frame Analysis.* New York: Harper and Row.
Hawk, B. (1992). *Africa's Media Image.* New York: Praeger.
Höjer, B. (2004). "The discourse of global compassion: the audience and media reporting of human suffering". *Media, Culture & Society*, 26(4): 513–531.
Jeffries, L. (2003). "Not a drop to drink: Emerging meanings in local newspaper reporting of the 1995 water crisis in Yorkshire". *Text*, 23 (4): 513–538.
Lakoff, G. (1987). *Women, Fire and Dangerous Things. What Categories Reveal about the Mind.* Chicago and London: Chicago University Press.
Lakoff, G. (1996). *Moral Politics: What the Conservatives Know that Liberals Don't.* Chicago and London: University of Chicago Press.
Lakoff, G. (2004). *Don't Think of an Elephant! Know Your Values and Frame the Debate.* Chelsea Green: White River Junction.
Lakoff, G. and Ferguson, S. (2006). "The framing of immigration". Published electronically: http://www.rockridgeinstitute.org/research/rockridge/immigration.
Lakoff, G. and M. Johnson (1980). *Metaphors We Live By.* Chicago, IL: Chicago University Press.
Langacker, R. W. (1987). *Foundations of Cognitive Grammar. Theoretical Prerequisites.* Stanford: Stanford University Press.
Langacker, R. W. (1990). *Concept, Image and Symbol. The Cognitive Basis of Grammar.* Berlin: Mouton de Gruyter.
Langacker, R. W. (2001). "Discourse in Cognitive Grammar". *Cognitive Linguistics* 12: 143–188.
Lennon, P. (2004). *Allusions in the Press. An Applied Linguistic Study.* Mouton de Gruyter.
Lippmann, W. (1922). *Public Opinion.* New York: Harcourt, Brace and Co.
Livingston, S., Eachus T. (2000). "Rwanda: U.S. Policy and Television Coverage". In: H. Adelman and A. Suhrke (eds.). *The Path of a Genocide: the Rwanda Crisis From Uganda to Zaire.* New Brunwick: Transaction Publisher: 209–28.
McCarthy, M. (1983). *Dark Continent: Africa as Seen by Americans.* Westport: Greenwood Publishing Group.
McLeod, D. M. and B. H. Detenber (1999). "Framing Effects of Television News Covergae of Social Protest". *Journal of Communication* 49(3): 3–23.
Minsky, M. L. (1975). "A framework for representing knowledge". In: Winston, P. H. (ed.). *The Psychology of Computer Vision.* New York: McGraw-Hill: 211–277.

Moeller, S. D. (1999). *Compassion Fatigue: How the Media Sell Disease, Famine, War, and Death*. London: Routledge.

O'Keeffe, A. (2002). "Exploring indices of national identity in corpus of radio phone-in data from Irish radio". In: A. Sanches Macarro (ed.). *Windows on the World. Media Discourse in English*. Valencia: University of Valencia Press: 91–113.

O'Keeffe, A. (2003). "Like the vise virgins and all that jazz" – using a corpus to examine vague language and shared knowledge". In: U. Connor and T. A. Upton (eds.). *Applied Corpus Linguistics. A Multidimensional Perspective*. Amsterdam: Rodopi: 1–20.

O'Keeffe, A. (2005). "You've a daughter yourself?" a corpus based look at question forms in an Irish radio phone-in". In: K. P. Schneider and A. Barron (eds.). *The Pragmatics of Irish English*. Berlin: Mouton de Gruyter: 339–366.

O'Keeffe, A. (2006). *Investigating Media Discourse*. New York: Routledge.

Pan, Z. and G. M. Kosicki (1993). "Framing Analysis: An Approach to News Discourse". *Political Communication* 10: 55–75.

Philo, G. (1990). *Seeing and Believing*. London: Routledge.

Schaefer, T. M. (2003). "Framing the Us Embassy Bombings and September 11 Attacks in African and Us Newspapers". In: P. Norris, K. Montague and J. Marion (eds.). *Framing Terrorism: The News Media, the Government, and the Public*. London: Routledge.

Scheufele, D. A. (1999). "Framing as a theory of media effects". *Journal of Communication* 49: 103–122.

Scheufele, D. (2004). "Framing-Effects Approach: A Theoretical and Methodological Critique". *Communications* 29: 401–28.

Schramm, W. (1949). "The nature of news". *Journalism Quarterly*, 26: 259–269.

Scott, M. (1998). "Focusing on the text and its key words". In Stephens, C. (ed.). *TALC 98 Proceedings* .Oxford: Humanities Computing Unit, Oxford University: 152–164.

Scott, M. (1999). *Wordsmith Tools version 3*. Oxford: Oxford University Press.

Scott, M. (2000). "Focusing on the text and its key words". In: Burnard, L. & McEnery, T. (eds.). *Rethinking Language Pedagogy from a Corpus Perspective*. Frankfurt am Main: Peter Lang: 103–122.

Sorenson, J. (1991). "Mass media discourse on famine in the Horn of Africa". *Discourse and Society* 2 (4): 223–242.

Stubbs, M. (1996). *Text and Corpus Analysis: Computer-assisted Studies of Language and Culture*. Oxford and Cambridge, Mass.: Blackwell.

Stubbs, M. (1997). "Whorf 's Children: Critical comments on Critical Discourse Analysis (CDA)". In: A. Ryan & A. Wray (eds.). *Evolving models of language*. Clevedon: BAAL in association with Multilingual Matters: 110–116.

Tannen, D. (1993). *Framing in discourse*. New York: Oxford University Press.

Tuchman, G. (1978). *Making News: A Study in the Construction of Reality*. London: Collier Macmillan.

Verschueren, J. (1985). *International News Reporting: Metapragmatic Metaphors and the U-2 (Pragmatics and Beyond 6/5)*. Amsterdam and Philadelphia: John Benjamins.

Hanna Pulaczewska

Łódź Academy of International Studies
University of Regensburg

SYNTACTIC REDUPLICATION AS AN ICONICALLY-DRIVEN PRAGMATIC PRINCIPLE IN THE SPOKEN LANGUAGE

Abstract: Reduplication of sound strings, based on "iconicity of repetition", can be used to intensify the illocutionary force of an utterance. The article describes the results of a contrastive corpus study of directives in Polish, English and German, showing cross-linguistic differences in the application of reduplication in certain types of directives, and the unique use of tone group-internal reduplication in Polish. It is discussed how universal iconic principles are subject to language-specific selection and conventionalisation.

Keywords: cross-linguistic study, directive, English, German, iconic, iconicity, Polish, reduplication, repetition, speech act.

1. Introduction

This paper presents the results of a contrastive study of reduplication (repetition of sound strings) in Polish, German and British English, based on the cognitive semantic principle of iconicity. The study is based on a set of small parallel multimedia corpora of conversational language compiled by the author, consisting of video recordings of the reality TV series Big Brother[1]. The corpora are matched in the speakers' age and gender, mixes of social backgrounds and informality of the situation. The analysis focuses on emphatic functions of syntactic reduplication in directive utterances. The original corpora comprise ca. 22, 14 and 12 hours of spoken interaction for British English, German and Polish, respectively. Transcripts of the video recorded material used in the

[1] In the coding of the quotations, the capital letters E, G, P signify the respective language of the sample and the number that follows refers to the number of the Big Brother series in the given language.

analysis include 625, 473 and 647 directive utterances included in the corpora for British English, German and Polish, respectively. Unlike earlier studies which dealt with reduplication on the level of word formation and morphosyntax, the focus of this study is on reduplications situated in the level of pragmatics, including pragmatic conventions rather than fully grammaticalized or lexicalized routines.

2. Reduplication and iconicity

According to Moravcsik (1992: 323), reduplication is "a pattern where the double or multiple occurrence of a sound string, syllable, morpheme, or word within a larger syntagmatic unit is in systematic contrast with its single occurrence, with the iterated elements filling functionally non-distinct positions." Reduplication can be total (a repetition of the whole meaningful constituent) or partial (a repetition of part of a constituent). The following examples from Kajitani (2005) (from Macdonald 1976: 32 and Murane 1974: 73) illustrate reduplication in word formation:

a. Total reduplication: Indonesian
orang 'human being' > *orang-orang* 'human beings'
b. Partial reduplication: Daga
nononga 'long' > *nonononga* 'very long'

Languages around the world employ reduplication as a way of expressing various meanings. For example, according to Dixon (1980: 326), it expresses approximation or pretension in Pitjantjatjara, a language spoken in Australia, (e.g. *wati* 'man' > *wati-wati* 'children playing at being adult men'). In English, the expressive meaning of lexical items displaying partial or complete reduplication such as *dum-dum*, *claptrap*, *nitwit* and *riffraff* includes the element of derogation and contempt.

In spite of this diversity of function, cross-linguistic studies have shown that there is a great deal of overlap in the meanings carried by reduplication across languages. Moravcsik (1978: 316) notes that although "there is no a priori reason why reduplication, or any other form device of language, should serve as the expression of some meanings rather than as that of others", in fact the particular meanings associated with reduplication reoccur across languages. According to Uspensky (1972: 70), the most frequently encountered semantic components brought by reduplication into the meaning of the lexical items are increase of quantity (augmentation) and increase of degree (intensification). Less frequent but recurring ones are decrease of quantity (diminution) and decrease of degree (attenuation).

It is unlikely that similarities such as these would occur by chance. From the perspective offered by the cognitive approaches to semantics, the claim of there being no "a priori reason" for preference of certain meanings over others lost a lot of its validity. The earlier Saussurian notion of the "arbitrariness of the sign" has been modified by the contention that many forms of linguistic expressions are motivated by their iconic relation to meanings. Iconicity holds if the signans "assigns a property to the signatum by virtue of having a similar property itself" (Posner 1986); in other words, in an iconic relation the sign evinces a degree of physical resemblance to its object of reference (cf. e.g. Peirce's 1985: 10–12). In her study of reduplication as a discourse structuring principle, Barbaresi (2000: 1) claims that "iconicity is a basic principle of language organization, a most elementary one. Iconic procedures in language are natural, efficient, preferred because it is proved that they allow easy planning, monitoring, immediacy of perception, memorization, and they are preferred by children, by foreign language learners … iconicity is, in this sense, a constitutive principle of language and text."

The most frequently quoted types of iconicity are:

- iconicity of quantity, where greater quantities in meaning are expressed by greater quantities in form,
- iconicity of complexity, where more complex meanings are expressed by more complex forms,
- iconicity of cohesion, where meanings that are semantically closer are expressed by more cohesive and less separable forms,
- iconicity of contiguity where forms that belong together semantically occur next to each other,
- iconicity of sequence where the sequence of forms matches the sequence of experiences,
- iconicity of repetition, where repetition of form expresses plurality or distribution.

Barbaresi (2000), who defines intra-textual iconicity as "syntagmatic equivalence or similarity among text constituents", uses the term "repetition" to refer to two different cases: 1) repetition of signantia (as lexical recurrence, structural parallelism); 2) repetition of signata (as synonymy, paraphrase). In this study, the notion of *reduplication* will be applied to refer to "repetition of signantia" without any form change, observing Moravcsik's (1992) definition according to which the iterated elements in reduplication fill "functionally non-distinct positions". We will speak of *repetition* when referring either to non-consecutive repetition of a sound string, i.e. with another string intervening between its two occurrences (unmodified repetition), or a partial iteration modified through deletion, insertion or exchange of some elements within the iterated string. The term *iteration* will be applied to refer to both reduplication and repetition.

Along with plurality, augmentative and intensifying functions of reduplication may be viewed as a subtype of the *iconicity of quantity*. From the iconic principle certain applications of reduplication follow quite straightforwardly, such as the expression of the interrelated concepts of repetition and multiplicity. Almost as straightforward is the link between reduplication and increase in intensity, following from the basic underlying relation "more is strong/intense". This relation is expressed for example in the co-existence of synthetical forms of the comparative for adjectives and adverbs with its analytical forms including the comparative quantifier *more* (or its equivalents) in many languages, e.g. in English: *smarter, more intelligent*. The same relation also underlies routinised syntagmas, such as e.g. in the Russian *bolshoe spasibo* "great thank you". The conceptual link between greater *intensity* and repetition (multiplicity) as an expression of greater *quantity* is well visible in the English collocation *many thanks*. An example of a collocation where multiplicity stands for intensity and is in itself expressed by verbal reduplication is *very very* + adj/adv. Apart from the word formation and routinised syntagmas, reduplication in iconic function can be found on the level of discourse structuring (cf. Barbaresi 2000, Israeli 1997 for Russian), in lexical phrases (cf. Borillo 1995 for French) and in syntax (cf. e.g. Lindström 1999 for Swedish, Wierzbicka 1986 for Italian).

3. Context of discovery

Some time ago, my ten-year old son, raised in Germany as a Polish-German bilingual, and I watched a Polish comedy in which a wanna-be film director complained about his lack of talent and managing skills:

MARYSIA: masz prawdziwy talent
you've got a real talent
YANEK: kto # ja? # mnie nawet nikt nie słucha # nie mam żadnego talentu
who # me? nobody even listens to me # I have no talent

To this, he received the following response:

MARYSIA: masz masz
you-have you-have

My son, who learned dialogues from this film by heart for their humour and originality, surprised me two days later when I stated that I couldn't buy him a present every day by saying:

ALEX: możesz możesz
you-can you-can

There could be no doubt that this was a case of deliberate (and humorous) intertextuality, as the utterance imitated the original intonation of MARYSIA's utterance, her emphatic way of speaking and her hyper clear pronunciation. The striking property of this imitation was that it did not involve quoting any lexical material; rather, it was the structural principle that the child acquired. It should be noted that in the meantime I also observed Alex extend the use of reduplication to another type of speech act, a reassuring response to a directive (e.g. *zrobię zrobię* – "I will do (it) I will do (it)").

4. Syntactic reduplication in Wierzbicka (1986)

Wierzbicka (1986) studied the pragmatic functions of syntactic reduplication in relation to cultural and cross-cultural, cross-linguistic issues. Working with various data including literary works and their translations, she described the reduplication of adjectives, adverbs and adverbial expressions in Italian as a device consistent with the abundant presence of other means of increasing expressivity in this language. She noted that in English translations syntactic reduplication was rendered by other, lexical means. Also, she noted the difference between "the repetition of the whole speech act" (as in "All right. All right.", ibid. 292), "clausal repetition": a reduplication of a part of utterance (a clause, a phrase) in a new tone group (as in "addagio, addagio"; ibid. 296), and "syntactic reduplication" in "pauseless expressions" ("addagio addagio", ibid.). While she used punctuation (dot, comma and no mark) rather than terms explicitly referring to prosody to mark the difference between the three types she distinguished, it is clearly prosodic distinctions that are at issue. Also, Wierzbicka noted that "it seems likely that in all languages which have the imperative as a grammatical category, imperatives can be repeated for emphasis."

Wierzbicka claimed that "whatever the exact meaning of the 'clausal repetition' is ... both the speakers of English and the speakers of Italian feel on occasion a need to convey it", yet, the speakers of Italian tend to do it more often (1986: 292). She postulated that "there may be a link between the enormous role of 'clausal repetition' in Italian discourse and the existence of the illocutionary device of 'syntactic reduplication' in Italian grammar" (ibid.). Wierzbicka related reduplication to the level of pragmatics both implicitly (by mentioning the imperative – and thus implying directive speech acts – as a frequent context of "clausal repetition"), and more explicitly by using notions such as "illocutionary grammar" and "illocutionary semantics" to refer to the form-function correspondence of syntactic reduplication. However, the pragmatic context of syntactic reduplication – the type of speech act in which it is embedded – does not play any role in her analysis. The following corpus study addresses the relationship between syntactic reduplication and speech act-specific illocutionary force.

5. Syntactic reduplication in the corpus

The following study analyses the intensifying function of non-lexicalised reduplication and compares the occurrence of reduplication cross-linguistically. The presence or absence of a tone group boundary between the first and second occurrence of the reduplicated text is also taken into account. While the above quoted pieces of Polish dialogues display the pragmatic act of refuting the contents of the immediately preceding statement, acts of this type occurred rarely in the multimedia data corpus. A preliminary analysis of the corpus data showed, though, that reduplication was often used as a means of emphasis in directive utterances (of both inhibitive and initiating sort). The study focuses on speech acts of this type. What is common to both types of speech act (refutation and directive) is that the intensification by means of reduplication pertains to the *illocutionary force* of the whole utterance that contains it.

In the study both reduplication within the head act of the directive utterance and its supportive moves is taken into account. Supportive moves are utterances adding some new propositional contents (e.g. stating personal preferences, insisting) and syntactically external to the "head act", the proposition that carries the directive illocutionary force.

Reduplication and repetition in directives occur in several functions that are unequally relevant to the conventions of language use, which concern us in this article:

i. In hesitations, where they are alternatives to silence or non-articulate gap-fillers; reduplications of words of phrases signal that the current speaker is searching for words but intends to continue (in conversation analytical terminology, "holding turn").
ii. In the service of maintaining the channel of communication, to assure that the addressee acknowledged the directive. A part of the message or the whole message is repeated.
iii. As a means of persuasion when the addressee has been reluctant to comply with the directive or neglected a part of it (e.g. regarding the manner of action) after the first formulation of the message. The message is repeated in a new tone group.
iv. As a means of emphasis, when there is no sign of the addressee's reluctance to comply before repetition:
    a. The message or its part is repeated in a new tone group.
    b. A single lexical item or a phrase is repeated within the same tone group.

Of these, (i) and (ii) are unrelated to emphasis and do not interact with the illocutionary purpose of the utterance. The function related to both iconicity and strategies of interpersonal rhetoric is (iv), where reduplication and repetition serve as modifiers (cf. Blum-Kulka *et al.* 1989) amplifying the illocutionary force of the directive (also "maximisation device", cf. Held 1989). It should be noted that functions (ii) through (iv a) are sometimes difficult to differentiate when they are embedded in action and/or simultaneous talk of several persons. I estimate that in the corpus data, up to ca. 10% of all cases of reduplication and repetition in directives might represent (ii) and (iii).

Reduplication in function (iv) is illustrated below by examples coming from all three languages:

ENGLISH

1-E4. **skid # skid for the lads # skid for the lads**

2-E3. M **don't let him # don't let him go # do- # do- # don't let him go** # cause he'll hurt himself # don't let him go

GERMAN

3-G4. **Jörg dein Beitrag # Jörg dein Beitrag**
Jörg your comment # Jörg your comment

4-G4. **Chrisi komm hier # Chrisi komm hier # ich muss es doch erst mal in die Packung tun**
Chrisi-FIRST NAME come here # Chrisi-FIRST NAME come here # I must put it into the cover first

POLISH

5-P3. **drugi drugi # dawaj dawaj**
second one second one # come on come on

6-P3. weź # **Madzia # Madzia** # przestań
come on # Madzia-FIRST NAME # Madzia-FIRST NAME # stop that

While all the uses of repetition and reduplication from (ii) to (iv) can be expected to be commonplace in all the three languages under analysis, and while (iv) indeed proved to occur rather frequently in directives in all of them, it may come as a surprise that some striking cross-linguistic contrasts also occurred.

In Polish and English, the intensification of the directive's illocutionary force by iteration was particularly frequent in inhibitive requestives uttered with the goal of either stopping the undesired current action by the addressee or preventing such an action in the future (cf. Table 1). About one sixth of requests of that type contained reduplication or repetition of the verb, verb phrase, emphatic, negation or affirmative particle, elliptical phrase, term of address, or adverbial of manner.

In German, the sum of repetition and reduplication occurred with roughly the same frequencies as in English and Polish in initiating directives (i.e., directives meant to initiate rather than prevent or stop an activity by the addressee or a joint activity).[2] However, compared to the other two languages both repetition and reduplication were strongly dispreferred in inhibitive directives. Reduplication occurred just once in the whole pool of German inhibitive directives, and there was no instance of repetition.

A look at the overall patterns of intensification shows that German speakers were by no means more reluctant to intensify their inhibitive utterances in general. Thus, their non-use of reduplication can hardly be interpreted as

[2] The figures are: 11.3 occurrences per hundred for English, 8.6 for German and 9.9 for Polish.

resulting from a less impositive, more "polite" interaction style. Modifiers increasing the directive illocutionary force were applied in German inhibitive requests as frequently as in the other two languages. Various means of intensification used in inhibitive utterances, such as e.g. vulgarisms and augmentatives, semantic intensifiers, conventional use of utterance-initial semantically empty verb in the imperative, lexical intensifiers and accompanying moves in the three languages under study occurred in ca. 51 to 58 per hundred utterances (with German in the lead), meaning that the overall cross-linguistic differences in the use of intensification were negligibly slight.

German made up for the very infrequent use of reduplication in inhibitive directives by much more frequent use of *lexical intensifiers* (9 x *doch*, 1 x *ja*, 1 x *echt*) than the remaining two languages and, compared to English, more frequent use of intensifying supporting moves. The discourse particle *doch* expresses emphasis by juxtaposing "is-state" and "should be-state" (usually, of the addressee's mental state or knowledge); *ja* is a discourse particle pointing out the obviousness of the proposition, while *echt* is an adverb meaning "really, truly". Supportive moves are utterances adding some new propositional contents (e.g. stating personal preferences, threatening) and syntactically external to the "head act", the proposition that carries the directive illocutionary force.

Table 1 illustrates the cross-linguistic differences in the use of intensifiers in inhibitive directives, focusing on categories of intensifiers for which these differences were significantly large: lexical intensifiers, repetition and reduplication, and intensifying supportive moves.

Table 1. The use of modifiers in inhibitive requests: a cross-linguistic comparison. Numbers in brackets show the number of inhibitive directives in each sample

Intensifies per 100 utterances	ENGLISH (164)	GERMAN (92)	POLISH (152)
lexical intensifier	0,0	12,4	3,4
supportive move	19,5	33,7	26,2
repetition and reduplication	16,5	1,1	16,6
other	21,1	19,1	15,9
total	51,2	58,4	55,2

Second, the analysis showed that while repetition occurred in German as frequently as in the other two languages, reduplication, fulfilling the definition by Moravcsik (1992) demanding that there be no new material between or within the iterated parts of the utterance, was rare in German.[3] Table 2 shows the use of reduplication, unmodified repetition (where a new string was inserted between the iterated part of the utterance but the part was not internally changed), and modified repetition. The notion "modified repetition" refers to cases of repetition modified by deleting a functional element from the iterated part, exchanging an element, or adding a new element, typically an adverbial, a term of address, a lexical intensifier or a mitigator.

Table 2. Reduplication and repetition in English, German and Polish: occurrences per hundred directive utterances

	ENGLISH (625)	GERMAN (473)	POLISH (647)
reduplication	7,4	2,1	5,9
unmodified repetition	0,2	0,4	0,9
modified repetition	4,0	3,8	3,2

The other issue analysed was the distinction between (iv a) and (iv b) above, pertaining to the prosodic characteristics of reduplication. All the quotations above illustrate type (iv a) where there is a tone group boundary between the reduplicated parts of the utterance. The hypotheses that this prosodic property might indeed constitute a cross-linguistic pragmatic difference was tested for directive speech acts. The quotations below contain all occurrences of reduplication of type (iv b), that is, reduplication within the same tone group found in the samples.

Syntactic reduplication within a tone group

POLISH

6-P3. F idź po te poduszki jeszcze # **idź idź** kochanie
do to fetch the pillows # go go darling

7-P3. M **właź właź** # ty # właź pierwsza tutaj
get in get in # you # get in first

---

[3] The difference in the occurrence vs. non-occurrence of reduplication in directives in English and German was significant at $p<0.001$, $df=1$, $chi^2 = 15.3$. The difference between Polish and German was significant at $p<0.005$, $df=1$, $chi^2= 9.1$. The difference between English and Polish was insignificant, $df = 1$, $chi^2 = 1.3$.

8-P3. F1 Andrzej # **zobacz zobacz**
Andrzej-FIRST NAME # look look

9-P3. halo # panie # nie spać # **chodzić chodzić**
hallo # mister # no sleeping # move move

10-P3. **czekaj czekaj czekaj** # żebym kogoś nie uderzył
wait wait wait # OPTATIVE I not hit someone

11-P3. **poczekaj poczekaj poczekaj**
wait wait wait

12-P3. **dawaj dawaj**
go on go on

13-P3. **drugi drugi # dawaj dawaj**
the next the next # go on go on

14-P3. **jazda jazda** # bo nie ma czasu
off off # there is no time

15-P3. **nie nie nie** # proszę wytłumaczyć mi- # wytłumaczyć mi tę kwestię
no no no # I ask you to explain to me # explain this issue to me

16-P3. **cicho cicho** # nic nie mów
quiet quiet # don't say anything

17-P3. **czekaj czekaj** # no nie bój się
wait wait # don't be scared

18-P3. **idziemy idziemy**
we-go we-go

The reduplicated elements included: the verb in the imperative and the infinitive; the negation particle; as well as an adverb (*cicho*), a noun (*jazda*) and a numeral (*drugi*) – as far as these words constituted the core realisation of directives in elliptical directive routine formulas or situational ellipsis.

ENGLISH

In English, reduplication within the same tone group was limited to the routine formula *wakey wakey* and the negation particle: *nono*, *nonono*, *nononono*. Prosodic boundary was in one case nearly unobservable in verb duplication in fast speech rate:

20-E3 **go on # go on # go on** # just keep going man # we are wasting so much time

The only case in which the speaker definitely failed to observe the phrase boundary after the third and further repetitions of a phrase involved "go on" articulated with increasing speech rate:

21-E4 **go on # go on # go on go on go on go on**

However, the data is not quite conclusive as the speaker had a Polish parent and may have overtaken the parent's pragmatic patterns of speech into her own idiolect (either through exposition to Polish, or the transfer of this routine into English by the parent).

GERMAN

In German, reduplication appeared with affirmative and negation particles: *jaja*, *nene*, *nenene*, inhibitive elliptical routine: *Moment Moment*, and the colloquial adverbial particle *dalli*:

22-G4. dann machst du halt Hans Rosenthal nach # und wir spielen trotzdem das Spiel # dalli # **dalli dalli**
then you mimic Hans Rosenthal # and we play the game all the same # off you go # off off

The data is inconclusive because "dalli", an emphatic particle expressing the sense of urgency, is a relatively recent neologism, which still has a status of a quotation rather than a lexical item for the generations of speakers aware of its authorship by the popular show moderator Hans Rosenthal. The expression "dalli dalli" was the title of Rosenthal's TV show in the seventies. It also was used in the show as a signal for the invited guests to start acting, and was articulated with a tone group-internal reduplication. It is likely to have been overtaken in this form from Russian or Polish (where "dalej", literally: "further", is used in the function of "go on", "hurry up", and "off you go"). Nowadays "dalli" is used by children and teenagers as an emphatic particle with and without reduplication, without any awareness of its origin as a show title.

Tone group-internal reduplication (iv b) occurred in Polish with a striking frequency (about once in an hour of spoken interaction) which suggests that we are dealing with a language-specific pragmatic convention, formalised on the syntactic and prosodic level. The existence of such a routine not only shows how universal iconic principles are subject to language-specific selection and conventionalisation, but also confirms the view of grammar as non-autonomous with respect to linguistic pragmatics.

6. Summary and final remarks

The qualitative analysis of the data showed that while syntactic reduplication is used in all three languages to intensify the directive force of directive utterances, cross-linguistic contrasts occur. First, unlike in English and Polish, the speakers of German made comparatively little use of reduplication in general, and of both reduplication and repetition in inhibitive directives. This suggests that the use of repetition and reduplication in the function of illocutionary force intensifier is to some extent conventionalised, i.e. language-specific in a context-sensitive way, rather than an unrestrictedly universal result of applying iteration as a basic cognitive and communicative principle. Secondly, reduplication of verbs and short elliptical phrases within the same tone group seems to be confined to Polish. It is a language-specific pragmatic routine of a particular type, which does not contain any lexicalised material but is merely a rule of formation whose application is restricted by syntactic and pragmatic (illocutionary) factors. Thus, it is situated at the interface of syntax (reduplication applies to some syntactic categories, in particular to the verb), pragmatics (it occurs in some types of speech acts and intensifies their illocutionary force), and semantics (it affects expressive meaning).

The routinisation can be rendered in terms of the following linguistic structure, comprising the formal, functional-semantic, and functional-contextual components of conventionalised reduplication as carriers, effects, and conditions of use:

1. Formal elements of the utterance structure which the convention applies to:

A. Phonology: reduplication of some phonological material
B. Prosody: reduplication within a tone group

2. Level of language structure affected by the device:

A. semantics: expressive meaning (affective component of meaning)

B. pragmatics: illocutionary force

C. "illocutionary semantics"? (cf. Wierzbicka 1986[4])

3. Level of language structure restricting/activating the application of the device:

A. pragmatics: type of speech acts

B. syntax: reduplication affects some grammatical categories – sentence constituents and word classes

While only directive speech acts were analysed cross-linguistically using the data corpus, other evidence suggests that the same conventionalised pragmatic pattern of intensification occurs in at least two other speech acts in Polish – refutation of a statement made by the addressee and confirmation of the intention to comply with a directive.

All this invalidates to a large extent the comment of Wierzbicka's (1986: 309) following her analysis of syntactic reduplication within one tone group in particular of adverbs and adjectives in Italian, and its functional effects:

> It is interesting to note … that while an uninhibited display of emotions paralleled by a rich system of expressive derivation is as characteristic of, say, Russian or Polish as it is of Italian, devices such as syntactic reduplication don't have any counterparts in Slavic languages – certainly not on the same scale. Russian and Polish are as emotional as Italian … Nonetheless, they don't seem to have any grammatical devices for conveying the kind of pragmatic force which is conveyed by expressions such as *bella bella* … How is this difference to be interpreted? Is it possible that the pragmatic principle of "interest", posited by Leech (1983: 146) in connection with overstatement, plays a greater role in Italian culture than it does in Slavic culture? Does Italian pragmatics give a special prominence to a desire for dramatic effects, or for vividness of speech?

Written in 1986, this evaluation was based on introspective data rather than a corpus analysis. While it might be true that the syntactic reduplication of adjectives and adverbial expressions within the same tone group does not play any considerable role in Polish, the corpus data presented in this paper invalidate the claim that syntactic reduplication as such occurs infrequently in this language. The misconception is clarified when Level 3, representing the syntactic and pragmatic conditions for the application of reduplication, is taken into account. The cross-linguistic difference seems to lie not so much in the occurrence of reduplication in Italian and its non-occurrence in Polish, but, rather, in the interrelated (A) and (B) characteristics on Level 3 – the types of

[4] It is questionable whether Wierzbicka's „illocutionary semantics" goes beyond (A) and (B).

speech acts, and the grammatical-functional categories affected by formally conventionalised syntactic reduplication in these speech acts.

At the same, Wierzbicka's suggestion that the occurrence or non-occurrence of syntactic reduplication within one tone group as a language-specific convention might correlate to a high degree with the frequency of "clausal reduplication" (reduplication in a new tone group) did not find support in the data. While clausal reduplication was found as frequently in English as in Polish, reduplication within the same tone group was characteristic of Polish only.

The "grammar of reduplication" is still a little known phenomenon. In spite of its apparent simplicity, the conventionalisation of reduplication as a means of intensifying an illocution lies at the interface of several levels of linguistic form and function. It would be desirable to analyse its occurrence and distribution in a whole range of speech acts in Polish as well other languages (Italian, Swedish) where similar phenomena have been shown to occur (cf. Wierzbicka 1986, Lindström 1999). Further research is needed to find out how frequent it is in related and in unrelated languages, and which cross-linguistic contrasts and similarities occur regarding the speech acts in which it is found. A promising field of study is the prosody of iterative speech, which could not be discussed here in detail.

Finally, if it proves to be a non-unique phenomenon recurring in languages of different origins, another interesting practical question will arise in the area of contact linguistics: how far is reduplication within the same tone group as a conventionalised means of intensifying directive and other speech acts susceptible to transfer from one language to another in situations of societal bilingualism?

REFERENCES

Barbaresi, Lavinia Merlini (2000). *Iconicity in language and text.* A paper read at ESSE5-2000 (The Fifth Conference of the European Society for the Study of English) at the University of Helsinki, Finland, 26. August 2000.

Blum-Kulka, Shoshana, Juliane House and Gabriele Kasper (eds.) (1989). *Cross-Cultural Pragmatics: Requests and Apologies.* Norwood: Ablex.

Held, Gudrun (1989). "On the Role of Maximization in Verbal Politeness". *Multilingua* 8 (2–3): 167–206.

Israeli, A. (1997). "Syntactic reduplication in Russian: A cooperative principle device in dialogues". *Journal of Pragmatics* 27: 587–609.

Kajitani, Motomi (2005). "Semantic Properties of Reduplication among the World's Languages". *LSO Working Papers in Linguistics 5: Proceedings of WIGL 2005*: 93–106.

Lindström, J. K. (1999). *Vackert, vackert! Syntactic reduplication in Swedish.* FD Dissertation.

Macdonald, R. Ross (1976). *Indonesian reference grammar.* Washington, D.C: Georgetown University Press.

Moravcsik, Edith, A. (1992). "Reduplication". In: William Bright (ed.). *International encyclopedia of linguistics*. Oxford: Oxford University Press: 323–324.

Murane, E. (1974). *Daga grammar: From morpheme to discourse.* Glendale, CA: The Church Press.

Nattinger, James R. and Jeanette de Carrico (1992). *Lexical Phrases and Language Teaching.* Oxford: Oxford University Press.

Peirce, Charles S. (1985) [1902]. "Logic as Semiotic: The Theory of Signs". In: R. E. Innis (ed.). *Semiotics. An Introductory Anthology*. London: Hutchinson: 4–23.

Posner, R. (1986). "Zur Systematik der Beschreibung verbaler und nonverbaler Kommunikation. Semiotik als Propädeutik der Medienanalyse". In: Bosshardt, H.-G. (ed.). *Perspektiven auf Sprache. Interdisziplinäre Beiträge zum Gedenken an Hans Hörmann*. Berlin/New York: 293–297.

Uspensky, B. A. (1972). "Subsystems in language, their interrelations and their correlated universals". *Linguistics: An International Review* 88: 53–71.

Wierzbicka, A. (1986). "Italian reduplication: cross-cultural pragmatics and illocutionary semantics". *Linguistics* 24: 287–315.

Part Three

MONOLINGUAL STUDIES

Kamila Turewicz

University of Stettin

A COGNITIVE GRAMMAR PERSPECTIVE ON JENNIFER COATES'S FINDINGS ON THE SEMANTICS OF ENGLISH MODALS

Abstract: The purpose of the present paper is to address issues that emerge at the interface of corpus findings and theoretical positions of researchers (re)analyzing the linguistic facts. The case in focus is Jennifer Coates's (1983) work on the semantics of English modals. Starting with crucial (though necessarily selected) characteristics of the findings, I comment on their position in the area of research on modality, illustrating certain pitfalls researchers may fall into if corpus findings are handled with inadequate precision. Next, the problem of possible interface between theoretical models and corpus analyses is addressed. To illustrate the issue I attempt to explicate correspondences between Coates's findings and relevant facets of Langacker's Cognitive Grammar.

Keywords: deontic modals, English, epistemic meaning, epistemic modals, fuzzy sets, modal auxiliaries, modality, root meaning, syntactic co-occurrence patterns.

1. Introduction

Jennifer Coates's book *The semantics of the Modal Auxiliaries* (1983) belongs to most important and illuminating works in the area of modality. The unique value of the work derives from extensive research into the English language data, upon which the author founded her arguments as regards semantics of English modal auxiliaries. Indeed, Coates defined her work as "a report of an investigation into the meanings of the modal auxiliaries in modern British English" (Coates 1983: 1). The investigation was based on written language materials from the 1 000 000 word Lancaster corpus (developed into Lancaster – Oslo – Bergen (LOB) corpus) and the Survey of English Usage, consisting of 725 000 words, from which the linguist excluded parts overlapping (in type) with the LOB corpus (i.e. written, published data), focusing her analysis on spoken and written – unprinted language materials.

As the author observes, the value in basing an analysis of modal semantics on corpora consists both in reliability of data and representativeness of the findings, and significance of related theoretical implications. As regards the former, i.e. the reliability of data and representativeness of findings, Coates stresses that "a corpus prevents the linguist from relying on his own invented examples (which tend to be clear-cut, central examples), and therefore from arriving at an unrealistically 'tidy' view of his subject." (Coates 1983: 3) Her position on the relevance of corpus findings in the context of theoretical stands is reflected in anther quotation:

It seems to me to be unquestionably one of the justifications of the corpus analysis that it brings to light indeterminate cases which cannot be dealt with by the 'tidy' models of linguistic theory. (Coates 1983: 22)

This does not mean that Coates rejects legitimacy of theoretical models, indeed, she postulates one, based on Zadeh's (1965) concept of 'fuzzy sets', to account for the findings. Rather, in her view "[c]orpus data brings the linguist face-to-face with indeterminate examples, which must be recognised if the model is to reflect reality" (Coates 1983: 3). In other words, the linguist is warning against biasing the process of gaining information by theoretical claims, and issuing a challenge to theoretical models to accommodate the findings she obtained.

2. Corpus findings on modal usage

Coates (1983) approached the facts collected in the corpuses without any particular theoretical perspective, focusing instead on a thorough examination of modal usage in both written and spoken types of discourse, from formal to various degrees to private texts. This theory-neutral perspective facilitated a number of discoveries, whose relevance consisted in providing better insights into modal usage, often questioning widely accepted beliefs, and/or challenging some predominating theoretical assumptions. Let us consider just a few examples selected from her thought-provoking corpus-based findings.

To begin, with respect to the distribution of English modals CAN and MAY,[1] Coates's findings show that the synonymy of CAN and MAY is clearly exaggerated as "in 74 per cent of cases, CAN cannot be substituted by MAY" (Coates 1983: 24). Next, the distribution of the two modals differs in terms of prosodic patterns, the factor generally ignored in the prior discussions of modal

[1] As the 25 year span is too short a period of time for significant changes in modal usage to occur, I present the findings as reflecting the modal usage of today's English.

semantics (e.g. Palmer 1979). Namely, CAN and MAY are related to different stress patters in that the former modal is not normally stressed, (i.e. its prevailing realization is kən / kŋ), while the latter, MAY, is. As the author stresses, "It should be noted that not only is MAY (= Epistemic 'Possibility') stressed in 79 per cent of all cases, but typically it is associated with fall-rise intonation, (…)" (Coates 1983: 104). Furthermore, the finding that "CAN is the only modal auxiliary, where we do not find the root-epistemic distinction" (Coates 1983: 85), i.e. no uses of CAN Epistemic Possibility had been found, whereas "MAY is primarily used, particularly in spoken English, to express Epistemic Possibility…" should have called for a serious re-analysis of the semantics of the two modals, traditionally characterized as largely overlapping, especially by authors of pedagogical grammars.

Also worth noting are discoveries made with respect to modals of obligation and necessity OUGHT and SHOULD. Contrary to Palmer's (1979) claim on contra-factive usage of SHOULD, the corpus data link the modal with the future, hence non-factivity: "the modal is not contra-factive but non-factive; the outcome of the directive is not known" (Coates 1983: 61). As for OUGHT, Coates's discoveries placed the predicate (categorized by Traugott and Dasher (2002: 107) with quasi-auxiliaries), among 'true' modals, with Epistemic and Root meanings, and argue that, although relatively infrequent, "OUGHT is less in danger of becoming obsolete than has sometimes been thought" (Coates 1983: 70) except that the modal was found more frequent in spoken language. Furthermore, the spoken corpus data analysis hinted at some role of prosody in the distribution of SHOULD and OUGHT (disregarded by Palmer (1979)). Namely, unlike SHOULD, in almost all examples with Epistemic OUGHT, the modal was found to "have stress of some kind, most commonly nuclear stress" (Coates 1983: 75).

As regards possible challenges corpus data create for linguistic theories, I would argue that Coates's findings with most significant implications for theoretical models are the syntactic co-occurrence patterns, which evidently systematize correlations between modal categories, Root and Epistemic, with the syntactic context of the modal involved. Thus, discussing the Epistemic and non-Epistemic modality, Coates states the following:

> the co-occurrence of the Epistemic modals and certain syntactic forms, such as HAVE + EN, BE + ING, etc., distinguish this category of modality from non-Epistemic. (Coates 1983: 20)

> Despite the range of meaning covered by the Root modals, their essential unity is confirmed by the syntactic patterns associated with them, which distinguish them from their Epistemic counterparts. For example, the features animate subject, agentive verb and passive voice are all linked with Root meaning. (Coates 1983: 21)

Another aspect of modal usage, which surfaced from the data due to availability of larger fragments of spoken discourse, are the interdependencies between the meanings assigned to respective modal predicates and aspects of extra-linguistic context of the utterance with the modal. Coates stresses the relevance of extra-linguistic context in deciding upon the meanings involved when she argues against Palmer's (1979) differentiation into dynamic / deontic within the category Root, postulating the 'cline' analysis of Non-epistemic meanings "from strong 'Obligation' (the core) to cases at the periphery where the sense of 'Obligation' is extremely weak":

Clearly, in certain contexts, where the authority structure is well-defined, such as when a mother speaks to a child, or a teacher to a pupil, a 'deontic' (Palmer 1979) or 'discourse-oriented' (Palmer 1974) interpretation is more appropriate, and in the contexts such as formal prose, where the participants are less clearly defined, such an interpretation would be less appropriate. (Coates 1983: 21)

In view of her findings, the work of Jennifer Coates should have inspired discussion aiming at a more accurate model of the semantics of English modals. First, uncovering the systematic relation between the formal (syntactic) aspects of language and the modal categories Root and Epistemic should have provoked questions about the syntax/semantics dichotomy, thus stimulating research into the nature of the interdependencies. Next, in view of Coates's interpretations of meanings of corpus sentences which foregrounded the role of extralinguistic factors in categorizing decisions, it seems legitimate to argue that semantic values assigned to the English modals, be it root/deontic, dynamic, epistemic, etc., should be analyzed as **meanings of utterances with modals,** i.e., composite meaning structures drawing from conceptual values of language expressions and relevant facets of speech situations. An implication of these interpretations could be that **meanings/ conceptual values/ of English modals need not be equated with the modal values / concepts assigned to them.**

The evidence that the semantic, modal categories arise in relation to both syntactic context and pragmatic information ought to have encouraged a more general dispute about the nature of borderlines between the respective levels of language structure. Especially since the corpus findings questioned the autonomy of syntax from semantics (or semantics from syntax) as well as semantics from pragmatics, thus, possibly, shed new light on issues of semantic indeterminacy such as: polysemy, ambiguity, merger, they should have opened a new chapter in the research on English modals and modality.

3. Coates's corpus findings in view of post 1983 research into modal phenomena

The literature on modality and modal phenomena published after 1983 leaves little doubt that Coates's findings have had a relatively modest impact on the more recent research into modal phenomena. Among probable reasons why the findings have not been adequately appreciated, could be the fact that they focused on the semantics of English modal auxiliaries, a language specific issue, whereas most influential works seem to have focused on more general theoretical issues related to typology of modality and subcategorization of the domain (Bybee, Perkins, Pagliuca (1994), van der Auwera and Plungian (1998), Frawley (2005)). In those works, if reference is made to Coates (1983), it is in the context of assumed subcategorization into root/epistemic meanings vis-à-vis the epistemic/deontic/dynamic classification, as propagated by Palmer (1979/2001), or categorization systems postulated by other authors (external/internal, speaker-oriented/agent-oriented modalities).

Another reason why Coates's findings appear not to have been adequately appreciated either in works on modality and/or English modals, could be the fact that they became a real challenge to predominating theoretical approaches, based on traditional (if not orthodox) conceptualizations of language structure. Indeed, there are reasons to argue that Coates's findings turned out to be 'too difficult to handle' for mainstream research, which might explain why the significance of correlations between syntactic features and semantic modal categories, on the one hand, and the role of extralinguistic context, on the other one, was either undermined or ignored. This is illustrated by the words of an Anonymous Reviewer (2006) of a paper in which Coates's findings were reinterpreted from a Cognitive Grammar perspective.

In my view, the author also partly misinterprets (or perhaps better, overrates) the findings of Coates (1983). Coates only speaks of 'syntactic co-occurrence patterns', which to a lesser or greater degree can be associated with the modal verb's semantics. The association is very outspoken for *must*, but less clear with other modals. (Anonymous Reviewer 2006)

A more thorough analysis of Coates's work might result in reconsidering this opinion, if only in view of the patterns discovered for MAY (the formula '$\supset^{100}$' reads: 'in 100 percent of examples', emphasis mine):

The discrete nature of Epistemic MAY is confirmed by **strong associations** found between syntactic and semantic features.

(i) Perfective Aspect $\supset^{100}$ Epistemic Meaning
I /may have put it there#/out of the way# (S.7.1A.10)

(ii) Progressive Aspect$\supset^{100}$ Epistemic Meaning
They /may be :reading something by Shakespeare # (S.5.10.38)

(iii) Existential Subject$\supset^{100}$ Epistemic Meaning
January I sup:pose there :may be an :interview round about January# (S.1.1.16)

(iv) Quasi –modal $\supset^{100}$ Epistemic Meaning
I "/may be 'able to leave here# and /still 'owe them my !notice# (S.7.3F.10)

(v) Stative Verb $\supset^{95}$Epistemic Meaning (Lanc:83)
/on the feries# . em. /I was always 'being 'told# you /may 'have a degree# but you're "/no better waiter than :I am# (S.5.9.28)

/I think he 'may be a very !violent !man# (V.5.1B.12)

(vi) Negation $\supset^{100}$ Epistemic Meaning (Lanc:77)
they /say !he may :[never work] again# be/cause he's 'got ə 'schizophrenia# (S.1.13.20)
(Coates 1983:137)

Widely cited proposals: Sweetser (1990), Langacker (1991), Goosens (2000), Traugott and Dasher (2002), Nuyts (2005), de Haan (2005) tend to acknowledge Coates's work to the extent that it can be referred to in the discussion on subcategorization of the modal domain and/or as a source of examples. Admittedly, an author of a publication makes decisions about what to refer to and how to support their own arguments through reference to other works. However, there is an interesting question worth addressing here. Is it appropriate to draw from an author's work without adequate acknowledgement of how this work may have contributed to advancement of the research area, to the effect that the author's achievement and value of the work are reduced to a source of reference only?

3.1. Problems with selective reference to Coates's corpus-based findings

As remarked above, Coates's work is often, if not exclusively, referred to in the context of discussions on most adequate subcategorization of modality and/or as a source of examples. Let us consider Traugott and Dasher (2002) as a case illustrating the problem. In one of the initial definitions in the chapter on modals, the authors state:

Deontic modality (from the Gk. deon "what is binding"); also widely known as "root" modality (e.g. Coates 1983, Sweetser (1990). This centrally involves obligation and compulsion

Traugott and Dasher (2002: 105–6)

There are two related problems with the statement. First of all, in view of her corpus-based analysis, Coates found the modal logic term *deontic* inappropriate, justifying her decision to employ the category Root as follows:

...it [*deontic*] refers to the logic of obligation and permission (cf. von Wright 1951). Typical Root modals, such as MUST and MAY, cover a range of meaning, of which 'Obligation' and 'Permission' represent only the core. Palmer (1979) attempts to overcome this problem by recognizing not just deontic but also dynamic and existential modalities. However, this fails to capture the fact that all the meanings of non-Epistemic MUST (for example) are related and can be shown to lie on a cline extending from strong 'Obligation' (the core) to cases at the periphery (where a more appropriate paraphrase would be 'it is important that ...'). (Coates 1983: 21)

Thus, clearly, for Coates *deontic* does not seem to have been 'recognized' as Root. To the contrary, in view of the language data she seems to insist that the two should be kept distinct. Another problem related to equating the modal logic category *deontic* with linguistic category Root[4] (hence overlooking Coates's arguments) is the confusion related to interpretations of the corpus examples which were both elaborately analyzed and categorized by Coates and employed and commented upon by Traugott and Dasher, without reference to the original account, regardless of how similar or different the two interpretations appeared to be. For example, Coates (1983: 33) postulates four features characteristic of core Root MUST:

(i) Subject is animate.
(ii) Main verb is activity verb.
(iii) Speaker is interested in getting subject to perform the action.
(iv) Speaker has authority over subject.

Coates (1983: 33)

These four features are employed in her analysis of twelve example sentences from both corpora as criteria whose presence or absence is indicative of the positions of respective uses on the cline, from strong 'core' where all (i)–(iv) are present, to periphery where only one of the features could be present:

1. a. ((C. 12) p. 35)
Clay pots /...../ must have some protection from severe weather (Lanc1-403)

[4] As regards the definition of category Root see Butler (1982) and Hofmann (1966).

b. (T&D (12)p.109)
Clay pots must have some protection from severe weather.
(Coates 1983: 35)

(1.a.) is Coates's example illustrating the weakest extreme of the (Root) cline, characterized as follows (emphasis mine):

Example (12) **has both third person inanimate subject and a non-agentive verb**. The sense of obligation is thus very weak, and the speaker's involvement is minimal.
(Coates 1983: 36)

(1.b.) comes from Traugott and Dasher (2002: 109), who, having acknowledged Coates's work as the source of the example, provide the following comment (emphasis mine): "**Subjects of deontics are sometimes not even human**", and generalize:

In MdE [Modern English] **deontic and epistemic modals**, unlike main verbs, **impose no selectional restrictions on their subjects or the verbs that follow them.** Subjects may be animate or inanimate, and syntax may be active or passive; these modals are neutral to *there*-construction, and other characteristics associated with main verbs.
(Traugott and Dasher 2002: 109)

Juxtaposing (1.a.) with (1.b.) creates a puzzle. Where Coates provides (1.a.) as an illustration of how contextual features (i) – (iv) help systematize "the range of meaning covered by the Root modals" due to "their essential unity (...) confirmed by the syntactic patterns associated with them", Traugott and Dasher use the same example sentence, identifying Coates's work as its source, apparently to argue to the contrary ("impose no selectional restrictions on their subjects or the verbs that follow them."), overlooking Coates's contextual findings.

Even more confusing results obtain when one juxtaposes Coates's (1983) and Traugott and Dasher's (2002) analyses of sentences in (2.a) and (2.b.) (emphasis mine):

2. a. (C. (27) p. 42)
this sort of conversation # əm - - / have you noticed president # that əm- - the boiled eggs # at Sunday breakfast # always hard # - - and president said# - //ah/ well# - **the simple truth is# that / if you're going to boil eggs communally# they must be hard# /..../** you/ have to crack the head of an egg when you take it out of the pan# otherwise it goes on cooking# (S.1.3.46)

b. (T&D.(16),p.111)
The simple truth is that if you're going to boil eggs communally they must be hard.
"it is necessary for the cook to boil eggs hard"

(Warner 1993: 14)

Coates provides the example to illustrate a rare case of objective Epistemic meanings, commented on in the following words (emphasis mine):

the cline associated with logical Necessity extends from a subjective core, meaning 'I confidently infer that x' (...) to an objective periphery meaning **'In the light of what is known, it is necessarily the case that x' Objective Epistemic MUST** is, however, extremely unusual in normal everyday language, and has been overlooked altogether by linguists

(Coates 1983: 41–42)

(2.b) is Traugott and Dasher's (2002) example (16), (and (23b)[5]), and clearly a part of the Survey example analyzed by Coates, except that the authors do not refer either to the Survey (S.1.3. 46) or Coates ((27): 42) as the source, but to Warner (1993: 14), who evidently reduced the information-rich version of the corpus example to a decontextualized fragment. As a result Traugott and Dasher analyze and paraphrase (2.b) as follows (emphasis mine):

> Among non-prototypical **deonic** sentences with ***must*** are general objective expressions like (16) meaning "it is necessary for X to do / be Y"
>
> (16) The simple truth is that if you're going to boil eggs communally they *must* be hard. " **it is necessary for the cook to boil eggs hard**"
>
> Warner 1993: 14
>
> (Traugott and Dasher 2002: 111)

Where the information-rich context of an utterance with a modal available in corpus data motivates the interpretation of modal usage as a rare case of (objective) Epistemic modality (Coates 1983: 41–2), an analysis of the same utterance reduced to a sentence with the modal may implicate contrasting categorization judgment, i.e., defining the modal meaning as *deontic* (Traugott and Dasher 2002: 111). The immediate lesson we could, or perhaps, should learn from the brief discussion presented above is that the validity of our arguments is a function of reliability our data. On more general grounds, the discussion of

---

[5] The Traugott and Dasher (2002: 113) example (23b) illustrates wide scope of the modal, paraphrased as "it is required, eggs boil till hard"

(1.a.) and (1.b.) shows that the selective reference to Coates's work disregarding her theoretical proposals may imply a rather incomplete and impoverished picture of the value of the study. This is unfair since besides numerous examples reflecting real usage, Coates offered a comprehensive and systematic account of the semantics of English modals, providing solid arguments for postulated categorization and a theoretical model for accommodating her findings.

4. Theoretical implications of Coates's findings

In the chapter 'Theoretical Considerations' Coates (1983: 10) summarizes her data analysis as follows:

> On the one hand, my data suggest that the Root-Epistemic distinction is a discrete one; the main indicators are: (i) the existence of ambiguous cases (where the two meanings are in either / or relationship (...)); (ii) the co-occurrence of the two categories, Root and Epistemic in distinct syntactic and semantic features (such as negation, aspect, etc,); (iii) the possibility of distinct paraphrases. On the other hand, it seems that both these categories involve indeterminacy: that is examples assigned to them cover a range of meaning.
>
> (Coates 1983: 10)

In view of the findings, she arrived at the conclusion that "a correct description of modal meaning must reconcile categorical and non-categorical approaches" (Coates 1983: 10). As a consequence, to accommodate the findings she postulated 'a fuzzy set' theoretical proposal, based on Zadeh's (1965) Fuzzy Sets Theory. This conceptualization allowed her to present the structure of postulated categories Epistemic and Root as fuzzy with respect to such parameters as subjectivity/objectivity and/or strong/weak. Coates characterized the structure of modal categories as organized around such notions as: core, skirt and periphery. A weakness of the model was that it did not adequately accommodate the discoveries relating both modal (sub)categories and their internal structure with patterns for contextual features. The correlations between syntactic features and semantic modal categories consisted in providing 'parameters' motivating subcategorization of the conceptual domain covered by English modals into Epistemic and Root, as well as 'fuzzy' internal structure of each of the categories, especially Root. What Coates's fuzzy set model did not account for was what and how syntactic and/or extra linguistic, pragmatic context contributed to the semantics of modals.

It should be borne in mind that Coates published her research results in the (linguistics) research context of 1983, the year when, on the one hand, a foundational assumption for linguistics was that form was qualitatively different from meaning, and on the other, a few researchers started questioning this generally accepted premise. Indeed, that was the year when Langacker's 'Space Grammar' circulated in and through some academic centers in Europe, almost with a status of a 'forbidden fruit'. In his (albeit preliminary) discussion on the nature of language Langacker both presented arguments for viewing grammar as symbolic on the par with lexicon and offered semantic definitions of such formal aspects of English as: profiles of simple verb forms, perfective/imperfective or conceptual values of auxiliaries and participial forms, DO, BE. HAVE, -ING and –EN. He explicated the nature of semantic integration, in which semantic values of composite language structures derive through integration and accommodation of conceptual values of language forms and lexical material. As regards English modals, Langacker (1978) offered a preliminary analysis of modals as epistemic/grounding predicates. All in all, Coates's (1983) work was illuminating in giving a promise that there might be some regularities in the system, thus making modal semantics to a reasonable extent predictable, whereas an early version of Langacker's theory, Space Grammar (Langacker 1978, 1983) offered a theoretical 'missing link' between the semantic complexity of modals and the syntactic co-occurrence patterns.

5. Coates's findings vis-a-vis cognitive linguistics

5.1. Modal categories in contexts

Coates (1983) shows that Root / Epistemic sub-categorization of a modal is related to its syntactic / formal context. For instance, discussing 'core' examples of Root MUST, illustrated by (3), Coates (1983: 33) observes that they share the four previously mentioned contextual features.

(3) "*You must play this ten times over*", Miss Jarrova would say, pointing with relentless fingers to a jumble of crotchets and quavers. (Lanc1-G3320)
Coates (1983: 37)

How significantly the syntactic context is associated with Root MUST is reflected by the corpus data:

I shall give here all the associations found with the high percentage value. Where the Survey and Lancaster material are not identical, the Survey value is given in parentheses.

Negation	$\supset^{100}$ + Root Meaning	
Passive	$\supset^{93}$ + Root Meaning	(60)
Agentive verb	$\supset^{91}$ + Root Meaning	(85)
Second Person Subject	$\supset^{87}$ + Root Meaning	(62)
First person subject	$\supset^{83}$ + Root Meaning	(92)"

Coates (1983: 37)

Undoubtedly, the discoveries of both the patterns and differences in their distribution in the two corpora deserve a thorough analysis. Because such an analysis is beyond limits of the paper, in what follows I would like to outline a cognitive grammar re-analysis of the contextual feature identified by Coates as 'Agentive verb'. The feature has been selected because the numbers indicating correlations between Root MUST and the feature in both corpora (i.e. 91 and 85 percent, respectively) imply that, together with first person subject, its presence can be considered highly indicative of the Root meaning.

5.2. Contextual features in view of Cognitive Grammar

Langacker ([1983] 1987, 1991) conceives of all language structure as symbolic in that every language structure has its conceptual content – semantic pole, symbolised by a phonological sequence – phonological pole. Accordingly, a verb form designating a process type is also a symbolic structure in that it profiles the verb's conceptual content in either of two way: as a **perfective** or **imperfective** process. Hence, with some verbs, a simple verb form can structure a scene in terms of a sequence of changing relations between participants (e.g. an agent (and an object)) within a limited span of time, so that all of the relations, each distinct from the others, including the initial and final ones, are conceptualised as equally salient. The effect of the type of profile is that none of the relations can legitimately represent the complexity of the process: "...perfectives lack the property of contractibility (hence the entire event – including its endpoints – must be profiled for it to count as a full instantiation of the process type)". (Langacker 1991: 252). Examples of verbs whose simple forms profile perfective processes are: *eat*, *go*, *come*, *bring*, *walk*, *sing*, etc.

In the case of verbs such as *be*, *have*, *know*, *love*, which profile imperfective processes, the form contributes conceptually to their meanings in that it 'adds' the following information: the situation is construed as stable, unchanging through a span time. Technically speaking, the imperfective profile imposes effective homogeneity on the conceptualised scene in that each of the phases/relations/'component states' of the scene under conceptualisation is conceived of as identical to others and, thus, all the phases can be represented by any of them. As Langacker (1991: 251) puts it "for any such process that extends through the time of speaking, those component states which fall within OS constitute a full instantiation of the process type."

An important implication of the two types of profile is that the conceptual contents of respective verb types are organized either as contemporaneous to the time of utterance or temporally incompatible with it. Namely, the imperfective profile designates a scene that 'is currently the case', i.e. overlapping with the time of speaking, whereas the perfective profile designates a scene 'to take place' i.e., whose full instantiation is still ahead of the time of speaking. Paraphrases of Root and Epistemic meanings of a modal seem to grasp the difference between perfective and imperfective profiles. With respect to Root MUST Coates states that 'a basic meaning can be identified which is common throughout; roughly 'it is necessary **for**..." (Coates 1983: 32) (emphasis mine), hence Root meaning relates to cases when the situation designated by the main verb 'is not the case as yet', rather, its accomplishment is still ahead.. The meanings identified for Epistemic MUST are "I confidently infer that x" and "in the light of what is known it **is** necessarily the case that x" (Coates 1983: 40) (emphasis mine), hence, Epistemic meanings apply when the scene designated by the main verb correlates with the actual time of speaking, i.e., 'is the case at the moment of speaking'. Thus, the perfective profile as defined by Langacker is immanent in Coates's category 'agentive verbs', whereas her categories 'stative verbs', perfect aspect and progressive aspect (Coates (1983: 20) HAVE + EN, BE + ING), correspond to imperfective processes.

What should be borne in mind at this point is that the contextual feature 'agentive verb' identified by Coates as related to Root modals, is essentially a feature stemming from the profile of the main verb, and thus, a conceptual value inherent in the context rather than a feature of the modal predicate. By the same token, Coates's syntactic features of Epistemic modal meaning appear to be largely determined by the imperfective profile (as in Langacker 1987, 1991) of the verb that follows the modal.

6. Discussion and concluding remarks

Correlating Coates's findings with Cognitive Grammar perspective on language structure allows us to discern the contribution of syntactic patterns to the semantics of modal auxiliaries. As illustrated above, and argued in Turewicz (1986, 2000), the Root/Epistemic distinction can be systematically linked to different profiles of the main verb (or, more appropriately, the verb phrase). Accordingly, Cognitive Grammar reanalysis of Coates's corpus findings formulated as (i) and (ii) (Coates 1983: 33) provides possible theoretical justification for viewing the two modal categories as sentence level categories. Analyzed from the perspective of Cognitive Grammar conception of symbolic nature of all language structure, Coates's syntactic co-occurrence patterns can be interpreted as templates sanctioning Epistemic or Root meanings, which emerge from lexical and 'formal' linguistic units through semantic integration processes. Essentially, as confirmed independently by traditional paraphrases, the component structures that differentiate between the two types of composite structures, deriving Root and Epistemic meanings, respectively, are perfective or imperfective profile of the main verb.

Plausible as the argumentation may be, it does not accommodate Coates's (1983: 33) features (iii) and (iv), which define parameters of extralinguistic context, i.e. pragmatic information, 'responsible' both for in-category indeterminacy, especially among Root meanings, and for cases such as (2.a) and (2.b) above, where one sentence with the modal can derive different utterance level meanings, Epistemic (Coates) or deontic (Traugott and Dasher), depending on the extralinguistic context.[7] Since (iii) and (iv) link modal semantics with parameters of actual speech acts, I find it legitimate to analyze modal categories as usage categories, hence, utterance level categories. In other words, the fact that a modal category emerges in the context of some kind of 'on-line' information, available only to actual speech act participants at 'the time of speaking' ('speaker is interested in getting subject to perform the action', 'speaker has authority over subject'), implies that modal categories are determined to a remarkable extent by information from beyond the language material. This fact still awaits its account.

Nonetheless, as the discussion above explicates, Coates's findings may significantly affect research into modal semantics. Specifically, if the differentiation into Root/Epistemic and the indeterminacy within each of the categories are related to conceptual contribution of the linguistic context analysed by speech act participants in a specific usage context, the issues of ambiguity, polysemy, indeterminacy need not be related to modal predicates per se. To the contrary, the conceptual content of the modal itself may be the same in each case, as suggested by traditional paraphrases for MUST: 'necessary for....', 'necessarily the case that...'. Should this be the case, it might be worthwhile to

[7] The 'extralinguistic context' for (2.b) is specified in (2.a).

re-address the old question of polysemy of English modals. If the categories Root/deontic/Epistemic, and others, are utterance level categories, each of the modal predicates may have a central meaning (Ehrman 1966). Furthermore, if the categories derive through semantic integration of a central meaning of the modal, conceptual value of its linguistic context and extralinguistic information, at least two more issues emerge that deserve serious considerations. If the modal categories assigned to modal predicates are not meanings of modals but utterance level meanings, *what precisely are the meanings of modals*? Moreover, should there be one meaning schema for each modal, *what are the processes which allow the 'one meaning schema' or 'central meaning' of a modal to sanction both Root and Epistemic (and indeed all other) modal values as utterance level meanings*?

What emerges from the above questions is the challenge for theoretical models to accommodate an account of modal semantics capable of reconciling categorical and non-categorical approaches. That is, reconciling the existence of semantic categories, with indeterminacy identified with respect to the semantics of respective English modals. The discussion of the extent to which Coates's syntactic patterns can be accommodated within the conception of language structure postulated by Langacker allows us to consider Cognitive Grammar as capable of facing the challenge, at least to the extent that it offers an explanation why and how syntactic context contributes to the emergence of a modal category as sentence level category, which thus can be distinct from the modal itself. What remains to be seen, however, is whether Cognitive Grammar can accommodate implications of Coates's features (iii) and (iv). Such descriptive/analytic devices as Ground and Subjectification, as well as the very concept of dynamic usage based semantics allow for incorporation of extralinguisic information into the meaning structure that emerges at the level of utterance. Thus, there is a promise that the model can account for the on-line meaning construction processes deriving utterance level semantic categories/meanings which have to be unambiguously recoverable to ensure successful communication.

To conclude, corpus linguistics and cognitive linguistics are methodologically independent branches of linguistic science, each functioning in its own right and each contributing to a better understanding of the complexity of language structure and usage. However, as the present discussion illustrates, each of them can remarkably affect the development of the other. First, a theoretical model capable of accommodating corpus findings in a general conception of language structure allows for significant generalizations of quantitative discoveries. Second, because the analytic power of any theoretical model is a function of its capacity to accommodate linguistic reality, the linguistic model whose analytic tools account for the facts can be considered as satisfying the requirement of explanatory adequacy.

REFERENCES

Butler, C. S. (1982). *The directive function of the English modals.* Unpublished PhD Dissertation. University of Nottingham.

Bybee, J. L., Perkins, R. D., Pagliuca, W. (1994). *The evolution of grammar. Tense, aspect and modality in the languages of the world.* Chicago and London: The University of Chicago Press.

Coates, J. (1983). *The semantics of modal auxiliaries.* London: Croom – Helm.

Ehrman, M. (1966). *The meaning of modals in present- day American English.* The Hague: Mouton.

Frawley, W. (ed.) (2005). *The expression of modality.* Berlin: Mouton de Gruyter.

Goossens, L. (2000). "Patterns of meaning extension, "parallel chaining", subjectification, and modal shifts". In: Barcelona 2000a: 149–169.

Hann, de F. (2005). "Typological approaches to modality". In: Frawley, W. (ed.). *The Expressions of Modality.* Berlin, New York: Mouton de Gruyter.

Hofmann, T. R. (1966). "Past tense replacement and the modal system". *Harvard Computational Laboratory Report to the National Science Foundation on mathematical linguistics and automatic translation.* NSF 17 Cambridge, Mass.

Langacker, R. W. (1978). "The form and meaning of the English auxiliary". *Language* 54: 853–82.

Langacker, R. W. (1983). *Foundations of Cognitive Grammar.* Chapter I and II reproduced by L.A.U.T

Langacker, R. W. (1987). *Foundations of Cognitive Grammar.* Vol. 1. *Theoretical Prerequisites.* Stanford: Sanford University Press.

Langacker, R. W. (1991) *Foundations of Cognitive Grammar.* Vol. II. *Descriptive Applications.* Stanford: Stanford University Press.

Lyons, J. (1977). *Semantics* .Cambridge: Cambridge University Press.

Nuyts, J. (2005). "Modality: Overview and linguistic issues". In: Frawley, W. (ed.). *The Expression of Modality.* Berlin, New York: Mouton de Gruyter.

Palmer, F. R. (1974). *The English verb.* London: Longman.

Palmer, F. R. (1979). *Modality and the English modals.* London and New York: Longman.

Sweetser, E. E. (1990). *From etymology to pragmatics: metaphorical and cultural aspects of semantic structure.* Cambridge: Cambridge University Press.

Traugott, E. C., Dasher, R. B. (2002). *Regularity in Semantic Change.* Cambridge: Cambridge University Press.

Turewicz, K. (1986). *Modal predicates in English: cognitive approach*. Unpublished doctoral dissertation. University of Gdańsk.

Turewicz, K. (2000). *Applicabity of Cognitive Grammar as a Foundation of Pedagogical-Reference Grammar*. Łódź: Wydawnictwo Uniwersytetu Łódzkiego.

Van der Auwera, J. and Plungian, V. (1998). "Modality's semantic map". *Linguistic typology* 2.1: 79–124.

Zadeh, L. A. (1965). "Fuzzy Sets". *Information and Control*, 8: 338–53.

Eliza Kitis

Aristotle University, Thessaloniki

EMOTIONS AS DISCURSIVE CONSTRUCTS: THE CASE OF THE PSYCH-VERB 'FEAR'

Abstract: In this paper, I concentrate on emotion predicates (*fear* psych-verbs) and trace back their original meanings to the domain of action (motion) rather than emotion. I show that emotional meanings are initially parasitic on actional predicates denoting external behaviour, whose senses gradually give way to emotional meanings as causative constructions give way to non-causative ones. In this sense, emotion meanings can be seen as outgrowths of action or motion meanings. Moreover, emotion predicates examined here are shown to have developed various syntactic constructions utilized in discourse to express not just emotions, but also a variety of cognitive functions approximating other cognitively weighted verbs of thinking, etc., and specific speech acts.

The findings of this study may have implications for Wierzbicka's research. If the original meanings of emotion verbs are to be found in their initial uses to signify motion rather than emotion, how can we claim that certain configurations of assumed universal cognitive cross-cultural concepts, such as 'think' and 'feel', will yield the emotion concepts encoded in lexemes *fear* and *afraid?* Besides, at which stage can we sever these lexical items (and/or their corresponding concepts) from their evolutionary course and, hence, from their variability of meaning and functions? Moreover, using conceptual primitives may go some way towards constructing a semantic analysis, but leaves off exactly where language takes over, i.e., when language is put to use. I show that emotion terms have multifunctionality in discourse, which remains unaccounted for in Wierzbicka's theory. Emotions in this perspective can be seen as discursive constructs reflecting institutionalized evolutionary processes. In effect, this paper presents evidence for the need to merge the cognitive with the functional aspects of language.*

Keywords: discourse, emotion predicates, fear, psych-verbs, Greek fear verbs, metonymy, (non-)causative constructions, pragmaticization, resemanticization.

---

* I wish to thank the editors, and especially Kat Dziwirek, for perceptive comments and criticism that greatly improved, hopefully, the paper. Also, Io Manolessou for help with sources, Alexandros Tantos for e-discussing worrying issues and help in aspects of his expertise, Anna Anastasiadi-Symeonidi for expert advice and Maria Theodoropoulou for helpful comments on the paper. All mistakes and shortcomings are mine.

1. Introduction

In enumerating the reasons for the neglect of particles in modern linguistics, Wierzbicka (1986: 520) blames it partly on the a-semantic, a-pragmatic orientation of much of modern linguistics which was "purposefully divorced from real-life communication involving full-blooded human beings (rather than automata), in an atmosphere when supreme value was placed on keeping apart 'language structure' and 'language use' "; and adds, resonating Mey (1986), that language is after all SOMEBODY'S language and that its structure, not only reflects, but is also shaped by its users and their needs.

In this paper, I would like to follow up on this remark by Wierzbicka and examine *fear* constructions, not so much as expressing emotion, but rather as discursive constructions used in everyday speech to perform various speech acts. The findings will have implications for Wierzbicka's (1999) claims regarding her programme of setting up definitional criteria of presumed universal applicability for emotion predicates across languages.

In this study, we will examine the interrelation between feelings, thoughts, and their utilization in the pragmatic domain of interpersonal meaning by examining *fear* predicates in English and Greek (*fear*, *afraid* for English, and *fovume* for Greek). After a classification of emotion verbs, we will trace briefly the evolutionary route of the *fear* predicates in Greek and English, noting their parallel morphosyntactic and semantic courses, and see how they came to be used as distinct constructions in mundane situations, not so much to express emotion, but rather to express thoughts and, ultimately, couch speech acts that might otherwise 'injure' (Butler 1995) the face of the addressee, or even to sanction or ratify specific speech acts that otherwise would not be clarified, perceived and taken up as such. In fact, they can be seen as assuming performativity. It will then become clear that Wierzbicka's analysis of the emotion of fear can be seen as only basically definitional, leaving a great deal to be desired in terms of the actual predicate's use in various structures functioning as discursive constructs in social situations.

2. Classification of emotion verbs

In recent years, scholars have been much intrigued by verbs of emotion or psychological states. This focus in linguistics ties in with burgeoning research in the field of emotions, cognition and, generally, consciousness, in the field of philosophy and cognitive science. Most of the literature on emotions analyzed linguistically is encountered in the field of lexical semantics bordering on syntax, as it is widely acknowledged that lexical structure affects syntactic configuration. (cf. Tenny and Pustejovsky 1999, among others). Within this field, verbs denoting emotion are usually called psychological (psych) verbs. The class of such verbs denoting emotions like fear, anger, hate, love, etc. is commensurate with the class of psych-verbs (fig. 1, A). In a broader interpretation, the category of psych-verbs also includes sub-classes of perception verbs (*hear*, *see*, *feel*, etc.), cognitive verbs (*think*, *believe*, etc.), and also evaluation verbs (*estimate*, *appreciate*, etc.) (Fig. 1, B) (Klein and Kutscher 2005):

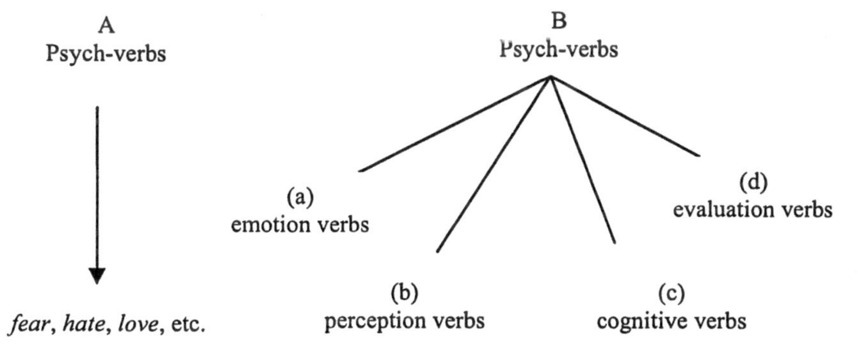

Fig. 1. The class of psych-verbs

Fear predicates are clearly emotion predicates since fear is one of the basic emotions. However, it has also been claimed (Kakouriotis and Kitis 1999; Kitis 2009; Tissari 2007) that emotion predicates such as *fear*, *be afraid*, in English and in Greek, have developed meanings beyond those of emotion. They have evolved into cognitive verbs of thought that are further utilized to express interpersonal meanings. These *fear* predicates have, moreover, spanned across domains, evolving from the semantic domain to the pragmatic domain of functions. *Fear* predicates provide evidence that there is a consistent and unidirectional evolution from emotion verbs (a) to cognitive verbs (c), and, further, to evaluation verbs (d) (fig. 1). This is not the whole story as these cognitive emotion meanings, originating from action meanings, are capitalized upon in the social domain to enact specific speech acts. In fact, it can be claimed that emotion verbs are a source of thought verbs and, further, of performative verbs. This route is unidirectional rather than bidirectional as Vender (1972) has argued (cf. Kakouriotis and Kitis 1999; Kitis 2009). In the next section, I will present Wierzbicka's analysis of the two main *fear* concepts.

3. Wierzbicka's emotion concepts of *fear*

A major focus of Wierzbicka's work in semantics has been the organization of knowledge domains in the human mind and their lexicalization in specific languages. More specifically, she set up a kind of presumably universal semantic alphabet consisting of indefinable primitives, the atoms of human thought, called Natural Semantic Metalanguage (NSM), various configurations of which can yield the semantic meaning of sets of words (corresponding to concepts) in specific languages (1996). Wierzbicka has implemented this method of semantic analysis in emotion words as well, claiming that NSM is a stabilizing factor in this respect across cultures and languages (1990, 1994, and 1999).

According to Wierzbicka (1990, 1999) the cognitive scenarios corresponding to the emotion concept of *fear* and *afraid* are as follows:

Fear (X felt fear)

(a) X felt something because X thought something.
(b) sometimes a person thinks:
(c) "I don't know what will happen
(d) some bad things can happen
(e) I don't want these things to happen
(f) I want to do something because of this if I can
(g) I don't know if I can do anything"
(h) when this person thinks this this person feels something bad
(i) X felt like this
(j) because X thought something like this

Afraid (X was afraid)

(a) X felt something because X thought something
(b) sometimes a person thinks about something:
(c) "something bad can happen to me because of this
(d) I don't want this to happen
(e) I don't know if I can do anything now"
(f) when this person thinks this this person feels something bad
(g) X felt like this
(h) Because X thought something like this

(Wierzbicka 1999: 75)

In the next section we will briefly trace back the evolutionary courses of these *fear* predicates in both English and Greek, using the Perseus corpus of Ancient Greek (AG) texts for Greek. The translational equivalent of both *fear* and *afraid* in Greek is *fovume.* I will then present the implications of my findings for Wierzbicka's cognitive scenarios of these two predicates.

4. The evolution of *fear* predicates

4.1. The evolution of 'fovume' in Greek[1]

As has been argued in Kitis (2009), the psychological Modern Greek (MG) verb *fovume* has its roots in the AG transitive causative verb of action *phobeô* meaning 'to put to flight', 'to strike with fear', 'to terrify, frighten, alarm', linked to its cognate object, the noun *phobos.*[2] While AG verbs ending in *-eô* are mainly intransitive, *phobeô* belongs to a small group of verbs with this suffix that are causative (Monro 2000: 56). This AG verb denoted movement away from a source, either by force or due to fear as in (1) and (2):

1. *ou men gar nun prôta podôkeos ant' Achilêos stêsomai, all' êdê me kai allote douri phobêsen ex Idês...* (Homer, *Iliad* book 20, 1.58)
   'Not now for the first time shall I stand forth against swift-footed Achilles; nay, once ere now he drave me with his spear from Ida.'

[1] I regard as translational counterparts those terms which occur more frequently as their translational equivalents and appear first in dictionaries: *fear* = fovos, tromos, etc.; *afraid* = fovismenos, etc., *be afraid* = fovame (Penguin-Hellenews English-Greek Dictionary, 1975); *fovos* = fear, fright, dread, anxiety; *fovume* = be afraid, be fearful, be/stand in fear of, etc. (Stavropoulos, 1988, Oxford Greek-English Learner's Dictionary, OUP). There are two morphological versions of the predicate: *fovame* and *fovume*, the latter being closer to its Ancient Greek equivalent form.

[2] *phobeô*; aor. *(e)phobêsa*; mid. pres. part. *phobeumenos*; fut. *phobêsomai*; pass. aor. 3 pl. *(e)phobêthen*; perf. part. *pephobêmenos*; plup. 3 pl. *pephobêato*: Act. 'put to flight', tina (=one)-3 sl.; mid. and pass., 'flee, be put to flight', *hupo tinos* or *hupo tini* (=by one); *tina*. Various forms such as *phobêsô, ephobêsa* go back to a period when the present was either *phobêmi* or *phobêô* (Monro 2000: 114). The noun *phobos* is assumed to derive from the verb *phebomai*. Transliteration key for AG (different from that for MG, the first sign is in AG, the second in transliteration, if a third, it is for pronunciation): β/b=v. φ/ph=f, ω/ô =o (long), η/ê=i (long), υ=u, θ/the=the (as in 'thing'), γ=g, δ/d=the (as in 'they'), ξ/x=ks, ψ=ps, χ=ch, as in Perseus. Breathings are not reflected. Underlining in examples reflects exact lexical correspondences. All AG examples derive from the Perseus corpus. Translations derive also from Perseus, but in some cases have been adapted to reflect more precisely the original structure and wording.

2. *ê mala dê kakotechnos amêchane sos dolos Hêrê Hektora dion epause machês, ephobêse de laous.* (Homer, *Iliad* book 15, 1.34)
'that art hard to deal with, it is the craft of thine evil wiles that hath stayed goodly Hector from the fight, and hath driven the people in rout.'

Also in Homer, we encounter the passive, rather poetic, form of the verb *phebomai*, meaning 'to be put to flight', 'to flee in terror', but only in the present tense and imperfective aspect.

3. *hôs Danaoi Trôas menon empedon oude phebonto.* (*Iliad* 3.31, book 5)
'even so the Danaans withstood the Trojans steadfastly, and fled not (were not driven away).'

As noted in Kitis (2009), the verb in Homer always denoted the action of fleeing away (not the emotion of fear). However, it is reasonable to assume that the thematic object denoting the affected (the object of the causative transitive verb, or the subject of the passivized form) also came to be the experiencer object in the sense that the affected (patient) also experienced the emotion of fear -world knowledge tells us that compulsory fleeing away is connected to fear (LeDoux 1996).

In later AG texts, however, the verb develops a middle form, *phoboumai,* in which the internal thematic object of the causative verb *phobeô*, meaning 'putting to flight', takes up the position of the subject of this middle verb (external theme as experiencer subject in the nominative). In fact, the former internal thematic object of the causative verb now becomes the external theme or nominative subject of the middle form verb. Apparently, this is due to a shift of focus from the causer or the agent of the action to the affected or experiencer object, which becomes the theme of the discourse. An experiencer subject in-the-nominative theme can be the topic of the discourse or the theme of the sentence as it is external to the structure, while an internal thematic object cannot. This specific shift may have been motivated by a more general shift in the discourse of the time from total concentration on descriptive accounts to accounts that also focus on more abstract domains of motives, fears, emotions and views of the characters. The following example from Thucidides is in the present perfect form of the middle verb *phoboumai* (as evolved from the causative transitive *phobeô*), and selects an object in the accusative as signifying the cause of the anxiety. The experiencer is the ellipted 'I' morphologically marked in the suffix of the verb.

4. *mallon gar pephobêmai tas oikeias hêmôn hamartias ê tas tôn enantiôn dianoias*. (*Thuc*. 2.37)
'I rather (have) fear(ed) more our mistakes than the enemies' thoughts' (what they're up to).

Not only did *phobeô* mean 'to put to flight' in the early AG texts (Homer), i.e., it selected an internal theme in object position as the afflicted party (patient), but also the noun *Phobos* 'fear' was originally the name of a mythical demigod, the son of the god of war, Ares, who drove people away. So the mutation from transitivity to middle form, applies to the noun *phobos* (*fovos* in MG), a cognate object noun (*phoboumai phobous aischrous* 'I fear nasty fears', Plato, *Protagoras* 360b), which in MG signifies the emotion of fear felt by the experiencer. In (5) we see an example from Homer's *Iliad*, where *Phobos* is a proper name denoting the dear son of Ares, who was valiant and 'turned to flight' (*ephobêse*) warriors.

5. *hoios de brotoloigos Arês polemon de meteisi, tôi de Phobos philos huios hama krateros kai atarbês hespeto, hos t' ephobêse talaphrona per polemistên*: (*Il*. Book 13, 1.40)
'And even as Ares, the bane of mortals, goeth forth to war, and with him followeth Rout [Fear], his son, valiant alike and fearless *[=atarbês]*, that turneth to flight a warrior'.

In fact (5) exhibits a metaphor whereby a specific individual carries out an action that ultimately is understood as causing the emotion of fear. It is a matter for further study to what extent emotion is represented in concrete terms (metonymized and metaphorized in action predicates and concrete entities for qualities) in very early Ancient Greek texts, in a culture where virtue and vice, as well as all emotions are conceptualized in the form of goddesses or demigoddesses, nymphs or muses.

Once the causative construction gave rise to a non-causative one in middle form, we witness the development of various syntactic structures the verb *phoboumai* enters into. It can select an object accusative as the source of anxiety (4), often followed by an *hoti*-causal clause (cf. Kitis 2009), or an infinitival complementizer (6), or a *mê*- 'lest'-complement clause (*phoboumai mê ou genêtai* 'I fear that it may not happen'),[3] all versions of these structures having equivalents in MG, used as distinct discourse constructions with distinct, even if related, functions.

[3] This is a complementizer that can be selected by verbs of fearing or by apprehension epistemic (Goodwin 1989; Lichtenberk 1995).

6. *egô men gar phoboumai sophistas phanai.* (Plato, *Sophist* 3.52)
'For I fear/hesitate to declare/say the sophists'

4.2. The evolution of 'fear' and 'be afraid' in English

Just like the AG *phobeô*, *fear* was originally a causative verb meaning 'to drive away by fear', 'to scare away'. Apparently, the emotion of fear was a resulting state of an action verb, as the following example testifies:

7. *Here Bugles boldely for to blowe, To fere the beestis.* (c1400 *Sowdone Bab.* 59)[4]

In Shakespeare, *fear* retains its causative meaning – listed first in Crystal and Crystal (2002) – together with its current meaning:

8. *Warwick was a bug that feared us all.* (*Antony&Cleop.* II.vi.24) (Crystal and Crystal, 2002)

In this agentive form, *fear* also acquired the meaning of deterring one from a course of action:

9. *He doth...fear us from putting any confidence in our own works.* (1531 FRITH *Judgm. Tracy* 251)

Like the AG *phebomai*, it is also encountered in the passive form:

10. *A Swallow flew about his head and could not be feared from him.* (1614 RALEIGH *Hist. World* II. IV. ii. §7. 152)

Just like its AG counterpart, *fear* soon turned from a causative verb (with its external theme in maximal agentive position, as in (7) and (8), Dowty 1991) to a reflexive one with the meaning of 'to be afraid' (11), or 'doubt' (12) from Shakespeare, a form that is obsolete nowadays.

11. *I fear me he is slain.* (1590 MARLOWE *Edw.* II, II. Iv)
12. *Fear you not her courage.* (*Hamlet* III.iv.7) (Crystal and Crystal 2002)

[4] All following examples in this section are from OED, unless otherwise specified.

The reflexive form is soon dropped and *fear* develops various meaning nuances in various constructions. Over time, its external thematic subject-nominative position comes to be occupied by the experiencer rather than the agent. As for its internal theme in object position, it can be seen as the stimulus or target of the emotion. So agentive causative frames with the experiencer in object position as in (13) appear almost at the same time as expletive constructions (14), and as frames with the exprериencer in external thematic subject position (*They*, 15):

13. *He feareth me above all the men lyvynge.* (1530 *PALSGR.* 547/2)
14. *It fereth me sore for to endyte.* (1503 HAWES *Examp. Virt. Prol.* 2)
15. *They feared not the enemy, but the narrownes of the wais.* (1563 GOLDING *Cæsar* 30b)

Later, selecting a *to*-infinite, the verb acquires the meaning of hesitating to do something, fearing the consequences. In this sense it approximates a cognitive state verb expressing an intentional mental state, rather than just an emotion, as (16) shows even though emotion can be caused by entertaining intentional mental states (thoughts) (cf. Theodoropoulou 2004):

16. *As if he feared to attediate..us.* (1603 FLORIO *Montaigne* 563)

This use is a current one, too. While a *to*-infinitive necessarily sets the time of the complement-event posterior to that of the main, *fear* also selects a *that*-clause, which does not restrict time setting of the clausal predicate (17).

17. *I feare sore that many chrysten people..do as the chyldren of Israel dyd.* (1526 *Pilgr. Perf.* (W. de W. 1531) 16b)

Since fear is considered a negative emotion (Langacker 1987: 151) it is expected that further evolutionary meanings are also judged on a negative scale. Once the psych-verb selects a *that*-complement clause, it expresses negatively assessed views and functions as an epistemic verb rather than a psych one expressing emotion (cf. Kakouriotis and Kitis 1999; Theodoropoulou 2003; Tissari 2007). In this construction, just as in the *to*-infinitival one, we witness emotions (unintentional mental states) rubbing shoulders with thoughts (intentional mental states, Searle 1983, 2002, 2004). While, however, the *to*-infinitival structure scores more highly on the emotion scale, the *that*-construction scores more highly on the epistemic scale, with emotion often being negligible or non-descript. Theodoropoulou (2003: 302) stresses that the

MG *fovume (h)oti* 'that' construction prioritizes the cognitive orientation of the utterance.

Turning now to the other *fear* predicate, *afraid*, it is a past participial form and as such it denotes a situation rather than an action. It initially meant 'disturbed, alarmed, frightened from a prior state of peace':

18. *Alle frayed he went fro that cite.* (1330 R. BRUNNE *Chron.* 323)

In Shakespeare, the verb appears as *affray*, meaning 'startle', 'frighten away', or as *affright*, meaning 'frighten', 'scare', and in adjectival form as *affrighted*, meaning 'alarmed', 'frightened' (Crystal and Crystal 2002):

19. *arm from arm that voice doth us affray* (*Romeo&Jul.* III.v.33).
20. *Let not our babbling dreams affright our souls* (*Rich. III* V.iii.309).
21. *th'affrighted globe / Should yawn at alteration* (*Othello* V.ii.101).

(Crystal and Crystal 2002)

It soon came to select a *to*-infinitival complement to express apprehension of the consequences (22), and later a *that*-complementizer, which can be also omitted (23):

22. *Moses couered his face, for he was afrayed to loke vpon God.* (1535 COVERDALE *Ex.* iii. 6)
23. *I am much afraid my Ladie his mother plaid false.* (1596 SHAKES. *Merch.* V. I. ii. 47)

Both *fear* and *afraid* came to be used as propositional attitude verbs, encoding the speaker's attitude towards the proposition rather than any emotion, (23), (24); from that stage on, they soon developed parenthetical functions, thus promoting their complement clauses to the status of the main (25), (26), (27).

24. *I fear they are troubled with King's evil.* (1658-9 *Burton's Diary* (1828) IV. 47)
25. *The account..will hardly, I fear, render my letters very interesting.* (1863 F. A. KEMBLE *Resid. in Georgia* 16)
26. *Disagreeable enough (as most necessities are) but, I am afraid, unavoidable.* (1740 GRAY *Let. 16 July (1900)* I. 76)
27. *She did not like it, but I did many a thing she did not like, I'm afraid – and now she's gone!* (1853 MRS. GASKELL *Cranford* iii. 47)

We therefore witness initially a shift in the semantic meaning of the *fear* predicates from the concrete domain of action to the more abstract domain of emotion. This process is one of re-semanticization and will be discussed in the next section.

However, quite apart from the semantic meaning of emotion, these verbs, both in Greek and in English, further developed functions in the pragmatic domain of interpersonal meaning.[5] This process is one of pragmaticization (Traugott 1989, 2003; Traugott and Dasher, 1987, 2002). These pragmatic readings are determined by their specific constructions, as we have seen (cf. Kitis 2009). As propositional attitude verbs or parentheticals, these verbs select a reading in the sense of 'I regret to say; I regretfully or apologetically admit, report, etc.; I suspect; I am inclined to think' (OED) (cf. Tissari), as in (28) dated 1959, and (29) from the MG corpus ILSP:

28. *It would be less kind, but true, I am afraid, to find in this book a quite invincible taste for the mediocre.* (1959 *Observer* 14 June 22/6)

29. *I apantisi, fovume, δen ine ikanopiitiki*
The reply, I'm afraid, not is satisfactory
'The reply, I'm afraid, is not satisfactory'

5. Action predicates acting as metonymies for the emotion

In this section, we will examine how the process of resemanticization of these predicates took place, namely how motion verbs were resemanticized as emotion verbs. I will claim that the main operation involved in this process is that of metonymization (Foucault 1966; Gibbs 1999).

Regarding *fear* predicates, we witness metonymic processes in meaning representation. We have seen how a cognate object of the AG verb is metaphorized as a war god's son. War begets fear or *Phobos* and, this feeling or perception is conveniently concretized in the received perception of its time that the war god, *Ares*, begets a son, *Phobos*.

We have seen that as far as Greek is concerned both the verb in its causative (and passive) forms, but also its cognate noun, have the actional causative

[5] In Homer the parenthetical use of *fear* verbs is served by other verbs such as *deidô*, surviving mainly in the perfective *δeδoika* in later AG texts but also (and mainly) by moods, e.g., subjunctive (see Monro 2000: 254–255). Indeed, in AG we observe a gradual lexicalization of grammatical features such as mood markings in expressing subjective meanings.

meaning of effecting an action (that of driving away, or being driven away, and, consequently, scaring) in an entity, which is the affected or experiencer in object position.

Clearly, fleeing away from a point is only a stage of a more holistic scenario to which this act can be seen as belonging. We can only surmise that the AG term *phobeô*, denoting the action – and only by implication the emotion of its evolved causative object experiencer verb – or its passivized form *phebomai*, signifying the affected's behaviour originally of fleeing, came to invoke a more comprehensive scenario concerning such actions. Individual experiences involving such actions can be evoked to invest words and their denotata with enriched meaning. On the basis of the data, it is reasonable to assume that the route of meaning was one from signification of the action alone to that of the action-cum-emotion at an interim stage, and, lastly, to that of the emotion alone. In time, it apparently became the norm, probably by conventionalization of implicatures (Grice 1989; Traugott 1989; Traugott and König 1991), to use the verb to evoke metonymically the whole scenario that stands for such situations, i.e. the entire model cognitively enriched by the speaker's personal experience of such situations and the condition of the experiencer. Indeed, fleeing away would be just one stage of the cognitive model (ICM) (Lakoff 1987) humans have internalized as a standard one occurring in cases of fear. Fleeing away from danger (often just a wish, since paralyzing effects are common in conditions of immense fear) does not appear as a stage in Wierzbicka's semantic analysis of *fear* (1990, 1999, see above). But she does note that *fear* "is more likely to mobilize one to action, in particular, to make one run away from a potentially dangerous situation (although it could also have a paralyzing effect), whereas being *afraid* is more likely to stop one from doing something" (1999: 74). (Also, cf. Kövecses 1990).

But what is at the root of this resemanticization process? I submit that the resemanticization of the predicates is motivated by the human unconscious urge to blend the objective with the subjective experience (cf. Nagel's notorious question: 'What is it like to be a bat?'). Subjective feelings relate to mental states like fear, pain, etc., while objective experience relates to perceptions of the world. We don't have a clue how a bat feels or senses the surrounding world, but we do when it comes to understanding and interpreting perceptions of outer external behaviours of similar creatures (other humans) because we can extrapolate from subjective experience. This is how we merge objective and subjective experience in understanding the surrounding world. This fact is a clear motivation for meaning enrichment then. The term signifying just the external behaviour (fleeing from a point) is first enriched to mean both the perceivable action but also to implicate the subjective experience of the entity afflicted (patient). Gradually, this added layer of meaning turns the (perceived) patient of the action to the (conceived) experiencer of the emotion, thus resemanticizing the term denoting the state.

6. From action to emotion, from the causative to the middle domain

The metonymic use of the *fear* verbs invoking the whole cognitive model of the experience (action for emotion, symptom for source) is coupled by the predicates' syntactic shift from a causative verb, initially to a passive form (as in Homer, cf. Kitis 2009, and example 10 for English), and later to a middle formation. Croft *et al.* (1987: 188) note that "the active, middle and passive domains are not autonomous: all three are related to each other, however distantly, through semantically intermediate uses." As the focus shifted from the agent of the action, or cause (stimulus) of the emotion, to the afflicted (patient) or the experiencer, or, in other words, as the focus of the discourse shifted from the more concrete domain of action to the more abstract esoteric cognitive domain of emotions, the experiencer entity shifted from the position of the internal thematic object to that of an external theme which possesses a higher syntactic position and can, consequently, be the topic of the discourse or a discourse theme, as we have seen. This thematic shift reflects a shift in type of force: from force exerted in the physical domain to force or cause or stimulus in the more abstract domain of cognitive or mental states. Indeed, causality in the relevant literature on these predicates is originally seen as a basic physical force that just extends to the cognitive domain (e.g. Croft 1991, 1993, 1998). The evolution of the predicates illustrates this process very clearly.

7. Parallel courses of verbs and selected prepositions

In MG, the action meaning of putting to flight is extinct for the verb *fovume*. The emotion verb *fovume* occurs only in the middle form designating emotion 'to feel fear', and we encounter the MG transitive form *fovizo*, meaning 'to frighten', (the MG denominal derivation with a MG verbal suffix) that selects an Experiencer in object position.[6] The passivized form of AG verb *phobeô*, *ephobêthen* (see note

[6] For discussion and a discourse-friendly analysis of these two Greek psych-verbs see Tantos 2006. He claims that considering Greek data will impose a unified analysis of psych-verbs.

2), is preserved as the past perfective *foviθika* of MG *fovume*, the only form that selects the *apo*-'from/by' Prepositional Phrase (PP), which ordinarily signifies the agent of an action in passive forms.[7] While *fear* predicates as experiencer-subject psych-verbs are states (Grimshaw 1990; Dowty 1991, amongst others), the past perfective *foviθika* of *fovume* is the only form of the predicate that is not characterized by stativity (quite understandably). It can be claimed that this past perfective form of *fovume*, with characteristics such as the inchoative and causative character (events) and lack of experiencer control (cf. Croft 1993), is a vestige of the original Homeric predicate testifying to its initial meaning in concrete domains and its derivational history as explained above.

As state predicates, *fear* verbs do not occur in the progressive (30) and do not license pseudo-cleft constructions perspectivizing the change of state within the event denoted by the verb (31) (see Klein and Kutscher 2002, 2005 for a review). The equivalent causative verb selecting an object experiencer occurs both in the progressive (in English, since there is no progressive in Greek) but also in pseudo-clefts:

30. **John is fearing floods.*
31. **What happened to John was that he feared the flood.*
32. *The lion is frightening John.*
33. *What happened to John was that the lion frightened him.*

Yet, while the imperfective forms of MG *fovume* follow the same pattern (34, 35), the (past) perfective form of the verb, *fovithika*, seems to be characterized by non-stative or actional features (36, 37):

34. *?Fovotan oli ti mera.*[8]
feared-3sImperf whole the day.
'S/he was afraid the whole day.'

35. **Auto pu tis sinevi itan oti fovotan.*
What that her happened was that feared-3sImperf.

36. *Fovithike jia ligo/pros stigmi/otan akuse ta nea.*
Was scared-3s/Perf for a while/for a moment/when heard-3s the news.
'S/he was frightened for a while/for a moment/when s/he heard the news.'

---

[7] Cf. also modal perfective forms *θa/na foviθo*, which behave like the perfective form discussed here, i.e. can select an *apo*-PP. Other non-perfective forms with *apo*-PP are rare though not impossible. (Thanks to M. Makri-Tsilipakou for data).

[8] Without a complement-clause or other qualifications. The only acceptable reading would be to interpret the verb as 'trembling'. Even if not so frequent, these constructions may occur: *Ke i Anna apopse fovotan*. 'Anna, too, was scared/afraid today'.

37. *Auto pu tis sinevi itan oti fovithike apo to sismo.*
What that her happened-3s was that feared-3s/Perf by the earthquake.
'What happened to her was that she feared/got frightened by the earthquake.'

As has been mentioned, this passive past perfective form, *fovithika* (-1person.sing.), is (with some minor exceptions) the only form of the verb that can select an *apo*-PP that ordinarily denotes the agent in passive voice. Preposition *apo* followed a similar evolutionary route to the *fear* verbs examined here, that is, it initially signified in the concrete domain (movement away from a certain point), and later developed meanings in the abstract domain (causality) as well. Similarly, we can claim that just as *fovithika* selects an *apo*-PP, English *fear* verbs select the preposition that seems to follow a route akin to the Greek preposition (e.g., 1400: *fear of*; *afraid of*).[9] It is instructive to recall that the main preposition of agency in Old English (OE) was *from*, whose function was taken over by the preposition *of* (11th c). Fraser (1987: 246–47) writes that "*from*..., with its insistence on the initial point of the action, tends to be reserved for verbs which themselves express movement. And he adds that while, "*from* focuses on the starting point from which the verbal operation initiates, *of* underlines rather the conduction of the operation itself." (245).

What emerges from all this is that the semantics of both *apo* and *of* converge with the semantics of original *phoboumai* (Homeric *phebomai*). Both signified motion from a certain point in space. While the semantics of the verb shifted from the source domain of motion to that of emotion, the prepositions developed secondary meanings, such as those of source of cause to cause to agency. Combined with *fear* verbs, they demonstrate a shift in meanings from force in the physical domain to force in the mental domain.

8. *Fear* verb-discursive constructions

In this section, I discuss those *fear*-constructions that are used, not so much to express emotion, but rather to perform specific speech acts. As has become clear by now, *fear* verbs initially signified actions in the physical domain, these

[9] The diagrammatic evolution of meanings of the prepositions and their relation:
Greek: *apo*=Sanskrit: *apa*>Lat: *ab*>OE: *af, oef, of*, etc. Original sense 'from'.
Domain of signification: *Place>motion>superficial motion> (similarity of the) cause or ground>of position (away from)>of the mind>...>of the cause* (L&S).
English: *of*=Old Fris.: *af, of, ofe*<Old Sax.: *aft*<MLGerm. *af*<....<OTeut.: *αδα* (unaccented by-form *ab*< Sanskrit: *ápa*. The primary sense of *of* was 'away (from)' (OED).

meanings gradually giving way to representations of sensation and emotion, while much later they developed concurrent functions in the domain of evaluation. So we witness a metaphoric (more specifically, metonymic) shift from the physical domain of action and sensation to the more mental domain of emotion and further to the intentional domain of evaluation. This evolution is accompanied by a concurrent evolution of *fear* verbs from signifying unintentional states of sensation and (uncontrolled) emotion to denoting intentional states of thought and evaluation.

Vender (1972), who includes *fear* together with *hope*, as emotively tinged and groups it together with *anticipate* as a 'putative' across the expositive *predict,* points up the "temporal connotations" of its class. The time setting of the complement clause introduced by *fear* verbs can either predate or postdate the time of the *fear* predicate. One must add that this temporal versatility and these temporal connotations are what have enabled both *fovume* and *fear* to act as predictive speech acts. It must be noted that, while in Greek *fovume* does service for both *fear* and *be afraid*, in English *fear* is used mainly for predictive speech acts, whereas *be afraid* can perform both predictive but also non-predictive speech acts:

38. *I fear that the council may not use the powers it has or is worried about the cost of an appeal..*
39. *I fear that I won't make a good father.*
40. *I am afraid that I won't be able to come.*
41. *I'm afraid that your application has been rejected.*
42.

Fovame	*oti*	*δen*	*piezun*	*tin*	*Ankira.* (ILSP)
I'm afraid	that	not	pressurize-3p	the	Ancara.

'I'm afraid that they do not pressurize Ancara'.

43.

Fovame,	*Kirie Ipurge,*	*oti*	*ehume*	*mia*	*ideologiki*
I'm afraid,	Mister Minister,	that	have-1p	an	ideological
epemvasi...	*ke*	*fovame*	*mipos*	*ine*	*proδromos*
intervention...	and	I'm afraid	that	is-3s	precursor
mias megalis	*strofis....* (ILSP)				
a-gen. great	U-turn				

'I'm afraid, Minister, that we witness an ideological intervention and I'm afraid that it might be a precursor of a significant U-turn'.

Pesetsky (1995: 56) noted that "[i]n general, a negative emotion ... entails a negative evaluation..." Indeed, we witness a parallel evolution of fear constructions ranging from signifying negative emotion, and consequently negative evaluation, to performing speech acts that have a specific impact on the world.

We witness a progression from nominal object constructions reflecting emotion to clausal complement constructions reflecting the psych verb's enriched meaning from emotion to thought (*to*-infinitival clauses) to evaluation and ultimately to performativity (*that*-clauses), as below:

Psych-verb+nominal object complement> psych-verb+to-clause complement> psych-verb+(that-)clause complement

I fear/'m afraid of earthquakes> I fear/'m afraid to do something>
I fear/'m afraid (that) I can't, etc.

As we move from left to right above, we witness a progression from emotion to negative views and negative valuation and lastly to performative function, this course reflecting initially resemanticization and gradually pragmaticization processes as the structures evidence a shift to more subjective discourse-based meanings. Following Traugott and Dasher (2002), we can claim that *fear* verbs develop performative uses and as such they have procedural functioning; they index the speaker-addressee interaction, and their function is to mitigate the threatening force of the propositional content (39, 40, 42), but also to secure the intended uptake of the couched speech act (41). Indeed, utterances like (41) may have a world-to-word direction of fit (Searle 1979) on account of the function of the *fear* verb. Rather than just mitigating the force of the threatening speech act, the *fear* verb may have a double-edged function serving also to ratify and consolidate the speech act as one issued by someone in authority or control over a course of action. What could otherwise be read as a statement now can be read as a rejection, etc. on the basis of the indexical function of the *fear* verb. This pragmaticization of the verb (acquiring specific performative force) is attested in the unacceptability of imposing duplicate illocutionary forces as in *?Honestly, I'm afraid I can't accept your application*, while illocutionary parentheticals are possible when the verb signifies emotion: (*Honestly, I'm afraid of dogs*).

Since *fear* verbs can function in a negative way (expressing negative feelings, desires, etc.) it is expected that the performative function they carry out will often be in conjunction with a negative particle (*I'm afraid not/so*, *I fear not*, etc.), and in conjunction with a preceding speech act. After all, *I promise* (the paradigm of performative verbs) does not perform any promising on its own, severed from a preceding part, unless it introduces a complement clause. As mitigating devices, *fear* verbs can often be the bastion of charitability preventing injurious speech (Butler 1995), and their omission might reach the point of social callousness.

Fear verbs in conversational institutional discourse have a formulaic role to play signalling a speech act that is deemed to be either adversarial in the circumstances or introducing a proposition that may have a negative impact on the interlocutor, as above.

Furthermore, as *fear* verbs take the pragmatic course, their syntactic position becomes more flexible: the complement clause is promoted to the status of the main message, while the *fear* verb is relegated to the much more subjective-indexing position of a parenthetical verb:

44. *This clears the way for a possible return to the top job 12 months later, opponents fear.* (*City*, 16.10.07)

9. Implications

Wierzbicka's programme of employing NSM to account for emotion concepts is of a definitional and explanatory nature. Her scripts of emotions, based on their lexical manifestation, namely on the main lexeme representing the emotion, try to analytically explain the meaning of the words used for those emotions. NSM includes primitives like 'feel' and 'think', used in abundance in the explication of those universal emotions.[10] As noted in Riemer (2006: 352), explaining the meanings of words is giving "an unexpected emphasis for a modern theory of lexical semantics", since it is not at all clear that understanding meaning should be equated with explanatory definitions or reductive paraphrases, important, though, these enterprises might be.

Moreover, Wierzbicka's approach is based on the assumed universal indisputable primacy of primitives, such as 'feel' and 'think', used in specifying the meanings of the emotion lexemes she sets out to explain and define. However, as we have seen, this predilection for a cognitively gravitating perspective prioritizing feelings and thoughts rather than instinctual responses may be unwarranted, especially in view of the account of the etymological and evolutionary profiles of the *fear* predicates examined here. Their original meanings, etymology and morphosyntactic development raise doubts as to the

[10] Wierzbicka talks of emotion concepts rather than meanings, but as these concepts correspond to specific predicates, we are entitled to assume that she equates concepts to meanings in this respect. Again, the use of the term 'concept' can be controversial given its long history in philosophy, but in the tradition in which Wierzbicka works, we assume it to refer to a mental representation. But it's not clear why she assumes universal concepts such as *think*, *want* and *feel* to be atomic, while those composed on their basis (e.g., *fear*, etc.) are probably supposed to be structured.

undisputed priority of the emotions *per se* designated by these terms. The evidence presented here does not necessarily support prioritizing feelings (in the sense of cognitive awareness rather than sensations) over and above demonstrable behaviour ultimately indicating those states. Consequently, it can be claimed that it is not necessarily true that the emotional behaviour takes priority over its purported byproducts (sensations or other external indications or behaviours).

Indeed, fear can be conditioned. It has been shown that humans can demonstrate emotional learning without their conscious cognizing as that spelt out in Wierzbicka's scripts (section 3). It has been claimed that feelings are primarily shadows of the outer behaviour of emotions (Damasio 2003); tracing the original senses of the *fear* verbs leads to denotata of concrete external behaviour rather than of esoteric mental or psychological states. Even if views like those of Damasio's may be taken with a pinch of salt, Wierzbicka's account, suffers from a cognitive bias of propositionalizing emotions, as she bases her semantic analysis on propositions weighted down to cognitive thinking and feeling (see the clauses of the scenario pivoting around the predicates 'think', '(don't) know', etc.). A similar critique is levelled against Wierzbicka's account by Theodoropoulou (2003: 189), who claims that the more experiential somatic domain of emotions is "buried" and subjected to the cognitive domain of thoughts.

While in the case of emotion, bodily responses can be integral to its processes, as regards *fear* predicates, we have shown that they initially denoted just these bodily responses ('to (be) put to flight', 'to drive away', etc.), and only later by extrapolation of subjective experience did they come to denote the actual subjective emotion. Therefore, based on linguistic evidence alone, we are not warranted to conclude that cognitive aspects of subjective feelings or emotions can have primacy over instinctive bodily responses to external stimuli (defence responses). To assume a reversal of this process by prioritizing cognitive aspects of fear approximating an almost psychopathologically-oriented interpretation of fear cannot be supported by the evolutionary semantics of *fear* predicates or the current wide range of the verb's semantics. Emotions can 'intrude' into our consciousness, but this 'intrusion' does not warrant our assumption that they evolved as conscious feelings (LeDoux 1996: 40), as Wierzbicka's scripts seem to suggest.

In any case, Wierzbicka's definitional account of *fear* words in English captures an unwarranted 'middle-of-the-road' interpretation that does not necessarily reflect core senses. Her definitional analysis of *fear* verbs does not capture senses reflecting instinctual defence-responses, or the verb's evolved pragmatic interpretations in social transaction. If we assume that in fear there is a chain from reaction to action, Wierzbicka stops the pendulum at the extreme of cognitive action, forsaking reaction senses of the verbs. But even so, she misses the further development of meaning and function of the verbs in the social domain. In effect, she misses the pragmatic uses of the verbs in the domain of performativity. It may be fruitfully suggested that the meaning range of the *fear* predicates can be more efficiently described, or even exhausted, in the context of the precise constructions in which they occur, as these were presented in the previous section (also see Kitis 2009). For, indeed, there is a great deal of conventionalized meaning differential between *fear/afraid* construction-types. *Fear/afraid+(that-)* complement constructions are much more cognitively-based (often meaning just 'think', or 'take the view') than *fear+nominal* ones, as the following examples illustrate. The latter, as well as the expressions in (50), may invoke a more somatic or behaviour reflecting concept reminiscent of the verb's semantic evolution:

45. *... but I'm afraid I am going to have to ask you to leave.*
46. *I fear that the battle is going to obscure the substance, ...*
47. *Do you fear, Hussein, there will be a similar worldwide effort to profile suspicious Middle Eastern-looking ...*
48. *Fear prophets ... and those prepared to die for the truth, ...*
49. *He feared the Panamanian people.*
50. *Fear of panic, fear for their lives, fear of snakes, shout of fear, fear pulled at his ribs, fear entered me like heroin had, a chill of fear*, etc.

(BUY)

Moreover, in Greek there is no differentiation between two distinct fear concepts corresponding to the two emotion lexes (*fear*, *afraid*), distinguished by Wierzbicka, as *fovume* does service for both. Are we then talking about distinct concepts corresponding to two lexes in English? This view would lead us to the claim that experiences of fear are distinct for Greeks who apparently do not lexicalize types of fear emotion corresponding to the *fear/afraid* distinction. Wierzbicka (1999: 73) explicitly professes to "analyze the concepts *fear*, [etc.] (as well as *afraid*, [etc.]), as they really function in English, recognizing them for what they are: folk categories rooted in the English language rather than some language-independent absolutes." If this is so, then questions may be raised as to the validity of claims that these words reflect English cognitive scenarios.

Moreover, what are the grounds for including some "experience-near" concepts such as *feel* and *want* within a universal language-independent inventory, while other "experience-near" concepts such as *fear* are considered language-specific, even though it is assumed that they occur in all languages? (see Wierzbicka 1999: 11, 286). Why are we entitled to distinguish between different types of fear, but not different types of feel or want/desire? After all, in cognitive science *fear* is used in a more or less generic sense to include within its genus a variety of fear-types (cf. the term 'the fear system of the brain'). Besides, it must be stressed that Wierzbicka's account disregards grammatical form as she does not distinguish between nouns and verbs in discussing emotion concepts corresponding to the words *fear* and *afraid*. But how can we differentiate between the two concepts encoded in the two lexemes (*fear/afraid*) disregarding the fact that *fear* is both a noun and a verb (while *afraid* does not nominalize), and as a noun it does service for all types of fear, ripping off the emotion from the experiencing subject and reifying it in its nominalized form? Might this nominalization not motivate Wierzbicka's claim that *afraid* is "inherently personal… whereas *fear* is not" (Wierzbicka 1999: 73).[11]

Adopting Wierzbicka's perspective admittedly resonates with a grander scheme of potent cultural implications than a meaning specification programme would involve, but the question is whether this option is warranted in view of the findings and discussion in this study. It appears that, indeed, Wierzbicka's account in this respect has to be reconsidered in light of the insights afforded by the diachronic account presented here.

Similar criticisms might carry over to Searle's (1983) account of *fear* as denoting intentional states (see Smith 2003 for discussion). The notation for *fear* verbs is as follows:

Fear (p) $\rightarrow$ *Bel (◊p) and Des (~p)*
(If one fears that p, then one believes that p is possible, and one desires not p).

Unsurprisingly, Searle is concerned with the *fear* verb as denoting thought and evaluation. But then the question that emerges is exactly the same as the one dogging Wierzbicka's account: at what stage of the verb's evolutionary process shall the theoretician pick on, and what criteria should be employed in order to sever a particular 'slice' of the whole range of the polysemy of the 'psych-'verb?

10. Conclusion

In this study, I have examined the diachronic trajectories of the main fear predicates in Greek and English. Our findings are astonishingly similar in both cases. *Fear* verbs in both languages appear to derive from similar concrete sources and further develop into more esoteric abstract domains of emotion

[11] Cf.: "…fascination with grizzlies has turned into fear. I was afraid to let my kids out of my sight." (BUY)

through processes of metonymy. They have been further shown to develop pragmatic functions in the interpersonal domain acting as performatives and parentheticals. We have, therefore, witnessed processes of resemanticization and pragmaticization in their evolutionary histories.

In discussing the semasiological development of verbs into performative verbs, Traugott and Dasher (2002: 195) claim that "verbs with speech act meanings are typically derived from verbs with non-speech act meanings. Once this meaning shift has occurred, a SAV [speech act verb] that reports some event or state of affairs, often an event of speaking or cognizing, can be used to perform that same act or a related one, given the appropriate conditions for performativity, including use in the appropriate linguistic construction." While Traugott and Dasher (2002) discuss this evolution with respect to verbs of thinking, I have provided evidence that, not only verbs of thought (fig. 1, c) can develop further functions as speech act verbs (SAV) and as performative ones, but also verbs of emotion (fig. 1, a) can be recruited in this service. I have demonstrated that emotion verbs (fig. 1, a) can first develop as cognitive verbs of thought and speech (fig. 1, c) and these latter can, in their turn, further develop functions as performatives totally devoid of any emotion meanings. My findings, therefore, corroborate and further extend Traugott and Dasher's (2002) thesis.

Predicates such as *feel,* but also *fear*, *afraid*, are not to be taken at face value as denoting emotions or feelings. As Kakouriotis and Kitis (1999) and Kitis (2009) have shown, *fear* predicates have been desemanticised and resemanticised throughout their evolutionary history both in English and Greek and have further developed concurrent meanings in the pragmatic domain that are used to enact functions in the interpersonal sphere of communication. If this is so, then to actually take just one current use (the one signifying emotion) as testimony to the predicate's referential or conceptual range is problematic. It is also significant that *fear* predicates, as shown here, started their lives as third-person descriptions of action before they shifted to first-person emotion predicates.[12] They are still used as third-person descriptions of emotions, and it is reasonable to claim that in this use *fear* predicates do not prime subjective meanings of fear but rather behavioural ones.

This study may also inform the debate on psych-verbs with respect to their structure, i.e. as to whether causative non-stative psych-verbs are linked to their respective non-causative stative ones syntactically or semantically. While the corresponding causative psych-verbs of fear are not examined here, it has been

[12] We can witness 'fear' in its causative agentive form as late as 1923 in spoken data: "Yet he will fear the Argentine to pieces in the early rounds." (BUY)

shown that the Subject experiencer psych-verbs of fear in both Greek and English are constructions that have their origins in metaphoric shifts from concrete domains to more abstract esoteric domains (cf. Klein and Kutscher 2005), from domains of action to domains of sensation, and have further developed functions in the more conversational domain of social transaction.

Furthermore, linguistic studies of emotion predicates can significantly inform studies of emotions in the field of cognitive science and philosophy. This study may make some contribution in this respect, too.

REFERENCES

Butler, J. (1995). "Burning acts, injurious speech". In: A. Parker and E. Kosofsky Sedgwick (eds.). *Performativity and Performance*. London: Routledge: 197–227.

BUY. BUY Corpus of American English. Mark Davies/Brigham Young University.

Croft, W. (1991). *Syntactic Categories and Grammatical Relations. The Cognitive Organization on Information*. Chicago: University of Chicago Press.

Croft, W. (1993). "Case marking and the semantics of mental verbs". In: J. Pustejovsky (ed.). *Semantics and the Lexicon*. Dordrecht: Kluwer: 55–72.

Croft, W. (1998). "Event structure and argument linking". In: M. Butt & W. Geuder (eds.). *The Projection of Arguments*. Stanford, California: CSLI: 21–64.

Croft, W., H. Bat-Zeev Shyldkrot and S. Kremmer (1987). "Diachronic semantic processes in the middle voice". In: Giacalone Ramat *et al.* (eds.): 179–192.

Crystal, D. and B. Crystal (2002). *Shakespeare's Words*. England: Penguin Books.

Damasio, A. (2003). *Looking for Spinoza. Joy, Sorrow, and the Feeling Brain*. New York: Harcourt.

Dowty, D. R. (1991). "Thematic proto-roles and argument selection". *Language* 67: 547–619.

Foucault, M. (2002/1966). *The Order of Things*. London and New York: Routledge.

Fraser, Th. (1987). "The establishment of *by* to denote agency in English passive constructions". In: Giacalone Ramat *et al.* (eds.): 239–249.

Giacalone Ramat, A., O. Carruba and G. Bernini (eds.) (1987). *Papers from the 7th International Conference on Historical Linguistics*. Amsterdam/Philadelphia: John Benjamins.

Gibbs, R. W. (1999). "Speaking and thinking with metonymy". In: K.-U. Panther and G. Radden (eds). *Metonymy in Language and Thought*. Amsterdam/Philadelphia: John Benjamins: 62–76.

Goodwin, W. (1889). *Syntax of the Moods and Tenses of the Greek Verb*. London: MacMillan.

Grice, P. (1989). *Studies in the Way of Words*. Cambridge, Massachusetts, London, England: Harvard University Press.

Grimshaw, J. B. (1990). *Argument Structure.* Cambridge/Mass: MIT Press.

Homer (1948/1898). *The Iliad.* Samuel Butler (ed.). ebooks@adelaide, 2006.

ILSP, Institute of Language and Speech Processing. Modern Greek Corpus.

Kakouriotis, A. and E. Kitis (1999). "The case of *fovame* and other psychological verbs". *Greek Linguistics. Proceedings of the 3rd International Conference on Greek Linguistics.* Amalia Mozer (ed.). Athens: Ellinika Grammata: 131–140.

Kitis, E. (2009). "From motion to emotion to interpersonal function. The case of *fear* predicates". In: H. Pishwa (ed.). *Language and Social Cognitio: Expression of the Social Mind.* Berlin/New York: Mouton de Gruyter: 417–436.

Klein, K. & S. Kutscher (2002). "Psychic verbs in German and the principle of lexical economy". *Arbeitspapiere des SFB 282 Theories des Lexicons, Nr. 122.* Düsseldorf: Universidad.

Klein, K. & S. Kutscher (2005). (Revs. Version of 2002). "Lexical Economy and case selection of psych-verbs in German", available at http://www.linguistics.ruhr-uni-bochum.de/~klein/papers/LexEconPsych.pdf

Kövecses, Z. (1990). *Emotion Concepts.* New York: Springer.

Lakoff, G. (1987). *Women, Fire, and Dangerous Things. What Categories Reveal about the Mind.* Chicago and London: The University of Chicago Press.

Langacker. R. (1987). *Foundations of Cognitive Grammar.* V. I. Stanford, California: Stanford University Press.

LeDoux, J. (1996). *The Emotional Brain.* New York: Simon and Schuster.

Lichtenberk, F. (1995). "Apprehensional epistemics". In: J. Bybee and S. Fleischman (eds.). *Modality in Grammar and Discourse.* Amsterdam/Philadelphia: John Benjamins: 293–327.

(L&S), Liddell Henry George and Robert Scott (1948). *A Greek-English Lexicon.* Oxford: Clarendon Press.

Mey, J. (1986). *Whose Language? A Study in Linguistic Pragmatics.* Amsterdam/ Philadelphia: John Benjamins. (Pragmatics and Beyond, Companion Series, 3).

Monro, D. B. (2000). *Homeric Grammar.* London: Bristol Classical Press.

Nagel, Th. (1974). "What is it like to be a bat?" *Philosophical Review* 83(4): 435–450.

(OED), *Oxford English Dictionary.* Oxford: Oxford University Press.

Pesetsky, D. (1995), *Zero Syntax. Experiencers and Cascades.* Cambridge, Mass: MIT.

Riemer, N. (2006). "Reductive paraphrase and meaning: a critique of Wierzbickian semantics". *Linguistics and Philosophy* 29: 347–379.

Searle, J. R. (1979). "The classification of illocutionary acts". In: Searle (ed.). *Expression and Meaning. Studies in the Theory of Speech Acts.* Cambridge: Cambridge University Press: 1–29.

Searle, J. R. (1983). *Intentionality.* Cambridge: Cambridge University Press.

Searle, J. R. (2002). *Consciousness and Language.* Cambridge: Cambridge University Press.

Searle, J. R. (2004). *Mind: A Brief Introduction.* Oxford/New York: Oxford University Press.

Smith, B. (2003). "From speech acts to speech activity". In: B. Smith (ed.). *John Searle*, Cambridge: Cambridge University Press: 1–51.

Tantos, A. (2006). "Rhetorical relations in verbal eventual representations? Evidence from Psych Verbs". In: *Proceedings of the 2004 Texas Linguistics Society Conference*, Pascal Denis *et al.* (eds.). Somerville, MA: Cascadilla Proceedings Project: 123–136. www.lingref.com, document #1511.

Tenny, C. and J. Pustejovsky (eds.) (1999). *Events as Grammatical Objects. The Converging Perspectives of Lexical Semantics and Syntax*. Stanford, California: CSLI.

Theodoropoulou, M. (2003). *Στα Γλωσσικά Μονοπάτια του Φόβου. Ψυχισμός και Γλώσσα [On the Linguistic Path to Fear. Psyche and Language]*. Athens: Nisos.

Tissari, H. (2007). "Compressing emotion to politeness: On I fear and I'm afraid". In: M. Rissanen, M. Hintikka, L. Kahlas-Tarkka and R. McConchie (eds.). *The Change of Meaning and the Meaning of Change*. Helsinki: Société Néophilologique de Helsinki: 59–90.

Traugott, E. Closs (1989). "On the rise of epistemic meaning in English: An example of subjectification in semantic change". *Language* 65 (1): 31–55.

Traugott, E. Closs (2003). "From subjectification to intersubjectification". In: R. Hickey (ed.). *Motive for Language Change*. Cambridge: Cambridge University Press: 124–139.

Traugott, E. Closs and R. Dasher (1987). 'On the historical relation between mental and speech act verbs in English and Japanese'. In: Giacalone Ramat *et al.* (eds.): 561–73.

Traugott, E. Closs and R. Dasher (2002). *Regularity in Semantic Change*. Cambridge: Cambridge University Press.

Traugott, E. Closs and E. König (1991). "The semantics-pragmatics of grammaticalization revisited". In: E. Closs Traugott and B. Heine (eds.). *Approaches to Grammaticalization*. Vol. 1. Amsterdam: John Benjamins: 189–218.

Vendler, Z. (1972). *Res Cogitans. An Essay in Rational Psychology*. Ithaca and London: Cornel University Press.

Wierzbicka, A. (1986). "Introduction". *Journal of Pragmatics*, special issue on Particles, ed. by Wierzbicka, 10(5): 519–534.

Wierzbicka, A. (1990). "The semantics of emotions: *fear* and its relatives in English". *Australian Journal of Linguistics* 10 (2): 359–375.

Wierzbicka, A. (1994). "Cognitive domains and the structure of the lexicon: The case of the emotions". In: L. A. Hirschfeld and S. A. Gelman (eds.). *Mapping the Mind. Domain Specificity in Cognition and Culture*. Cambridge: Cambridge University Press: 431–452.

Wierzbicka, A. (1996). *Semantics: Primes and Universals*. Oxford: Oxford University Press.

Wierzbicka, A. (1999). *Emotions Across Languages and Cultures: Diversity and Universals*. Cambridge: Cambridge University Press.

Agnieszka Kaleta

University of Humanities and Natural Sciences, Piotrków Trybunalski

ENGLISH ASPECTUAL VERBS AND THEIR COMPLEMENTS: THE CASE OF 'BEGIN'

Abstract: The present paper is concerned with the gerundive and infinitival complementation patterns of the aspectual verb 'begin'. Underlying the study is the assumption that syntax is not an arbitrary system but has semantic basis. Our main aim is to substantiate this thesis with linguistic evidence drawn from the British National Corpus. In particular, we analyze the distributional properties of 'begin' with respect to the structure of events and semantic roles evoked by the utterance in which 'begin' occurs. This analysis provides the basis for comparing and contrasting the two complementation patterns basing on semantic criteria. The main point of reference in the research is Langacker's (1987, 2002) distinction between *perfective* and *imperfective processes* and strictly related to it notion of conceptual *boundedness*. It is our conviction that many seemingly puzzling aspects of the distribution of gerundive and infinitival complementizers can be systematically traced back to bounded and unbounded construal as defined and elaborated on by the founder of Cognitive Grammar.

Keywords: aspectual verbs, bounded construal, complementation patterns, gerunds, infinitives, imperfective process, Langacker, perfective process, unbounded construal.

1. Introduction

The complementation patterns of English aspectual verbs have received a considerable amount of attention within studies concerned with the properties of English sentential complementation. The cognitively oriented research into this area is represented by a number of important contributions, including Dirven (1989), Dixon (1991, 1995), Duffley (1999, 2000, 2003), Hamawand (2002, 2003), Horie (2000), Smith and Escobedo (2001), Verspoor (1996, 2000), and the extremely influential chapter by Wierzbicka (1988).[1] Interesting and

[1] We use the label of cognitively – oriented research loosely to include functionalists (e.g. Dixon, Duffley, and Wierzbicka).

revealing as all the studies in question might be, they seem to suffer from one common shortcoming. That is, they are based on a rather limited and arbitrarily selected collection of utterances. The point is that the use of isolated examples produced by the authors on ad hoc basis or drawn from other studies on the same topic can hardly be considered a sufficient enough basis for broad generalizations or far-reaching conclusions.

The issue of methodology becomes even more pertinent if one takes into account the usage-based thesis as advocated by cognitive linguists (cf. Langacker 1987, 2002) Specifically, the usage-based model grounds language in actual instances of language use (usage-events) specifying that broad generalizations or high-level schemata emerge via the process of abstraction from specific usage-events. Hence, to see how a given pattern or schema comes into being we need access to the complex reality of language in use. The most straightforward way of gaining such an access seems to be through the application of corpus methods of data extraction and analysis, which is the approach adopted in the present paper. In particular, we present a case study investigating the gerundive and infinitival complements of 'begin' – the most prototypical representative of the category of aspectual verbs of beginning. The reservation to be made at this point is that the study is a part of larger project aimed at developing a comprehensive picture of the semantics of English aspectual verbs with particular focus on their complementation patterns.

Here is a brief outline of the paper. In the first section to follow we set the scene for the more detailed discussion by clarifying the methodological issues, presenting the frequency data, and delineating the main line of reasoning followed throughout the study. Sections three and four are concerned with the two main complementizers of 'begin' – *to*-infinitives and gerunds, and are followed by a section comparing and contrasting these two. The paper concludes with a section summarizing all the main insights gained throughout the study and comments on the merits of the methodology employed.

2. Preliminary remarks

The analysis is based on a sample of 250 random occurrences of 'begin' extracted from the British National Corpus (BNC) by means of the concordancing software XAIRA.[2] The sample has been manually tagged for

[2] The ceiling of 250 occurrences has been set to make the task of manual analysis of the data manageable. It needs to be emphasized that tracing the subtle differences in the conceptualization

a number of features including, naturally, the syntactic category of the complements of 'begin' but also the semantic properties of the referents co-occurring with 'begin' – its subject and the complement verb.

The application of corpus methodology has the important merit of allowing insight into the frequencies with which particular patterns occur in authentic discourse. Below we present the relevant quantitative data as extracted from the sample under consideration (the two complements which will be our focus in the present study have been marked in bold):

Table 1

Begin +	
to-infinitive	**130**
gerund	**24**
noun phrase	26
intransitive	70
TOTAL	250

As can be seen 'begin' is most strongly associated with infinitival complements which account for as many as 130 occurrences in the sample consisting of the total of 250 occurrences (over 50%), gerundives and nominal phrases lagging far behind with only 24 and 26 occurrences respectively. It is worth noting in passing that the sample has also yielded a considerable number of intransitive uses of the lemma. As already indicated we limit our discussion in this paper only to infinitival and gerundive complements and our major aim is to demonstrate that the distributional patterns they follow are not a matter of chance or arbitrary syntax but have strong semantic foundations.

Furthermore, underlying the present study is the assumption that to understand and fully appreciate the conceptual potential of any verbal

patterns coded by almost synonymous constructions (i.e. begin + infinitive / begin + gerund) requires careful consideration of a variety of factors motivating the occurrence of one and not the other form in a particular discourse context. This, in turn, involves manual inspection of every single occurrence of a given form. Consequently, the overabundance of corpus data could blur the underlying patterns of conceptualization instead of making them explicit to the human researcher. Additionally, the fact that the analysis concerns a single matrix verb is not without significance. Here, the semantic properties of gerundive and infinitival complements come to light more readily than in the case of their combinations with a variety of different matrix verbs (with their own semantic contributions), the analysis of which would undoubtedly require a more substantial sample. It is also worth mentioning that some renowned corpus linguists, most notably Biber *et al.* (1998: 96), did not hesitate to use rather restricted samples (of 250 occurrences) for their semantic investigations if they required hand-editing or manual handling.

predication, we first need to understand the structure of the events or states coded by the clauses in which this predication occurs. This, in turn, requires the consideration of the (theta) roles played by all the major participants of a given situation[3] (most notably those in the subject and complement position) as well as the relationships holding between them. In doing so, we draw on the classification of situation types presented in Radden and Dirven (2007: 267–301), which reflects Fillmore's (1968, 1977) and Langacker's (1987, 2002) well-known conceptions of events and semantic roles played by their participants.[4]

The other essential point of reference is Langacker's conception of the verb defined as "a symbolic structure whose semantic pole profiles a process" (1987: 494)[5]. Here is a schematic representation of the semantic structure of 'begin' as presented by Langacker (2002: 198):

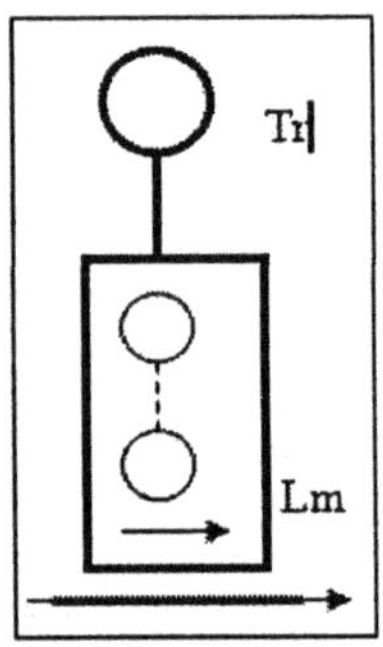

Fig. 1

All that we can read from this highly general schema is that "[BEGIN] profiles a process in which the trajector is a thing (spelled out by the subject nominal) and the primary landmark is another process." (2002: 198) Thus, it

---

[3] The notion of situation is used in cognitive linguistics literature as a technical term to denote "events that happen or states that things are in." (Radden and Dirven 2007: 47).

[4] In particular, among the different types of events we find the *action schema* which involves an intentionally acting agent who instigates and carries out the action, *emotion schema* which describes emotional states experienced by a sentient human being, *cognition schema* associated with different types of cognitive experiences, and finally *processes* which may be dynamic, that is involving a change of state (e.g. She fell in love) or steady (e.g. It has been raining).

[5] The notion of process as used by Langacker is not to be confused with the same term used to denote a type of event schema, as mentioned above. On Langacker's account process is a generic label for any type of situation denoted by a verbal predication. (for a detailed discussion see Langacker 1987: 244–274)

remains to be seen how this skeletal representation is elaborated on by concrete trajectors and landmarks as they emerge from the corpus data.

3. Begin and to infinitives

The pattern [begin + to infinitive] is associated with a few different types of situations. The most prominent seems to be the *action schema*, which "describes events in which a human agent deliberately and responsibly acts upon another entity, the theme" (Radden and Dirven 2007: 284). Consider the following examples:

1. Marcus (...) relaxed his pose and *began* to massage his left hand with his right
2. She *began* to read by the mooned light of the torch ...
3. No one else spoke. A little servant girl *began* to cry.
4. He *began* to stroll round the park, observing the lewd behaviour of the couples lying on the grass ...

The prototypical action has been described by cognitive linguists, most notably by Langacker, as an energetic event involving the transmission of energy from a sentient human being, the so called *energy source*, to the entity passively absorbing this energy, labeled as *energy sink*. (cf. Langacker 2002: 213). This prototypical conceptualization tends to be extended or elaborated on in a number of ways. Out of the examples cited above, only the first one seems to conform to the prototype, with 'Marcus' and 'his left hand' acting as energy source and energy sink respectively. Utterances (2)–(4) depart from this prototype primarily in that they make no mention of the entity directly affected by the action. However, in (2) the affected entity is implicitly there – it is quite clear that the action of reading involves some written work. But, being conceptually salient and easily recoverable from the context, it is not coded linguistically. In (3) and (4) we have to do with situations in which the affected entity figures neither at the conceptual nor at the linguistic level. The agent generates some energy, but it is either dispersed, as in (3) or absorbed by the agent himself and used to carry out the action, as in (4). What follows from the above is that the prototypical action described as the *energy flow* (cf. Langacker 2002: 238) is subject to different elaborations, all of which are, however, linked to the prototype by the presence of an agent – a volitional human being acting as an instigator and performer of the action.

The other point that should be made here concerns the time relationship between the event expressed by the matrix verb 'begin' and the event coded by its infinitival complement. In utterances (1)–(4), this relationship is that of simultaneity and immediacy, which is to say that the two events coincide in time. This point, should become clearer if one considers the following utterances.

5. (…) long after acquiring Belle Vue Cottage she *began* to search for a piece of land in the Cotherstone …
6. Out of a desire to protest against the 'oppression and exploitation' he saw around him, he *began* to write short stories, by the time of his death over a hundred had been published.
7. (…) those who had objected to the physical changes introduced during the previous decade *began* to destroy altars, rails, and stained glass …

In (5)–(7), we have to do with a series of events extending over a period of time. For instance, 'searching for a piece of land' is not a single continuous event but implies a succession of separate instances of 'searching'. Moreover, there is no implication of immediacy, that is to say the actual performance of the action coded by the infinitive does not (necessarily) coincide with the 'starting point' coded by the matrix verb. Thus, the examples under consideration involve two different conceptualizations of the schematic landmark of 'begin', which are presented below as fig. 2 and fig. 3:

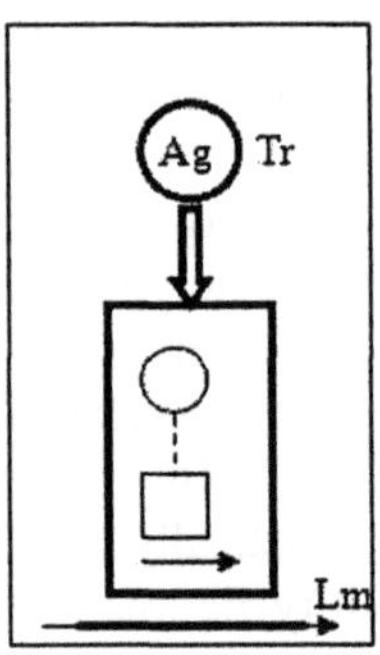

Fig. 2

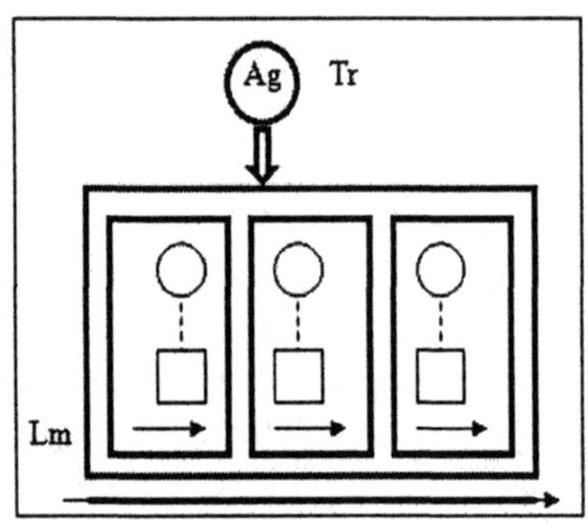

Fig. 3

Both landmarks are atemporal processes as defined by Langacker and symbolized by the thin arrow(s) inside the landmark box. (cf. Langacker 1987: 214–243). However, in fig. 2 it is conceptualized as a single durative event whereas in fig. 3 it involves a sequence of recurrent events happening at intervals (symbolized by separate components of the atemporal landmark). What the two schemas have in common is the role of the agent that fills the subject position (i.e. schematic trajector). The double arrow depicts the transmission of energy generated by the agent.

Yet another common elaboration of the schematic landmark is the one in which the event coded by the infinitival complement is construed of as a durative abstract *process*, with a clearly delineated notion of change. The following examples illustrate the point being made:

8. Mr Clarke has *begun* to change the culture of our body educational.
9. (...) so that we can *begin* to renew a sensitivity to areas of stylized feeling from the past
10. (...) the very fact that historians are at least *beginning* to make some progress in the study.

In (8)–(10) the situations denoted by the infinitives can hardly be construed of as a sequence of episodic events, which, however, does not mean that they do not actually consist of such events. After all, 'changing culture', 'renewing someone's sensitivity', or 'making progress in a study' all presuppose a series of specific actions on the part of the human agent. However, all the specifics of those actions are effectively suppressed in favour of a more holistic conceptualization of the event as an on-going, purposeful process of change. This is schematically represented in Fig. 4:

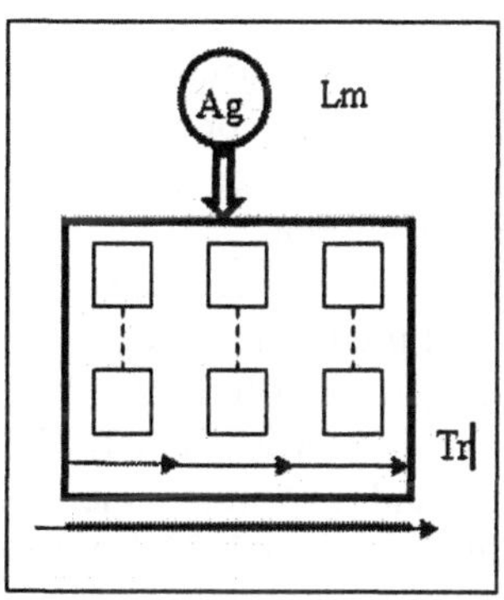

Fig. 4

Fig. 4 differs form fig. 5 in that it hides the borderlines between particular events, which are no longer viewed as individualized entities but rather as an ongoing process of transition from one state to another.

Having discussed the main conceptualization patterns associated with the *action* schema, we now turn to what Radden and Dirven refer to as 'situations in the psychological world' (2007: 281). Subsumed under this heading are *emotional*, *perceptual* and *cognitive* experiences people have or are subject to. Here are some corpus examples:

11. I, too, *began* to fear for my life as I stooped over the lavatory bowl.
12. Nutty *began* to feel sorry for him.
13. (…) it was only much later on that he *began* to wonder how Thomas knew about Alice atte Bowe.
14. the EEC (…) had also *begun* to consider how it might accommodate the remaining EFTA states
15. Now I was *beginning* to see that it didn't necessarily have to be that way.

In the utterances above, the subject is no longer an instigator of an action, but assumes a more passive role of an experiencer. The category of experiencers is not a uniform one but has a radial structure as many other conceptual categories. The key aspect seems to be here the degree of control a sentient human being is able to exert over his/her experience. Specifically, the lower the degree of control the more prototypical the experience is. This, seems to be the case with emotional experience where the subject is thought of as having only little or no control over his/her experience, as in examples (11) and (12). However, the situation is quite different in the case of cognitive events as illustrated in (13)–(15), where the subject is much more in control. For instance, while we can hardly exert conscious control over emotions such as fear or pity, cognitive events (e.g. wondering or considering something) are by no means independent of our conscious volition.

So far, we have been mostly concerned with the cases in which the role of the trajector of the relational predication 'begin' is performed by a human being, construed variously as an agent or experiencer. It is time now to turn attention to the second major class of instances, namely those which have non-animate entities as their subjects and instantiate the broadly-conceived category of *processes* (cf. Radden and Dirven 2007: 344). Here are some examples:

16. (…) population and inflating prices for necessaries *began* to increase the burden on rate-payers from (…).
17. (…) religious authority and the authority of the husband all *began* to totter.

18. Traffic was *beginning* to build up on the main road.
19. (…) her pale abdomen, not yet *beginning* to swell with the new life inside her
20. Soon it would *begin* to grow dark, and she hadn't seen to the house yet.

What the above utterances profile are dynamic processes of change involving a gradual transition from one state to another. The processes might be either abstract, in which case the subject position is occupied by an abstract noun as in (16)–(17), but they might also concern physical entities as in (19), or other situations available to sensory perception e.g. atmospheric phenomena, as illustrated in (20).

In this section of the paper we have shown that [begin + *to*-infinitive] pattern is associated with three major schemas, that is *action*, *emotion/cognition*, and *process* schema. In the next section we conduct a similar analysis with respect to [begin + gerund] pattern.

4. Begin and the gerund

It should be stated at the beginning that the gerundive complement is by no means as wide-ranging as the infinitival one in terms of its conceptual potential. The corpus data point to its compatibility mainly with the *action* schema. Here are the relevant examples:

21. (…) but when I *began* experimenting I was unable to get convincing results …
22. Hertfordshire-based AI International Ltd says it's *begun* shipping ParcPlac Software Systems…
23. In 1979, she and Branson *began* talking about establishing an independent label…
24. Early in 1831 he *began* transplanting mature trees, becoming expert in their removal…

The events profiled by the above utterances are all conceptualized as a series of recurrent events instigated and carried out by a human agent at some intervals. (cf. fig. 3). In addition to this major pattern, we have recorded some isolated instances of actions conceptualized as a single durative event (cf. fig. 2), as illustrated in (25).

25. Taylor ran down the aisle and, seizing a microphone from the prison chaplain, *began* haranguing inmates about the system.

Finally, the sample has yielded two instances of the *process* schema with a human being and inanimate entity as patients in the subject position.

26. (…) she murmured as her eyes closed and she *began* drifting slowly off to sleep.
27. Firemen were called to Hartlepool marina yesterday after a 30ft fishing boat *began* taking in water.

Having outlined the main conceptualization patterns associated with the infinitival and gerundive complements of 'begin', we are now in a position to compare and contrast these two types, basing our conclusions on the semantic profiles presented in the two preceding sections.

5. To-infinitive vs. gerund as the complements of 'begin'

The first and most straightforward conclusion that follows from what has been said so far is that the infinitival pattern has a much wider range of applications than the gerundive one. First of all, the latter has not been found to refer to emotional and cognitive events. Hence, out of the two examples to follow, only the first one is felicitous in a default context.

28. Nutty *began* to feel sorry for him.
29. *Nutty began feeling sorry for him.

The same concerns the onsets of situations conceptualized as stative, or in Langacker's terminology, as 'imperfective processes'.

30. The word *began to mean* 'natural' rather than 'barbaric'.
31. *The word *began meaning* 'natural' rather than 'barbaric'.

On Langacker's account the most important criterion that allows one to distinguish imperfective processes (states) from perfective processes (activities, accomplishments, achievements) is the absence or presence of change. Specifically, "a perfective process portrays situation as changing through time, while an imperfective process describes the extension through time of a stable situation" (2002: 86). The other essential criterion is that of bounding – perfective processes are conceived of as bounded in time (likely to come to an end) while the prototypical imperfectives profile situations that may extend indefinitely, and thus are viewed as unbounded. This distinction is instrumental in explaining why imperfective processes do not normally occur in progressive aspect. As Langacker puts it: "The basic reason is simply that progressive is imperfectivizing, hence its occurrence with imperfectives would be superfluous" (2002: 91). It is our conviction that the principle of 'imperfectivizing' applies not only to progressive but to all ING constructions including gerunds and present participles. Following this line of reasoning, (29) and (31) are unacceptable because they imposes unbounded construal on unbounded event, which is evidently superfluous. The same explanation seems to apply to cognitive events, which are typically classified as imperfective process:

32. (...) the baby's unified perceptions are shattered and she *begins* to understand herself as a subject disturbingly distant from the external world
33. *the baby's unified perceptions are shattered and she *begins* understanding herself as a subject disturbingly distant from the external world.

The case of cognitive events however merits some further attention since not all instances are as unambiguous as the ones above. Wierzbicka (1988: 85–87) in her interesting analysis of similar cases presents the following counterargument:

34. In my second year in Alice Springs, I started *understanding* what people were saying in Aranda.[6]

Wierzbicka's account is based on the general assumption that "gerundive complements of aspectual verbs are limited to the predicates which can be interpreted (in a given context) as referring to on-going processes rather than to mere states" (1988: 86). She further elaborates on this description specifying that ING complements are inextricably linked with "constant possibility of change" (ibid.). This explanation is clearly in line with Langacker's suggestion that progressive constructions are compatible with perfective processes which are inherently dynamic and changeable. However, the mere notion of change proves insufficient to account for the situation in (33), which is dynamic and on-going, just like the one in (34), yet can hardly be combined with the gerund. The key to

[6] Wierzbicka uses in her example 'start', not 'begin' – this however does not seem to constitute an obstacle in illustrating the main point, that is the flexibility of some predications expressing mental states to be used either as gerunds or infinitives.

solving this puzzle is to realize that the distinction between perfective and imperfective processes is sometimes blurred, a fact recognized both by Langacker (2002: 93) and Wierzbicka (1988: 86). Hence, in (33) the meaning of 'understand' is more imperfective than perfective whereas in (34) it is the other way around. More specifically, in the former case the situation is that the role of the subject (she) is that of an experiencer who has little control over her experience. The meaning of 'understand' can be roughly paraphrased here as 'to realize', or 'be aware'. In (34), on the other hand, the subject is much more in control of the situation. In fact, he/she is more agent-like than experiencer-like, which is to say that 'understanding' is not simply the realization of something, but it is construed as a much more dynamic process involving some cognitive effort on the part of the subject, and thereby is more perfective. Consequently, the use of gerund seems justified in this case. Yet, the distinction between perfective and imperfective processes in not always instructive enough to account for the flexibility of cognition verbs to take either *to*-infinitive or gerund. Consider the following examples:

35. (…) it was only much later on that he *began to wonder* how Thomas knew about Alice atte Bowe …
36. While John Carter waited in custody, local police *began wondering* about the strange disappearance of the farmer's second wife.

The situations portrayed by the two utterance can hardly be distinguished on the basis of the degree of the subject's control over her experience, which is relatively high in both cases. However, even here the choice of one form and not the other one is not a matter of an arbitrary decision on the part of the speaker. Wierzbicka (1988: 64) accounts for similar cases tracing the semantics of gerunds to what she refers to as 'sameness of time'. That is to say, the event denoted by the gerund takes place at roughly the same time as the main clause event. *To*-infinitives, on the other hand, are described as suggesting 'a sequence of times', which is to say that one event follows the other one. This observation seems to provide a good explanation of why gerund is used in (36) and not (35) – only the former portrays the two events as overlapping or concurrent in time. Basing on such instances, Wierzbicka elevates the notion of temporal overlap to the semantic invariant of the gerundive constructions, that is a stable component of their semantic potential. This, however, seems to be too far-reaching a conclusion in the light of corpus data. Consider the following instances:

37. Asimov taught himself to read English at five, and *began writing* soon afterwards.

38. Soon after moving in Hunt *began reading* Minton's copy of Delacroix's Journals .

The above utterances profile 'sequence of times' rather than 'sameness of time', yet the gerund has been used instead of the infinitival complement. However, it should be noted that in (37) and (38) we have to do with an immediate succession of events, as opposed to (35) where the time lag is much more conspicuous. Hence, it should be concluded that Wierzbicka's observation applies mainly to the situations in which there is a marked temporal gap between two events. When one event immediately follows another one, on the other hand, gerund seems more likely, or perhaps we should say as likely as infinitive, as evidenced by the following utterances:

39. He took up a pen and *began to write* quickly.
40. He reached for a sheet of paper, picked up a pen and *began writing*.

The closely related notions of 'sameness of time' and 'immediacy' constitute an important part of the semantic structure of gerunds. However, they are more realistically described in terms of prototypicality rather than as stable and invariant aspects of the semantics of ING constructions, a point we shall return to while discussing the gerundive complements of 'begin' as listed in section 4.

It is important to point out here that the quantitative discrepancy between infinitival and gerundive complements is very significant, the latter accounting for only 24 occurrences as opposed to 130 instances of the former in the corpus sample (see table 1). It is our conviction that this discrepancy is not a matter of chance or arbitrary syntax, but has a semantic basis. More specifically, it can be traced back to the semantics of the matrix verb – given that 'begin' in itself denotes the starting point of a durative event, it should be quite clear that ING is simply superfluous. This is analogous to the incompatibility of prototypically imperfective processes with the progressive aspect, as mentioned earlier. Using Langacker's terminology we might thus say that 'begin' is 'imperfectivizing' just like progressives, which results in its much lesser propensity to co-occur with gerundive constructions.

Nevertheless, the cases of such a co-occurrence have been recorded. As argued in section 4 they are mainly instantiations of *action* schema construed either as series of recurrent events (examples 21–24) or, more marginally, as a single durative event (example 25). Hence, this is an area where we can expect some overlap with *to*-infinitive complements (cf. section 3). However, a closer consideration of the relevant linguistic materials suggests that the gerundive complements differ slightly from the infinitival ones and this subtle difference can be traced back, as we believe, to the notion of boundedness as associated with perfective processes (cf. section 3). This point should become clearer if we return to the examples provided in section 4. In particular, events such as experimenting, shipping, talking, transplanting trees, can be easily conceptualized as consisting of a certain number of episodic events (i.e. experiments, shipments, talks etc.). What is even more important those events, albeit durative in nature, do not normally continue over a very long period of time (e.g. a single conversation or experiment is typically a matter of minutes or hours but not days or months). This construal contrasts in some subtle ways with the one imposed on the conceived scene by *to*-infinitive construction where the notion of boundedness seems slightly less clearly delineated. Let us, for example, consider utterance (6) repeated here as (41):

41. Out of a desire to protest against the 'oppression and exploitation' he saw around him, he *began to write* short stories, by the time of his death over a hundred had been published.

The point is that writing a book, even a short one, tends to be conceptualized as an effortful activity taking a considerable amount of time (in any case more than a single experiment or conversation). Besides, there is a clear indication that the process of writing short stories continued over a large part of the writer's life. Consequently, the conclusion to be drawn on the basis of this and other similar instances is that the difference between the construals evoked by the two complementizers with respect to the *action* schema resides in the degree of salience of the notion of boundedness. That is to say, the easier it is to construe a given scene as an episodic, bounded event, the more likely is the occurrence of gerundive complement. Conversely, the events that have more duration, or are not easily conceived of as individualized situations tend to be coded with *to*-infinitives (cf. examples 5–8). The same line of reasoning seems to apply to instances (26)–(27) which represent *process* rather than *action* schema. The point is that both 'falling asleep' and 'taking in water' proceed quite rapidly and hence are conceptualized as rather short in duration. Consequently, the notion of the end-point (telicity) is quite salient in both cases, which seems to justify the choice of the gerundive complement rather than the infinitival one.

The conceptual link holding between gerunds and the notion of boundedness should not come as a surprise here because it is inherent in Langacker's description of ING constructions. As noted earlier, ING forms are primarily associated with imposing unbounded construal on bounded (that is perfective) events. The point, however, is that the boundaries associated with perfective processes do not disappear – they are defocused, but implicitly there. Radden and Dirven (2007: 177) aptly describe the basic meaning of progressives (which we extend here to all ING constructions) as 'unboundedness with implicit boundaries',

The above conclusions also allows us to rationalize the use of to infinitives rather than gerunds with events discussed under the heading of *processes* or change of state situations (cf. examples 16–20) which can hardly be broken into discrete events, and even more importantly, tend to be conceptualized as slow or gradual. Thus, the notion of conceptual boundedness is effectively suppressed here, which explains the rather awkward nature of (43) and (45):

42. Soon it would *begin to grow dark*, and she hadn't seen to the house yet
43. ? Soon it would *begin growing dark*, and she hadn't seen to the house yet

44. (...) religious authority and the authority of the husband all *began* to totter.
45. ?(...) religious authority and the authority of the husband all *began* tottering

6. Conclusion

The analysis presented in the sections above shows that the process of complement selection by 'begin' is semantically motivated. Specifically, the infinitival and gerundive complementizers are not features of arbitrary syntax but exhibit some semantic potential, which determines their compatibility or incompatibility with different types of events. Our main aim in this paper has been to establish which types of events are most compatible with which complementation pattern. The corpus-based methods of obtaining linguistic materials have proved invaluable in this respect, enabling the creation of a detailed semantic profile for 'begin' as it co-occurs with infinitive and gerundive constructions. This fine-grained semantic analysis has revealed certain tendencies in the distribution of the two complements and provided the basis for their contrastive analysis.

The two complementizers can be effectively distinguished on the basis of the degree of boundedness they impose on the conceived scene. Hence, gerundive constructions (like the other ING constructions i.e. progressives and present participles) are prototypically associated with 'unboundedness with implicit boundaries' which makes them particularly compatible with actions rather than emotional or cognitive events. In the case of infinitives 'the implicit boundaries principle' does not apply. Consequently, they tend to co-occur with prototypical imperfectives i.e. mental/cognitive states, or change of state situations. They are also frequent with perfective processes (i.e. different types of agentive actions), in which case they should be easily substitutable for gerunds. Yet, even here the 'implicit boundaries' construal seems instructive in that the events coded by gerunds tend to be conceptualized as 'more bounded' (that is shorter in duration or having an implicit end-point) than the ones expressed with infinitives. This, in turn, explains the high degree of compatibility between gerunds and activities construed as rapid or instantaneous, on the one hand, and infinitivals and events which are slower or more gradual, on the other. Related to this is the observation that gerunds are likely to be associated with the notions of 'sameness of time' and 'immediacy' as opposed to infinitives which are more likely to co-occur with 'sequence-of-times' events.

The important point made in the study is that that the distinction between bounded and unbounded construal is by no means clear-cut, and there are many borderline cases which are somewhere in between these two extremes. The binary notions such as telicity/atelicity, limited duration/extended duration, simultaneity/sequence of times are all relative in nature, that is they are most usefully seen in terms of a continuum rather than sharp oppositions. This, in turn, inevitably, leads to the final conclusion that in some cases the choice between gerundive and infinitives might be a matter of the speaker's perceptions of a situation – that is, whether he construes it as more bounded-like or more unbounded like – rather than the 'objectively' existing aspects of the scene.

The approach taken in this paper departs in an obvious way from the one to be found in the majority of publications devoted to English complementation. Instead of looking for some major generalizations cutting across many different classes of English verbal predications, we have focused on a single representative of a single class of English aspectuals. Underlying the present study is the conviction that broad generalizations can only be formulated on the basis of the detailed knowledge of specific instances. Large, computerized corpora of texts, allowing a quick and relatively efficient access to the distributional properties of particular items, seem particularly well suited for this task. However, the knowledge gained through the application of corpus based methods is not an end in itself but only a means to a more fundamental end, that is, the underlying patterns of conceptual organization as they emerge from the corpus data. The sample research presented in this paper has been intended as a small step towards this goal. However, the conclusions we have drawn need to be verified by comparisons with the distributional properties of other aspectual verbs and other classes of verbs taking both gerunds and *to*-infinitives as their complements.

REFERENCES

Dirven, R. (1989). "A cognitive perspective on complementation". In: D. Jaspers *et al.* (eds.). *Sentential Complementation and the Lexicon: Studies in Honour of Wim de Geest*. Dordrecht: Foris Publication: 113–139.

Dixon, R. M. W. (1991). *A New Approach to English Grammar, on Semantic Principles*. Oxford: Clarendon Press.

Dixon, R. M. W. (1995). "Complement clauses and complementation strategies". In: F. R. Palmer (ed.). *Grammar and Meaning. Essays in Honour of Sir John Lyons*, Cambridge. Cambridge University Press: 175–220.

Duffley, P. J. (1992). *The English Infinitive*. London. Longman.

Duffley, P. J. (1999). "The use of the infinitive and the -ing after verbs denoting the beginning, middle, and end of an event". *Folia Linguistica*, 33: 295–331.

Duffley, P. J. (2000). "Gerund versus infinitive as complement of transitive verbs in English: the problems of 'tense' and 'control' ". *Journal of English Linguistics* 28: 221–248.

Egan, T. (2003). *Distance and Direction: A Usage-Based Study of Infinitive and -ing Complement Clauses in English*. Oslo. Unipub AS.

Fillmore, C. J. (1968). "The case for case". In: E. Bach & R. T. Harms (eds.). *Universals in Linguistic Theory*. New York: Holt, Rinehart and Winston: 1–88.

Fillmore, C. J. (1977). "Scenes-and-frames semantics". In: A. Zampolli (ed.). *Linguistic Structures Processing*. Amsterdam: North-Holland: 55–81.

Freed, A. F. (1979). *The semantics of English aspectual complementation*. Dordrecht: Reidel.

Hamawand, Z. (2002). *Atemporal Complement Clauses in English. A Cognitive Grammar Analysis*. München: Lincom Europa.

Hamawand, Z. (2003). "The construal of atemporalisation in complement clauses in English. *Annual Review of Cognitive Linguistics* 1: 59–85.

Horie, K. (ed.) (2000). *Complementation. Cognitive and Functional Perspective*. Amsterdam/Philadelphia: John Benjamins.

Langacker, R. W. (1987). *Foundations of Cognitive Grammar*. Vol. I. *Theoretical Prerequisites*. Stanford: Stanford University Press.

Langacker, R. W. (1991). *Foundations of Cognitive Grammar*. Vol. II. *Descriptive Applications*. Stanford: Stanford University Press.

Langacker, R. W. (2002). *Concept, Image, and Symbol. The Cognitive Basis of Grammar*. 2nd edition. Berlin/New York. Mouton de Gruyter.

Mair, Ch. (2003). "Gerundial complements after begin and start. Grammatical and sociolinguistic factors, and how they work against each other". In: G. R. Rohdenburg & B. Mondorf (eds.). *Determinants of Grammatical Variation in English*. Berlin/ New York. Mouton de Gruyter: 29–345.

Miller, D. G. (2002). *Nonfinite Structures in Theory and Change*. Oxford: Oxford University Press.

Newmeyer, F. J. (2003). "Grammar is grammar and usage is usage". *Language* 79/4: 682–707.

Newmeyer, F. J. (1975). *English aspectual verbs.* The Hague: Mouton.

Radden, G. & R. Dirven (2007). *Cognitive English Grammar.* Amsterdam/Philadelphia: John Benjamins.

Radden, G. (1989). "Semantic Roles". In: R. Dirven (ed.). *A User's Grammar of English: Word, Sentence, Text, Interaction.* Frankfurt: Lang: 421–472.

Smith, M. B. & J. Escobedo (2001). "The semantics of to-infinitival vs. -ing verb complement constructions in English". In: M. Andronis, Ch. Ball, H. Hellston & S. Neuvel (eds.). *The Proceedings from the Main Session of the Chicago Linguistic Society's Thirty-seventh Meeting.* Chicago: Chicago Linguistic Society: 549–565.

S. Verspoor, M. (1996). "The story of -ing: a subjective perspective". In: M. Pütz & R. Dirven (eds.). *The Construal of Space in language and Thought.* Berlin/New York. Mouton de Gruyter: 417–454.

Verspoor, M. (2000). "Iconicity in English Complement concstructions: conceptual distance and cognitive processing level". In: K. Horie (ed.). *Complementation. Cognitive and Functional Perspective*: 1999–225.

Wierzbicka, A. (1988). *The Semantics of Grammar.* Amsterdam/Philadelphia: John Benjamins.

Lily I-wen Su and Louis Wei-lun Lu

National Taiwan University

A NEW LOOK AT ANALOGOUS WORDS: A CORPUS-BASED APPROACH*

Abstract: This paper demonstrates how a corpus-based approach differs from a traditional introspection-based approach in distinguishing analogous words, with an illustration of WORRY and BOTHER. We begin with statistics automatically generated by a corpus query system, the Sketch Engine, to point out that the lemma WORRY is comparatively more time-stable and homogeneous in its inherent meaning than BOTHER. In addition to the homogeneity exhibited by WORRY, the Sketch Engine also shows a tendency to collocate with modifiers with a negative meaning as a distinct lexical property of BOTHER. Manual examination is used not only to remedy the statistics given by an automatic corpus query system but also to sort out representative syntactic patterns associated with WORRY and BOTHER in a small corpus. With the results derived from the manual search, an overarching explanation is given that the surface differences, including the homogeneity of WORRY, are actually rooted in the different perspectives taken by WORRY and BOTHER. The results and discussion show that introspection may serve as a starting point of linguistic research, but a corpus-based methodology can give solid and surprising evidence to form a better generalization than intuition. In addition to claiming the advantage of a corpus-based methodology, we further propose that a word should be known not only by the company it keeps but also by the perspective it takes.

Keywords: analogous word, linguistic context, the Sketch Engine.

1. Introduction

Analogous words present great difficulties for many language learners, with various guides to related words and usage dictionaries dazzling especially second

* We would like to thank Prof. Kathleen Ahrens, Prof. Kat Dziwirek, Prof. Barbara Lewandowska-Tomaszczyk and Prof. Sebastian Loebner for valuable comments. Sincere gratitude also goes to our lab members of NTU Cognitive Pragmatics (NTU CoPra) for useful suggestions. All possible inadequacies remain our own responsibility. Correspondence and requests for reprints should be addressed to iwensu@ntu.edu.tw.

and foreign language learners. According to *Webster's Dictionary of Synonyms*, analogous words are terms that are closely related in meaning and share much the same implications. The following typical instances illustrate the interchangeability of analogous words in context.

(1a) It really worries me that we are being exposed like this.[1]
(1b) It really bothers me that we are being exposed like this. (constructed example)
(2a) I'm not particularly worried about how I look. (constructed example)
(2b) I'm not particularly bothered about how I look.

From pairs (1) and (2), it is obvious that the two words do share similar meanings in certain contexts. Several usage dictionaries have also noticed their similarity in use. *Worry* and *bother* are listed as analogous words in *Webster's Dictionary of Synonyms*, as synonyms in *The Synonym Finder* (Rodale *et al.* 1978), and as related words in *Use the Right Word: Modern Guide to Synonyms and Related Words* (Hayakawa 1968). Facing a pair of semantically similar words like these, a typical intuition-based approach would render a distinction between the pair in the following way:

> [*Bother* is] often used in both active and passive senses. On the passive scale, *bother* usually indicates a minor complaint that may come and go... [*Worry* is] largely confined to the passive implication of being upset about something... *worry* suggests less clear-cut reasons for uneasiness, specifically implying suspense over the outcome of something. (Hayakawa 1968: 61)

Hayakawa's explanation is the only generalization we found that a typical intuition-based approach has generated, but it is too vague to contribute much to the understanding of the pair of analogous words *in use*. An intuition-based approach thus seems to reach its limitation against instances (1)–(2): when two lexical items are interchangeable in certain contexts, it becomes difficult to tell them apart. An intuition-based approach furthermore cannot give enough evidence in support of the distinctions it claims to make. We take up this issue to propose our research questions:

1. Given the vagueness of the traditional introspection-based method, is there any other way to clearly and objectively describe the differences between analogous words?

[1] Most of the instances employed in this paper are authentic data from the British National Corpus (BNC). Occasionally constructed instances are used to provide illustration. Such instances are specifically indicated.

2. Can this proposed method present further evidence that points to an underlying explanation for the surface differences observed?
3. Can this proposed method help language learners understand the differences between analogous words better than the traditional intuition-based approach?

Our hypothesis in response to these questions is that intuitions can serve as a preliminary direction of linguistic research, but may fall short when finer-grained distinctions between analogous words need to be made and when more concrete descriptions need to be given, whether theoretically or pedagogically. We hypothesize that an approach based on corpora (e.g. Gries 2006; Kemmer 2001; Stefanowitsch 2003) may help shed light on the complex structure of analogous words in use and may additionally help language learners acquire typical usage patterns of individual members of a set of analogous words.

2. Methodology

To verify our hypothesis, we rely on two research methods in the collection of data: a corpus query system that automatically derives statistics from a large corpus and a manual examination of a small corpus. The first method takes advantage of a corpus query system to provide results for grammatical and collocational analyses. The query system used in this study is the Sketch Engine[2], an online query system that accesses the entire British National Corpus (henceforth the BNC). The Sketch Engine is used to automatically sort out the distributional and collocational patterns of the words compared.

In addition to the statistics automatically generated by a query system, we need manual examination to complement our methodology. The idea that a rigorous cognitive semantic study cannot rely completely on a fully automated approach has been mentioned in other corpus-based studies (e.g. Gries and Divjak, To appear). The reason for the manual search is that the Sketch Engine generates only exact matches, and the design of its algorithm and the way parts of speech are tagged does not completely suit the purpose of the present paper as a cognitive semantic study. We encountered difficulty when we tried to search

[2] The Sketch Engine provides at least three useful functions for the purpose of the present study: The function of Concordance generates all tokens of data that contain the target word or phrase. Word Sketch generalizes the behavioral patterns of the target word (for nouns, verbs and adjectives only). Sketch-Diff compares the behavioral patterns of two target words to derive their most prominent collocations that distinguish the target words (also for nouns, verbs and adjectives only). Details of the Sketch Engine have been introduced by Kilgariff, Rychly, Smrz and Tugwell (2004).

for WORRY[3] within the construction [Subj V Obj] where the pattern generally means '(For the subject) to disturb the peace of mind of, or to be on the mind of (the object)'. A one-click search for such uses is not possible given the design of the query system, since the Sketch Engine generates only exact matches. The problem of "exact matches only" happened to other syntactic patterns. Hence, as far as such highly schematic constructions are concerned, we had to manually examine the data in our small corpus to find the distributions of the verbs.

In order for a more comprehensive picture of the syntactic patterns which WORRY and BOTHER participate in, we established a small corpus with data extracted from the BNC and manually scrutinized the tokens for the syntactic patterns that the target words participated in. We employed as our database the first 200 tokens given by a Concordance search for WORRY and BOTHER each as a verb. We excluded some unidentifiable tokens, tokens that were mistakenly tagged as verbs, and idioms, such as *Don't worry your head about that*. There were eight such tokens for BOTHER and ten such tokens for WORRY out of the original corpus of 200 tokens each.[4]

3. Results automatically generated by the Sketch Engine

In this paper, we study WORRY and BOTHER used as different parts of speech to find out their individual inherent meanings. Our underlying assumption is in line with Langacker's (1999: 11–12) discussion on the different profiling and relations of the various uses of the English word *yellow*. Langacker argues that the use of *yellow* as a noun, as an adjective, as a verb and *yellowed* as a participle involve different ways of profiling and, in the case of verbal use, a processual change in the color domain. Albeit the above differences, we observe that in Langacker's discussion the various uses of *yellow* as different parts of speech share a common conceptual content of "a region in color space" (1999: 11). The point of our studying WORRY and BOTHER as different parts of speech is to extrapolate the shared characteristics of the underlying conceptual content for each lemma. This section discusses the large-scale corpus-driven statistics automatically generated by the Sketch Engine regarding WORRY and BOTHER.

---

[3] Capitalization represents the concept of a lemma. For instance, the lemma WORRY can occur in the forms of *worrying*, *worried*, *worries* and *worry*.

[4] Sinclair (2004) proposes that the sketch of a word's usage require at least 20 tokens for not specifically polysemous words and 50 tokens for average words in English. Based on Sinclair's suggestion, our corpora are large enough for decisions regarding usage.

3.1. The more frequent occurrences of WORRY as nouns

This section is based on the statistics given by the function of Concordance of the Sketch Engine. In the BNC, both WORRY and BOTHER can be used as verbs and nouns. (3) and (4) are typical instances where they are used as nouns.

(3) 'I'm afraid there's been a bit of bother, Mrs. Mitchell,' he said.
(4) But the biggest worry for Taylor must be Platt.

However, despite the common nominal use of WORRY and BOTHER, their ratio of use as nouns is different in the BNC, see Table 1.

Table 1. Nominal occurrences of WORRY and BOTHER in the BNC

	WORRY	BOTHER
Tokens occurring as nouns	1,838	215
Total tokens in the BNC	7,702	4,178
Percentage in the BNC	23.86%	5.15%

In the BNC, 1,838 hits of WORRY occur as nouns, which accounts for almost 24% of the 7,702 hits of the lemma. This is over four times as many as the percentage of nominal use of BOTHER, with only 215 hits out of the 4,178 hits of the lemma in the entire BNC. Given the statistics presented in Table 1, we can claim that the lexical property of WORRY is more noun-like than BOTHER.

3.2. Only participles of WORRY occur as attributive adjectives

The results presented in this section are also derived by the function of Concordance. Among the various usage patterns of WORRY and BOTHER, another crucial distinction is whether their present and past participles can serve the grammatical function of attributive adjectives. We observe that in the BNC, only participles of WORRY can occur as attributive adjectives, exemplified by (5) and (6). For BOTHER, on the other hand, no such token was found. Although we found 112 tokens of *bothered*, they were all for predicative use, as in (7).

(5) Niall McDiarmid reports on a worrying trend.

(6) Headmaster Geoffrey Wilson blamed the problem on worried parents facing salary cuts.
(7) Well she wasn't too bothered.

Note that the corpus-driven algorithm did not reflect a precisely accurate picture of the distribution of *worrying* and *worried* as attributive adjectives. The function of Concordance generated results that contain 271 tokens of *worrying* followed by an NP and 296 tokens of *worried* followed by an NP. Out of the original search results, we manually deleted unrelated tokens such as *What is **worrying** farmers most is that nature has a nasty habit of having a sting in the tail* and *Crime has persistently interested and **worried** people…*, where the participles happen to occur right before the nouns but are in fact not a part of the noun phrases. The search results are listed in Table 2.

Table 2. Participles of WORRY and BOTHER as attributive adjectives

	Tokens	Total tokens of the lemma in the BNC	Percentage
Worrying + NP	260	7,702	3.38%
Worried + NP	266	7,702	3.45%
Bothering + NP	0	4,178	0%
Bothered + NP	0	4,178	0%

The figures in Table 2 reflect the distribution of *worrying* and *worried* followed by an NP. With a manual check, we have complemented the possible loopholes of corpus-driven statistics that are sometimes flawed due to the incorrect tagging or inappropriate design of the algorithm of the query system.

3.3. The collocations of BOTHER: modifiers with a negative meaning

The results presented from 3.3 to 3.5 are all based on the function of Sketch-Diff in the Sketch Engine. Sketch-Diff is a function that generates patterns that are specific to each word input as a member of the target pair under investigation. The results in 3.3 to 3.5 are all based on collocations that are in exclusive syntagmatic relation to only one member of the pair compared.

What tops the list of collocations of BOTHER as a verb are adverbs used in conjunction with the concept of negation, including *hardly*, *anyway*, *rarely*, and *no longer*.[5] Table 3 shows that the above four adverbs out of the top five, *hardly*, *anyway*, *rarely*, *particularly* and *no longer*, exhibit such property.

Table 3. Top five modifiers in BOTHER-only patterns

Collocations with BOTHER as a verb			Collocations with BOTHER as a noun
Modifier	Tokens	Significance	N/A (no modifiers found in the result)
Hardly	24	28.5	
Anyway	11	24.7	
Rarely	11	21.3	
Particularly	15	19.8	
No longer	9	17.2	

Note that *anyway* does not itself carry a negative meaning, but in the BNC it always occurs with *not*, an adverb carrying a negative meaning, as in (8), or in a question. (9) is another instance of BOTHER with an adverb with a negative meaning. A constructed instance without such modifier, as in (10), sounds awkward.

(8) I'm pleased he's not bloody bothered anyway.
(9) 'Yes,' replied Evans, hardly bothering to sound convincing.
(10) *'Yes,' replied Evans, bothering to sound convincing. (constructed example)

The tendency of BOTHER to occur with modifiers used in conjunction with a negative meaning is a very special property associated with this lemma. With help from a corpus query system, a learner can easily familiarize himself or herself with the pattern.

3.4. Collocations of WORRY tend to implicate a sense of continuity

Among the collocations in the WORRY-only patterns, WORRY is found to exclusively attract some modifiers that carry the meaning of a continuous state, which is absent from the BOTHER-only patterns. On the lists of the top five

[5] At first glance, the adverbs *hardly* and *rarely* may cast some doubt. But in WordNet, *hardly* has a meaning of 'almost not' and *rarely* means 'not often', which both carry a negative meaning.

modifiers of WORRY as a verb and as a noun, we have identified two such modifiers on each list: *increasingly* and *constantly* for WORRY as a verb and *nagging* and *constant* for WORRY as a noun. Table 4 summarizes the most representative collocations of WORRY used as a verb and as a noun that distinguish it from BOTHER.

Table 4. Top five modifiers in WORRY-only patterns

Collocations with WORRY as a verb			Collocations with WORRY as a noun		
Modifier	Tokens	Significance	Modifier	Tokens	Significance
Unduly	16	34.0	*Nagging*	9	28.3
Increasingly	11	19.0	*Relegation*	12	27.9
A bit	10	17.7	*Biggest*	21	27.7
Seriously	7	16.0	*Financial*	31	25.4
Constantly	6	15.8	*Constant*	16	23.7

According to the results from the WORRY-only patterns, two of the top five modifiers that collocate with the verbal use of WORRY denote a sense of continuity: *constantly* 'without variation or change; without interruption', and *increasingly* 'advancing in amount or intensity':[6]

(11) [S]he worried constantly about whether she was, whether they both were, working hard enough.
(12) Many photographers are currently becoming increasingly worried about the impact of electronics on the industry.

The modifiers in (11) and (12) both code a sense of continuity. In (11), the disturbance in the subject's mind remains as time goes by. The mental discomfort of the subject in (12) grows as shown by the use of *increasingly*.

In addition to occurrences of WORRY as a verb, such collocations are also found to relate closely to the nominal use of WORRY. (13) and (14) are typical adjectival collocations that denote a sense of continuity.

(13) This latter point had occurred to Jane, as a nagging worry.

[6] The meanings of these modifiers are based on WordNet. Note that the meaning of *nagging* cannot be found in WordNet or other major dictionaries such as *American Heritage*, *Collins Cobuild* or *Webster's*. However, all usages listed under the entry of *nag* as a verb carry meanings of 'constancy'.

(14) Toomey's childhood was dominated by constant worry about money, but it spurred him on.

In (13) and (14), the modifiers *nagging* 'constant' and *constant* 'unvarying in nature' also both denote a sense of continuity. Out of the top five modifiers that collocate with WORRY as a noun but not with BOTHER, namely *nagging*, *relegation*, *biggest*, *financial* and *constant*, two modifiers carry the meaning of continuity. The same is true for modifiers of WORRY as a verb. Based on the above evidence, we can conclude that the lemma WORRY is closely associated with modifiers with a sense of continuity. Such a tendency is not found among the BOTHER–only patterns.

3.5. Self-collocations of WORRY

Among the patterns generated by the function of Sketch-Diff, another difference in the collocational patterns of WORRY and BOTHER is that only WORRY is found to collocate with itself (in the sense of Sinclair *et al.* 2004: 83–84) in the BNC. (15) is a typical example.

(15) Apart from having his home, his place taken over like this. Worry, worry, Alice sat worrying.

The function of Sketch-Diff gives 11 such tokens for WORRY, but does not give a similar result for BOTHER.

3.6. Summary: WORRY as relatively more time-stable and slow-changing

We can generalize, according to the above usage patterns, that the inherent meaning of the lemma WORRY is relatively more time-stable, slow-changing and homogeneous than the lemma BOTHER, based on the following four reasons. The first piece of evidence is the fact that the percentage of WORRY found to appear as a noun is higher than that of BOTHER. Based on Langacker's (1999: 8–12) discussion of lexical classes, the above difference in percentage can be understood as a reflection of the different tendencies of WORRY and BOTHER to profile the conceptual content of emotion as a particular kind of thing, i.e. a region in the domain of emotion and in addition atemporal given its non-verbal nature. The higher percentage of WORRY used as a noun than BOTHER means that WORRY is used to profile a feeling as being atemporal more often than BOTHER and is thus more static and time-stable in nature than BOTHER. The second piece of evidence is that WORRY allows its participles to function as attributive adjectives, while no such pattern is identified for BOTHER. Following Langacker (1999: 11–12), the fact that the participles of WORRY occur as attributive adjectives but those of BOTHER do not indicates that only WORRY can occur in modification of a noun to construe the conceptual content in the domain of emotion in an atemporal and non-verbal way, while BOTHER does not allow such occurrences. The exclusive distribution of the lemma WORRY as an attributive adjective can be considered a reflection of its greater tendency for profiling the conceptual content in the domain of emotion in an atemporal and time-stable way. BOTHER on the other hand shows less tendency of such profiling given its comparatively limited distribution. Based on the statistics presented in 3.1 and 3.2 concerning its frequent nominal use and the behavior of its participles, the inherent meaning of the lemma WORRY is more time-stable and more slow-changing than BOTHER.

Our third and fourth pieces of evidence echo our preliminary generalization above. WORRY, whether in nominal or verbal use, is found to collocate frequently with modifiers which carry a meaning of continuity, which is compatible with its quality of being time-stable. WORRY furthermore collocates with itself, which iconically (Haiman 1980) reflects a sense of continuity. Since the quality of WORRY is more stable and involves less change over time, the lemma is as a result more homogeneous in nature.

As for BOTHER, in addition to being relatively more fast-changing and temporally less stable, and as a result more heterogeneous, than WORRY, a prominent characteristic of BOTHER is that it often occurs with modifiers signaling a negative meaning, which is missing in traditional usage dictionaries based on intuition.

4. Results based on the manual examination of a small corpus

The second part of our paper is based on the manual examination of a small corpus in search of schematic grammatical patterns associated with the verbal use of WORRY and BOTHER. The point of this examination is to establish patterns that cannot be detected by a corpus-driven algorithm. In this section, we present the grammatical patterns where WORRY and BOTHER occur as a verb, in order to see whether the results can reveal any further differences between the pair. With a manual examination with reference to WordNet, we have generalized three types of patterns for WORRY, [Subj WORRY], [Subj WORRY Obj] and [Subj BE *worried*], and five types of patterns for BOTHER, [Subj BOTHER], [Subj BOTHER Obj], [Subj

BE *bothered*], [Subj BOTHER *to* Infinitive/Gerund] and [Subj BE *bothered to* Infinitive/Gerund], and the general meaning of each pattern, which will be addressed in 4.1 and 4.2 respectively.

4.1. The syntactic patterns associated with WORRY as a verb

The most prominent syntactic pattern associated with WORRY as a verb is the active intransitive construction of [Subj WORRY], which accounts for 75.26 percent, or 143 tokens out of the total of 190. The relative frequency of this cluster of use in comparison to the other types of syntactic patterns is shown in Table 5.

Table 5. The syntactic patterns associated with WORRY as a verb

Grammatical pattern	Meaning[7]	Token	Percentage
[Subj WORRY]	'(For the subject) to be concerned, anxious, troubled or uneasy'	143	75.26%
[Subj WORRY Obj]	'(For the subject) to disturb the peace of mind of, or to be on the mind of (the object)'	33	17.37%
[Subj BE *worried*]	'(For the subject) to be afflicted with, or mentally upset over, anxious uneasiness or trouble or grief'	14	7.39%
Total		190	100%

The overwhelmingly frequent pattern [Subj WORRY] carries only the experiencer as the main argument of the verb, followed by an optional prepositional phrase. Typical examples include (16), an intransitive instance without a prepositional phrase and (17), where a prepositional phrase, *about* NP, is present.

(16) They pretend for my sake they don't worry.
(17) [W]e no longer had to worry about having the exhaust pipes running…

The use of WORRY profiles the participant roles of [Stimulus] and [Experiencer].[8] But we can further observe that the grammatical preference of

[7] The meanings presented here are based on the definitions found in WordNet. WordNet provides both the sentence frames and the several meanings of *worry* and *bother*. The meanings in Table 5 and 6 are organized according to the syntactic patterns associated with each cluster of usage.

[8] The participant roles Experiencer, Stimulus presented here and Effect, to be discussed in 4.2, are all based on the terminology of FrameNet.

WORRY as a verb indicates that between the two roles, WORRY tends to profile, more often, the role of the experiencer.

In addition to profiling the two typical participant roles in the structure of an event of emotion, another characteristic of the syntactic patterns associated with WORRY is worth noting. Out of the 190 tokens, 83 tokens of WORRY are followed by a prepositional phrase, *about* NP, which specifies the general topic that concerns the experiencer. Given the high frequencies of [Subj WORRY] and the prepositional phrase that follows WORRY in the corpus, the speaker's use of WORRY in coding the event not only profiles the experiencer of the emotion but also mentions a general topic about which the experiencer is emotionally provoked. This pattern is also what can be identified by a corpus-based approach but cannot be readily provided by introspection.

4.2. The syntactic patterns associated with BOTHER

The most salient feature of the syntactic patterns associated with BOTHER as a verb is its frequent occurrence followed by another verb. In our small corpus, BOTHER occurs in the grammatical patterns of [Subj BOTHER *to* Infinitive/Gerund] and [Subj BE *bothered to* Infinitive/Gerund], which altogether account for 85 tokens, or almost 45 percent, out of the total of 192 tokens. The distribution of the syntactic patterns associated with BOTHER as a verb is given in Table 6.

Table 6. The syntactic patterns associated with BOTHER as a verb

Form	Meaning	Token	Percentage
[Subj BOTHER]	'(For the subject) to trouble or inconvenience oneself'	49	25.52%
[Subj BOTHER Obj]	'(For the subject) to cause annoyance in (the object)'	26	13.54%
[Subj BE *bothered*]	'(For the subject) to be caused to show discomposure'	32	16.67%
[Subj BOTHER *to* Infinitive/Gerund]	'(For the subject) to trouble or inconvenience oneself to do something'	75	39.06%
[Subj BE *bothered to* Infinitive/Gerund]	'(For the subject) to be caused to show discomposure to do something'	10	5.21%
Total		192	100%

In the occurrences in [Subj BOTHER *to* Infinitive/Gerund] and [Subj BE *bothered to* Infinitive/Gerund], BOTHER occupies the position of the main verb whether in the active form or in its participle form. What follows BOTHER is either a *to*-infinitive or a gerund, which codes the effect brought about by the stimulus. (18) and (19) are typical instances.

(18) Yet she wasn't afraid and didn't even bother to open her eyes to find out...
(19) Jay wanted to say then don't bother calling.

As shown in Table 6, BOTHER linguistically realizes the roles of [Stimulus], [Experiencer] and [Effect]. But a closer look reveals that among these three participant roles, BOTHER tends to focus on the roles [Experiencer] and [Effect], given the more frequent occurrences of BOTHER as the first verb in constructions like (18) and (19), where [Experiencer] and [Effect] become the profiled elements.

4.3. A unifying account: perspectivization of events

With a close manual examination of a small corpus, we have been able to generalize the syntactic patterns associated with the verbal use of WORRY and BOTHER with a view to sorting out their most representative usages. We have established that WORRY most frequently occurs in the intransitive construction of [Subj WORRY], which profiles the role of [Experiencer] in an event of emotion. BOTHER on the other hand is often followed by a *to*-infinitive or a gerund specifying both the role of [Experiencer] and the [Effect] caused by the stimulus. Here we shall relate the conceptual profiling of WORRY and BOTHER back to the inherent meanings observed from the corpus-driven results discussed in Section 3.

We shall argue that in comparison to BOTHER, the more slow-changing and time-stable, and as a result more homogeneous, meaning of the lemma WORRY can be attributed to the different ways of presenting conceptual contents in a semantic frame (Fillmore 1982). According to Fillmore, the use of the verb *sell* in a commercial transaction frame is to present the situation from the perspective of the seller, while the verb of *buy* views the event from the viewpoint of the buyer. Different choices of the verb reflect the perspective from which the speaker chooses to construe the transaction, with different participants in the frame linguistically realized. We argue that the concept of framing from a certain perspective is readily applicable to the lexical choice between WORRY and BOTHER, with a distinct perspective taken by each verb. The prototypical perspectives taken by WORRY and BOTHER are shown in Figure 1a and 1b respectively, where the bold frames represent the profiled elements in the structure of an emotion event.

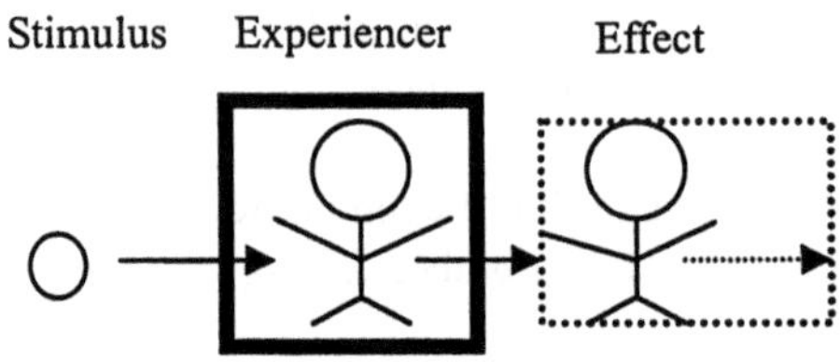

Fig. 1a. The perspective taken by WORRY on an emotion event

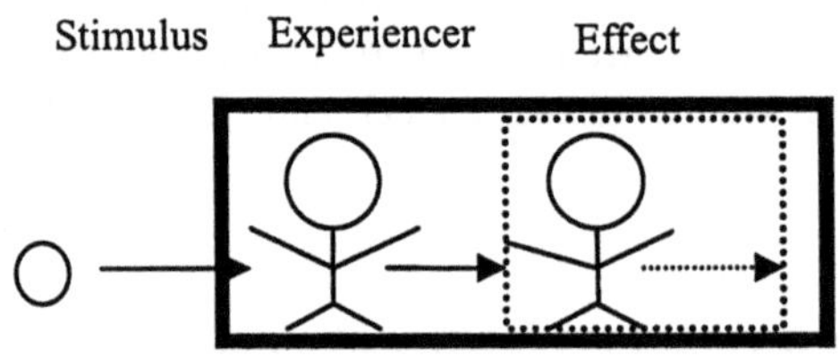

Fig. 1b. The perspective taken by BOTHER on an emotion event

As Figure 1a shows, WORRY takes a more narrow perspective than BOTHER on the event to profile only the [Experiecer] of the emotion, and such a narrower perspective allows WORRY to focus mostly on the internal state of the experiencer and thus lends WORRY a highly time-stable and homogeneous lexical property. On the other hand, Figure 1b demonstrates that the perspective taken by BOTHER is not as narrow as that taken by WORRY so that it can include both the [Experiencer] of the emotion and the [Effect] brought about by the stimulus. The inherent meaning, as compared to WORRY, is as a result more compact and more heterogeneous, involving more change over time. Looking into how each verb takes its own perspective on an event of emotion allows for an overarching explanation for the surface differences between WORRY and BOTHER addressed from Section 3 to 4.2.

5. A corpus-based approach to analogous words: A new look

The corpus-based methodology is what sets this paper apart from the traditional introspection-based approach. A corpus-based approach to analogous words can generate the most representative patterns in order for language learners to quickly grasp the crucial differences between the pair, or among the set (if more than two). The methodology in this paper includes both automatically generated corpus-driven results and corpus-based manual examinations. The two types of methodology complement each other to further provide an overarching explanation regarding the differences in the behavior of the lemmas WORRY and BOTHER. This is in perfect response to our research questions and to our hypothesis proposed previously: introspection may serve as a starting point of linguistic research, but provides neither solid evidence nor a unifying explanation for the surface differences between analogous words. Corpus-driven statistics are quick and convenient, and are capable of showing a comprehensive picture by extracting typical patterns from an extremely large range of data. This, however, should be complemented by manual examination, which can remedy minor errors of large-scale corpus-driven statistics and is capable of uncovering schematic patterns within a small corpus that cannot be identified by the algorithms of an automatic query system.

In addition to studying how analogous words interact with their respective immediate linguistic context, such as their collocations and syntactic patterns, our study further provides a unifying explanation for their surface differences. We conclude that the different perspectives taken by WORRY and BOTHER result in the majority of the differences in their behavior in the corpus. From a pragmatic point of view and from the observations made so far, the choice between WORRY and BOTHER in the domain of emotion can be considered the speaker's perspective on conceptual contents, i.e. to selectively present or to ignore certain elements in the conceptual domain in daily interactions. By gearing a corpus-based methodology toward a cognitive analysis, we conclude that a word is not simply known by the company it keeps; a word should also be known by the perspective it takes.

REFERENCES

Fillmore, Ch. (1982). "Frame semantics". *Linguistics in the Morning Calm*, ed. by Linguistic Society of Korea: 111–138. Seoul: Hanshin.

Gries, S. (2006). "Corpus-based methods and cognitive semantics: The many meanings of *to run*". *Corpora in Cognitive Linguistics: Corpus-based Approaches to Syntax and Lexis*, ed. by S. Gries and A. Stefanowitsch: 57–99. Berlin; New York: Mouton de Gruyter.

Gries, S. and D. Divjak (To appear). "Behavioral profiles: A corpus-based approach towards cognitive semantic analysis". *New Directions in Cognitive Linguistics*, ed. by Vyvyan Evans and Stephanie S. Pourcel. Amsterdam; Philadelphia: John Benjamins.

Hayakawa, S. I. (1968). *Use the Right Word: Modern Guide to Synonyms and Related Words*. Pleasantville: Reader's Digest Association.

Kemmer, S. (2001). "Causative constructions and cognitive models: The English *make* causative". *First Seoul International Conference on Discourse and Cognitive Linguistics: Perspectives for the 21st century*: 803–846. Seoul: Discourse and Cognitive Linguistics Society of Korea.

Kilgarriff, A., P. Rychly, P. Smrz, and D. Tugwell (2004). "The Sketch Engine". *Proceedings of the Eleventh EURALEX International Congress*. Lorient: 105–116.

Langacker, R. (1999). *Grammar and Conceptualization*. Berlin; New York: Mouton de Gruyter.

Sinclair, J. (2004). "Corpus and text: Basic principles". *Developing Linguistic Corpora: A Guide to Good Practice*, ed. by M. Wynne: 1–16. Oxford: Oxbow Books. (Electronic version available at http://ahds.ac.uk/guides/)

Sinclair, J., S. Jones, R. Daley and R. Krishnamurthy (2004). *English Collocation Studies: The OSTI report*. London; New York: Continuum International.

Stefanowitsch, A. (2003). "Constructional semantics as a limit of grammatical alternation". *Determinants of Grammatical Variation in English*, ed. by Gunter Rohdenburg and Britta Mohndorf, 413–443. Berlin; New York: Walter de Gruyter.

Usage dictionaries and internet resources consulted

The Synonym Finder (1978). ed. by J. I. Rodale, Laurence Urdang, Nancy LaRoche, and Faye C. Allen. Emmaus: Rodale Press.

Webster's Dictionary of Synonyms. (1951), Springfield, MA: Merriam-Webster.

FrameNet (http://framenet.icsi.berkeley.edu/)

The Sketch Engine (http://www.sketchengine.co.uk)

WordNet 3.0 (http://wordnet.princeton.edu/)

Giuliana Fiorentino

Università degli Studi del Molise

THE ORDERING OF ADVERBIAL AND MAIN CLAUSES IN SPOKEN AND WRITTEN ITALIAN

Abstract: Using corpus data of written and spoken Italian, the paper argues in favour of a different ordering distribution of adverbial and main clauses partially due to cognitive restrictions on written and spoken language.

After analysing the cognitive factors such as weight effects that, according to some relevant psycholinguistic models, can interact with the ordering of linguistic constituents the paper argues in favour of a multiple explanation for data. Cognitive motivations by themselves are not sufficient to explain all cases of ordering of adverbial clauses and it is also necessary to refer to a semantic analysis of adverbial clauses and to pragmatic or discourse motivation for explaining some specific cases.

The article also supports the idea that corpus-based analysis of languages is a successful way of testing psycholinguistic hypotheses on different degrees of syntactic complexity that spoken and written language can afford.

Keywords: adverbial clauses, causal clause, conditional clause, main clause, pragmatics, processing, spoken language, temporal clause, word order, written language.

1. Introduction

The comparison between spoken and written language has been a focal issue in European linguistic research since the first years of the XIX century (see for example 1929 Frei, *La grammaire des fautes*). A special sensibility to the differences among spoken and written language arose in studies on variability in language (in Romance research on the *français populaire* or the *italiano popolare*). In all these pioneering works data were taken from real spoken language and compared to the standard realisation of the language (better represented in the written language).

The development of technologies, related to the possibility of recording spoken language and storing data on hard disks in order to form electronic archives, shed a new light on the study of written and spoken languages.

In this article my main aim is to demonstrate how the comparative analysis of spoken and written language can take advantage of large corpora-based studies (see Biber (1988), Miller & Weinert (1998), among others). This is especially true for syntax, as we know that the main differences between spoken and written varieties of a language at this level are related not only to the preference accorded to different constructions (spoken Italian, for example, avoids nominalizations, the gerund and the subjunctive, uses the present tense instead of the future, generalises the use of *che* in relative clauses for all syntactic functions and does not use the relative pronoun *il quale*), but even to a greater frequency in the use of the same constructions (for instance, free participles as in *Sitting at the window*, I noticed a car at the bank, *Covered in confusion*, he apologized, are less frequent in spoken English than in written English, see Miller & Weinert 1998: 340).

Sometimes the different degrees of syntactic complexity in spoken and written varieties of the same language are explained by the pressures of on-line processing which are stronger in the spoken language because of short term memory restrictions. This explains the lack of long sentences with lots of subordinate clauses in spoken language. This kind of sentences are complex not only from the point of view of the speaker, who has to plan long sentences and a complex architecture of clauses, but also from the point of view of the hearer. If differences between spoken and written language can be explained as differences in processing, they have their basis in cognitive motivations. We hypothesize that another difference between spoken and written language is a different preferential ordering of linguistic elements. In this paper we will investigate this last point applied to the relative ordering of adverbial and main clauses in spoken and written Italian (see § 2–4).

It is also well known that testing the effect of processing on language structures can take advantage of corpus-based analysis and not only from experiments carried out in laboratories (for a critical approach to this point see Hawkins 1994, 2004). In this sense a secondary aim of this article is to (indirectly) support the idea that corpus-based analysis of language is a successful way of approaching the different cognitive restrictions related to the spoken or the written language.

2. A general overview on the ordering of adverbial clauses in Italian

Before discussing the results of the analysis, it can be useful to have a general overview of subordination in Italian and of the ordering of elements in the sentence.

Since Greenberg's (1963) work on word-order correlations it has been common to correlate the ordering of the linguistic elements with the order of Verb and Object. For instance, in languages where O precedes V (henceforth OV languages) adpositions follow NP and genitives precedes the head noun. Languages where V precedes O (henceforth VO languages) present the opposite situation: genitives follow the head noun and adpositions precede the NP.

On this basis in Italian, a VO language, we expect subordinate clauses to follow their main clause when they are complement clauses (with both finite (*So che tu sei del Belgio* 'I know that you are from Belgium') and nonfinite verbs (*Penso di non venire domain* 'I think not to come tomorrow.')). We also expect that relative clauses, like noun modifiers, will follow the clause containing the head noun.[1] Likewise, adverbial clauses, which correspond to adjuncts, might either precede or follow the main clause as adjuncts commonly do.

Regarding the ordering distribution of main and adverbial clauses Diessel (2001) makes some relevant predictions for large-scale crosslinguistic investigations. His conclusion, based on the analysis of a sample of forty languages of the world,[2] can be summarised as follows:

> there are two major crosslinguistic ordering patterns: (1) either a language uses adverbial clauses both before and after the main clause/predicate (and both orders are common), or (2) the adverbial clause usually precedes the main clause/predicate. [...] When both orders are common the position of the adverbial clause varies with its meaning or function: conditional clauses usually precede the main clause/predicate; temporal clauses may precede or follow it; causal clauses tend to occur in sentence-final position, but occasionally they are preposed; and result and purpose clauses almost always follow the associated element (Diessel 2001: 433–434).

According to Diessel, pattern (2) only occurs in OV languages, while pattern (1) applies to VO languages and a minority of OV languages. The distribution of adverbial clauses also correlates with the position of the subordination particle. Adverbial clauses with a final subordinator tend to occur before the main clause/predicate, whereas an initial subordinator can correlate with both orders.

To sum up, on the basis of Diessel's typological work we can predict that Italian adverbial clauses will both precede and follow the main clause/predicate and that the preferred order will probably depend on the semantic value of the clause.

---

[1] It must be noticed that Italian can also embed a relative clause into the main clause, and this second possibility is less frequent in spoken language because of processing motivations (Prideaux and Baker 1986).

[2] Italian has not been included in Diessel's sample of languages (see Diessel, Appendix A 2001: 449).

There is another possibility to explain the distribution of linguistic elements, which has been explored by Hawkins (1990, 1994, 1998, 2004). Hawkins offers a systematic description of the ordering of linguistic elements as primarily processing-based. According to him, information structure is relevant to constituent order only if two alternative orders are equally difficult to process. He hypothesizes that the ordering of adverbial clauses has to do with the relative length of the adverbial clause and the main clause. The longer the adverbial clause, the higher the possibility that the subordinate clause will follow the main clause.

Wasow (2002) argued that the ordering of postverbal elements in English involves more factors (syntax, semantics, pragmatics, and lexicon; see also Wasow 1997a, 1997b). Diessel (2005) also argued that the 'positioning of finite adverbial clauses is affected by multiple forces that are in conflict with each other. Specifically, it is shown that the ordering of main and adverbial clauses is determined by the interaction between processing, discourse pragmatics, and semantics." (Diessel 2005: 450).

In this article we are applying Hawkins's hypothesis integrated with Wasow's and Diessel's corrections but at the same time we will put a stronger emphasis on the different ordering in written and spoken language. If our results support a clear difference in the ordering of adverbial clauses between the two varieties we will be able to integrate the general cognitive hypothesis that lies behind Hawkins model with a further integration on the different impact of processing on spoken and written language.

3. Corpus

This research is based on two corpora of contemporary Italian. A written corpus made of articles from a daily newspaper published in Northern Italy (*La Stampa*, *Torino*, the articles are from 1997) and a selection of a spoken corpus called *LABLITA corpus*, which has been collected at the University of Firenze (Cresti & Moneglia 2005).[3]

The size of the corpora is over 58.000 words (the written corpus is over 26.000 words and the spoken corpus is over 32.000 words).

[3] The corpus is a very varied one. It includes conversations among friends, conversations in public places among strangers (offices, stores, markets, etcetera), different types of public discourses (in the court, at school, at the university), some texts are monologues.

I individuated a list of over 40 items that are the commonest conjunctions introducing subordinate clauses in Italian and then I counted how many tokens of each type recur in the two corpora. I found that 90% of the total amount of clauses is introduced only by 11 conjunctions out of 40 so I decided to analyse in detail these 11 cases.

The total list of conjunctions is as follows: *a condizione che, a patto che, a tal punto che, acciocché, affinché, anche se, appena, benché, come, comunque, così che, dove, eccetto che, finché, fuorché, giacché, laddove, malgrado che, mentre, nonostante, perché, poiché, purché, qualora, quando, quanto, quantunque, salvo che, se, sebbene, senza che, seppure, siccome, talmente che, tanto che, tranne che.*

See table 1 for the list and the number of occurrences of the 11 most used conjunctions:

Table 1. List of more common conjunctions

	written corpus	spoken corpus	
anche se	10	10	**20**
appena	7	4	**11**
come	69	120	**189**
comunque	4	21	**25**
dove	49	14	**63**
mentre	23	10	**33**
perché	36	139	**175**
quando	39	51	**90**
quanto	19	13	**32**
se	72	123	**195**
siccome	–	12	**12**
Total			**845**

The conjunctions belong to four main semantic areas: temporal (*appena, mentre, quando*), causal (*siccome, perché*), conditional (*se*), modal or comparative (*come, quanto, comunque*). I also considered concessive adverbial clauses introduced by the conjunction *anche se*.

Some of the conjunctions, for example *dove, perché, quando, come*, can also function as interrogative adverbs in direct (1) or indirect (3) questions or as relative adverbs (2)–(4):

(1) CAR: *Come* andò domenica a Milano? (spoken corpus)
'how did you do on Sunday in Milan?'

(2) Come, il 24 settembre 1864, *quando* seppero reagire alla perdita della propria Capitale, fra i morti della strage di piazza San Carlo (written corpus)
'It was like on September 24th 1864, when they knew how to react to the loss of their own capitol city even with so many dead in the massacre of Piazza San Carlo
(3) non sapendo *dove* lasciare il figlio durante le vacanze di Natale (written corpus)
'as he did not know where his son could spend Christmas Holidays'
(4) ecco *perché* il pubblico ministero parte da una ricerca (spoken corpus)
'that is why the pubblico ministero starts with an investigation'

When behaving like relative or interrogative adverbs they have been excluded because their position is a fixed one and there is no possibility of alternative positions.[4] I excluded from the analysis *that*-complement clauses (even if they are the commonest type of subordinate clauses) for the same reason. In fact, they have a fixed position after the main clause (they very rarely precede their main clause, and preferably when they are Subject clauses like in (5)):[5]

(5) [che tu sia stato promosso]$_{Sub}$ / [mi fa molto piacere]$_{Main}$
'[That you have been promoted] is a pleasure for me'

And finally I excluded *if*-complement clauses, to say indirect interrogative clauses that are commonly ordered after the main clause containing a verb of 'asking'.

(6) Non so se te ne ricordi (spoken corpus)
'I do not know if you remember it'

---

[4] We also excluded the use of conjunctions when they work in the discourse without any syntactic function as subordinate particles. This is the case of *comunque* in cases like 'Con me presidente, *comunque*, Bagni non ci sarà' 'If I am the president, *anyway*, Bagni will not be in the team' or *perché* used as an explicative element in cases like: '*perché* se io sto interpretando un film, un personaggio io realmente devo essere quell personaggio' 'because if I am playing in a movie as a character, I really have to become that character', where the clause is a conditional one introduced by *se* 'if' while *perché* is synonymous of *in fact*.

[5] Complement clauses can also precede the main clause in Italian: *Che Gianni arrivi in orario è tutto da vedere;* 'that Gianni will arrive in time is not sure'; *che tu possa partire domani non lo credo proprio* 'that you can leave tomorrow I do not believe at all'. But the initial position seems really very rare or even impossible to be found in spoken language. Miller & Weinert 1998 notice that in spoken English complement clauses can occur as object clauses but less frequently as subject clauses and rarely precede the main clause.

The reason for all these exclusions is the objective of the research: to analyse the ordering of subordinate clauses in relationship to the main clause, we have to consider cases where both positions, before or after the main clause, are possible. Thus only adverbial clauses have been the object of this analysis.

4. Data

The 845 occurrences of the 11 conjunctions listed in Table 1 have been analysed and above half of them have been excluded as they represent cases of relative and interrogative adverbs or cases of discourse markers (like the examples of *comunque* or *perché* seen in the footnote 4).

The remaining 400 cases have been analysed in detail. Some 90 cases have been again excluded because they are instances of 'interrupted' clauses. Under this definition we put both cases of interrupted clauses that are not analysable (*MAU: ecco dunque se*, end of the turn of speaker MAU), and special cases of interrupted clauses that typically occur in spoken language. In this last case the adverbial clause is complete, but the sentence includes only it and there is no main clause to which the subordinate clause refers. In Italian, this phenomenon has been widely considered for conditional clauses (see Lombardi Vallauri, 2004a, 2004b, 2005), but I found some cases for other types of adverbial clauses. See (7), where the conditional clause occupies the whole turn of the speaker MDR:

(7) MDR: *se* una volta al giorno fossero puliti e lavati (spoken corpus)
'if they were cleaned and washed once a day'

Finally the last group of 24 clauses has been excluded because the clauses are embedded in the main clause, so their position is neither initial nor final. This is the case of parenthetical clauses introduced by *come* 'as, like', and some few cases of *se* 'if', *quando* 'when'. See examples in (8)–(11):

(8) Il problema infatti, *come* spiega Fabio Evangelisti (pds), (written corpus)
'In fact, the problem, *as* Fabio Evangelisti is explaining,'

(9) anche se *come* dicevo sono delitti fortemente e ragionevolmente territorializzati (spoken corpus)
'even if *as* I was saying they are crimes strongly and reasonably tied to some specific territories'

(10) il pentito aveva detto di avere visto nel suo ufficio, *quando* l'onorevole era pubblico ministero a Savona, un sacchettino con della cocaina (written corpus)

'the (person who) repented told that *when* the 'onorevole' was working as a judge in Savona, he saw a small bag with some cocaine in the office of the judge'

(11) Stamane Karembeu dovrebbe allenarsi per l'ultima volta con la Samp. "Venerdì poi, *se* il mio procuratore confermerà di avere trovato l'accordo con il presidente Sanz, raggiungerò il Real Madrid
'This morning -Karembeu should train for the last time with the Samp football team. "On Friday, if my lawyer confirms that he signed an agreement with president Sanz I will join the Real Madrid'

Table 2 summarises the ordering distribution of adverbial and main clauses for the resulting amount of 303 adverbial clauses. Data from spoken and written corpus are given separately.

Table 2. The ordering distribution of adverbial and main clauses

		Main + Adverbial	Adverbial + Main
anche se	written corpus	4	0
	spoken corpus	4	4
appena	written corpus	2	0
	spoken corpus	1	2
come	written corpus	12	0
	spoken corpus	14	4
comunque	written corpus	0	0
	spoken corpus	0	1
dove	written corpus	0	0
	spoken corpus	0	0
mentre	written corpus	10	1
	spoken corpus	2	2
perché	written corpus	27	0
	spoken corpus	62	2
quando	written corpus	8	13
	spoken corpus	10	27
quanto	written corpus	4	0
	spoken corpus	3	0
se	written corpus	11	17
	spoken corpus	9	46
siccome	spoken corpus	0	1
Total		183 60%	120 40%

The preferential ordering registered in the remaining 303 adverbial clauses is Main clause + subordinate clause in 60% of cases and the opposite ordering in the remaining 40%.[6]

If we consider separately spoken and written language we observe that the preferential ordering is chosen in the 71.5% of cases in the written corpus and in 54.1% of cases in spoken corpus. Even if the final adverbial clause is the commonest position in both corpora, the data deserves more comments as we would expect the spoken language to show highest percentages of the preferential ordering.

The preferential ordering (main + adverbial clause), apart from the general typological considerations that have been proposed in §2, is consistent with Hawkins's predictions deriving from his *performance theory of order and constituency* (Hawkins 1990, 1992, 1994, 1998, 2000). According to Hawkins

> Grammars have conventionalized syntactic structures in proportion to their degree of preference in performance, as evidenced by patterns of selection in corpora and by ease of processing in psycholinguistic experiments (2003: 122 and 2004: 3).[7]

Efficient processing of dependency relationships in Hawkins's model predicts, on the basis of two main principles (minimize domains and maximize on-line processing), that a dependent element clearly marked by a syntactic particle at the beginning will be better and easier processed if it is put to the right of the element that assigns the dependency relationship to it. So the Main + Adverbial clause ordering fits with this prediction better and more efficiently. In fact, it allows the parser to faster and easier recognize the two constituents (the main clause and the adverbial clause). As soon as the parser ends the processing of the main clause and reaches the adverbial subordinator she/he can close the processing of the first constituent and start the processing of the second one. In the opposite ordering, the parser starts the processing by knowing in advance that there is a complex sentence (in fact the sentence starts with a subordinate conjunction) but as this is a dependent constituent he has to keep it in the short term memory until the parser has recognized the main clause. So the processing takes longer and is harder for the short term memory. According to this model

---

[6] Diessel's (2005) research on English data presents very similar results. Adverbial clauses occur in final position in all types of corpus: conversations (67.9%), fiction (62.4%) and in written texts (56.3%). Initial adverbial clauses are usually shorter than the main clauses on which they depend, whereas final adverbial clauses are usually longer than their main clauses (see Figure 2 in Diessel 2005: 453).

[7] This is what Hawkins calls the *Performance-Grammar Correspondence Hypothesis*, which is the main core of his theoretical proposal.

and simplifying it a little, shorter elements come before longer elements because the shorter a constituent is the quickest a parser can reach the borders of the subsequent constituent and recognize it (in Hawkins model this is the Early Immediate Constituents (EIC) principle, predicting that structures with a short recognition domain carry a lower processing load than longer structures).[8]

In complex sentences the EIC works as shown in (12)–(13). If the adverbial clause precedes the main clause (12) the parser will be able to start the processing of the second expected constituent only after that she/he has processed all the words of the adverbial clause plus the first word of the second one (*Mary*), the Subject of the main clause. So it takes 5 words before the parser reaches the starting of a second Immediate Constituent. In the opposite ordering (13) it takes only one word to pass from the first constituent to the second one:

(12) [When Peter came home] [Mary was working in the garden]
2 IC : 5 words (When Peter came home Mary) = 0.4
(13) [Mary was working in the garden] [When Peter came home]
2 IC : 1 word (when) = 1

As already observed, the prediction of the model regarding the preferred ordering main + adverbial clause is satisfied in our corpus. But in over 40% of cases the prediction is not satisfied and there are some other criteria that can be considered. One of them, as it is also clear on the basis of the EIC principle, is the length of the adverbial clause. The model predicts that an adverbial clause which precedes the main clause should be shorter than its main clause.

The length of each clause for each ordering has been measured and 6 possibilities have been considered (see Figure 1). The first and the fourth columns in Figure 1 refer to cases where the two clauses, main and adverbial, differ in less than 3 words in length. In the other four cases the main clause or the adverbial clause is longer than the other clause for more than 3 words.[9]

[8] Diessel (2005) on the basis of Wasow (1997a, 1997b) observes that Hawkins's 'processing theory accounts for constituent order primarily from the hearer's perspective' (2005: 458). But even taking into account the speaker's perspective the prediction does not change. In fact, if it is true that 'speakers tend to arrange constituents in orders that do not require an early commitment to a specific syntactic structure, which will involve an extensive amount of utterance planning' (2005: 458), the planning of utterances will be one clause at a time. Starting a complex sentence with an adverbial clause means that the speaker is planning at least two clauses (adverbial + main clause). This explains why an opposite ordering does not commit the speaker to a complex sentence or to be involved in planning it from the beginning. In sum, both from the speaker's and the hearer's point of view the final position is the best one for adverbial clauses.

[9] The idea of considering more than 3 words as a cut off point for considering one clause longer than the other is found in Diessel (2005) too.

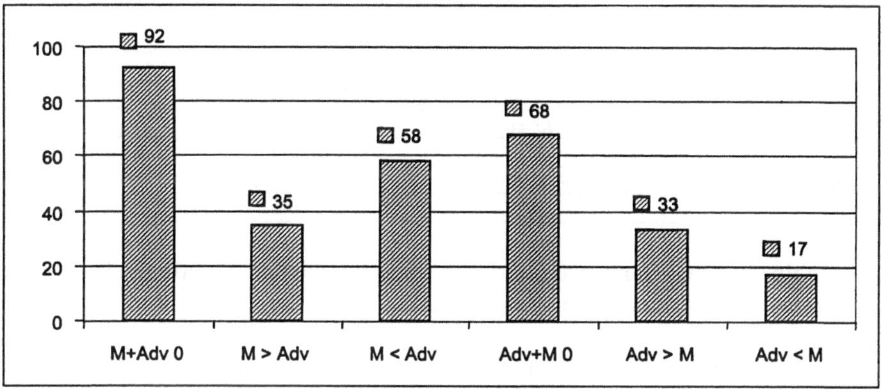

Fig. 1. Relative lenght of initial and final adverbial clauses

Figure 1 suggests that the ordering with the adverbial clause following the main clause is preferred when the two clauses have the same length (92 cases, 30% of the total). But under the same conditions (two clauses with similar length), the opposite ordering is also favoured (68 cases, 22.4% of the total).

When the length of the two clauses is not equal, there is a preference for the adverbial clause to follow the main clause independently of the relative length of the two clauses. The 58 cases (19.1%) of final adverbial clauses longer than the main clause and the 35 cases (11.5%) of final adverbial clauses shorter than the main clause are the third and fourth highest values in our data.

The prediction that the longest element tends to occupy the final position independently of its syntactic value is satisfied by our data, even if with a slight difference in percentage. In fact, if we add up the third and the sixth column where the longest element comes after the shortest one, we reach the average of 24.7%, while the sum of the second and the fifth column (where the longest element precedes the shortest one) gives 22.3%.

It is relevant to highlight that the lowest percentage in Figure 1 corresponds to the 17 cases (5.6%) in column 6 where a longer main clause follows a shorter adverbial clause (and this is in contradiction with Diessel's data according to which an initial adverbial clause is shorter than the main clause in 52.1% of the total).

The quantitative analysis has to be integrated by a semantic analysis. We consider the 4 semantic types of adverbial clauses represented in our data in Table 3.

Table 3. The ordering distribution of adverbial clauses according to the semantic type

	Main / Adverbial		Adverbial / Main	
causal (*siccome, perchè*)	89	97%	3	3%
modal and comparative (*come, quanto, comunque*)	33	87%	5	13%
conditional (*se*)	20	24%	63	76%
temporal (*appena, mentre, quando*)	33	42%	45	58%
total	175		116	

Table 3 shows how differences in the ordering of adverbial clauses are related to the semantic value of the clause and to differences within a semantic type.

Causal clauses in our corpus follow the main clause in all cases, are almost exclusively introduced by *perché* and integrate the main clause event with a sort of explanation more than a cause. We did not find other causal conjunctions such as *dato che, poiché, dal momento che* (corresponding to English *as, since*) which are typically found in scientific texts and introduce a cause which determines the effect described in the main clause. A few examples from the corpus are given below:

(14) Io non guardo quasi mai la tv *perché* ho perso l'abitudine, (written corpus)
'I do not watch the TV because I got out of the habit'

(15) questa qui è morbida // *perché* viene girata con questo filetto (spoken corpus)
'this stuff is soft because it has been turned with a special instrument'

The preference for *because* clauses to occupy the final position has been found for English too. Hawkins (p. c.), who is collecting data on adverbial clauses in English and American English, observes that *because* clauses follow main clauses with an average of 93% (while *as* and *since* clauses often precede it). *Because* in English is favoured with backgrounded causes, as opposed to *as* and *since* where the cause is more central to the proposition in the main clause.

Modal and comparative clauses more frequently occur after their main clause. The few cases of a modal clause preceding the main clause have been found in the spoken corpus. See an example in (16):

(16) *come* tutti sanno / *come* tutti ricordano venti giorni fa in questa città si è celebrato si è solennizzato il trentesimo anniversario dell' alluvione // (spoken corpus)
'as everybody knows, as everybody remembers / 20 days ago in this town we celebrated the 30th year since the flood'

Pragmatic and rhetoric reasons in (16) justify the position of the modal clause before the main clause. The modal clause has the effect of focusing on the main clause and persuading the listener that what is mentioned in the main clause is well known to everybody. So in this case the modal clause precedes the main clause. When modal clauses follow the main clause, they often have a parenthetical value as in (17):

(17) ecco se questa è una premessa esatta *come* siamo convinti (spoken corpus)
'if this is a right premise as we believe'

Conditional clauses more commonly precede their main clause for semantic reasons again. This result is confirmed by English data, too. The *if* clause often introduces a precondition relative to which the main clause is true. In (18) the precondition is presented first. In this way the main clause can be fully interpreted in real time with the precondition accessible at the time of main clause processing:

(18) *se* all' otto 'un è tornato / s' avverte i carabinieri (spoken corpus)
'if at 8 o'clock he is not back home we can inform the police'

The preference for the initial position of conditional clauses in our data is independent of weight factors. In (19) a very long conditional clause easily precede its main clause:

(19) [e *se* poi nella lettura c' è qualcosa di oscuro o di / poco chiaro / o o di / ambiguo / o che si presti a interpretazioni diverse] [si chiede chiarimenti] (spoken corpus)
'and if in reading there is something oscure not very plain or ambiguous or can be interpreted in different manners] [we ask for clarifications]

Temporal clauses can either follow or precede main clauses. This is partially related to the conjunction and the specific semantic value of it. *Appena*, 'as soon as' which introduces some temporal circumstance that precedes the temporal collocation of the event in the main clause commonly precede the main clause. *Mentre* 'while' preferably follows the main clause and express a temporal frame in which some main event is co-located or a temporal circumstance that co-occurs with the event in the main clause. *Quando* in our data can occupy both positions, but preferably introduces an initial adverbial clause. Compare the different values of the following temporal clauses:

(20) [*appena* so qualcosa] [ti chiamo / però] (spoken corpus)
'*as soon as* I know something / I call you'
(21) [Tutto accade] [*mentre* la bimba di 4 anni dorme] (written corpus)
'Everything happens *while* the 4 years old baby is sleeping'
(22) *Quando* avremo il quadro decideremo. (written corpus)
'*When* we will have the picture we will decide'
(23) I giornalisti arrivano allo 8, *quando* tutto è finito. (written corpus)
'Reporters arrive at 8 o'clock *when* everything has come to an end'

Comparing our data with Diessel's and Hawkins' data we can notice how the distribution of initial to final subordinate clauses in languages with clause-initial subordinators follows the performance preferences of English almost exactly:

(24) INITIAL Adverbial clause : Conditionals
FINAL Adverbial clause: Causals (generally)
BOTH: Temporals

5. Conclusion

The idea of multiple motivations for the ordering of adverbial and main clauses, which has been suggested by Diessel, Wasow and Hawkins, receives confirmation in our data. Furthermore, our data support the general hypothesis about the ordering of linguistic elements that we discussed in paragraph 2.

Like SVO languages with clause-initial subordinators, Italian can allow adverbial clauses both to follow or precede the main clause. The final position seems the preferred option in our data and weight effects seem not so relevant.

Semantic and pragmatic factors also seem influence the positioning of adverbial clauses. The ordering of clauses is strongly related to the semantic type of the adverbial clause and is highly iconic, with conditions preceding their consequences, causes following them, and temporal circumstances both following or preceding the main event on the basis of the specific temporal frame represented.

Contrary to our expectations, the data do not support the idea of strong differences between spoken and written language, that we would connect to different degrees of processing pressures. This result can be due to the fact that for the written language we only considered one type of texts (from newspapers). Further research on this topic will be necessary in order to better discuss this last point. Differences among written and spoken language that emerged in our discussion concern some other aspects of syntax, that are not focal here. For instance, the possibility of allowing 'interrupted' adverbial clauses which are clearly interpretable by the hearer even without an explicit main clause. For the moment we are not able to give any positive support to the claim that cognitive differences between spoken and written language have a direct impact on the ordering of adverbial clauses.

REFERENCES

Biber, D. (1988). *Variation across Speech and Writing*. Cambridge, Cambridge University Press.

Cresti, E. & M. Moneglia (eds.) (2005). C-Oral Rom. Integrated Reference Corpora for Spoken Romance Languages. Amsterdam / Philadelphia, Benjamins.

Diessel, H. (2001). "The ordering distribution of main and adverbial clauses: a typological study". *Language*, 77, 2: 433–455.

Diessel, H. (2005). "Competing motivations for the ordering of main and adverbial clauses". *Linguistics*, 43, 3: 449–470.

Frei, H. (1929). *La grammaire des fautes*. Paris-Geneve-Leipzig, Reprint Geneve, 1971.

Greenberg, J. (1963). "Some universals of grammar with particular reference to the order of meaningful elements". *Universals of Language*. Cambridge: MIT Press: 73–113.

Halliday, M. A. K. (1985). *Spoken and Written Language*. Oxford, Oxford University Press.

Hawkins, J. A. (1990). "A parsing theory of word order universals". *Linguistic Inquiry* 21: 223–261.

Hawkins, J. A. (1992). "Syntactic weight and information status in word order variation". *Linguistische Berichte* (special issue 4): 196–219.

Hawkins, J. A. (1994). *A Performance Theory of Order and Constituency*. Cambridge: Cambridge University Press.

Hawkins, J. A. (1998). "Some issues in a performance theory of word order". In: A. Siewierska (ed.). *Constituent Order in the Languages of Europe*. Berlin and New York: Mouton de Gruyter: 729–780.

Hawkins, J. A. (2000). "The relative order of prepositional phrases in English: going beyond mannerplace-time". *Language Variation and Change* 11: 231–266.

Hawkins, J. A. (2004). *Efficiency and Complexity in Grammars*. Oxford, Oxford University Press.

Lombardi Vallauri, E. (2004°). "Grammaticalization of syntactic incompleteness: free conditionals in Italian and other languages". *SKY Journal of Linguistics* (The Linguistic Association of Finland), 17: 189–215.

Lombardi Vallauri, E. (2004b)." 'Pragmaticizzazione' dell'incompletezza sintattica nell'italiano parlato: le ipotetiche sospese". In: F. Albano Leoni, F. Cutugno, M. Pettorino, R. Savy (eds.). *Il parlato italiano.* Atti del convegno nazionale di Napoli. Napoli, M. D'Auria Editore, 2004, B08 (CD-rom).

Lombardi Vallari, E. (2005). "Come era il parlato di lingue antiche: le ipotetiche libere". *SILTA*: 225–255.

Miller, J. & R. Weinert (1998). *Spontaneous Spoken Language. Syntax and Discourse.* Oxford, Clarendon Press.

Prideaux G. D. & W. J. Baker (1986). *Strategies and Structures. The processing of Relative Clauses.* Amsterdam-Philadelphia, Benjamins

Sornicola, R. (1981). *Sul parlato.* Bologna, Il Mulino.

Wasow, Th. (1997a). "Remarks on grammatical weight". *Language Variation and Change*, 9: 81–105.

Wasow, Th. (1997b). "End-weight from the speaker's perspective". *Journal of Psycholinguistic Research*, 26: 347–361.

Jerzy Gaszewski

University of Łódź

POLISH PARTICLES *TAK* AND *NIE* AS POLYSEMOUS WORDS: A CORPUS-DRIVEN STUDY

Abstract: The subject of the analysis is the polysemy of the Polish response particles: *tak* 'yes' and *nie* 'no'. As a theoretical basis the paper employs the concepts of radial categories and radial networks of meaning. The analyzed material is retrieved from the spoken conversational section of the PELCRA Reference Corpus of Polish.

The paper discusses the discernible functions of *tak* and *nie* in the corpus sample. The discussion opens with the most basic and most obvious function of answering a polar question. Then the author proceeds to responses to other speech acts, non-responsive functions (e.g. back-channel cue) and non-interactional functions (e.g. the rhetorical use of the particles to answer one's own question immediately after uttering it).

The concluding section discusses syntactic, pragmatic and semantic properties of the particles as used in the presented functions. The author proposes semantic links between the functions and presents a radial network of meanings that combines all the functions of the particles.

Keywords: corpus research, polysemy, Polish particles, radial categories, response particles, speech event.

1. Introduction

The present paper focuses on the Polish particles *tak* 'yes' and *nie* 'no', which are used as answers to polar questions[1] in the language. These two words are not limited to this usage, but have a number of discourse functions in spoken Polish. My goal here is to present the picture of this polysemy.[2] The distinction of the functions as well as their analysis is based on the data retrieved from the

[1] Throughout the paper I follow Pope (1976) and apply the term *polar question* to questions more commonly known as *yes-no questions*.

[2] That a word has different functions (i.e. is polyfunctional) does not automatically mean that it is polysemous. Yet, in case of *tak* and *nie*, the different functions cannot be reduced to one meaning.

PELCRA Reference Corpus of Polish developed at the University of Łódź. Unless mentioned otherwise, all examples in this paper are excerpts from the spoken-conversational subsection of the PELCRA corpus. The theoretical framework employed for the analysis of the polysemy of the particles is the concept of radial networks of meaning introduced by Lakoff (1987).

Particles *tak* and *nie* have not been studied extensively (cf. the remarks in Dobaczewski 1995: 151), especially taken together as an answering system (for single-particle studies see e.g. Dobaczewski 1995 or Bugajski 1981). Existing studies do note different functions of the two words, but not exhaustively. The only in-depth typological analysis of the problem I know of is included in Pope (1976). As for studies of polysemy, they mostly focus on major lexical classes. Among minor classes (grammatical words) only prepositions have received considerable attention (e.g. case study 2. in Lakoff 1987; Przybylska 2002). This produces a gap worth filling as many words of minor lexical classes are polysemous.

The major argument for using language corpora in this (and any) study is that they offer authentic language material. The linguist relies on the assembled data and not on invented sentences. Sorting, categorising and analysing corpus data allows one to observe linguistic facts that could otherwise be unnoticed. Thus, methodologically, this study was largely corpus-driven, i.e., there was no initial hypothesis to be checked against the corpus data (Lewandowska-Tomaszczyk 2005: 133). The observations and categorisations made in the paper are based on the interpretation of the retrieved language samples. The main focus is the variety of meanings of *tak* and *nie* in spoken language and not numerical properties of their distribution. Consequently, I make few statistical remarks referring only to striking observations. Still, there is statistical support for the analysis I present. Due to space limitations only few examples can be given, but they are representative of the data in the corpus.

The examples from the corpus are given in their original form, which does not always follow standard Polish orthography and, more conspicuously, ignores standard punctuation. A single full stop appears where there is a short pause in the utterance, double full stop renders a longer pause, question mark represents rising intonation.

The term *particle* (Pol. *partykuła*) is itself somewhat problematic. It has served in Western linguistics as a traditional, poorly defined umbrella term (EJO 1999: 423). Modern categorisations of Polish lexical classes have brought clear criteria and added new more specific categories. According to them *tak* and *nie* are labeled *dopowiedzenie*. A *dopowiedzenie* is an uninflected, syntactically independent lexeme that implies the existence of preceding discourse, typically a polar question (Laskowski 1984: 30; Grochowski 1986: 39–40). These distinctions are not followed by contemporary dictionaries of Polish, which choose to employ the traditional set of parts of speech. Some classify *tak* and *nie* as particles (USJP 2003 2: 894–6, 4: 11), some as interjections (Pol. *wykrzyknik*; ISJP 2000 1: 975–6, 2: 803), and some count *tak* as the former and *nie* as the latter (WSPP 2004: 609–10, 1162). In English terminology, the best equivalent of *dopowiedzenie* is *response particle*. The terms *minimal direct answer* (Pope 1976: 111) and *pro-sentence* (Schachter 1985: 32) have also been used. Yet, as we shall see, these terms do not fit all the functions of *tak* and *nie* described here. Therefore, I shall be content to call the two words particles, bearing in mind the reservations stated here.

2. Polysemy

Apart from providing answers to polar questions, the words *tak* and *nie* perform a number of other functions in Polish. This polysemy is the major point of interest in this paper. At this point, I must clarify what I intentionally omit here. Consider:

(1) `Boże wyobrażasz sobie tak jeździć teraz?`[3]
Oh God can you imagine driving like that now?

In this example *tak* means 'so; like that; in this way'. It is an adverb. Such use is syntactically and semantically very distant from the positive answer to a polar question. The two are too divergent to be discussed as functions of one word. Both the adverb and response particle do stem from the same etymological source (Boryś 2005: 625–6), but from a synchronic perspective they are homonyms (cf. Taylor 1995: 103). This distinction is kept in Grochowski 1986 and Dobaczewski 1995.

With *nie* the situation is similar:

(2) `ja to obiadu nie będę jadł Arek..`
I won't eat dinner, Arek

Again, there exists a homonym of the response particle – a preverbal negation. As with *tak* above, the syntactic discrepancy between the two makes them

---

[3] In the paper I follow the convention of marking corpus examples by a separate font (`Courier New`).

separate lexemes. Moreover, the two *nie*'s are not even identical etymologically (Bańkowski 2000: 292).

2.1. Radial networks of meaning – an approach to polysemy

The basis for the analysis of polysemy used here is the concept of radial networks of meaning. It was first proposed in Lakoff (1987) and used to analyse noun classes in Dyirbal, an aboriginal Queensland language which in its traditional form had confusingly heterogeneous noun classes. One of the major principles of the construction of radial networks is centrality. In each category some elements are central. The classes are expanded via semantic links between the central elements and the peripheral ones. This leads to chaining of elements: the central element 1 is linked to element 2, which is linked to element 3, etc. (Lakoff 1987: 95). Non-adjacent elements (e.g. 1 and 3) are not directly connected and need not share any properties (cf. Lakoff 1987: 96).

Lakoff applied this concept to grammatical categories, but it has also been used to explain the phenomenon of lexical polysemy (e.g. Dirven and Verspoor 1998: 32–37). Dirven and Verspoor postulated four cognitive processes which are the basis of the links. They are: metonymy, metaphor, generalisation and specialization (Dirven and Verspoor 1998: 33–35). These four processes were postulated with regard to the polysemy of words of major lexical classes and it remains to be seen how well they can describe the relations between the functions of *tak* and *nie*.

Let us summarise the cognitive approach to polysemy with this quote: "word senses are linked to one another in a systematic way through cognitive processes so that they show an internally structured set of links" (Dirven and Verspoor 1998: 32). It is my intention to establish such "sets of links" for the two analysed particles.

3. Responsive functions of *tak* and *nie*

In this paper I divide the functions of the particles *tak* and *nie* into responsive and non-responsive ones. I discuss each group in a separate section (3 and 4 respectively). It is then necessary to define what is a response and what is not. A key concept for the distinction is the notion of adjacency pair. As a discourse structure, an adjacency pair is a pair of utterances in which the first one requires the occurrence of the second one. For example, a question requires an answer, a greeting requires a greeting etc. By response I understand only such an utterance that closes an adjacency pair. Note that not every reaction in verbal communication is a response, but a response is necessarily a reaction.

3.1. Answers to questions

The question-answering function of *tak* and *nie* can be exemplified by the following excerpts from the corpus:

(3) `słuchaj czy ty głowę myłeś wczoraj?`
Listen, did you wash your hair yesterday?
`tak`
yes

(4) `ale macie ten IRTS?`
but have you got this IRTS?
`nie..`
no

In these interactions the two words function as answers to polar questions. Let us now consider what properties answers have. First of all, they are strictly interactional, that is they are directly related to the interpersonal communicative aspect of language. Furthermore, an answer is not a reaction appearing randomly in discourse, it constitutes a response to the preceding speech act, a question. The answer is, as it were, forced on the speaker by the question. We must also note that an answer has declarative modality. It presents the speaker's knowledge (or belief) about the state of affairs in the external world. When the particles *tak* and *nie* are used as answers, they recapitulate the semantic content of the preceding polar question (with or without negation) in a form of a statement. Thus, in (3) the particle renders the sense of *Myłem głowę*. 'I washed my hair' and in (4) that of *Nie mamy IRTS-u*. 'We don't have the IRTS'.

Then, if we consider semantic relations, the two particles are antonyms. We can supplant one for the other to obtain an opposite answer:

(5) słuchaj czy ty głowę myłeś wczoraj?
Listen, did you wash your hair yesterday?
nie
no

(6) ale macie ten IRTS?
but have you got this IRTS?
tak..
yes

Lastly, a characteristic grammatical property of the two words is their syntactic independence: they stand for whole sentences and function as full utterances on their own. This is what Schachter (1985) called a *pro-sentence* (cf. the concept of *dopowiedzenie*). The properties listed in this section characterise the particles *tak* and *nie* in the question-answering function.

3.2. Responses to other speech acts

Responses utilising the words *tak* and *nie* are not restricted to answers to questions. Both particles appear in other contexts as well:

(7) `chcesz dolać ci soku?`
Do you want [me to] pour you more juice?
`nie..`
no

(8) `to jak chcecie lodziku?`
So, do you want some ice?
`tak`
yes

In (7) and (8) *tak* and *nie* do appear after interrogative utterances, but these are not really questions in pragmatic sense. Sp1[4] is not interested in obtaining information, but rather makes an offer to sp2, which is a different speech act.

The next set of examples diverges even more from the question-answer adjacency pair. Consider:

(9) `nie przesadzaj.`
Don't exaggerate.
`tak oczywiście`
yes, of course

[4] When analysing the examples in the paper I refer to the speakers in the cited interactions as sp1 and sp2.

(10) `daj jeszcze jedną..`
give [me] another one
`nie..`
no

(9) and (10) contain an order and a request respectively and focus on desired actions of sp2.

Let us now move to the last set to be analysed in this section:

(11) `aleź Asiu przecież ty masz ich` (=adoratorów) `całe mnóstwo..`
but Asia you have plenty of them [= suitors]
`tak no niestety..`
yes, unfortunately

(12) `da ci spokój na jakiś czas..`
[he]'ll leave you alone for some time
`nie..`
no

These two exchanges feature statements to which sp2 reacts using a response particle.

As has been demonstrated, the words *tak* and *nie* appear as responses after various speech acts. Since each of the speech acts has different pragmatic properties, we can assume that responses to these speech acts differ accordingly. Consider the particle *tak* as a positive answer in (3) and as an acceptance of an order in (9). The former represents only the sp2's knowledge about the situation mentioned by sp1, whereas in the latter the particle means submission to sp1's will. Agreement with a statement as in (11) is still different. Here, the most important aspect is that the view on the discussed matter is shared by sp1 and sp2. Similar differences can be observed between the occurrences of *nie* in the above examples.

3.3. Establishing links between the functions

If we compare the functions from section 3.2 to the prototype of an answer to a question, we notice more similarities than differences. All the speech acts discussed so far introduce (or at least allow for) a polar choice (positive answer vs. negative answer, acceptance vs. rejection, etc.). Consequently, in all these functions the particles are antonymous. They are also interactional and grammatically independent.

A noteworthy fact is the relative rarity of occurrences of *tak* after orders, requests and offers and *nie* after orders and requests in comparison to answers to questions and reactions to statements. This could be explained by non-verbal communication in these contexts. Consider orders and requests: if they call for an immediate action, the action itself is a sufficient response. Offers also allow for an immediate acceptance by an action. Body language (e.g. nodding) may also be used. Other lexemes that normally serve as responses are also available: possibly *dziękuję* 'thank you' is more entrenched as a reaction to an offer than *tak*. Similarly, *dobrze* 'OK' may be a better response in the context of a request. Thus, answers to questions and reactions to statements seem to be of higher significance than the other functions.

If we consider semantic links between the functions discussed so far, we intuitively feel they are related. In fact, in spoken language it is difficult to delineate sharply what is a question and what is not (Boniecka 2000: 10). We can create a series of utterances (and responses) that gradually change from a prototypical question e.g. *Is Joe at home?* via biased questions like *Joe is at home, isn't he?* and qualified statements as *Joe is at home, I think.* to a prototypical statement *Joe is at home.* (Givón 1986 cited after Taylor 1995: 155). This series shows there is a semantic continuum between questions and statements. For the responses, this is a <u>continuum of contexts</u>. Since there is no clear boundary between one speech act and another, the use of the particles *tak* and *nie* as responses easily spreads over the whole continuum. One can also envisage similar continua linking an answer to a question to other speech acts (Givón 1986 cited after Taylor 1995: 155).

4. Non-responsive functions of *tak* and *nie*

4.1. Expression of disbelief

As we have seen above, the response particles *tak* and *nie* often appear as reactions to statements. Yet, we also find a number of examples of *tak* which are considerably different from what we have seen so far. Consider the following:

(13) `Elka dzwoniła i mówiła że jest taki etat w takiej szkółce przyjemnej dosyć. to z rok temu..`
Elka phoned and said there was a post in a fairly nice school. It was about a year ago.

`tak?`
really?
`no mówiła..`
yeah, she said so

Here sp2 reacts with a *tak*, but not to express agreement with sp1, as in (11). Rather, they express disbelief. This prompts sp1 to reaffirm the message. The effect of rendering disbelief is obtained by using interrogative intonation. The particle *tak* does not close an adjacency pair here, but itself needs a response. In (13) we can observe a sequence of utterances, forming a distinct discourse pattern: statement – expression of disbelief – reaffirmation. Such triads are common in the corpus:

(14) `Olechowski był drugi..`
Olechowski was second [in the election]
`tak?! to nie Krzaklewski?`
really? and not Krzaklewski?
`coś ty Krzaku to taka kompromitacja że to teraz krzyczą na niego żeby zrezygnował z przewodnictwa w Awuesie`
well, Krzaklewski['s performance] was such an embarrassment that they now want him to give up the [party] leadership of AWS

Still, we also find ones like the following:

(15) `mój ojciec ma znajomego lakiernika w Kaliszu wiesz?`
My father knows a car painter in Kalisz, you know?
`tak? ja mam chyba drugiego wujka lakiernika muszę się zapytać mamy..`
Really? I think I have an uncle [who is] a car painter, I must ask mum.

Here, sp2 is somewhat surprised to learn about an acquaintance painter, but does not find this surprising or important enough to require reaffirmation. The particle *tak* expresses some surprise, but the information is easily accepted by sp2, who continues to talk. If we compare (15) and (14), we note that the attitudes that can be expressed by *tak* in this function range from mild surprise to shock.

Let us now consider the relation of this new function to the ones distinguished earlier. A conspicuous difference is related to modality. Unlike in section 3, here the particle is not declarative. This is clearly visible in (13) and (14) where *tak* actually turns into a direct interrogative and requires an answer and forms a three-utterance pattern mentioned above. We even find exchanges where *tak* is answered by *tak*:

(16) `on się ze mną chciał kłócić o prawo karne..`
he wanted to argue about criminal law with me
`tak`**?**
really?
`tak`
yes

There are also essential similarities to be noted. The particle *tak* in responsive functions invokes the content of a whole sentence which is retrievable from the context. This happens here too: the phrase *tak?* in (14) is equivalent to *Olechowski był drugi?* 'Was Olechowski second?' much as the particle in (3) is equivalent to *Myłem głowę wczoraj* (see section 3.1). The expression of disbelief is pro-sentential like the previous functions. The major difference is the modality of this content.

The particle as expression of disbelief necessarily occurs after a statement. It thus shares its context with the function of reaction to statement. Semantically, the contrast is between the declarative and the interrogative, which are differentiated by intonation in speech. In fact, the interrogative character is what marks the function of expressing disbelief.

So far we have only dealt with *tak*. The particle *nie* is used as expression of disbelief after negative statements:

(17) `może pani zlecenia nie dałam do tego Rychlika..`
maybe I haven't given you the order for this Mr. Rychlik
`no to chyba nie..`
then I think you haven't
`nie? no to piszę`
I haven't? so I'll write [it now]

It would seem then that as expression of disbelief the particles are distributed complementarily, each questioning statements congruent in polarity. However, there are cases like the following:

(18) `on nie ma nic przeciwko jakoś..`
somehow he has nothing against [it]
`tak?`
really?

yhm..
mm

Here, *tak* invokes a negative sentence *On nie ma nic przeciwko?* 'Does he have nothing against it?'. We must then revise our conclusion: *tak* may appear after all statements as an expression of disbelief, and *nie* only after negative ones. The sense relation between the particles could then be described as meronymy.

4.2. Back-channel cues

Let us begin the analysis of the next function with the following example:

(19) Alusia jak Jutek zacznie patrzeć..
Alusia, when Jutek starts watching
tak..
yes
to jak zacznie latać po tych programach to ja i tak nic nie wiem i tak nic nie wiem..
when he starts switching from one channel to another, I don't know anything anyway.

Sp2's reaction here is a textbook example of a back-channel cue. The particle *tak* does not bring any semantic contribution to the interaction, but it marks sp2's attention to what sp1 is saying. Its role is only to maintain contact between the speakers, which is a manifestation of the phatic function of language. The exchange exhibits the pattern: topic introduction – phatic signal – continuation. Sp2's reaction, placed where it is in (19), shows interest in the topic.

It is interesting to note that such precise placement of back-channel cues is not always possible. Consider:

(20) słuchaj. masz kubeczek. w kubeczku jest woda z sokiem..
Listen. You have a cup. In the cup there's water with juice
tak
yes
przykrywasz tym kubeczkiem drugi kubeczek gdzie się parzy kawa.
with this cup you cover the other cup where the coffee is brewing

and its alternative version:

(21) słuchaj. masz kubeczek.
Listen. You have a cup.
tak
yes
w kubeczku jest woda z sokiem.. przykrywasz tym kubeczkiem drugi kubeczek
In the cup there's water with juice. with this cup you cover the other cup
tak
yes
gdzie się parzy kawa.
where the coffee is brewing

Both are equally legitimate stretches of discourse. We could propose other manipulated versions of (20) altering the place and number of *tak*'s (within reasonable limits, of course) and the communicative result would be practically the same. Thus, the choice when to utter back-channel cues in (20) is largely an arbitrary decision of sp2.

Evidently, the back-channel cue in (19) is not placed as freely as in (20). Sp1 makes a longer pause, as if inviting sp2 to show attention and interest. However, the cue is not obligatory. The option of remaining silent seems readily available in (19), although less likely. This is in sharp contrast with exchanges involving questions, where failing to provide an answer is an evident breach of the conversational maxim of politeness (cf. Leech 1983).

Let us now compare this function to the previous ones. The first major difference is that the back-channel cue is phatic in character. Another characteristic is that its placement is not rigidly determined (as shown by (20) and (21)). This results from the fact that it is a reaction to the whole situation rather than to any particular element of what the interlocutor says (in the way an answer is a reaction to the question utterance).

We must also notice two facts. First, only *tak* appears in this function and *nie* is totally absent. Secondly, as in section 4.1, in this function the particle appears after a statement. These observations suggest how back-channel cues can be linked to other functions. Apparently, the phatic *tak* does bear a very weak value of agreement. Indeed, if a speaker shows attention and encourages continuation, they implicitly accept what has been said. The weakening agreement is the semantic link between the function of back-channelling and reaction to a statement. This also explains why only *tak* is used as a back-channel cue. Obviously, *nie* as a marker of disagreement could not follow this path. This line of reasoning is supported by the existence of exchanges like the following:

(22) `słuchaj pożyczyłaś mi bardzo fajną książkę do angielskiego..`
listen, you've lent me a very nice English book
`tak..`
yes
`którą też przeczytałam całą. tylko mi się rozkleiła na kawałki. więc kupiłam ci drugą..`
which I read whole, but it fell into pieces, so I bought you a new one

The structure of the exchange in (22) is strikingly similar to (19), we can observe the same tripartite discourse pattern. The particle is clearly a signal of attention which encourages sp1 to continue speaking. Yet, there is also a distinct secondary element of agreement to sp2's utterance. She is in a position to agree or disagree. (22) is a border case, combining both functions: back-channel cue and reaction to statement.

4.3. Reactions to summons

Let us again start with an excerpt from the corpus:

(23) `Kasia..`
Kasia
`tak?`
yes?
`to sobie zjedz..`
Eat this

Like in 4.2, *tak* is used here to mark attention. (23) is an opening of a conversation formed by an adjacency pair: summons – response to summons; *tak* is used as the latter. The summons triggering such use of *tak* might be verbal as above or non-verbal (e.g. a phone call or raising a hand). The next example comes from a phone conversion with my sister. While we were talking, my mother wanted to ask her about something, so I had to hang on for a short while. When my sister was able to speak to me again, the very first thing she said was:

(24) tak tak już jestem.
yes, I'm [back] already

Note that there was no formal summons, but the awareness of me waiting for her (implicit summons as it were) was enough to trigger such a re-opening.

This function is very close to that of back-channel cue. Both are phatic and both have only occurrences of *tak*. Yet, a major difference is that in (23) and (24) the particle plays a role in establishing contact, it does not just maintain it. Thus, the two functions differ primarily in the context in which the particle appears (the very start of an interaction vs. the middle). This difference accounts for the semantic link between the two. The contexts are different and so is the function of the particle. Back-channel cue only shows attention and understanding, making the communication easier. The response to summons is necessary for the subsequent interaction to take place at all.

Lastly, a reaction to summons is a response to a speech act and hence its placement in discourse is fixed and its appearance obligatory (though it need not be expressed by *tak* or any verbal form). This is much like an answer coming after a question and unlike a back-channel cue.

4.4. Shift of focus

Consider the following exchange:

(25) `dorobię jeszcze górę segmentu na duże książki..`
I'll add some upper shelves for big books
<u>`tak`</u> `i ona będzie te encyklopedie wsadzać na wysokość`
yes and she will be putting these encyclopedias so high

Here the utterances of sp1 and sp2 are not very closely connected. Sp2 uses *tak* not to express agreement, but to mark an utterance relating to a different aspect of the situation mentioned by sp1. In fact, the typically agreeing *tak* introduces a rather disagreeing statement here.

Similar examples utilising *nie* are easily found as well:

(26) `już się robi tak ciemno szaro brzydko. znaczy są takie miłe momenty ale. nie cierpię tego..`
It's getting so dark, grey, ugly. I mean there are nice moments but I hate it
<u>`nie`</u> `normalnie jak wychodzę z jakiegoś języka już ciemno to łzy w oczach od razu.`
no when I simply leave a language [course and] it's so dark [that I have] tears in my eyes at once.

Here, sp2 sticks to the topic (short daytime during the winter), but shifts the focus to his/her situation. The particles *tak* and *nie* in (25)–(26) introduce utterances which bring some new perspective to the discussed topic. In (25) the change was from merits to demerits of an idea, in (26) from the feelings of sp1 to those of sp2. Below we can observe a shift from a general description of a place to a request for information on a specific aspect:

(27) obecnie jest tak że. jest duży korytarz się wchodzi. z prawej strony od razu jest y. nie ubikacja później jest łazienka..
now it's like that: there's a big corridor [when] you enter, the first room on the right is umm no the toilet, and then the bathroom
tak ale chodzi mi o to czy to jest wycięte jakby z bryły korytarza czy to są oddzielne pomieszczenia?
yes but what I want to know is if this is sort of cut out of the space of the corridor or are they separate rooms on their own?

In the above examples the particles *tak* and *nie* function as discourse markers of shift of focus. They mark utterances that contribute a new perspective to the interaction. It must be stressed that this usually does not mean a change of topic.

In this function there is little, if any, difference in meaning between the particles. Consider:

(28) tak normalnie jak wychodzę z jakiegoś języka już ciemno to łzy w oczach od razu.

and

(29) nie ale chodzi mi o to czy to jest wycięte jakby z bryły korytarza czy to są oddzielne pomieszczenia?

These are acceptable reactions in (26) and (27). Reversing the particles does not cause a change of meaning. We must then view *tak* and *nie* in this function as (near) synonyms.

In order to anchor this function to others, we will resort to a strategy of finding border examples (cf. (22)). Consider:

(30) no jest przypakowany znaczy sprawny facet widać..
You can see the guy is brawny I mean fit

sprawny tak. i teraz no się cieszy bardzo bo wychowuje dziecko
fit, yes. and now he's very happy because he's bringing up a child

Here, *tak* clearly expresses agreement (about an acquaintance of the speakers' being fit), but sp2 immediately proceeds to talk about a rather distant aspect of the man's life (raising a child). Arguably, the use of *tak* is twofold: it is both an agreement and a shift of focus. In the whole context of (30) it seems that the agreement, though straightforward, is secondary. We can then assume that shift of focus may develop semantically from a weak agreement.

This explanation may work for *tak*, but it cannot account for the use of the particle *nie* in this function. First, this would be illogical. In (30) shift of focus naturally develops from a disinterested agreement. It is unlikely that disagreement could ever be as disinterested. Second, such an idea seems counterfactual: in (26) *nie* has no trace of disagreement and we must propose a different link for *nie*. The shift of focus in the interaction as illustrated by (25–30) consists in distancing the preceding discourse. The marker of the shift 'cuts off' the interlocutors from the previous perspective (or topic) and introduces new content. This is how we can link the use of *nie* as a marker of shift of focus to its prototypically negative use. Negativity is conceptualised by a couple of schemas, one of which can be called *disjoining* (as opposed to *conjoining* which is positive; Lewandowska-Tomaszczyk 1996: 34). Thus, a sense of disjunction or disconnection underlies negation and surfaces in the particle *nie* when it marks a shift of focus.

4.5. Tag questions

Note the two occurrences of *nie* in the following example:

(31) jakbyś miał dobry to mogliby ci umorzyć trochę pożyczki nie?
if you had good [results] they could cancel some of your loan, couldn't they?
nie
no

They are pronouncedly different. The latter is a typical instance of answer to question, while the former is a part of the question itself.

Let us consider further examples:

(32) `ten ten bardzo charakterystyczny bazyliszek skandynawski w tympanonie..`
this characteristic Scandinavian basilisk in the tympanum
`no właśnie. znaczy ta poczwara to jest bazyliszek tak?`
exactly. so this monster is a basilisk, isn't it?
`tak`
yes

(33) `to jest kraj generalnie górzysty nie?`
it is mostly a mountainous country, isn't it?
`tak..`
yes

(34) `to jakby definitywnie już postanowiłaś że odchodzisz tak?`
so you've finally decided to quit [the job], haven't you?
`nie..`
no

In (32–34) we can observe the interplay of two different functions of response particles. Both *tak* and *nie* may be appended to a question.

Let us consider the character of the new function. Essentially, all the above examples contain biased questions. This is directly related to the presence of *tak* and *nie*. Let us analyse the composition of (33):

(35)

Table 1

	to jest kraj generalnie górzysty	nie?
structure	clause [Subj Cop Subj Compl]	particle
semantics	proposition	biased interrogative
intonation	typical of declarative but unfinished	rising

Compare (35) to a neutral question:

(36)

Table 2

	czy	to jest kraj generalnie górzysty?
structure	particle	clause [Subj Cop Subj Compl]
semantics	plain interrogative	propositional content
intonation	rising	

What we can infer is that the particles *tak* and *nie* function as constituent elements of questions. Unlike *czy* 'whether' they appear sentence-finally rather than initially. They also create a semantically distinct type of question, a clearly biased one. *Tak* and *nie* in (31–34) are equivalents of English tag questions.[5]

In a sense, the function of tag questions is the antithesis of the question-answering function. The former is used to ask a question, the latter to answer it. From the point of view of syntax, the former belongs to the grammatical structure of the sentence, whereas the latter is a free pro-sentence. Consider also the sense relation between the particles. Compare the following altered versions of (31) and (34):

(37) jakbyś miał dobry to mogliby ci umorzyć trochę pożyczki <u>tak</u>?
(38) to jakby definitywnie już postanowiłaś że odchodzisz <u>nie</u>?

Swapping the particles does not change the meaning. The meaning of the biased questions stays the same. Both particles are used to form biased questions. Thus, the particles as tag questions seem to be synonymous, while as answers to questions, *tak* and *nie* are a paradigm example of antonymy.

Yet, if we try to change the particle in (32), the result is unacceptable:

(39) ten ten bardzo charakterystyczny bazyliszek skandynawski w tympanonie..
znaczy ta poczwara to jest bazyliszek * <u>nie</u>?
tak

This exchange shows that the synonymy of *tak* and *nie* in tag questions is not absolute. In (32) sp2 asks the question about something they sincerely have no knowledge of. The question is biased only because of sp1's earlier utterance. This is a consultative question and as such cannot be accompanied by *nie?*, which appears to imply the speaker's own knowledge behind the bias. Compare also (34) and (38). In the original (with *tak?*) the speaker seems to be less sure than in the altered version (with *nie*). We must then conclude that as a tag question *nie* forms a stronger bias than *tak*.

We shall now seek semantic links that account for the use of *tak* and *nie* as tag questions. This function and the question-answering one are to some extent antithetical. Surprisingly enough, answer to question seems to be the source from which we can derive the function of question tag. So far, I have focused on the discrepancies between the two functions. Yet, we must also note the obvious

[5] Of course, they are not the only words that can be used for creating biased questions; consider for example *prawda* 'truth' used in this way.

closeness of the two functions in (31–34, 37–39) or, to be more precise, their adjacency in discourse. The particle as a tag question seems to be a "clone" of the answer. I shall now propose a development of the tag from the answer. Consider a proto-question for (32):

(40) ta poczwara to jest bazyliszek?
is this monster a basilisk?
tak.
yes

This question may be neutral or biased, depending on intonation. If the latter is the case, sp1 may mark the bias syntactically as well. One of the ways of doing this is to utter the expected answer as an ancillary question:

(41) ta poczwara to jest bazyliszek? tak?
is this monster a basilisk? yes?
tak.
yes

The particle from the answer is thus imported to the preceding utterance. The adjacency in discourse enables the diametrical change of the particle's properties (most notably, declarative vs. interrogative) and the establishment of a new function. Questions like the one in (41) get compressed into a single syntactic structure.

Can we use the same route of development for the particle *nie* as a tag? Note that (31) ends with a *nie*, but the expected answer is positive. The particle's appearance is not anticipatory but pre-emptive in nature. Still, it is based on a possible (though disfavoured) answer. The use of the negative combined with the interrogative to suggest the positive is widespread. For example, in English a negative tag marks an expectation of a positive answer (and vice versa). Compare also the German tag *nicht (wahr)?* lit. 'not (true)' and the French one *n'est-ce pas* lit. 'isn't it', which are used to create biased questions.

4.6. Non-interactional applications of *tak* and *nie*

This section analyses a group of uses appearing in a similar context but not representing a single function. What they all have in common is that they are not directly related to the interactional aspect of language. They do not appear at turn-taking points (as the previous functions), but inside speakers' utterances.

4.6.1. Tag questions inside an utterance

Most of these functions have a small frequency in the corpus sample I analysed. The only exception is the function described in the present subsection. Let us start with the following example:

(42) `to wiesz to jest taki typowy kawał nie? jak się na przykład pytasz o godzinę i ktoś trzyma herbatkę tam ..`
you know, this is such a typical practical joke, isn't it? for example, when you ask about the time and someone is holding [a cup of] tea [in their hand]

In the excerpt we only have one speaker, who is talking for some time and includes a tag question in their utterance. This tag quite clearly does not create a true question, since the speaker continues to talk and does not expect an answer. It seems that by faking the form of the question the speaker tries to engage the listener's attention. Upon hearing an interrogative, people automatically focus on the formation of an answer. In this way, even if the speaker does not really want any answer they launch the process of its formation in the listener's mind. This keeps the listener attentive.

In a way, such use of question tags is the reversed version of the function of sustaining contact, where it is the listener who gives short phatic signals and assures the speaker of their attention. What is noteworthy, examples of *nie* in this function are surprisingly more frequent than those with *tak*.

4.6.2. Other functions

We shall now briefly describe the remaining functions. Consider the examples:

(43) `no nie no wczoraj w Abece to ja się na ten sklep obraziłam. ja tam. tak no. chyba przestanę chodzić.`
well you know, yesterday [I was] in ABC I'm angry with the shop I will, yes, I will stop going there

(44) `na szesnastą chyba nie na piętnastą trzydzieści..`
[I have classes] at four p.m., I think, no, at half past three

Here, the speakers comment on their own statements. In (43) by using *tak*, they reassert their bad feelings about a shop. In (44) by contrast, *nie* is used for self-correction.

Another function is exemplified by the following:

(45) `jest coś takiego że. jest jakieś stężenie tak tego? tak musi być stężenie we krwi. po prostu ten lek musi się wiesz wchłonąć`
There is something like... Is there some concentration of it? Yes, there has to be some blood concentration of it, simply the medicine has to be absorbed.

(46) `są jeszcze ogródki na Piotrkowskiej? chyba nie ja nie będę siedziała w ogródku na pewno..`
Are there still beer gardens in Piotrkowska Street? I don't think so, [anyway] I won't sit in a garden for sure.

In the above excerpts, the speakers ask questions and give answers themselves without any action on the part of the listener. This seems to combine the effect of mobilising attention and somewhat rhetorical way of speaking. When the speaker asks the question, it provokes more attention on the part of the listener. The answer produced at this point is thus emphasised.

The last function of the present group is presented by the following excerpts:

(47) `cerkiew katedralna jaka ta Łódź ładna.. pod wezwaniem świętego Aleksandra Newskiego. tak a zdjęcie jest robione z ostatniego piętra hotelu Centrum..`
The orthodox cathedral, how beautiful Łódź is, dedicated to Saint Alexander Nevsky yes, and the picture was taken from the top floor of the Centrum hotel

(48) `też cały czas tak mówiłam a potem dziewczynka była. nie ale ty musisz mieć chłopca..`
I kept saying this too and then it was a girl no but you must have a boy

Here, the speakers use the particles when they change the focus of their monologue. In (47) the shift is from the building in a photograph to the site where the picture was taken. In (48), the speaker talks about her predictions about the baby's sex during her previous pregnancy, then inserts the particle and shifts to the listener's present pregnancy.

The functions described in this section are simply applications of the interactional functions in the context within an utterance: (42) goes back to question tags, (43) and (44) to reactions to statements, (45) and (46) to the question-answering function, whereas (47) and (48) to the function of shift focus.

5. Conclusions

The examples in the paper show the wide range of the usage of the particles *tak* and *nie* in spoken Polish. Undeniably these two words are multifunctional and polysemous. The following table sums up relevant properties of the discussed functions.

(49)
Table 3

section no.	function	modality	syntactic character	discourse position	sense relation between the particles
3.1.	answer to a question	declarative	pro-sentence	response	antonymy
3.2.	reaction to an offer	declarative	pro-sentence	response	antonymy
3.2.	reaction to an order	declarative	pro-sentence	response	antonymy
3.2.	reaction to a statement	declarative	pro-sentence	response	antonymy
4.1.	expression of disbelief	interrogative	pro-sentence	reaction	meronymy
4.2.	back-channel cue	N/A	discourse marker	reaction	N/A
4.3.	reaction to summons	N/A	discourse marker	response	N/A
4.4.	shift of focus	N/A	discourse marker	reaction	synonymy
4.5.	tag question	interrogative	interrogative particle	cue for reaction	synonymy
4.6.1.	tag question inside an utterance	N/A	interrogative particle	inside utterance	synonymy
4.6.2.	reaction to one's own statement	declarative	pro-sentence	inside utterance	antonymy
4.6.2.	answer to one's own question	declarative	pro-sentence	inside utterance	antonymy
4.6.2.	shift of focus inside an utterance	N/A	discourse marker	inside utterance	synonymy

The functions discussed in section 3 are very close and share all of the relevant properties. By contrast, the functions in section 4 are a more heterogeneous group. In the radial network of meanings the former set will constitute the core of the network and the latter its peripheries.

While discussing particular functions, I proposed semantic links that join different functions to one another. Put together, they form a radial network shown in the following diagram.

(50)

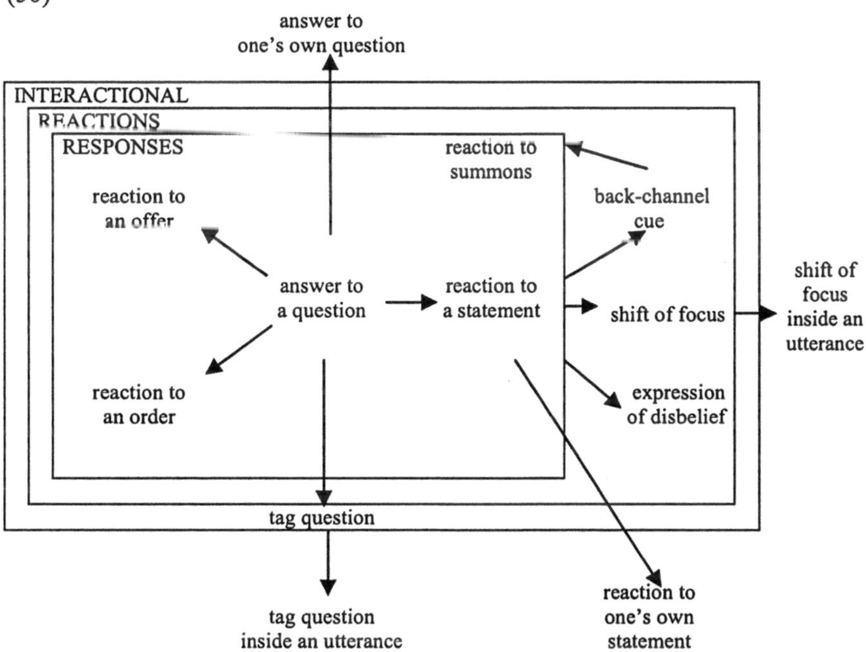

The central element is the answer to a question. It seems to be the most entrenched function – it comes first to mind when one thinks of the words *tak* and *nie*. It is also the most frequent in statistical terms. All other functions are derived from it, either directly or through chaining. I will now track the details of the development of the network. "Development" of the network and "derivation" of one function from the other refer to the cognitive links that join the different ways of using the particles and allow the speakers to perceive them as instances of the same word. This is thus an attempt at describing a small section of the organisation of language knowledge that constitutes language competence of native speakers of Polish.[6]

The functions from section 3 are linked by context continua (section 3.3). In all of them, *tak* expresses some particular aspect of a broad semantic concept of agreement, whereas *nie* an aspect of disagreement. The functions merge into one another. All of them are also responses in adjacency pairs. Using Dirven and Verspoor's (1998) term this is a case of generalisation. The forms used prototypically as responses to one speech act (question) are also used to respond to a broader set of speech acts. In these functions the particles represent the two options of a polar choice introduced by the preceding utterance.

The functions of expression of disbelief (section 4.1), back-channel cue (section 4.2), as well as shift of focus (section 4.3) can all be derived from the function of reaction to statement. They all appear after statements, that is, they share the discourse context with the source function and with one another. Hence, the semantic differences between these four functions depend solely on the changes within the utterances including the particles. This situation is different from the one with responsive functions, each of which exists in the context of a different adjacency pair.

The emergence of the function of expression of disbelief from the reaction to statement can be explained by a regular syntactic-semantic operation. The difference between the two boils down to a difference in sentential modality (see section 4.1). Thus, it can be seen as a difference on the level of the sentence, and not a new quality of the particle itself. As for the back-channel cue and shift of focus, these result from some kind of internal semantic development of the particles. None of the cognitive processes listed by Dirven and Verspoor (1998) (section 2.1) fits these three functions.

The function of response to summons (section 4.4) is notionally closest to the back-channel cue. Both are manifestations of the phatic function of language. They both have no propositional content and are restricted to the particle *tak*. The difference between them is the exact position in the interaction i.e. the context. It seems then that the link between the two can be described as an instance of generalisation.

As far as the function of tag question is concerned, it is to be derived from an answer to a question. The two appear in different positions within the same adjacency pair and the link between these functions relies on their adjacency in discourse. Thus, the same form is used for close elements that together constitute

[6] The links could also possibly reflect the historical development of the meanings of the particles. However, since the functions discussed here are typical of spoken language, it is practically impossible to verify such an assumption against historical data.

a larger whole. Within Dirven and Verspoor's framework this counts as metonymy.

Like most of the functions, the non-interactional ones (section 4.6.) are obtained by changing the context in which the particles *tak* and *nie* appear. However, it is a different kind of context change. It is neither just a different though analogously structured adjacency pair (responsive functions) nor the opposite position in the same adjacency pair (tag question). The difference of context consists here in putting typically interactional elements out of place (inside a single speaker's utterance). In this new context, the particles develop new tasks. For example, an answer to a question normally serves to provide information. If a speaker asks a question and answers it immediately in the same utterance, the particle's role is clearly different – it adds emphasis and engages the listener's attention. Again, this type of link is not accounted for well by Dirven and Verspoor's cognitive processes.

In conclusion, it seems that for the study of polysemy of words like the Polish particles *tak* and *nie*, the model of cognitive links proposed by Dirven and Verspoor (1998) is not sufficient. These words are closely related to the interaction between speakers. One of the major criteria that is relevant when describing how they are connected to one another is the difference of the context. In fact it seems crucial for the identification and description of the links between the functions.

It seems that apart from being words with a considerably developed polysemy, the particles *tak* and *nie* are also very well entrenched as a pair. This is nothing but obvious with responsive functions, where there are naturally two options of the choice, a positive and a negative one. However, it is not so with other functions. Still, only two of all the discussed functions are restricted to one of the two particles. It must also be borne in mind that even if the two words are a pair in many functions, they need not be a pair of antonyms. Throughout the paper we have seen a gallery of different sense relations that can be established between *tak* and *nie*.

REFERENCES

Bańkowski, A. (2000). *Etymologiczny słownik języka polskiego.* Vol. II. Warszawa: PWN.

Boniecka, B. (2000). *Struktura i funkcje pytań w języku polskim.* Lublin: UMCS Press.

Boryś, W. (2005). *Słownik etymologiczny języka polskiego.* Kraków: Wyd. Literackie.

Bugajski, M. (1981). „Niektóre funkcje składniowe morfemu *nie*". *Acta Universitatis Lodziensis. Folia Linguistica* 2: 17–29.

Dirven, R. and M. Verspoor (1998). *Cognitive Exploration of Language and Linguistics.* Amsterdam: John Benjamins.

Dixon, R. M. W. (1982). *Where Have All the Adjectives Gone?* Berlin: Walter de Gruyter.

Dobaczewski, A. (1995). „Cechy semantyczne leksemów dopowiedzeniowych *tak i owszem*". In: M. Grochowski (ed.). *Wyrażenia funkcyjne w systemie i tekście. Materiały konferencji naukowej (Toruń 21–23 X 1993).* Toruń: UMK Press: 151–158.

[EJO] (1999). *Encyklopedia językoznawstwa ogólnego.* K. Polański (ed.). Wrocław: Ossolineum.

Givón, T. (1986). „Prototypes: Between Plato and Wittgenstein". In: C. Craig (ed.). *Noun Classes and Categorization.* Amsterdam: John Benjamins: 77–102.

Grochowski, M. (1986). *Polskie partykuły. Składnia, semantyka, leksykografia.* Wrocław, Warszawa, Kraków, Gdańsk, Łódź: Ossolineum.

[ISJP] (2000): *Inny słownik języka polskiego.* Vol. 1–2. M. Bańko (ed.). Warszawa: PWN.

Lakoff, G. (1987). *Women, Fire, and Dangerous Things: What Categories Reveal about the Mind.* Chicago: CSLI.

Laskowski, R. (1984). „Podstawowe pojęcia morfologii". In: R. Grzegorczykowa, R. Laskowski, H. Wróbel (eds.). *Gramatyka współczesnego języka polskiego.* Vol. 2. *Morfologia.* Warszawa: PWN: 9–58.

Leech, G. (1983). *Principles of Pragmatics.* London: Longman

Lewandowska-Tomaszczyk, B. (1996). *Depth of Negation. A Cognitive Semantic Study.* Łódź: University of Łódź Press.

Lewandowska-Tomaszczyk, B. (ed.) (2005). *Podstawy językoznawstwa korpusowego.* Łódź : University of Łódź Press.

Pope, E. (1976). *Questions and Answers in English.* The Hague: Mouton.

Przybylska, R. (2002). *Polisemia przyimków polskich w świetle semantyki kognitywnej.* Kraków : Universitas.

Schachter, P. (1985). "Parts-of-speech systems". In: Shopen, T. (ed.). *Language typology and syntactic description.* Cambridge: Cambridge University Press. Vol. III. *Grammatical categories and the lexicon*: 3–61.

Taylor, J. R. (1995). *Linguistic Categorization. Prototypes in Linguistic Theory.* 2nd edition. Oxford: Clarendon.

[USJP] (2003). *Uniwersalny słownik języka polskiego.* Vol. 2, 4. St. Dubisz (ed.). Warszawa: PWN.

[WSPP] (2004). *Wielki słownik poprawnej polszczyzny.* A. Markowski (ed.). Warszawa: PWN.

Martine Delorge

Ghent University

A DIACHRONIC CORPUS STUDY OF THE CONSTRUCTIONAL BEHAVIOUR OF VERBS OF RECEPTION IN DUTCH

Abstract: Though modern cognitive research pays a lot of attention to the meaning of grammatical patterns and the interaction of verbal and constructional semantics, there is still a lack of detailed *diachronic* studies. In this paper, a contribution to filling up this gap is made by focussing on the developmental path, the shifts and evolutions in the grammatical possibilities of reception verbs. More specifically, the focus will be on the constructional evolution of four verbs of reception in Dutch: *verkrijgen* 'get', *ontvangen* 'receive', *verwerven* 'obtain' and *begeren* 'desire'. The synchronic constructional behaviour of these verbs will be compared with that of earlier linguistic stages of Dutch.

Keywords: argument structure constructions, corpus based, diachrony of constructions, Dutch, form/meaning-relationship, verbs of reception.

1. Introduction[1]

Until fairly recently, the view that the lexicon is the sole determining factor in the form/meaning-relationship dominated traditional linguistics. That is to say, the overall meaning of a sentence was taken to be projected from the lexical-semantic properties of the individual words. The surge of paradigms like Cognitive Grammar (Langacker 1987, 1991) and Construction Grammar

[1] This article is based on the presentation given at the 10th International Cognitive Linguistics Conference in Krakow (July 15th–20th 2007) entitled 'The constructional behaviour of verbs of reception in Dutch: a diachronic corpus study'. I would like to thank those who attended the presentation for their feedback. I would also like to thank Timothy Colleman and Bernard De Clerck for their valuable comments on earlier drafts of this paper.

(Goldberg 1995, Kay & Fillmore 1999) has led to the recognition of the grammatical construction as a meaningful element in its own right. Neither Cognitive Grammar nor Construction Grammar assume a rigid division between syntax and semantics. According to Langacker (1999), for instance, the interaction between the form of sentences and word groups and their meaning is the most crucial issue in contemporary linguistics.

This paper fits within these approaches and focuses on the constructional variation attested with Dutch verbs of reception, both synchronically and diachronically and examines possible differences in their constructions semantics.

2. Definition

Verbs of reception are a subtype of what Levin (1993: 138) calls *verbs of change of possession*. Like verbs of giving, they express the transfer of an object to a new possessor. The agent instigating this transfer is typically (but not necessarily) the original possessor. In a reception event, the following three semantic roles can be discerned: (i) recipient, (ii) theme and (iii) agent (and/or original possessor), as illustrated in (1):

(1) Zij (*recipient*) krijgt een cadeau (*theme*) van haar vriend (*agent/original possessor*).
'She (*recipient*) gets a gift (*theme*) from her friend (*agent/original possessor*)'

Both in international typological research as well as in more specific specialised literature on Dutch grammar, verbs of reception have received considerably less attention than verbs of giving, undoubtedly the most prototypical verbs of transfer of possession (see e.g. Newman 2005 for argumentation). Verbs of reception, however, constitute a challenging area of investigation as well, since they display interesting variation. They are, for instance, semantically trivalent, but syntactically they mostly occur with two participants only, which indicates that there seems to be an imbalance in the relationship between syntax and semantics. The next section gives an overview of the constructional variation found with verbs of reception in Dutch.

3. Constructional variation with verbs of reception: an overview

3.1. Synchronic variation

The most frequent syntactic pattern attested with Dutch verbs of reception is the simple monotransitive construction in which the recipient appears as the subject and the theme as the direct object, as in (2).

(2) Tijdens de voorbereidingen krijgt ze de laatste raadgevingen.
'During the preparations she gets the last pieces of advice'

The third participant, the agent of the profiled event, remains in the background and is often not expressed. If the original possessor is explicitly referred to, it is encoded as a prepositional phrase headed by the source preposition *van* 'from', as illustrated in (3).

(3) Hij verkreeg informatie van een Pakistaan.
'He received information from a Pakistani'

The double-object construction, which encodes both theme and recipient as nominal objects as in (4), is primarily associated with verbs of giving.

(4) Hij geeft haar een boek.
'He gives her a book'

Some verbs of dispossession can also appear in this construction, like in (5), in which theme and source are nominal objects (see Delorge & Colleman 2006).

(5) Hij ontneemt haar een boek.
'He takes away a book from her'

Verbs of dispossession are semantically related to verbs of reception: both denote a transfer of an entity out of somebody's sphere of control or possession. Despite this semantic similarity, these two groups of verbs do not always behave in the same way syntactically: unlike verbs of dispossession, verbs of reception do not occur in the double-object construction, as is shown by the ungrammaticality of (6).

(6) *Hij ontvangt haar een boek.
*'He receives her a book'

3.2. Diachronic variation

From a diachronic point of view, verbs of reception display some interesting variation. Firstly, in older phases of Dutch, the source of the reception event could also be encoded by another type of prepositional phrase. The citation database of the *Middle Dutch Dictionary* (MNW) shows that verbs of reception, such as *verkrijgen* 'get' and *ontvangen* 'receive' could occur with the original possessor in a PP headed by the 'contact' preposition *aan* (cognate of English *on*, German *an*), as exemplified in (7).[2]

(7) So vercreegh si aen onsen Heer, dat si met heme soud deelen de pine. (*Leven van Sinte Christina de Wonderbare*, 14th or 15th century)
'So she obtained from our Lord, that she would share the pain with him'

Example sentences like (7), however, do not occur in the WNT from the 18th century onwards.[3] This would mean that the construction disappeared at the latest in the course of the 17th century.

Secondly, unlike in present-day Dutch, verbs of reception could occur in a double-object construction in older phases of the language. In such constructions, the indirect object generally refers to the beneficiary of the transfer (rather than to the original possessor), as illustrated in (8).

(8) Maria keyserinne, vercrijcht mi ws kints minne. (*Marialegenden*, 14th century)
'Mary empress, obtain your child's love for me'

However, instances with the nominal indirect object referring to the source of the transfer cannot be entirely ruled out, as shown in (9).

(9) Dat hi der ioncfrouwen iet begherde. (*Lantsloot van der Haghedochte*, 14th century)
'That he desired something from the young woman'

[2] In the example the older spelling with *ae* is used (*aen* instead of *aan*).

[3] The WNT is the diachronic *Dictionary of the Dutch Language* which contains material dating from the 16th to 20th century.

To summarize, both the double-object construction and the construction with *aan* could be used with verbs of reception in older phases of Dutch, possibilities which have since largely disappeared from the language.

Section 4 presents a more detailed diachronic corpus study of a number of verbs of reception. Cognitive Grammar has provided us so far with many meaningful insights on the semantic structure of constructions. These constructions are, however, constantly in development. Our understanding of the relationship between verbs and the constructions they occur in will benefit from looking at these shifts and tendencies. This diachronic study fits in with the wider scope of research on the syntax-semantics interface with Dutch verbs of reception and dispossession in which I want to gain insight into the constructional behaviour and the developmental path of these verbs.

4. Case study: *verkrijgen, verwerven, ontvangen* and *begeren*

As a preliminary investigation, I looked into the use of four verbs of reception: *verkrijgen* 'get', *verwerven* 'obtain', *ontvangen* 'receive' and *begeren* 'desire'. Although *begeren* expresses a desire to get something rather than an act of actual getting, I nevertheless added it to the list, since there is definitely a connection with a reception event: the goal is to get something from an original possessor. It is of course not unlikely that this verb will behave somewhat differently syntactically due to its different semantics.

On the basis of the data from the dictionaries referred to above a number of questions can be raised, which are at the centre of this paper:

(i) When exactly did the *aan*-construction and the ditransitive fall out of use with these verbs of reception?

(ii) Which (semantic and/or other) explanations can be given for this reduction of the constructional possibilities?

(iii) Were changes restricted to the *aan*-construction and the ditransitive or did these verbs undergo other structural changes as well?

For the analysis of the verbs, the following corpora of different periods of Dutch were used:

- a 10 million words corpus of Middle Dutch, mainly consisting of literary texts taken from the CD-ROM version of the *Middle Dutch Dictionary* (13th–15th century)
- a 1.4 million words corpus of 16th century literary Dutch, consisting of texts archived from the Internet (mainly downloaded from the Digital Library for Dutch Literature <www.dbnl.org>)

- a 3.1 million words corpus of 17th century literary Dutch (<www.dbnl.org>)
- a 3.8 million words corpus of 18th century literary Dutch (<www.dbnl.org>)
- a 9 million words corpus of 19th century literary Dutch (<www.dbnl.org>)
- the *27 million Words Corpus* of the Institute for Dutch Lexicology (INL), which is entirely made up of material from the Dutch newspaper *NRC Handelsblad*, representing present-day Dutch

All forms of the four verbs were automatically retrieved from the corpora, using the WinConcord concordancer for the older corpora and the built-in search facilities for the INL corpus. The results were manually filtered and labelled according to syntactic construction. In the following subsections, I shall first present the corpus results for present-day Dutch and then take a closer look at the results for Middle Dutch. Finally, I will discuss the intervening periods. For reasons of clarity and cohesion, I purposefully deviate from a default chronological order.

4.1. Present-day Dutch

Table 1 below gives an overview of the different constructions these verbs have been attested in in present-day Dutch.

Table 1 shows that the four verbs mainly occur in the monotransitive construction with a single direct object. The original possessor is encoded as an (optional) *van*-PP. *Ontvangen* and *verwerven* can exceptionally appear with a PP headed by *bij* 'with' to refer explicitly to the source of the transfer, as in (10).

(10) Beiden reizen door Europa om steun te verwerven bij hun collega-regeringsleiders.
'Both travel through Europe to obtain support from their colleague government leaders'

This is not a specific characteristic of these two verbs: *bij* can be used with a wide range of verbs to introduce the source: e.g. *iets halen bij iemand* 'obtain something from someone', *iets vinden bij iemand* 'get something from someone', etc. The difference between *bij* and *van* seems to have something to do with possession: the relationship between the direct object and the prepositional object is less exclusive, less 'possessive' with *bij*; *van* expresses separation, removal (see Colleman 2006).

Table 1. Results from INL corpus

Verb	Construction[4]	Frequency
verkrijgen	NP__NP	508
	NP__NP van NP	23
	NP__NP voor NP	7
	other[5]	7
verwerven	NP__NP	1043
	NP__NP van NP (voor NP)	48
	NP__NP voor NP	34
	NP__NP bij NP	3
	NP__NP NP (van NP)	132
	NP__NP NP voor NP	1
	other	2
ontvangen	NP__NP	1811
	NP__NP van NP (voor NP)	413
	NP__NP voor NP	181
	NP__NP bij NP	1
	NP__datPfin	1
	other	45
begeren	NP__NP	86
	NP__NP van NP	1
	NP__tePinf	2
	other	3

It should be noted that the verb *verwerven* does occur in a double-object construction. These occurrences, however, are subjected to the following restriction: the indirect object is always a reflexive pronoun, see (11).

[4] The codes in the second column are based on the system for coding verbs patterns used in the *Contragram Dutch-French-English Verb Valency Dictionary* <www.contragram.ugent.be/cvvd.htm>. The horizontal bar represents the verb, the NP to the left of the bar represents the subject and the codes to the right of the bar the inner complements. NP__NP van NP, for instance, refers to a construction with a subject, a nominal object and a PP introduced by *van*. The codes 'datPfin' and 'tePinf' refer respectively to a subordinate clause introduced by *dat* 'that' and an infinitival clause introduced by *te* 'to'.

[5] The label 'other' refers to other constructions which are not relevant for the present discussion, such as the absolute use of the verb *ontvangen* in (i).

(i) Wij moeten geven, anders zullen we niet ontvangen.
'We must give, otherwise we will not receive'.

(11) House is een eigen cultuur geworden, een nieuwe vrijheid die jongeren zich proberen te verwerven.
'House has become a culture on its own, a new freedom that the young try to obtain for themselves'

Perhaps a more appropriate term for this structural possibility is therefore 'transitive-reflexive construction'. The reflexive pronoun combines two roles in one: agent and beneficiary (*not* source). The underlying reason for the verb *verwerven* to occur in the transitive-reflexive construction, may be explained in terms of the semantics of the verb. More so than the other verbs, *verwerven* entails a notion of effort in its meaning. This implies that the recipient-subject can also be the agent of the 'obtaining event' (the agent/recipient takes possession of a theme), which makes the verb more compatible with the semantics of the double-object construction (see footnote 8).

Going back to the structural possibilities, note that the beneficiary role can also be expressed as an oblique constituent in these verbs. In that case, the PP is headed by *voor* 'for', as in (12).

(12) Zij wilden meer kabinetszetels verkrijgen voor Tutsi-politici.
'They wanted to obtain more cabinet seats for Tutsi-politicians'

4.2. Middle Dutch

Table 2 summarizes the results of the Middle Dutch corpus query.

Similar to present-day Dutch, the monotransitive construction accounts for the majority of the occurrences. In Middle Dutch, the object of transfer may also appear as a subordinate clause, which can be either a finite complement clause (mostly a *that*-clause, exemplified in 13) or an infinitival clause.

(13) Eerste salmense versoecken, vanden ende visitieren ende verwerven dat men bi hem come. [Dirc van Delf, *Tafel van den kersten ghelove*, 15th century]
'First they will invite them, find and visit them and get them to come to him'

Table 2. Results from Middle Dutch corpus

Verb	Construction	Frequency
verkrijgen	NP_NP	649
	NP_NP(gen.)	6
	NP_NP van NP	49
	NP_NP aan NP	6
	NP_NP voor NP	2
	NP_NP bij NP	1
	NP_NP NP (van/aan NP)	16
	NP_datPfin (van/aan NP)	32
	NP_datPfin voor NP	1
	NP_(NP) tePinf (van NP)	3
	other	7
verwerven	NP_NP	164
	NP_NP(gen.)	6
	NP_NP van NP	19
	NP_NP aan NP	14
	NP_NP op NP	1
	NP_NP NP (van/aan NP)	23
	NP_(NP) (dat)Pfin (van/aan NP)	27
	NP_tePinf	1
	other	2
ontvangen	NP_NP	2176
	NP_NP(gen.)	18
	NP_(NP) van NP (voor NP)	461
	NP_(NP) aan NP	17
	NP_NP voor NP	11
	NP_NP op NP	3
	NP_NP NP	4
	NP_datPfin (van/op NP)	11
	NP_tePinf	2
	other	76
begeren	NP_NP	1487
	NP_NP(gen.)	144
	NP_NP van NP	90
	NP_NP aan NP	35
	NP_NP op NP	14
	NP_(NP) voor NP	7
	NP_NP NP	4
	NP_(NP) (dat)Pfin (van/aan/op NP)	294
	NP_(dat)Pfin voor NP	2
	NP_(NP) (te)Pinf (van/aan/op NP)	744
	NP_naar NP	3
	other	75

Though not visible from our data, this type of direct object can occur in present-day Dutch as well.[6] If *verwerven* and *verkrijgen* are followed by a sentential direct object, they get a resultative interpretation: 'to reach something, to get something done'. The subject is agentive and it is the causer of the resultative state.

Example (14) shows that the direct object in Middle Dutch could get a genitive case marking. The *-s* in *mins doits* is clearly a reflex of the genitive case, confirmation of which is found in Stoett's (1923: 108) Middle Dutch Syntax, where *begeren* is included in a list of verbs that govern the genitive. He further observes that the construction with a genitive object is rather rare (Stoett 1923: 113) which is borne out by the low number of occurrences in the Middle Dutch corpus. Note that genitive objects do not occur in present-day Dutch as it is not a case language any more.

(14) Mi is beter dat ic sterue dan ic so lange leuede dat ic mins doits begerde.
[*Nederrijns moraalboek*, 13th century]
'It is better for me to die than to live so long that I would desire my death'

As already indicated by the *Middle Dutch Dictionary*, the source of the transfer, the default *van*-PP, can also be realised as an *aan*-PP. Table 3 below, however, shows that the number of *aan*-PP's is rather low in comparison with the number of *van*-constituents. Only *verwerven* seems to be more compatible with *aan* than with *van*. In comparison with the other verbs, the percentage of *aan*-constructions with *verwerven* is extremely high. Possible explanations for this different behaviour will be given in section 5 below.

Table 3. Percentages of *aan*- and *van*-constructions

verb	aan		van	
	%	#	%	#
verwerven	10.5	27	8.2	21
verkrijgen	1.3	10	7.1	55
ontvangen	0.6	17	16.7	465
begeren	1.8	53	4.2	122

[6] Even though the INL-corpus did not yield any instances of *verkrijgen* followed by a that-clause, a quick search on the Internet produced several good examples, such as the one in (ii).
(ii) Zij hebben verkregen dat ook een "masters Erasmus Mundus"-project wordt gelanceerd. <www. europarl.europa.eu>
'They also obtained the launch of a "masters Erasmus Mundus"-project'.

Table 2 further shows that in Middle Dutch, there is yet another structural possibility to encode the original possessor: the source-object can also occur in a PP headed by *op* 'on', exemplified by (15).

(15) Ende wat gi op my begeert, dat sel ic doen. [*Old Testament in Northern Dutch translation*, 14th century]
'And what you desire from me, that I will do'

However, this type of construction is rather rare and almost exclusively occurs with *begeren*. In addition, *begeren* also differs from the other verbs in that it – unlike the other verbs – also allows a construction in which the theme is realised as a *naar* 'to'-PP. As a possible explanation for these extended structural possibilities, reference can be made to the semantics of the verb *begeren* which has a sense of direction (the act of 'desiring' is always *directed at* something or someone) and is therefore better compatible with a PP headed by a directional preposition.[7] In present-day Dutch, the *naar*-PP still occurs with e.g. the semantically related verb *verlangen* 'long'.

The other verbs of reception also entail direction/motion. While the direction with *begeren* is two-way (not only is the desire of the subject directed at the object, but the goal of the subject is also to *receive* the object: subject ↔ object), the direction of transfer with the other verbs of reception is only one-way: it starts from the object and is aimed at the subject, the subject receives the object (object → subject).

(16) Menich wacht ende begheert na dat hem niet en mach gheschien. [Jacob van Maerlant, *Historie van Troyen*, 13th century]
'Many wait for and desire what they cannot have'

Another important finding visible from Table 2 – and one which is different from the present-day Dutch data – is that the double-object construction occurs with all four verbs. The indirect object need not necessarily be a reflexive pronoun (like with *verwerven* in present-day Dutch), but can also appear as a 'full' NP. Most double-object constructions are actually benefactive constructions, like in (17): the indirect object refers to the beneficiary of the transfer.

---

[7] Unlike *naar*, *op* is not really a directional preposition. In older phases of Dutch, however, *op* could also express direction. According to the *Dictionary of the Dutch Language*, *op* can be equivalent to *naar* when it expresses direction, as in (iii).

(iii) Die vader ghinc mede op dat meer. [Dirc Potter, *Der minnen loep*, 15th century]
'The father came to the lake'.

(17) Ende an die ghebenedide moeder ende maget maria Want si is die ons die ewighe regnacie verwerven mach. [*Marialegenden*, 14th century]
'And to the blessed mother and virgin Mary because she is the one who can obtain eternal dominion for us'

There are some double-object examples, however, in which the nominal indirect object does not refer to the beneficiary, but to the source of the transfer. This is the case in (18), in which the 'giver' is marked by a genitive case ending:

(18) Ende beghert hulpe ende ghebed alre goeder menschen. [Jan van Ruusbroec, *Een spiegel der eeuwigher salicheit*, 14th century]
'And desire help and prayer from all the good people'

4.3. 16th and 17th century

Tables 4 and 5 below present an overview of the structural possibilities in the 16th and 17th century respectively.

The results of the 16th and 17th century corpus queries are similar to those of the Middle Dutch period. First of all, the monotransitive construction again occurs most frequently. Secondly, the direct object can also appear as a subordinate clause. Genitive objects still occur in the 16th century, but seem to have disappeared in the 17th century, which indicates that the use of cases in Dutch decreased during this period (i.e. the time of the standardization of the language, see Weijnen 1974 and van der Wal & Van Bree 1992).

Fourthly, as in Middle Dutch, *aan* appears next to *van* to introduce the original possessor, but it is again attested less frequently than *van* (on average, *aan* occurs 3.6 times less than *van*). The few occurrences of the source object in an *op*-PP are mainly found with *begeren* (similar to Middle Dutch). In a couple of instances, the original possessor is encoded by a PP headed by *bij*, as is also the case in Modern Dutch.

Finally, most double-object constructions are benefactive constructions. The prepositional 'counterpart' with *voor* occurs occasionally and less frequently than the double-object construction.

Table 4. Results from 16th century corpus

Verb	Construction	Frequency
verkrijgen	NP__NP	98
	NP__NP(gen.)	2
	NP__NP van NP	21
	NP__NP voor NP	2
	NP__NP bij NP	1
	NP__NP NP (aan NP)	13
	NP__(dat)Pfin	3
verwerven	NP__ NP	160
	NP__NP van NP	13
	NP__(NP) aan NP	5
	NP__NP NP (van/aan NP)	16
	NP__(NP) datPfin (aan NP)	6
	NP__NP tePinf	1
ontvangen	NP__NP	370
	NP__NP(gen.)	1
	NP__(NP) van NP	84
	NP__NP op NP	2
	NP__NP voor NP	2
	NP__NP aan NP	1
	NP__NP NP	2
	other	3
begeren	NP__NP	263
	NP__NP(gen.)	8
	NP__NP van NP	27
	NP__NP aan NP	22
	NP__NP op NP	5
	NP__NP voor NP	2
	NP__naar NP	1
	NP__(NP) (te)Pinf (van/aan/op NP)	143
	NP__(dat)Pfin (van/aan/op NP)	54
	other	3

Table 5. Results from 17th century corpus

Verb	Construction	Frequency
verkrijgen	NP__NP	146
	NP__NP van NP	22
	NP__NP voor NP	4
	NP__NP aan NP	2
	NP__NP bij NP	2
	NP__NP op NP	1
	NP__NP NP (bij NP)	6
	NP__(dat)Pfin (van/aan NP)	10
	NP__datPfin voor NP	1
	NP__tePinf van/aan NP	2
	other	1
verwerven	NP__NP	148
	NP__NP van NP	12
	NP__NP bij NP	8
	NP__NP voor NP (bij NP)	6
	NP__NP op NP	2
	NP__NP aan NP	1
	NP__NP NP (van/bij NP)	19
	NP__datPfin (van NP)	3
	NP__tePinf	1
	other	2
ontvangen	NP__NP	134
	NP__NP van NP	45
	NP__NP NP(gen.)	1
	other	10
begeren	NP__NP	199
	NP__NP van NP	36
	NP__NP aan NP	6
	NP__NP op NP	3
	NP__NP voor NP	3
	NP__NP bij NP	1
	NP__NP NP	1
	NP__(te)Pinf (van/aan NP)	106
	NP__(dat)Pfin (van/aan/op NP)	81
	other	1

4.4. 18th and 19th century

Tables 6 and 7 summarize the results of the 18th and 19th century corpus queries.

Table 6. Results from 18th century corpus

Verb	Construction	Frequency
verkrijgen	NP__NP	416
	NP__NP van NP (voor NP)	26
	NP__NP voor NP	6
	NP__NP op NP	3
	NP__NP bij NP	2
	NP__NP NP	13
	NP__datPfin (van/op NP)	4
	NP__(te)Pinf van/op NP	20
verwerven	NP__NP	84
	NP__NP van NP	10
	NP__NP voor NP (bij NP)	6
	NP__NP bij NP	2
	NP__NP NP	22
ontvangen	NP__NP	407
	NP__NP bij NP	2
	NP__(NP) van NP	127
	NP__NP voor NP	9
	other	25
begeren	NP__NP	148
	NP__NP van NP	11
	NP__NP op NP	1
	NP__NP voor NP	1
	NP__naar NP	1
	NP__(dat)Pfin (van NP)	30
	NP__tePinf (van NP)	64
	other	2

Table 7. Results from 19th century corpus

Verb	Construction	Frequency
verkrijgen	NP__NP	468
	NP__NP van NP (voor NP)	56
	NP__NP op NP	13
	NP__NP voor NP	12
	NP__NP bij NP	4
	NP__NP NP (op NP)	5
	NP__(dat)Pfin (van NP)	31
	NP__datPfin voor NP	1
	NP__tePinf van/op NP	17
	other	7
verwerven	NP__NP	193
	NP__NP van NP	27
	NP__NP voor NP	11
	NP__NP bij NP	5
	NP__NP op NP	1
	NP__NP NP (van/bij NP)	88
	NP__Pfin	1
ontvangen	NP__NP	1286
	NP__NP van NP (voor NP)	370
	NP__NP voor NP	33
	NP__NP bij NP	2
	NP__NP aan NP	**1**
	NP__NP NP	2
	NP__(dat)Pfin	7
	NP__tePinf	1
	other	51
begeren	NP__NP	211
	NP__NP van NP	13
	NP__NP voor NP	6
	NP__naar NP	3
	NP__(dat)Pfin (van NP)	31
	NP__tePinf	66
	other	1

A constant throughout the evolution of the reception verbs is the dominance of the monotransitive construction. Also in the 18th and 19th century, this type of construction accounts for the majority of the occurrences. The direct object appears rather frequently as a subordinate clause, especially with *begeren*. As already observed in the 17th century, no genitive objects were found anymore. This observation agrees with Brill (1881). In his 19th century Grammar, Brill (1881: 64) mentions that the number of verbs that govern the genitive is very limited in the 'present-day' (i.e. 19th century) language. Only reciprocal verbs such as *zich bekommeren* 'concern oneself' could still occur with a genitive.

These periods deviate from the older phases of Dutch with regard to the *aan*-construction. Only one occurrence of *aan* was attested in the 19th century corpus, where the original possessor is encoded as an *aan*-PP with *ontvangen*. However, even this single occurrence is somewhat dubious, since the *aan*-PP in (19) could also be interpreted as a locative phrase ('at the bank').

(19) Eens heeft hij aan de bank zeventien gulden teveel ontvangen, en, hij bracht ze terug. [Multatuli, *Max Havelaar*, 1860]
'Once he received 17 gilders too much ?from/at the bank, and, he brought it back.'

The fact that this example occurs with *ontvangen* and not with *verwerven*, for instance, which fits better with *aan* in semantic terms, enhances the possibility that the *aan*-PP refers to a location.

Occasionally, as is the case in the other periods of Dutch, the preposition *bij* is used to signal the original possessor. Source objects introduced by *op* still occur until the 19th century.

In the majority of the double-object constructions found in the 18th and 19th century, the indirect object is – like in present-day Dutch – a reflexive pronoun. Moreover, like most double-object constructions found in all phases of Dutch, they are all benefactive constructions.

5. Discussion

The developmental path of *verkrijgen, verwerven, ontvangen* and *begeren* is especially marked by the disappearance of the *aan*-construction. In older phases of Dutch – especially in the Middle Dutch period – *aan* could be used to introduce the original possessor in the reception event. In present-day Dutch, only *van* is found in this role. In line with the data from the *Dictionary of the*

Dutch Language, the corpus data show that the culmination point of this historical change clearly lies between the 17th and 18th century.

How then can we account for this change? First, we start from the observation that the semantics of the *aan*- and *van*-constructions is largely determined by the meaning of the prepositions. *Aan* implies a notion of 'contact'. *Van*, on the other hand, implies a notion of 'separation, removal' from a source (Schermer-Vermeer 1991, Colleman 2006, *inter alia*). The semantics of the verbs of reception (which denote getting something *from a source*) is clearly more compatible with the semantics of *van* than of *aan*. In present-day Dutch, *aan* is mainly found with verbs of giving to refer to the recipient (in which case there is contact with the *endpoint* of the transfer). However, in older phases of Dutch, *aan* seemed to have a wider interpretation. The *Middle Dutch Dictionary* indicates that *aan* could also signal that an object lies *within* a person or object, which is the *source* of it. The object is desired or obtained from the source. The objects of transfer found in the *aan*-construction in the case study are often concepts like *mercy*, *grace*, *comfort*, etc. which are more or less intrinsic qualities of someone (i.e. they lie 'within a person or object'). Throughout the centuries, this use of *aan* (in which there is contact with the *source* of the transfer) seems to have diminished and disappeared. This would also explain why it occurs less frequently and eventually disappears in combination with reception verbs.

The (changing) semantics of the verbs in question also explain their appearance in the *aan*-construction. In the Middle Dutch corpus, it is striking that *verwerven* occurs rather often with *aan* (see Table 3, section 4.2). This is possibly due to the notion of effort which was an intrinsic part of the meaning of *verwerven* in older phases of Dutch (and to a large extent still is). As already mentioned before (see section 4.1), this implies that the recipient-subject is also an agent (the subject has to exert himself to obtain the desired object).[8] With an agentive subject and a more or less passive source-object in the PP as a result, the situation in the *aan*-construction with *verwerven* partially resembles the situation of a 'giving'-event as the subject in the latter is also agentive and the recipient in the *aan*-PP is also passive. There is, however, an opposite direction of the transfer with verbs of reception such as *verwerven*. This would also explain the low amount of *aan*-PP's with *ontvangen*, which does not entail such

[8] The notion of effort and the occurrence of an agentive subject can also account for the (sporadic) occurrence of *verwerven* in a double-object construction today, as already observed in section 4.1. According to Goldberg (1995: 143), one of the constraints on the double-object construction is that the subject argument must intend the transfer. Therefore, it has to be a volitional agent. In older benefactive examples with the other verbs we also find a clear agentive subject.

a clear notion of effort and does not (or hardly) occur with an agentive subject. With *ontvangen*, the subject-recipient is (mostly) passive and the transfer generally happens on instigation of the original possessor. Future research, involving more verbs of reception will corroborate whether this hypothesis can be extended to the category as a whole.

Another element that may explain the observed difference between *verwerven* and *ontvangen* in Middle Dutch is the presence of the prefixes *ver-* and *ont-*. It may well be that since *ver-* itself indicates 'separation, removal', there was no need in Middle Dutch to signal this again by means of *van*. In such cases, locative *aan* could have sufficed for reasons of economy and avoidance of redundancy. This line of thought, however, needs further research into the semantic history of the prefixes.

In any case, a sort of systematization has occurred, by which *aan* is used to indicate the new possessor with verbs of giving, while *van* is used to indicate the old possessor with verbs of reception and dispossession. The rise in the use of *aan* with all sorts of verbs of giving is primarily a 17th century innovation (see Weijnen & Gordijn 1970, Duinhoven 2003), and precisely then the other use of *aan* diminishes.[9]

Furthermore, we observed that the benefactive construction was more common in older periods of the language. In present-day Dutch this construction has two limitations: (1) it only occurs with *verwerven* and (2) the beneficiary is a reflexive pronoun. From the 13th to the 19th century, the benefactive construction appears with all the verbs in the case study. Moreover, the beneficiary can also occur in the form of a 'full' NP. A possible explanation for the decrease of the double-object construction can be related to the disappearance of case marking in Dutch. As indicated by Colleman (2002: 514), in Middle Dutch almost any transitive verb could occur with a dative nominal object which referred to the beneficiary. This was called a 'dativus commodi'. With the disappearance of the case system in Dutch, the 'dativus commodi' or beneficiary gradually lost ground in subsequent evolutions of the Dutch language. The disappearance of the benefactive double-object construction with verbs of reception can be situated within the general decline of the possibilities of the benefactive ditransitive with all sorts of transitive verbs. The conditions for using the benefactive construction are much stricter in the present-day language: not just any situation with a beneficiary can be encoded by a double-object construction. So, as was the case with the *aan*-construction, systematization has occurred.

---

[9] In view of this, the present-day use of *aan* with verbs of dispossession such as *ontnemen* 'take away' can be considered as a relic.

6. Conclusion

In this paper I have focussed on Dutch verbs of reception. To conclude, I will sum up the main findings of the case study.

First of all, we noticed that the monotransitive construction dominates throughout the centuries, which leads us to believe that in a reception event, the most important roles have always been the recipient and the theme, not the 'giver'.

Secondly, it has been observed that in the course of the centuries a constructional systematization has occurred, in which the double-object construction has lost ground and has become prototypical of dative (= 'give'-) relationships.

Thirdly, and finally, the use of prepositions has also been systematized: *aan* has become the default preposition to introduce the recipient role in dative constructions, *van* has become the default preposition to refer to the source role in receptive constructions.

REFERENCES

Brill, W. G. (1881) *Nederlandsche Spraakleer. Ten gebruike bij inrichtingen van hoger onderwijs. IIde deel: Leer van den volzin (Syntaxis)*. Third Edition, Leiden: E.J. Brill.

Colleman, T. (2002). "De benefactieve dubbelobject-constructie in het 19de-eeuws Nederlands". In: R. Willemyns (ed.). *De taal in Vlaanderen in de 19de eeuw. Historisch-sociolinguïstische onderzoekingen* (theme volume *Verslagen en mededelingen van de Koninklijke Academie voor Nederlandse Taal- en Letterkunde* 112): 509–528.

Colleman, T. (2006). *De Nederlandse datiefalternantie: een constructioneel en corpusgebaseerd onderzoek*, PhD, University of Ghent.

Delorge, M. & T. Colleman (2006). "Constructions with verbs of dispossession, a corpus-based case study". *Studies van de Belgische Kring voor Linguisitiek* 1.
<http://webhost.ua.ac.be/linguist/online/paps2006/del2006.pdf>

Duinhoven, A. M. (2003). "Actieve en passieve indirect objecten. Een kwestie van analyse en synthese". *Nederlandse taalkunde* 8: 199–230.

Goldberg, A. E. (1995). *Constructions: A Construction Grammar Approach to Argument Structure*. Chicago: University of Chicago Press.

Kay, P. & J. Fillmore (1999). "Grammatical Constructions and Linguistic Generalizations: The What's X Doing Y? Construction". *Language* 75: 1–33.

Langacker, R. (1987). *Foundations of Cognitive Grammar*. Vol I. Stanford: Stanford University Press.

Langacker, R. (1991). *Foundations of Cognitive Grammar*. Vol II. Stanford: Stanford University Press.

Langacker, R. (1999). *Grammar and Conceptualization*. Berlin: Mouton de Gruyter.

Levin, B. (1993). *English Verb Classes and Alternations: A Preliminary Investigation*. Chicago: The University of Chicago Press.

Newman, J. (2005). "Three place predicates: A cognitive-linguistic perspective". *Language Sciences* 27: 145–163.

Schermer-Vermeer, E. C. (1991). *Substantiële versus formele taalbeschrijving: het indirect object in het Nederlands*. Amsterdam: PhD UvA.

Stoett, F. A. (1923). *Middelnederlansche Spraakkunst*, 's Gravenhage: Martinus Nijhoff.

Verwijs, E. & J. Verdam. *Middelnederlandsch Woordenboek*. 11 delen, 's Gravenhage: Martinus Nijhoff, 1885–1952.

Wal, M. J. van der & C. Van Bree (1992). "Dialect and standard language in the past: the rise of Dutch standard language in the sixteenth and seventeenth centuries". In: J. A. van Leuvensteijn & J. B. Berns (eds.). *Dialect and standard language*. Amsterdam, Oxford, New York, Tokyo: 119–129.

Weijnen, A. A. (1974). *Het Algemeen Beschaafd Nederlands historisch beschouwd*, Assen: Van Gorcum & Co.

Weijnen, A. A. & A. M. J. Gordijn (1970). "Het binnendringen van het voorzetsel in het indirekt objekt in het Nederlands". *Leuvense Bijdragen* 59: 125–30.

WNT = M. De Vries, L. A. Te Winkel *et al.* (red.). *Woordenboek der Nederlandsche Taal*, 's Gravenhage: Martinus Nijhoff [etc.], 1882–1998.

Part Four

COGNITIVE CONTRASTIVE STUDIES

Dagmar Divjak and Stefan Th. Gries

University of Sheffield and University of California at Santa Barbara

CORPUS-BASED COGNITIVE SEMANTICS A CONTRASTIVE STUDY OF PHASAL VERBS IN ENGLISH AND RUSSIAN[1]

Abstract: In this paper we will present a corpus-based cognitive-semantic analysis of five verbs that express 'begin' in English and Russian, i.e. *begin*, *start*, *načinat'/načat'*. *načinat'sja/načat'sja* and *stat'*. On the basis of a quantitative analysis of data extracted from the ICE-GB and the Uppsala Corpus we conclude that the prototype for each verb and each set of verbs in each language revolves around different characteristics altogether: the difference between *begin* and *start* is lexical in nature, that between *načinat'/načat'* and *stat'* can be described as aspectual, whereas the differences between *načinat'/načat'* and *načinat'sja/načat'sja* involve argument structure. Because these dissimilarities are of an entirely different order, they can only be picked up if a methodology is used that adequately captures the multivariate nature of the phenomenon. The Behavioral Profiling approach we have developed and apply here does exactly that.

Keywords: Behavioral Profiling, complementation, English, ID tag, near-synonymy, polysemy, prototype, Russian, verb sense.

1. Introduction

Ever since the emergence of Cognitive Linguistics as a research paradigm, the analysis of semantic structures has been a priority on the cognitive linguistic agenda. Early studies, which shaped the field for many years, investigated the degree to which, for example, metaphor could be used to account for meaning extension. Radial categories allowed for new insights into the linguistic

[1] We would like to thank Steven Clancy, Laura Janda and the editors of this volume for a variety of useful comments on earlier drafts of this paper. The usual disclaimers apply. While working on this project, Dagmar Divjak was an honorary postdoctoral fellow of the F.W.O. – Vlaanderen (Science Foundation, Flanders, Belgium); their support is gratefully acknowledged.

organization – if not also mental representation – of polysemy, and to a lesser extent near-synonymy.

Yet, despite these advances that promoted a unified analysis of semantic phenomena, semanticists working on polysemy or near-synonymy within a cognitive linguistic framework also faced problems. Polysemy requires the researcher to determine whether two usage events are identical or sufficiently similar to be considered a single sense, what the degree of similarity is between different senses, where to connect a sense to others in the network, and which sense(s) to recognize as prototypical one(s). Linguists interested in (near) synonymy do not only face these four issues, albeit at word level, but, in addition, have to decide what the differences are between the near-synonyms as well as what the relation is between semantically similar words in a domain.

By and large, three different approaches to these problems can be distinguished, i.e. (i) approaches that are not based on empirical data, (ii) approaches that are partially based on empirical data, and (iii) fully empirical approaches. We will discuss these in turn in Section 1.1, then go on to presenting the Behavioral Profile approach, our corpus-based answer to some problems of cognitive semantics in Section 1.2.

1.1. Some background

The best known example of what we, admittedly provocatively, classify as a **non-empirical** approach is Lakoff and collaborators' (1987) full-specification approach. In this approach, minimal perceived differences between usage events constitute different senses. While this approach results in very detailed lexical semantic analyses, it also leads to a difficult-to-constrain proliferation of senses and distinctions, the cognitive reality of which may be hard to establish. In an attempt to rectify some shortcomings of the full-specification approach, Kreitzer's (1997) partial-specification approach claims that minimally different usage events need not constitute different senses. However, while Kreitzer's approach is somewhat more rigorous, both approaches rely largely on decontextualized data, collected by means of introspection and analyzed using intuitions regarding what constitutes a semantically or even cognitively relevant distinction or a prototypical sense, or what the exact structure of a postulated sense network looks like.

An example of a **partially empirical** approach is Tyler and Evans' (2001) and Evans' (2005) principled-polysemy approach. This approach presents a substantial improvement over any non-empirical approach in two ways. First, the approach is more stringent since a meaning criterion rules out adding senses *ad libitum*: it requires a new meaning component to be compared to other already established senses. Second, the approach makes testable predictions regarding both conceptual elaboration and grammatical distribution.

Within the class of empirical approaches, two strands can be distinguished, depending on whether the data used in the analysis are elicited or non-elicited. Prime examples of cognitive lexical semantics based on **experimental** data are Sandra and Rice (1995) as well as Rice (1996) who present lexical analyses based on data from sorting or sentence generation tasks and judgment elicitation techniques. Another example is work by Raukko (1999, 2003), who uses sentence generation and paraphrasing tasks and elicits prototypicality judgments for his polysemy-as-flexible-meaning approach (cf. Gries and Divjak, forthcoming b, for more discussion).

Within cognitive semantics, **corpus-based approaches** that use non-elicited data are few and far between. One early cognitive-semantic corpus-based approach relevant for the present paper is Kishner and Gibbs' work (1996) on *just* and Gibbs and Matlock (2001) on *make*. These studies rely on collocate analysis (words at R1, i.e. the first word to the right of the head word) as well as colligation analysis (i.e., the syntactic structure of the word combination) and correlate different senses with collocations and colligations. Their "findings suggest the need to incorporate information about [...] lexico-grammatical constructions in drawing links between different senses of a polysemous word" (Gibbs and Matlock 2001: 234). Other more recent work includes the papers published in Stefanowitsch and Gries (2006) and Gries and Stefanowitsch (2006), in particular Schönefeld (2006), who investigates the translational equivalents of the basic posture verbs *sit*, *stand*, and *lie* in English, German, and Russian with regard to how these languages have conventionalized the same physiologically determined perceptual experiences. Her investigation is based on approximately 8,000 collocations of the relevant posture verbs, and her work's crosslinguistic orientation has been a source of inspiration for the present study.

Yet, citations in corpus data have more to offer than just individual collocations and colligations: restricting the collocate/colligation analysis to the first word to the right of the head word is a heuristic blind to the wider syntactic structure the keyword occurs in. Corpus linguists realized this long ago, and corpus-based approaches to lexical semantics in the field of corpus linguistics have consequently produced impressive results. Take for example Atkins' (1987) study on *danger*. Her study includes an extensive collocation (words at L7 to R7, i.e. seven words to the left and seven words to the right of the head word) and colligation analysis as well as part of speech characteristics of the head word. Furthermore, she introduced "ID tags", or a collocation/colligation that correlates (probabilistically or perfectly) with a particular sense. In his study on *urge*,

Hanks (1996) extended Atkins' analysis: starting from a collocation and colligation analysis and "sense triangulation", i.e. the correlation of collocates in different clause roles, he arrives at 'Behavioral Profiles' or the totality of complementation patterns of a word that determines its semantics (Hanks 1996: 77). The full capacity of this approach is not exploited, however, and we will return to this topic in Section 1.2.

To summarize, it can be stated that, by and large, cognitive semantic studies have traditionally been based on decontextualized data, collected and analyzed by means of introspection. As a consequence, the findings may be empirically problematic: not all fine-grained sense distinctions are necessarily supported by the data (cf. Gries and Divjak, forthcoming b). In addition, reliance on introspection as a means of data collection and intuition as the main analytic method has prevented the development of a rigorous and objectively applicable methodology. Corpus-based or computational-linguistic studies, on the other hand, have always relied on large data collections, yet their studies may be less interesting from a linguistic point of view, and this for four reasons: first, corpus-based studies are often restricted to words with few different senses or small sets of semantically similar words (*almost* vs. *nearly*, *high* vs. *tall*, *between* vs. *through*; cf., e.g, Kjellmer 2003, Taylor 2003, Kennedy 1991), they typically focus on topics that are of little interest to theoretical linguistics such as semantic prosody (cf. Xiao and McEnery 2006), they tend to be based on impoverished subsets of data available and, fourth, those data are likely to be noisy or skewed given (semi-) automatic preprocessing tools.

In the present study, we argue strongly for more corpus-based work in lexical semantics in general and cognitive semantics in particular, a domain that is considered by many not to be particularly well-suited for corpus-linguistic studies. We present our Behavioral Profile approach, which we believe combines the best of both the cognitive and corpus linguistic traditions, i.e. a precise, quantitative corpus-based approach that yields cognitive-linguistically relevant results. We will bring the Behavioral Profile approach to bear on polysemous near-synonyms that express 'begin' in a contrastive English-Russian analysis. Hence, the focus of the study is on presenting a corpus-based methodology that can be used to pursue cognitively-inspired lexical semantic analyses and that yields results relevant to cognitive linguistics, rather than on presenting a cognitive-semantic analysis of verbs that express 'begin' in itself.

1.2. Our proposal

The key assumption underlying the Behavioral Profile (BP) approach (Divjak 2003, 2004, 2006, Gries 2003, 2006, Divjak and Gries 2006, Gries and Divjak, forthcoming a, Divjak and Gries 2008, Gries and Divjak forthcoming b) relies on the parallelism between the distributional and functional planes. Starting from the retrieval of all instances of a word's lemma from a corpus, we proceed with a (largely) manual analysis of morpho-syntactic, syntactic and semantic properties of the head word, its collocates, and the hosting clause/sentence. In other words, we extend Hanks's (1996) form of behavioral profile from being restricted to complementation patterns and roles to include a comprehensive inventory of elements co-occurring with a word within the confines of a simple clause or sentence in actual speech and writing. In this way, we arrive at a maximally comprehensive behavioral profile of the lexical items studied. The BP approach differs in two important respects from previous corpus-based studies, both within and outside of cognitive linguistics: the fine granularity of the annotation goes beyond most previous work as does the subsequent evaluation of the data that is statistical in nature. The resulting semantic description is hence entirely data-driven, and delays the need for arguably personal interpretations until the very last stage of the analysis, if not bypassing it altogether.

The first purpose of the present application is to strengthen support (see the studies quoted above) for the BP approach as a powerful method that provides as *objective* a basis for the semantic analysis of both polysemous and synonymous items as possible. By *objective* we mean that even if the classification of the data points can be considered subjective to some degree,

- the amount of data to be investigated has been determined objectively, i.e. a (randomly chosen sample of a) complete concordance is used;
- the annotation of these data can be made explicit (e.g., by a set of coding instructions/criteria; cf. Table 2) and tested for consistency;
- the analysis of the data is obtained by means of statistical techniques (cf. Section 4).

This way, we postpone intuition until the stage of result interpretation (Section 5). The second purpose is to show that this approach can also be applied to the notoriously difficult area of cross-linguistic comparisons. In order to achieve this two-fold aim, the approach will be put to the test by attempting a simultaneous within-language description and across-languages comparison of polysemous and near-synonymous items belonging to different subfamilies of Indo-European, i.e. English and Russian.

2. Schmid (1993)

The current project was partially inspired by Schmid (1993), one of the first large-scale corpus-based cognitive semantic analyses. Schmid (1993) provides an in-depth corpus-based analysis of *begin* and *start* using 318 instances of the lemma *start* and 472 instances of the lemma *begin* extracted from the Lancaster-Oslo-Bergen corpus. Each instance is annotated in terms of

- the inflectional form of the verb;
- clause type: intransitive, intransitive with adverbials, transitive;
- the syntax of the complement: zero, AdvP, *ing*-clause, NP, PP, *to*-clause;
- the semantics of the subject and the semantics of the complement:[2] abstract, action, animate, cognition, human, institution, locative, manner, object, process, state, temporal;
- verb sense: 'be far from', 'begin a career', 'begin as', 'begin to speak', 'cause to begin', 'introduce', 'jump', 'protrude', 'set going in a conversion', 'set in motion', 'set out', 'set out (fig.)', 'set up', 'start a race', 'start running', 'start time unit', 'inchoative'.

Of particular interest is the correlation between the choice of phasal verb and the kind of syntactic complement. Table 1 is an excerpt of Schmid's (1993: 228) Table 4.

Table 1. Cross-tabulating transitive phasal verb with type of complement

	begin	*start*	Totals
NP	48	96	144
ing-clause	24	53	77
to-clause	256	39	295
Totals	328	188	516

These data show that *begin* correlates with *to*-constructions whereas *start* prefers *ing*-constructions (cf. Schmid 1993: 239). Following Quirk *et al.*'s (1985: 1192) classification of *to* as signalling potentiality and *ing* as indicating performance, Schmid relates those features to the respective preferences of *begin* and *start* given the strong correlation the two verbs show with *to* and *ing*

[2] Note that Schmid only distinguishes between subject and complement, but not between the semantic roles of Beginner and Beginnee. Thus, Schmid's discussion of intransitive clauses (with or without adverbials) does not distinguish agentive from non-agentive subjects.

respectively.[3] *Begin* then gives a view into the state after the onset of the action: it expresses modality/intentionality and refers to later states of affairs. It typically applies to cognitive-emotive events and non-perceivable things. *Start*, on the other hand, focuses on the actual action, the actual beginning, the very moment of transition from non-action to action. It is dynamic and applies to visible changes and actions.

---

[3] Quirk *et al.* (1985) and Biber *et al.* (1999) should more reliably be summarized as relating *ing*-constructions to generality, actuality, simultaneity, and direct action while relating *to*-constructions to specificity, potentiality, futurity, and indirect action. In order to be able to support/reject Schmid's claims on independent grounds, we will analyze the two dichotomies present in the dataset separately: we will first deal with the constructional complementation preferences (*ing* vs. *to*) of *begin* and *start*, then proceed to the lexical complementation preferences of *begin* and *start*. In order to arrive at a more comprehensive picture concerning the phasal verbs' preferred complementations, we decided to look at a larger corpus, the 100-million words British National Corpus World edition. With an R script, we extracted all instances of any form of *begin* or *start* tagged as a verb (either with an unambiguous tag or a portmanteau tag) followed by a word tagged as a verb gerund as well as of any form of *begin* or *start* tagged as a verb (either with an unambiguous tag or a portmanteau tag) followed by *to* (tagged as "to0") followed by a word tagged as a verb infinitive. On the basis of the concordance, we were able to look at the data in more detail in two different ways:

1) We counted how often each verb was attested with each of the two complementation patterns. The result is summarized in the table below (with expected frequencies in parentheses) and shows a highly significant correlation of *begin* with *to* and *start* with *ing* (χ^2 = 5,491.6; df = 1; p <. 001, Cramer's V = 0.38). These results conform to Schmid's (1993) LOB data as well as Wulff and Gries's (forthcoming) data. Since cognitive linguistic/construction grammar approaches assume that structures co-occur (or are inserted into each other) to the extent that their meanings are compatible, this adds to the body of evidence that associates *begin* with potentiality etc. and *start* with actuality.

	begin	*start*	Totals
ing-complementation	2,780 (5,738.4)	6,239 (3,280.7)	9,019
to-complementation	21,458 (18,499.7)	7,618 (10,576.4)	29,076
Totals	24,238	13,857	38,095

2) We also counted how often each of the two phasal verbs was attested with each verb in the two complementation patterns. The resulting co-occurrence table was evaluated with a distinctive collexeme analysis using Coll.analysis 3.2 (cf. Gries 2004, Gries and Stefanowitsch 2004). The analysis by and large confirms Schmid's findings based on the semantic complement classes. *Begin* likes *be* and verbs that express cognition (*understand, realize, wonder, see, feel, find, recognize, suspect, experience, dawn, doubt, consider*), perception (*appear, emerge, seem, show*) as well as some other situations such as *fail, dissolve*. *Start*, on the other hand, likes less abstract verbs and takes a larger variety of verbs: it is found with basic general purpose verbs (*go, do, get, come, try, make, put*), verbs that express communicative activities (*talk, say, ask, cry*), and other, more dynamic activities such as *use, play, work, buy, smoke, look, fight, train, throw*, which we label 'other' because they either did not constitute a class of their own (e.g., *look* is the only verb having to do with perception) or because they are more specific than the general purpose verbs listed above but not specific enough to fall into some natural class.

Schmid's approach is comparable to our BP approach in that it involves a rather fine-grained annotation of instances obtained through an exhaustive corpus search. However, it differs in terms of the rigor with which the data are evaluated. With very few exceptions, Schmid (i) does not systematically evaluate the data statistically[4] and (ii) restricts his attention to bivariate co-occurrence patterns (sometimes even within nested tables) underutilizing the large amount of data at his disposal.

In the next section, we will demonstrate how the language-internal behavior of phasal verbs in English and Russian was investigated. In Section 4, we will show how those data can be used to contrast lemmas and senses language internally.

3. Profiling the behavior of phasal verbs

The current application of the BP approach features a contrastive analysis of 5 polysemous near-synonymous verbs that express 'begin': for English all 298 instances of the lemma *begin* and 531 of the lemma *start* were extracted from the ICE-GB; for Russian all 321 examples of the lemma *načinat'/načat'*, 173 of the lemma *načinat'sja/načat'sja*, and 156 with the lemma *stat'* were collected from the journalistic part of the Uppsala Corpus of Russian.[5]

Let us look at some examples that illustrate the main complementation patterns available: not surprisingly, and as discussed by Schmid, *begin* and *start* can be used intransitively (cf. (1a)), transitively (cf. (1b)), and as quasi-aspectual verbs (cf. (1c–d)); (2) presents the corresponding examples with *start*.

(1) a. *The land campaign has* therefore *begun*.
b. It's not thirty-two hours since *she began her shift*.

[4] Even on occasions where Schmid performs statistical tests, his methodological choices are not always optimal. For example, the interpretation of the data that are cited in connection with the most important semantic difference between *begin* and *start* (Schmid's (1993: 238) Table 6.9) involves the computation of a standard deviation for three percentages that are taken out of a larger and higher-dimensional table.

[5] We are aware of the fact that comparing written and spoken data might not be ideal, yet ICE-GB type spoken data is currently not available for Russian. In addition, the issue of how situationally-defined registers differ from each other with regard to near synonyms remains unresolved. It has been shown for English (i) that journalism resembles spoken language as far as some linguistic features, relevant in this analysis, are concerned (e.g., frequency of present perfects; cf. Gries 2006: 121) and (ii) the variation within the spoken mode and within the written mode can be so large as to make between-register variation pale by comparison (cf. Gries 2006: 121, 135).

c. And who would expect *the character to* [...] *begin writing* a letter?
d. *Accidents were beginning to happen.*

(2) a. Well, *war hasn't started* yet.
b. *What* are we going to give ourselves *to start this song*?
c. I'm glad *you've started wearing* the T-shirts.
d. So *I started to think* about the Crystal Cave.

In the first two Russian examples, *načinat'/načat'* is used, once followed by an infinitive in (3) and once by a noun in (4). In (5) *načinat'sja/načat'sja* is illustrated – it only opens up a subject position – and (6) illustrates that fact that *stat'* only combines with infinitives.

(3) Буквально с первых часов космического полета *организм человека начинает приспосабливаться* к невесомости.
[Literally from the first hours of a space flight *the human organism begins to adapt* to weightlessness.]

(4) 18 апреля в Лондоне *начинает работу* общеевропейский Информационный *форум*.
[On April 18th in London the Pan-European information *forum begins its activity*.]

(5) Сафронов был лишен депутатского иммунитета, и *следствие началось*.
[Safronov was deprived of his deputy immunity and *the investigation began*.]

(6) Из двигателя общества *она стала превращаться* в тормоз его развития.
[From being the motor of society *she started to turn into* the brake of its development.]

The corpus-based method we will introduce to analyze sentences such as the ones listed above focuses on co-occurrence information of symbolic units: the symbolic unit is considered the basic unit within a cognitive linguistic approach and co-occurrences of symbolic units are easily extractable from corpora. Secondly, our approach hinges on the assumption that the words or senses investigated are part of a network of words or senses. In this network, elements which are similar to each other are connected and the strength of the connection reflects the likelihood that the elements display similar syntactic and semantic behaviour; distributional similarity is generally considered a good proxy for functional and conceptual similarity.

In total, 1,479 English and Russian sentences were annotated for 73 properties, listed summarily in Table 2; these properties capture the syntax and semantics of the verbs and their immediate surroundings.[6]

Table 2. Annotation table

Kind of ID tag	ID tag	Levels of ID tag
finite verb	lemma	*načinat'/načat', načinat'sja/načat'sja, stat', begin, start*
	aspect	Russian: imperfective vs perfective English: na
	mood	indicative, imperative, infinitive, gerund, participle, conditional/subjunctive
	tense	Russian: past, present, future English: past, present
	person	English: base form, third person singular Russian: na
	sense	have a beginning, cause to have a beginning, operate, cause to operate, first part characterized by
	voice	active, passive
complement	noun	
	verb	Russian: infinitive English: *ing*-form vs infinitive
argument structure	type	Russian: ot+gen, s+gen, s+gen (time), s+instr English: copula construction, intransitive, monotransitive, complex transitive, ditransitive, transitive
clause	type	main vs dependent
sentence	type	declarative, interrogative, exclamation
semantic roles	Beginner and Beginnee	abstract, action, animate being, change of state (self), communication, event (has natural endpoint), perception/ emotion, human being, illness, intellectual/mental, linguistic_unit (e.g., *texts*, *words*), military_action (e.g., *war*, *campaign*), motion_other, motion_other (metaphorical), motion_self, motion_self (metaphorical), social/group, perception/emotion, process (lacks natural endpoint), temporal, inanimate thing, nothing that is explicitly expressed

[6] Not all features were coded identically in both languages, yet this is solely due the nature of the corpora from which the data were retrieved and does not have any theoretical or methodological significance.

Here are some examples of the sense distinctions available for both English and Russian. Given that the senses are extremely coarse there were very few (if any) problematic cases:

(7) have a beginning: *He started accusing her.*

(8) cause to have a beginning: *She began her shift.*

(9) first part characterized by (i.e., typically the Beginnee is an activity or a time span, whose beginning exhibits characteristics that are introduced by the *begin/start* phrase): *One must begin with examining ..., I had expected the day to begin with a phone call,* or *the fit itself may begin with an aura ...*

In addition, English *begin* and *start* occur in the 'operate' and 'cause to operate' sense that their Russian counterparts lack. They cover a wider semantic spectrum than Russian *načinat'/načat'*, *načinat'sja/načat'sja* and *stat'*, hence are polysemous to a larger extent.

(10) operate: *It wouldn't start.*

(11) cause to operate: *He started the car.*

The result of this extensive annotation is a table with co-occurrence frequencies that contains quavtitative behavioral profiles for each verb and verb-sense and can be used for quantitative analysis. For a detailed description of the procedure we refer to Gries and Divjak (forthcoming a); a program for converting annotated data into behavioral profile vectors and computing cluster-analytic statistics is now available (Gries 2008). In Section 4 we will present some techniques for extracting relevant semantic information from these quantitative behavioral profiles.

4. Contrasting the behavior of phasal verbs

In this section, we will rely on the information contained in the behavioral profiles for each verb and verb sense in order to arrive at an accurate and largely objective description of what defines each verb and verb sense and what differentiates them from each other. In Section 4.1, we will present contrastive results obtained for each verb and verb sense in English; in Section 4.2, we will look at the Russian data in more detail.[7]

4.1. English

4.1.1. Plotting the BP for each lemma

Overall, there is no large difference in terms of semantic variety between *begin* and *start*: when corrected for frequency, both verbs are attested with about the same number of senses. A different picture emerges when individual ID tags are considered, however. In order to compare the individual ID tag levels of *begin* and *start*, we first computed the differences between each of the 53 behavioral profile percentages for *begin* and *start*. For example, within the ID tag 'Beginner'/'what begins', 57.82% and 37.25% of all entities doing the beginning are human beings for *start* and *begin* respectively. The difference is therefore – 20.57%, which is the largest difference between all pairwise compared percentages observed in our dataset for English and, correspondingly, reveals the most pronounced difference between *begin* and *start*. By contrast, the difference for 'Beginnee'/'what begins' for all time units (e.g., *this week*) is only 0.34%, which means that with regard to this tag *begin* and *start* behave very similarly in our data. The inspection of the differences of the behavioral profile reveals strong ID tag levels and candidates for prototypical uses:

- *begin* is preferentially used in main clauses, in the present participle/ progressive aspect, when nothing that is explicitly expressed or a concrete object (Beginner'/'what begins': thing or 0) begins to initiate a change of state of either itself ('Beginnee'/'what's begun': change of state (self)) or of something abstract ('Beginnee'/'what's begun': intellectual/mental, linguistic unit, war, abstract); other Beginnees close to the top also support that pattern: 'Beginnee'/'what's begun': event, percepts, processes, …;
- *start*, on the other hand, is preferentially used transitively and in subordinate clauses, in the infinitive, when a human instigator ('Beginner'/'what begins': human) causes an action (in particular communicative actions) to take place or, a bit further down the list, causes a concrete object to operate (which nicely corresponds to the specific sense of *start* exemplified in *He started the bike*).

[7] All computations and graphs were performed and created with R for Windows 2.5.1 (cf. R Development Core Team 2007).

In order to present the overall tendencies in a way that allows for a straightforward comparison with the Russian data to be discussed in the following section, Figure 1 summarizes the behavioral profile for both *begin* and *start* using only the ID tags that apply to both the English and the Russian data. Each ID tag and its level (separated by three underscores) is plotted on the *y*-axis coordinate of the difference between that ID tag's value for *begin* and that ID tag's value for *start*. The ID tags are rank-ordered on the basis of the size of that difference from left to right with the ranks displayed on the *x*-axis. Highlighting (right or left) indicates the most distinctive ID tags for each verb. For example, the rightmost data point at –0.21 indicates that the entity *beginning* an action is a human 37.25% of the time, while the entity *starting* an action is a human 57.82% of the time, hence the difference of approximately 21%.

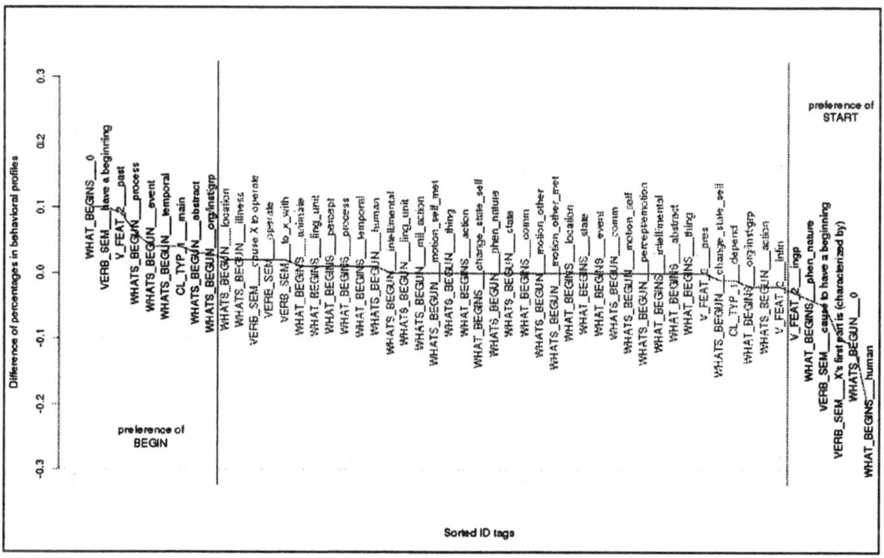

Fig. 1. Snake plot of the most distinctive ID tags for each verb

In the next section, we will briefly address the issue of how different senses of *begin* and *start* are related to each other.

4.1.2. Clustering the BPs for each sense

Contrary to Schmid, and in line with more recent and more rigorous attempts to avoid positing large numbers of senses, we have restricted our sense annotation to the five high-level senses listed in Table 2. As in our previous work, we have applied a hierarchical agglomerative cluster analysis to the complete behavioral profile (similarity measure: Canberra metric, amalgamation rule: Ward's algorithm); we found that the five different verb senses ('have a beginning', 'cause to have a beginning', 'first part characterized by', 'operate', 'cause to operate') form two clear clusters. The left panel of Figure 2 contains the dendrogram showing these two clusters, while the right panel visualizes average and individual silhouette widths (indicated by the grey step function lines and the vertical black lines respectively) for all possible cluster solutions;[8] the maximum silhouette width is obtained for a two cluster solution, as the numbers in the plot specify.

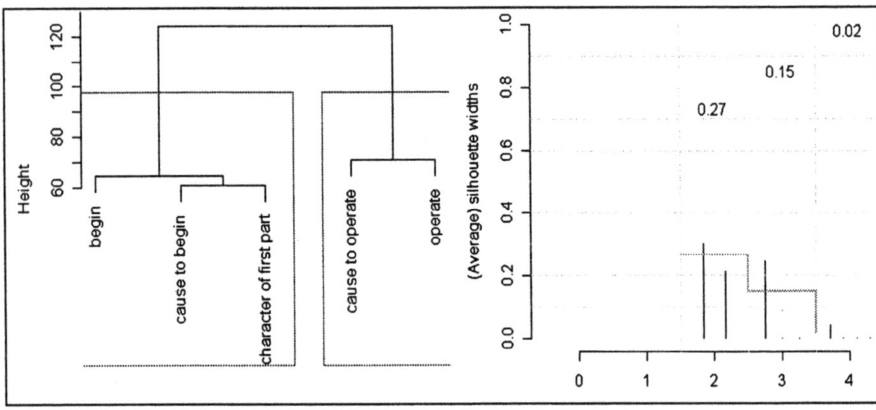

Fig. 2. Cluster-analytic results of begin's and start's senses

Here, different (high-level) senses of the verbs *begin* and *start* are clustered on the basis of overall semantic similarity, while in Gries (2006) different fine-grained senses of the verb *run* were mainly distinguished in terms of causativity/transitivity. This difference may in large part be due to the fact that the five senses of the two phasal verbs exhibit a very high degree of semantic similarity – much more so than many of the semantically very different senses of the verb *run*. When overall semantic similarity is low, distinguishing senses

[8] Silhouette widths are a means to assess the quality of a cluster-analytic solution. They are based on comparing the average similarity of an element to the other elements in the same cluster to the average similarity of an element to the elements in all other clusters. The larger the average silhouette width for a solution, the better the clustering; cf. Kaufman and Rousseeuw (1990) for details.

along a fundamental parameter such as causativity/transitivity can account for much of the variation. However, when overall semantic similarity is high, as with the phasal verbs, causativity/transitivity simply does not add much discriminatory power – lower-level semantic features are more important.

In the following section, we will perform similar analyses for our Russian data and finally, proceed to comparing the results cross-linguistically in Section 5.

4.2. Russian

Given that Russian has three verbs to express 'begin', this section will be structured slightly differently. First, we will cluster the three verbs *načinat'/načat'*, *stat'* and *načinat'sja/načat'sja* to find out which verbs are more similar to each other (Section 4.2.1); next (Section 4.2.2), we will plot the BPs of the three verbs against each other to reveal in which respects these verbs resemble each other and in which respects they differ from each other. Finally, we will turn to analyzing the verbs' senses (Section 4.2.3): clustering the BPs facilitates selecting the most distinctive ID tags per verb sense.

4.2.1. Clustering verbs

Out of all 73 assignable ID tag levels, 69 are contained in the behavioral profile (BP) for *načinat'/načat'*, 41 in the BP for *načinat'sja/načat'sja* and 44 in the BP for *stat'*. Yet, given that *načinat'/načat'* is by far the most frequent, i.e. it is used in 50% of all occurrences, all three verbs should be considered equally versatile.

Cluster analysis shows that *načinat'/načat'* and *stat'* form one cluster, while *načinat'sja/načat'sja* is distinct. This partition reveals a strong influence of the semantics of the argument structure on the clustering, i.e. *načinat'sja/načat'sja* lacks a syntactic/semantic subject position, i.e. it lacks a Beginner, whereas *načinat'/načat'* and *stat'* have both Beginner and Beginnee. We will return to this difference below.

4.2.2. Plotting the verbs' BPs

As above for *begin* and *start*, we computed pairwise differences of behavioral profile percentages of ID tag levels. In order to be able to compare the English and the Russian data, we provide a snake plot of the ID tags attested in both languages (hence aspect will not show up in the plot). Figure 3 contrasts *načinat'/načat'* and *stat'*.

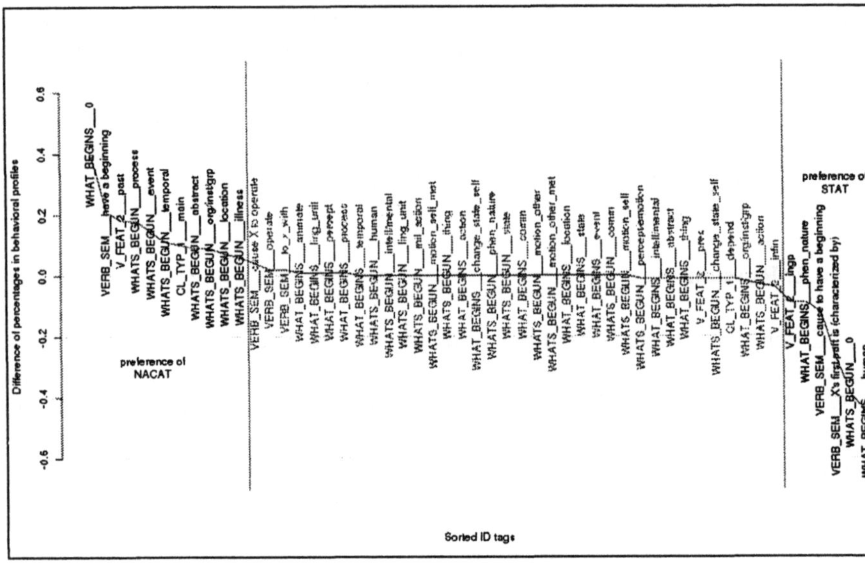

Fig. 3. Snake plot of the most distinctive ID tags for načinat'/načat' vs stat'

The following is a discussion of the top 17 distinctive properties between the behavioral profiles for the two most similar verbs *nacat'* and *stat'*.

- *Načinat'/načat'* differs from *stat'* in that it is found in the imperfective, as a gerund or infinitive, and in the present tense; it is often found in combination with *s* followed by a genitive ('since'), expressing a situation that has a clear source or begins at a specific moment in time. The beginning applies to both nouns and verbs expressing abstract concepts and changes of state instigated by the unknown or by nature. *Načinat'/načat'* expresses all three senses, i.e. "have a beginning", "the first part is characterized by" as well as something has been "caused to have a beginning".
- *Stat'*, on the other hand, prefers the perfective, the indicative and the past, is instigated by human beings and is aimed at actions in general as well as at communicative activities. Different from *načinat'/načat'*, *stat'* is restricted to expressing that something, in particular an event, has a beginning. Supporting this finding is that fact that *stat'* is never encountered with nouns or without Beginnee altogether.

Several of the differences revealed by an analysis of the BPs correspond to traditional interpretations (Flank 1987, Paillard 1998, Dickey 2000, Padučeva 2001) claiming that the verbs differ with respect to the phase of action that is referred to: *stat'* is said to defocus the beginning and to express a smooth transition into a new state, whereas *načinat'/načat'* is typically thought to foreground the beginning as an independent event.

Nacat' expresses a situation that begins at a specific moment in time; the beginning it expresses is ongoing and can be observed, hence it is an action in its own right. The preferences of *stat'*, on the other hand, can be interpreted as an indication of the fact that *stat'* itself expresses a completed action. At the same time, *stat'* is restricted to expressing that something has a beginning: it requires a second action in order to render phasal meaning (in combination with a noun in the instrumental case, *stat'* means "become"). The reliance of phasal *stat'* on that second action backgrounds the beginning while foregrounding the second event.

Načinat'/načat' differs from the third verb to which it is morphologically related, *načinat'sja/načat'sja.* The properties that distinguish best between *načinat'/načat'* and *načinat'sja/načat'sja* are summarized in Figure 4.

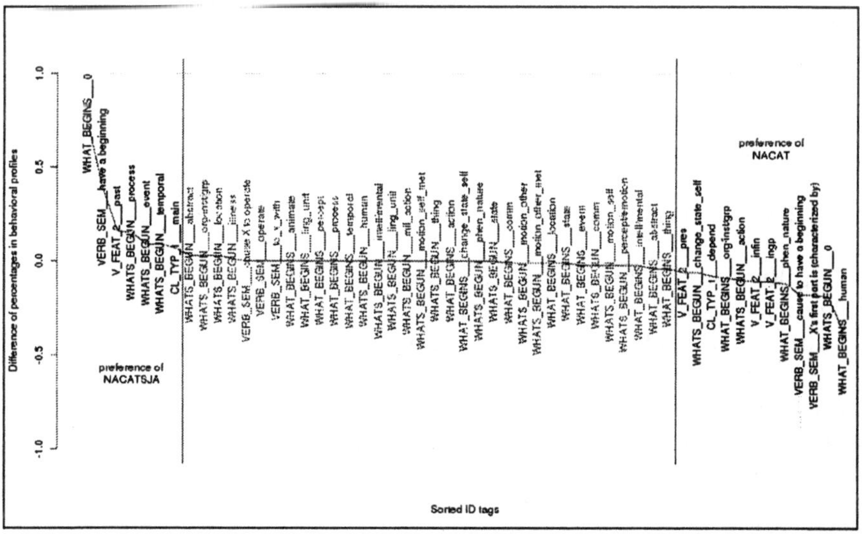

Fig. 4. Snake plot of the most distinctive ID tags for načinat'sja/načat'sja vs načinat'/načat'

- the first distinctive property for *načinat'sja/načat'sja* is the lack of a Beginner, the second distinctive property signals that *načinat'sja/načat'sja* is restricted to expressing the meaning "have a beginning"; the following properties highlight that this meaning is typically expressed in a main clause, with *načinat'sja/načat'sja* in the past tense; *načinat'sja/načat'sja* applies to processes, events and time-related situations.

- compared to *načinat'sja/načat'sja*, *načinat'/načat'* favors the present tense and dependent clauses; it conveys a wider range of senses including "causing something to have a beginning" and "characterizing the first part of X"; *načinat'/načat'* is instigated by human beings, groups/institutions or phenomena of nature and is typically applied to actions and changes of state that affect the self, yet the Beginnee does not need to be explicitly expressed.

Načinat'sja/načat'sja, being restricted to a Beginnee, lacks an overt active Beginner. These argument structure restrictions signal that *načinat'sja/načat'sja* embodies an externally imposed, agentless beginning (cf. Padučeva 2001: 34); it applies exclusively to obligatory nominal Beginnees that express events and processes. *Načinat'/načat'* is *načinat'sja/načat'sja*'s inverse: it has slots for both Beginner and Beginnee, and can choose to fill up either or both positions with elements from a variety of semantic groups.

In this section, we have briefly touched upon how the three verbs, i.e. *načinat'/načat'*, *načinat'sja/načat'sja* and *stat'*, correlate with the three different senses 'have a beginning', 'cause to have a beginning' and 'characterize the first part of X'. In the next section, we will investigate how the senses themselves relate to each other and which ID tags and levels of ID tags are involved in defining and distinguishing senses.

4.2.3. Clustering verb senses

In Russian, all three verbs express the sense 'have a beginning', whereas only *načinat'/načat'* can render 'cause to have a beginning' and 'characterize the first part of X'. Yet, a hierarchical agglomerative cluster analysis (dendrogram not shown) reveals that the senses 'have a beginning' and 'cause to have a beginning' cluster together – as they do for English – and are more similar to each other than either of them is to the sense 'characterizing the first part of X'. Clearly, argument structure plays an important role here and semantic differences caused by diathesis alternations are rightly considered highly influential.

Grammatically speaking, in Russian, the sense 'have a beginning' scores high (values ranging from 0.6 up to 0.99) for the following ID tags and levels: declarative main clause, perfective indicative finite verb and active infinitive. 'Cause to have a beginning' is typically expressed by perfective *načat'* when combined with a noun and is encountered in the indicative mood in declarative main clauses. Finally, the sense 'characterizing the first part of X' is most typical of declarative sentences with imperfective present *načinat'* followed by a noun.

As far as the semantic roles of Beginner and Beginnee are concerned for these three Russian verbs, human beings, phenomena of nature and nothing that is explicitly expressed tend to begin actions, processes and mental activities. Human beings, social entities or nothing that is explicitly expressed cause a process or event expressed by a noun or a communicative act to have a beginning. And finally, human beings and nothing that is explicitly expressed tend to have a first part that is characterized by or begun with or from something.

5. A cognitive cross-linguistic comparison

Overall, the within-language similarity between verbs is higher than between language similarity: in an across language cluster analysis including only properties attested in both languages, *begin* and *start* cluster together as *načinat'/načat'* and *stat'* do, while *načinat'sja/načat'sja* is kept separately.

Yet, the underlying dissimilarity matrix reveals that, while *begin* and *start* may well be most similar to each other within one language, seen across languages *načinat'/načat'* and *begin* are most similar. From this it does, however, not follow that *stat'* and *start* are equivalent. When we look at *stat'* in more detail, we see that it does indeed resemble *start* in that it prefers the past tense and certain types of Beginnee, i.e. actions, communications and mental activities. At the same time, *stat'* resembles *begin* in that it highlights the "view into the state after the onset of the action", as we characterized *begin*. These findings highlight the fact that a one-to-one lexical and/or conceptual mapping between phasal verbs in Russian and English may well be non-existing, a conclusion that is supported by our overall conceptual findings.

The prototype for each verb and set of verbs in each language seems to revolve around a different set of characteristics altogether: this difference is clearly revealed by the snake plots. In English (Figure 1), 12 out of the 15 most distinctive properties for *begin* and *start* relate to the type of Beginner and Beginnee; English *begin* is concerned with more abstract, less tangible/non-perceivable processes whereas *start* is associated with more dynamic and concrete actions instigated by humans. In Russian (Figures 3 and 4), however, only 6 out of the 17 (for *načinat'/načat'* versus *stat'*) and 8 out of the 19 (for *načinat'/načat'* versus *načinat'sja/načat'sja*) most distinctive ID tags relate to lexical preferences of the phasal verbs; the majority of distinctive properties relates to the aspectual and argument structure peculiarities of the verbs. The two Russian verbs *načinat'/načat'* and *stat'* differ with respect to the phase of action that is referred to: given that each of the structural verb-related differences account for a relatively large portion of the variation between *stat'* and *načinat'/načat'*, *stat'* can be said to defocus the beginning and to express a smooth transition into a new state, whereas *načinat'/načat'* is typically thought to foreground the beginning as an independent event. The difference between *načinat'/načat'* and *načinat'sja/načat'sja*, on the other hand, clearly revolves around the concept's compatibility with agentivity: *načinat'/načat'* does take Beginners, *načinat'sja/načat'sja* does not. In other words, the difference between *begin* and *start* may be termed lexical, whereas that between *načinat'/načat'* and *stat'* seems aspectual in nature (cf. Zaliznjak & Šmelev 2002: 219–222, and in less overt terms Černova 1999: 165–169), and the difference between *načinat'/ načat'* and *načinat'sja/načat'sja* relates to argument structure.

Verbs that express 'begin' in English and Russian are but one example of languages' tendency to carve up (a comparable) conceptual space in a unique way and to opt for a different division of labour between the lexemes available to express similar concepts. This can lead to dissimilarities that are of an entirely different order and are bound to be overlooked by comparative cognitive semanticists unless a methodology is used that adequately captures the multivariate nature of the phenomenon; behavioral profiling does exactly that.

6. Conclusion

In this study, we have put our BP approach to the test by applying it to the study of polysemous near synonyms in English and Russian that express 'begin'. We hope to have achieved three goals.

First of all, we have provided a detailed usage-based characterization of *begin*, *start*, *načinat'/načat'*, *načinat'sja/načat'sja* and *stat'* that captures what we have termed the verbs' behavioral profile. Snake plot summaries facilitate an immediate identification of the most central usage characteristics of these five verbs and of the related prototypical scenarios they evoke. These findings are of interest to both theoretically-oriented cognitive linguists and practically-oriented lexicographers. Secondly we have illustrated how, within a semantically homogenous set of verbs and senses, clusters of verb senses exist, and these may be revealed on the basis of distributional characteristics collected in BPs. The skeptic might argue that a cluster analysis will *always* yield clusters. While this is true, there are many possible cluster solutions, but only a few make sense, and the ones we obtained are probably the most or the second-most sensible solutions one could have wished for. Finally, we have shown how the objective annotation of comparable semantic and distributional ID tags of translational equivalents across languages enables us to take first steps toward a more rigorous cross-linguistic and cognitive-linguistic analysis.

While corpus-linguistic methods are more frequently applied in cognitive linguistics than in many other linguistic frameworks, their utility has not been sufficiently, let alone uniformly, recognized. Among others, Raukko (1999, 2003) launches a ferocious attack at corpus linguistic methods, but such criticism typically throws out the baby with the bathwater especially now that corpus linguistics is evolving towards a methodologically more mature and quantitatively more sophisticated state; the present study applies some of these quantitatively more refined methods to the study of near synonyms in a cognitive-linguistic framework.

Quantitative rigor does not imply that the job is done, however. There are both methodological and conceptual steps left to take. We have illustrated, albeit in an early footnote, that both the BP approach to *begin* and *start* as well as previous approaches are supported and enriched by additional analyses. The analysis of data from a different and much larger corpus than has been used for this paper and with a method that has been shown to be sensitive to lexical and constructional semantics confirms the patterns and interpretations found as well as the conclusions derived from the behavioral profiles. On the methodological side, the results from behavioral profiles must be tested against other empirical data, and the level of detail present in an objective data collection of this kind makes this task feasible. In the present case, for example, additional corpus data from English-Russian parallel corpora may help to determine how well our BP approach has succeeded in identifying the relevant dimensions of variation and hence in predicting the choice for one or the other available alternative. Alternatively, a reasonable next step would be to pursue a more fine-grained sense coding (possibly along the lines of Schmid 1993) to see with which distributional patterns, if any, the sense distinctions are correlated. The data-driven nature and comprehensiveness of behavioral profiles offer many different avenues of research, waiting to be explored by cognitive linguists.

REFERENCES

Atkins, B. T. S. (1987). "Semantic ID tags: Corpus evidence for dictionary senses". *Proceedings of the Third Annual Conference of the UW Centre for the New Oxford English Dictionary*: 17–36.

The British National Corpus, version 2 (BNC World) (2001). Distributed by Oxford University Computing Services on behalf of the BNC Consortium. http://www.natcorp.ox.ac.uk

Černova, S. V. (1999). "Fazisnye glagoly kak predikaty otražajuščie celenapravlennuju dejatel'nost' čeloveka". *Semantika. Funkcionirovanie. Tekst.* Kirov: 158–173.

Dickey, S. (2000). *Parameters of Slavic Aspect: A Cognitive Approach.* Stanford: CSLI Publications.

Divjak, D. (2003). "Ways of Planning Actions. A Cognitive Semantic Approach to Near Synonyms in Russian". Paper presented at the International Cognitive Linguistics Conference 2003. Universidad de La Rioja, 22 July 2003.

Divjak, D. (2004). *Degrees of verb integration. Conceptualizing and categorizing events in Russian.* Unpublished Ph.D. Dissertation, K.U. Leuven (Belgium).

Divjak, D. (2006). "Ways of intending: Delineating and structuring near synonyms". In: Gries, S. Th. & A. Stefanowitsch (eds.). *Corpora in Cognitive Linguistics: Corpus-Based Approaches to Syntax and Lexis.* Berlin, New York: Mouton de Gruyter: 19–56.

Divjak, D. & St. Th. Gries (2006). "Ways of trying in Russian: clustering behavioral profiles". *Corpus Linguistics and Linguistic Theory* 2(1): 23–60.

Divjak, D. & St. Th. Gries (2008). "Clusters in the mind? Converging evidence from near-synonymy in Russian". *The Mental Lexicon* 3(2): 188–213.

Evans, V. (2005). "The meaning of *time*: polysemy, the lexicon and conceptual structure". *Journal of Linguistics* 41(1): 33–75.

Flank, S. (1987). "Phase subdivisions and Russian inceptives". *Die Welt der Slaven* 32(2): 310–16.

Gibbs, R. W. Jr. & T. Matlock (2001). "Psycholinguistic perspectives on polysemy". In: Cuyckens, H. & B. Zawada (eds.). *Polysemy in Cognitive Linguistics.* Amsterdam, Philadelphia: John Benjamins: 213–39.

Gries, St. Th. (2003). "The many meanings of *to run*: cognitive linguistics meets corpus-based linguistics". Paper presented at the International Cognitive Linguistics Conference 2003. Universidad de La Rioja, 22 July 2003.

Gries, St. Th. (2004). Coll.analysis 3.2. A program for R for Windows.

Gries, St. Th. (2006). "Corpus-based methods and cognitive semantics: The many meanings of *to run*". In: Gries, St. Th. & A. Stefanowitsch (eds.). *Corpora in Cognitive Linguistics: Corpus-Based Approaches to Syntax and Lexis.* Berlin, New York: Mouton de Gruyter: 57–99.

Gries, St. Th. (2006). "Exploring variability with and between corpora: some methodological considerations". *Corpora* 1(2): 109–51.

Gries, St. Th. (2008). BP. A program for R (for Windows).

Gries, St. Th. & D. Divjak (forthcoming a). "Behavioral profiles: a corpus-based approach to cognitive semantic analysis". In: Evans, Vyvyan & Stephanie S. Pourcel (eds.). *New directions in cognitive linguistics.* Amsterdam, Philadelphia: John Benjamins.

Gries, St. Th. & D. Divjak (forthcoming b). "Quantitative approaches in usage-based cognitive semantics: myths, erroneous assumptions, and a proposal".

Gries, St. Th. & A. Stefanowitsch (2004). "Extending collostructional analysis: a corpus-based perspective on 'alternations' ". *International Journal of Corpus Linguistics* 9(1): 97–129.

Gries, St. Th. & A. Stefanowitsch (eds.) (2006). *Corpora in Cognitive Linguistics: Corpus-Based Approaches to Syntax and Lexis*. Berlin, New York: Mouton de Gruyter.

Hanks, P. (1996). "Contextual dependency and lexical sets". *International Journal of Corpus Linguistics* 1(1): 75–98.

Janda, L. A. (to appear). "What is the role of semantic maps in cognitive linguistics?" In: P. Stalmaszczyk and W. Oleksy (eds.). *Festschrift for Barbara Lewandowska-Tomaszczyk*.

Kennedy, G. (1991). "*Between* and *through*: the company they keep and the functions they serve". In: Aijmer, K. & B. Altenberg (eds.). *English Corpus Linguistics*. London: Longman: 95–110.

Kishner, J. M. & R. W. Gibbs Jr (1996). "How *just* gets its meanings: Polysemy and context in psychological semantics". *Language and Speech* 39(1): 19–36.

Kjellmer, G. (2003). "Symomy and corpus work: on *almost* and *nearly*". *ICAME Journal* 27:19–27.

Lakoff, G. (1987). *Women, Fire, and Dangerous Things*. Chicago, IL: The University of Chicago Press.

Kreitzer, A. (1997). "Multiple levels of schematization: a study in the conceptualization of space". *Cognitive Linguistics* 8(4): 291–325.

Norvig, P. & G. Lakoff (1987). "Taking: a study in lexical network theory". In: Aske, J., N. Beery, L. Michaelis, & H. Filip (eds.). *Proceedings of the Thirteenth Annual Meeting of the Berkeley Linguistics Society*. Berkeley, CA: BLS: 195–206.

Padučeva, E. V. (2001). "Fazovye glagoly i semantika načinatel'nosti". *Izvestija Akademii Nauk. Serija literatury i jazyka* 60 (4): 29–39.

Paillard, D. & F. Fici Giusti (1998). "L'inchoation en Russe: entre préverbes et auxiliaries". *Le Langage et l'Homme* 33(1): 79–94.

Quirk, R., S. Greenbaum, G. Leech, & J. Svartvik (1985). *A Comprehensive Grammar of the English Language*. London, New York: Longman.

R Development Core Team (2006), *R: A language and environment for statistical computing*. R Foundation for Statistical Computing, Vienna, Austria. ISBN 3-900051-07-0, URL http://www.R-project.org.

Raukko, J. (1999). "An 'intersubjective' method for cognitive-semantic research on polysemy: The case of *get*". In: Hiraga, M. K., C. Sinha, & S. Wilcox (eds.). *Cultural, Psychological and Typological Issues in Cognitive Linguistics*. Amsterdam, Philadelphia: John Benjamins: 87–105.

Raukko, J. (2003). "Polysemy as flexible meaning: Experiments with English get and Finnish pitää". In: Nerlich, B., Zazie T., Vimala H. & David D. Clarke (eds.). *Polysemy: Flexible Patterns of Meaning in Mind and Language*. Berlin: Mouton de Gruyter: 161–93.

Rice, S. (1996). “Prepositional prototypes”. In: Pütz, M. & R. Dirven (eds.). *The Construal of Space in Language and Thought*. Berlin, New York: Mouton de Gruyter: 135–65.

Sandra, D. & S. Rice (1995). “Network analyses of prepositional meaning: mirroring whose mind – the linguist’s or the language user’s?” *Cognitive Linguistics* 6(1): 89–130.

Schmid, H.-J. (1993). *Cottage and co., idea, start vs. begin*. Tübingen: Max Niemeyer.

Schönefeld, D. (2006). “From conceptualization to linguistic expression: where languages diversify”. In: Gries, St. Th. & A. Stefanowitsch (eds.). *Corpora in Cognitive Linguistics: Corpus-Based Approaches to Syntax and Lexis*. Berlin, New York: Mouton de Gruyter: 297–344.

Stefanowitsch, A. & St. Th. Gries (2006). *Corpus-based approaches to metaphor and metonymy*. Berlin, New York: Mouton de Gruyter.

Taylor, J. R. (2003). “Near synonyms as co-extensive categories: *high* and *tall* revisited”. *Language Sciences* 25(3): 263–84.

Tyler, A. & V. Evans (2001). “Reconsidering prepositional polysemy networks: The case of *over*”. *Language* 77(4): 724–65.

Xiao, R. & A. McEnery (2006). “Collocation, semantic prosody and near synonymy: a cross-linguistic perspective”. *Applied Linguistics* 27(1): 103–29.

Wulff, S. & St. Th. Gries (forthcoming). “Psycholinguistic and corpus linguistic evidence for L2 constructions”. *Annual Review of Cognitive Linguistics*.

Zaliznjak, A. A. & Šmelev, A. D. (2002). „Semantika ‘načala’ c aspektologičeskoj točki zrenija”. *Logičeskij analiz jazyka. Semantika načala i konca*. Moskva: Indrik: 211–224.

Katarzyna Dziwirek

University of Washington, Seattle

Barbara Lewandowska-Tomaszczyk

University of Łódź

LOVE and HATE – UNIQUE TRANSITIVE EMOTIONS IN POLISH AND ENGLISH

Abstract: In this paper we investigate several Polish and English verbs from the domain of LOVE and HATE. We argue that in both languages these verbs form a unique class of emotion predicates. They are syntactically transitive (passivize, take accusative and genitive objects in Polish), yet unlike most transitive emotion predicates they are not causative. Even though, like intransitive emotion predicates they express feeling, not causing the emotion, they are different when it comes to syntactic behaviour, specifically complement types. We also compare the Polish and English LOVE and HATE verbs and conclude that English *like* and Polish *lubić* present a similar range of referents and complement types. Polish *kochać* and English *love* on the other hand show only *partial* equivalence, and like *uwielbiać* and *adore* are semantically close, even though they do not always share the same structural patterns. While Polish does not employ HATE verbs in politeness routines, the English politeness *preparatory* use is quite frequent in the corpus.

Keywords: emotions, English, Polish, transitive.

In most emotion domains transitive verbs mean 'to cause the emotion' (Pol. *(roz)złościć kogoś* 'to anger sb', *(z)martwić kogoś* 'to sadden/depress sb', etc.), but not so in the LIKE/LOVE and DISLIKE/HATE fields. Here, transitive verbs, like the intransitive ones, mean 'to feel the emotion', e.g. the subjects of both *kochać się* 'to be in love' and *kochać* 'to love' are experiencers. Why this should be the case is not immediately clear. While LOVE and HATE are other-oriented, their objects can often denote causes just like objects of intransitive emotion predicates, e.g. *Nienawidzę psów* 'I hate dogs' and *Boję sie psów* 'I am afraid of/fear dogs', they are encoded differently morphosyntactically and exhibit different syntactic behaviors (passivization, complement types). In this paper we focus on complements of predicates from the LIKE/LOVE and DISLIKE/HATE fields. Our data come from four corpora: PELCRA (Polish and English Language Corpora for Research and Applications), the PELCRA Sampler, the British National Corpus, and the Longman Corpus Network. We analyze 6 Polish verbs and their English equivalents: *uwielbiać* 'to love/adore', *kochać* 'to love', *lubić* 'to like', *nienawidzić* 'to hate, *nie znosić* 'can't stand/bear', and *nie cierpieć* 'can't stand'. Corpus studies such as this have implications for linguists as well as language teachers, as they document the most frequent constructions, and illuminate the nuances in conceptualizations of different verbal complements and related cultural differences.

1. Why LOVE and HATE are unique

As mentioned above, verbs in the LIKE/LOVE and DISLIKE/HATE fields are unusual among emotion predicates in Polish and English. In Polish, the experience of emotion is expressed most often by intransitive, often reflexive, verbs, while in English the majority of experienced emotions are conveyed by adjectives or participles. In both languages the Experiencer (E) is the subject of the emotion predicate, which might also have a Stimulus (S) or cause (Dixon 2006).

(1) Adam **boi się**, że go zwolnią.
Adam **is afraid** that he will get fired.
E S

In both languages transitive verbs in most emotional domains are causative. For example, *to depress, to worry, to frighten, to anger,* etc. all mean to cause the emotion of *depression, worry, fear, anger*. Typically, the Stimulus is the subject of a transitive causative emotion clause, Experiencer is the object.

(2) Sytuacja w pracy **martwi** Ewę.
The situation at work **worries** Eve.
S E

The LIKE/LOVE and DISLIKE/HATE emotional domains are different. They are transitive, yet not causative. They align semantically with the intransitive verbs or adjectives (Experiencer Subject, Stimulus Object). Yet they are unquestionably transitive according to some diagnostics: their objects are accusative or genitive in Polish (see (3)–(4)) and they are passivizable (see (9), (18), (25) and (32)).[1]

(3) Adam **kocha** mamę.
Adam **loves** his mom.
E S

(4) Adam **nienawidzi** szefa.
Adam **hates** his boss.
E S

With respect to complementation properties however, verbs in the LIKE/LOVE and DISLIKE/HATE fields pattern with other transitive emotion predicates, in that they do not allow *że/that* complement clauses, and in general permit few finite clause complements. The contrasts between intransitive emotion predicates, transitive emotion verbs, and LIKE/LOVE and DISLIKE/HATE verbs are summarized in (5).

(5)

	intransitive predicates, e.g. *bać się/be afraid*	transitive verbs, e.g. *przestraszyć/frighten*	LIKE/LOVE & DISLIKE/HATE
Experiencer subject	+	–	+
Transitive	–	+	+
Causative	–	+	–
że/that finite complements	+	–	–

In this paper we focus on the complements of LIKE/LOVE and DISLIKE/HATE verbs. The meaning and complementation patterns of LIKE/LOVE in English and Polish exhibit similarities and differences. In both languages the

[1] There are a few other transitive emotion verbs with Experiencer Subjects in English and Polish. English *fear* can be used transitively*: She knew that I would never withstand her, and that **I feared her** too*, but is most often found in other constructions, such as intransitive: ***As I feared**, the handholds were wet in places, notably below the overhang.*, with *when* clauses: ***I feared when** Cormac was made bishop.*, with prepositional objects: *I like Benny. And **I fear for him**.*, with *that* clauses: ***I feared that** when I went shopping people would abuse me, spit at me.*, and with infinitives*:* ***I fear to** even say it.* Verbs in the LIKE/LOVE and DISLIKE/HATE domain are primarily used as transitive verbs with nominal objects.

semantic distance between *adore* and *love* (*uwielbiać* and *kochać*) is similar, while *like* and *enjoy* in English and *lubić* in Polish (Polish does not have a lexicalized equivalent of *enjoy*), show certain parallelisms in the conceptualization as well. The selection of their complementation patterns on the other hand is not equivalent.[2]

(6) LIKE/LOVE: English

Meaning:

Complement types:

(7) LIKE/LOVE: Polish

Meaning:

Complement types:

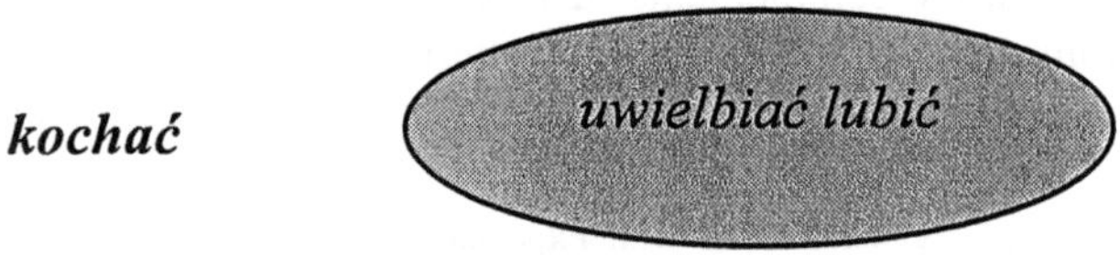

---

[2] Our data come from the British National Corpus (100 million words) and PELCRA (Polish and English Language Corpora for Research and Applications) Sampler (15 million words) and are thus not directly comparable. We focus on percentages of complement types rather than numbers of examples.

2. LIKE/LOVE

2.1. LIKE/LOVE: Polish

The main three verbs in this field in Polish are *lubić* 'to like/enjoy', *kochać* 'to love' and *uwielbiać* 'to love/adore'. They are unmistakably transitive: they take direct objects in the accusative (8) and can be passivized (9).

(8)a. Lubię matematykę.
I like math.

b. Kocham moją mamę.
I love my mom.

c. Uwielbiam teatr.
I adore the theatre.

(9)a. Nie **jesteśmy lubiani** przez społeczeństwo.
We are not liked by society.

b. **Był** ceniony i **kochany** przez żonę i przyjaciół.
He was valued and loved by his wife and friends.

c. Jackson **jest uwielbiany** przez dzieci bo nosi w sobie zwykłą dziecięcą radość.
Jackson is adored by children because he carries in him a simple childish joy.

None of the three verbs under consideration can take a *że*/that complement clause, but *uwielbiać* and *lubić* frequently occur with infinitival complements:

(10)

	lubić 'to like/enjoy'	***kochać*** 'to love'	***uwielbiać*** 'to love/adore'
number of examples	3503	1733	362
complex sentences	794 (22%)	9 (0.5%)	68 (19%)
że clauses	0	0	0
infinitives	742 (21%)	9 (0.5%)	64 (18%)
gerunds	4	3	1
'when'	52 (1.5%)	0	4 (1.1%)

Let us consider *kochać* first. It is in many ways the most 'concrete' and least hyperbolic of the three verbs and is directed prototypically towards people. What is observed here is a tendency to greater reification of complements, as *kochać* mostly occurs with nominal objects and rarely refers to activities. What/whom do Polish people love? Mostly Poles *kochają* other people (family members have highest frequency and mothers and children highest of all), arts and sports (*kino, teatr, balet, filmy, futbol, sport*), animals (*zwierzęta* 'animals', *koty* 'cats', *chomiki* 'hamsters'), nature (*góry* 'mountains', *morze* 'sea'), things (*rowery górskie* 'mountain bikes'), school subjects (*matematyka*), places (with special attention to patriotic concepts *Polska, ojczyzna* 'motherland', but also *moje miasto* 'my city', *Lwów*). A significant number of examples with *kochać* refer to God and Jesus, either in the context of God's love for people or people's love for God and Jesus (*Pan Jezus*).[3]

We found only 9 examples of *kochać* with the infinitive (11) and only three examples with gerunds (12).

(11)a. **Kocham patrzeć** na zegarmistrzowską precyzję Meryl Streep.
I love to watch the clockwork-like precision of Meryl Streep.

b. Autorka książki „Anoreksja, bulimia, otyłość" twierdzi, że one **kochają jeść**, ale potrafią rygorystycznie panować nad apetytem.
The author of the book "Anorexia, bulimia, obesity" claims that they love to eat, but are able to rigorously supress their appetite.

c. **Kocham grać** na fortepianie, ale nie odpowiada mi bycie zawodowym muzykiem.
I love to play the piano, but I do not want to be a professional musician.

(12)a. Teraz, gdy obie swoje restauracje sprzedałem, **kocham gotowanie** jeszcze bardziej.
Now, when I sold both of my restaurants, I love cooking all the more.

b. Chciał latać. **Kochał latanie**.
He wanted to fly. He loved flying.

[3] In Polish the love for God is often invoked in the phrase *Jak Boga kocham*, lit. 'As I love God', which is meant to confirm the veracity of what the speaker is saying (akin to English *I swear to God*).

c. Całe życie pracowałam i kochałam swoją pracę. Nie będę mówić, że **kochałam robienie** sweterków za pieniądze...
I worked hard and I loved my work. I won't say that I loved knitting sweaters for money...

Before we leave the verb *kochać*, we need to address the question of "I love you". Polish *Kocham cię* is very rarely used in direct statements to an addressee. It is reserved for serious, emotionally laden, romantic contexts, and is not used by moms leaving their children at preschool, or family members hanging up the phone, the way *I love you* is used in English. It is uttered by Polish people very rarely, possibly only a few times in their lifetime. In our corpus we found only 19 examples of *Kocham cię* out of 1733 instances of *kochać* (1.1%), of which 2 were from letters, and thus not exactly direct speech, 3 were in the context of "I could say that I love you" (but won't), 2 were uttered by children to parents, and 2 were directed to God. This can be compared to 667 examples of *I love you*, which constitute 7% of the 9273 British English uses of *love*. Even taking into account expressive derivation and a rich system of endearments that Polish speakers have at their disposal to show warm feelings to others, the fact that an overt declaration of love is rare among Poles is very curious. That it is so much more prevalent among English speakers seems to contradict Wierzbicka's (1999) claim that they are less outspoken, sincere and spontaneous than Slavic speakers.

Turning to *lubić* 'to like/to enjoy', it is the most common and in many ways least discriminating of the three Polish verbs. Poles like other people (though not parents and children, for whom this verb is not strong enough), their jobs, other nationalities, music, books, authors and artists, foods, and they like to do things: 21% the complements of *lubić* are infinitives:

(13)a. Ma tę słabostkę, że bardzo **lubi mówić**.
He has a weakness: he likes to talk a lot.

b. Piłsudski czytywał Marksa, **lubił rozprawiać** o teorii ewolucji społecznej.
Piłsudski read Marx, he liked to discuss the theory of social evolution.

c. Bardzo **lubię czytać** artykuły Adama Wajraka.
I really like to read Adam Wajrak's articles.

We found only 4 verbal nouns/gerunds as complements of *lubić*:

(14)a. Najbardziej **lubił zbieranie** chrabąszczy.
He liked collecting June bugs most.

b. Czytelnicy **lubią podpatrywanie** salonów.
Readers like spying on the elites.

c. Jest to złota era dla mężczyzn **lubiących majsterkowanie**.
This is the golden age for men who like (lit. 'liking') tinkering.

d. Po książkę sięga tylko ten, kto umie czytać na tyle by **lubić czytanie**.
The only person who will reach for a book is a person who knows how to read well enough to like reading.

Even though the verb *uwielbiać* has the fewest number of examples in the corpus (362 as compared with 3503 for *lubić* and 1733 for *kochać*), we sense that it is slowly gaining in Polish, as the closest equivalent of the English "LOVE"/"ADORE", as in "I love/adore movies, ice cream, chocolate", etc., and, in fact, is often used with foods and favourite artists. It has the "over the top", hyperbolic quality in most examples, though its literal sense of "to adore" is still preserved in religious contexts. It is often used with infinitive complements (18%), indicating activities.

(15)a. Premier Berlusconi pozostał miłośnikiem francuskiej piosenki. **Uwielbia czarować** słuchaczy własnym śpiewem.
Prime Minister Berlusconi remains a fan of French songs. He loves/adores to charm listeners with his singing.

b. Gazety **uwielbiają dawać** bankowcom nagrody, statuetki, specjalne tytuły.
Newspapers love to bestow awards, statuettes, special titles on bankers.

c. Co mnie bawi? **Uwielbiam latać**. Mam trzy wspaniałe samoloty.
What amuses me? I love/adore to fly. I have three great planes.

Only one example with a verbal noun was found in the corpus:

(16) Chłopiec **uwielbia pieczenie** ciasteczek czekoladowych.
The boy adores/loves baking chocolate cookies.

In summary: Polish verbs in the LOVE/LIKE field do not allow *że/that* complements at all, the frequency of *kiedy/gdy* 'when' finite complement clauses is very low, and so are verbal noun complements. As indicated in (7) semantically *kochać* and *uwielbiać* group together despite of a number of parameters that are distinct for each, and refer to more INTENSIVE emotions, while *lubić* and *uwielbiać* are close syntactically. They allow infinitive complements (roughly 1/5 of all examples for each verb) and often focus on activities, while *kochać* does so very infrequently (0.5%). *Uwielbiać* is most hyperbolic, *lubić* most mild and thus most common, *kochać* most serious and concrete (people or object/concept oriented).

2.2. LIKE/LOVE: English

(17)

	Like	*love*	*enjoy*	*adore*
number of examples	18600	9273	12132	518
complex sentences	14010 (75%)	1527 (16%)	16 (0.1%)	2 (0.4%)
that clauses	0	0	0	0
Infinitives	13890 (75%)	1488 (16%)	0	2 (0.4%)
Gerunds	Over 1000[4]	135	248	3
it when clauses	102 (0.5 %)	39 (0.4%)	16 (0.1%)	0

There are many similarities between the 3 Polish verbs discussed above and their 4 English counterparts. The English verbs are also transitive and non-causative, have Experiencer subjects and are passivizable:

(18)a. Sam was a generous person, **liked by everyone.**

b. I need to be wanted and **loved by the audience**.

c. The visit was very much appreciated by the South African Area and **enjoyed by those who went.**

d. He married and had four children and was **adored by his family**.

Comparison of corpus statistics reveals further similarities in the LIKE/LOVE domain in the two languages. Like its closest Polish counterpart *lubić*, the English *to like* is the most common of the 4 English verbs in this field (18600 per 1 hundred million words). Its popularity in English is probably due to

[4] The numerical values for gerund constructions with *like* could not be automatically retrieved due to the ambiguity of the word *like* (Verb/Adverb) and the following *-ing* constructions. POS tags used did not provide desirable results.

the fact that our search did not distinguish between *like* and *would like*. The latter is often used in politeness routines and does not always constitute an emotion verb as such. The construction *would like to* probably also accounts for the very high number (75%) of infinitival complements found with the verb *to like*.

(19)a. You can get drunk and sing with the rest, and yet you **like to be** on your own.

b. He **likes to talk** in terms of percentages.

c. We **liked to visit** Mr Macauley's shop because his furious brother George played cricket for Yorkshire.

d. She **liked to save** any money she got off Nigel and had her own private account in a building society the other side of London.

The verb *to love* also allows infinitives fairly frequently (16% of examples):

(20)a. He **loves to devour** huge meals; washed down with Chianti wine.

b. Nearly every child if properly taught **loves to draw** and paint.

c. I **love to watch** the things grow.

We have found no examples of infinitival complements with *to enjoy* and only two with *to adore*, one of which is less than coherent.

Regarding other clausal complements, none of the four English verbs allows *that* complement clauses. Finite *it when* clauses are rare and only attested with *like* (21)a–b, *love* (21)c–d and *enjoy* (21)e–f:

(21)a. He always **liked it when** she wore a certain shade of lipstick, coral, not cherry.

b. She **liked it when** he came to her room.

c. It's exciting and stimulating; with a private client I **love it when** she trusts me.

d. They **love it when** the pupils spontaneously show affection or appreciation.

e. I really **enjoy it when** we play quietly like this.

f. I didn't **enjoy it when** it happened the first time.

We have found no examples of *for-to* infinitives with the four English verbs. That is sentences like (22) did not occur in the BNC sample.

(22)a. I'd love for him to come to our party.
b.For him to do it is surprising.

Polish and English verbs are categorized according to their lexical semantic properties and the complementation patterns, which impose distinct imagery on the event represented in an utterance. While *to enjoy* never occurs with the infinitive in English, *to adore* – rarely, *to like* and *to love* are often used with the infinitive, which indicates a preference for more abstract senses in the object, such as those referring to generalizations, (projected) future, and hypothetical meanings. The verb *to enjoy* stands out as it co-occurs exclusively with gerunds, which express an action in progress, frequently simultaneous and co-temporal with the main verb. Semantically, *to like* and *to enjoy* go together in opposition to *to adore* (rare) and *to love*, which express more intensive emotions.

(23)a. We adore to travel. We adore to get out, get away.
[generalized/projected future, more abstract]

b. I adore reading.
[factual, conceptualization of the action in progress, possibly co-temporal]

c. The Princess likes looking at people's collections.
[durative action/action in progress/action performed in the past]

Finally, the verb *to enjoy* is unique in that it can be used in the imperative, either by itself (*Enjoy!*) or in combination with a noun phrase *Enjoy your meal/visit/trip!* This construction has been discussed in a recent paper by Bednarek and Bublitz (2007), who argue that the imperative use of *to enjoy* suggests that "the grammar promotes the ideology of fun" and helps convey the "message that having fun is good." (Bednarek and Bublitz 2007: 129). None of the other English emotion verbs and none of the Polish emotion verbs can be used in the imperative.

The table in (24) summarizes our findings regarding complements of LIKE/LOVE verbs in both languages. None of the verbs take finite *że/that* complements. In Polish *lubić* and *uwielbiać* and in English *like* and *love* allow infinitival complements expressing more abstract things, projected future/ hypothetical scenarios and generalized statements. The same verbs allow (although with much smaller frequency) finite *(it) when* complements. English *like* and Polish *lubić* turn out to be the closest equivalents (except for the Polish *podobać się*, not discussed here). They have a similar range of referents and complement types. Polish *kochać* and English *love* on the other hand, considered to be dictionary equivalents are in fact *partial* ones. Similarly, *uwielbiać* and *adore* are do not show *constructional correspondences* even though they are semantically very close: the former occurs frequently with complement clauses, the latter takes nouns and nominals as objects.

(24)

	Polish			**English**			
	lubić	***kochać***	***uwielbiać***	***like***	***love***	***enjoy***	***adore***
complex sentences	22%	0.5%	19%	75%	16%	0.1%	0.4%
że/that clauses	0	0	0	0	0	0	0
infinitives	21%	0.5%	18%	75%	16%	0	0.4%
gerunds	0.1%	0.2%	0.2%				
(it) when	1.5%	0	1.1%	0.5%	0.4%	0.1%	0

What is worth noting is the virtual absence of the more intensive verbs of emotion in negative constructions in both languages, particularly with complex complements such as ?*Nie kocham czytać 'I don't love to read'* ?*Nie uwielbiam Janka/czytać 'I don't adore John/to read* (except for specific contrastive contexts e.g. *(Nie to, że) Nie UWIELBIAM Janka, ja go po prostu LUBIĘ '(Not that) I don' ADORE John, I simply LIKE him*).

3. DISLIKE/HATE

3.1. DISLIKE/HATE: Polish

The three key verbs in this domain in Polish are *nienawidzić* 'to hate', *nie znosić* 'can't stand/bear', and *nie cierpieć* 'can't stand'. All three take genitive objects and are passivizable, though passive sentences with these verbs are quite rare in the PELCRA Sampler. Instead, passive participles are used in the modifying function.

(25)a. Newt Gingrich, przez jednych kochany, przez innych **nienawidzony** za swój ostry język i szybką myśl.
Newt Gingrich, loved by some, hated by others for his sharp tongue and quick wit.

b. Mnistrem oświaty jest powszechnie **nie cierpiany** półinteligent Gonella.
The minister of education is the widely disliked idiot Gonella.

When it comes to complements, the Polish HATE verbs are very concrete, they allow very few complement clauses of any kind, as can be seen in (26). By far the largest number of complements of Polish HATE verbs are people. Other objects are political systems (*reżimu, komunizmu, systemu*), other nations, places, qualities (*hipokryzji, tępoty* 'stupidity', *chamstwa* 'insolence') and things, see (27)–(29). Complement clauses of any kind are exceedingly rare with the three Polish verbs: no finite *że* clauses are possible, and infinitives, *when* clauses, *żeby* clauses, and gerunds combined account for 2.3% – 8% of all examples for a given verb.

(26)

	nienawidzić 'to hate'	*nie znosić* 'can't stand'	*nie cierpieć* 'can't bear'
number of examples	365	165	109
complex sentences	6 (1.6%)	7 (6.6%)	4 (3.6%)
że clauses	0	0	0
Infinitives	4 (1%)	6 (3.6%)	2 (2%)
when clauses	2 (0.5%)	4 (2%)	1 (1%)
Gerunds	3 (0.8%)	3 (1.8%)	1 (1%)
żeby clauses	0	1 (0.6%)	1 (1%)

(27)a. Arabowie **nienawidzili nas.**
The Arabs hated us.

b. Nie wszyscy Mongołowie **nienawidzą Rosjan.**
Not all Mongols hate Russians.

c. Ona **nienawidzi Stawskiej,** nie wiem nawet za co.
She hates Mrs Stawska, I don't even know why.

d. Niemcy pewno dlatego **ich tak nienawidzili,** że ich było tak dużo.
Germans probably hated them so much, because there were so many of them.

e. **Nienawidzę stoików** – rzekł Nero.
I hate the stoics, said Nero.

f. Czego Pan **nienawidzi? Nieuczciwości.**
What do you hate? Dishonesty.

g. **Nienawidzę walki**, ale jeszcze bardziej **nienawidzę agresji.**
I hate fighting, but I hate agression even more.

h. **Nienawidzę, gdy** wyją syreny. Boję się.
I hate it when the sirens are wailing. I am afraid.

i. Moja matka była z natury niecierpliwa i **nienawidziła czekania.**
My mother was impatient by nature and hated waiting.

(28)a. Ludzie **nie znoszą moralistów** pouczających innych.
People hate moralists, who tell others what to do.

b. Ja wiem, że ty **jej nie znosisz**, ale na moim pogrzebie musisz ...
I know that you cannot stand her, but at my funeral, you must ...

c. Barbarzyńskie narody **nie znoszą cudzoziemskich obyczajów**.
Barbaric nations hate foreign customs.

d. **Nie znoszę siedzieć** bezczynnie.
I can't stand sitting around and doing nothing.

e. Sam **nie znoszę robić** zakupów.
I myself hate shopping.

f. Nade wszystko **nie znosił, by** się co w domu zmieniało.
Most of all he hated for anything to change at home.

g. **Nie znosi podawania** ręki przy powitaniu:
He hates to shake hands.

(29)a. **Nie cierpię scen** i skandali.
I cannot stand scenes and scandals.

b. Mincel był bardzo porządny, **nie cierpiał kurzu.**
Mincel was very tidy, he hated dust.

c. Dyzma **nie cierpiał dzieci.**
Dyzma couldn't stand children.

d. Dlaczego tak **Jurka Owsiaka nie cierpią**?
Why do they hate Jurek Owsiak?

e. **Nie cierpię reżimu**, monopartii.
I hate the regime, the one party system.

f. **Nie cierpię pisać** o sobie.
I hate writing about myself.

g. **Nie cierpiał, żeby** cokolwiek było sprzątnięte.
He hated for things to be picked up.

h. **Nie cierpi zakłamania**, potrafi z nim otwarcie walczyć.
He can't stand mendacity, he knows how to fight it openly.

In summary, all three verbs expressing HATE occur very rarely with complement clauses in Polish. We observe that it is *noun concepts* that are more prototypical in this construction. The complementizer *żeby* when it occurs with HATE (as with other negative verbs), introduces future, hypothetical, undesired scenarios.

3.2. DISLIKE/HATE: English

Two key English verbs in this field are *to hate* and *to dislike*. Our findings are summarized in the table in (30).

(30)

	hate	***dislike***
number of examples	3722	876
complex sentences	464 (12%)	3 (0.3%)
That clauses	0	0
Infinitives	403 (11%)	1 (0.1%)
'when'	61 (1.6%)	2 (0.2%)
Gerunds	27 (0.8%)	26 (0.8%)

Like the Polish HATE verbs, English *to hate* and *to dislike* are very concrete and refer mostly to people and things. They can be very direct and personal: we found 106 examples of *I hate you*, 3% of all instances of *to hate* (there were no examples of *Nienawidzę cię* 'I hate you' in the PELCRA Sampler). The verb *to hate* does allow infinitival complements (11%), and while many of them can be said to refer to activities (31), quite a few are passive infinitives (32); many, especially the first person present tense utterances are politeness expressions (33),[5] while others still occur in set phrases: *hate to see, hate to think*, and *hate to say it* (34).

(31)a. He **hated to throw them away** when they got old.

b. That was the psychological moment: but she also remembered another, a turning-point in physical ageing, 'when I began to **hate to look at myself** in the glass.'

c. Also, I love animals and **hate to see them suffer**.

(32)a. He **hated to be boxed** up.

b. John never really conformed to the way of life in South Africa, and hated **to be tied down**.

(33)a. Miss Braithwaite; he turned towards her with warmth 'I realise of course that you're on holiday and I **hate to intrude** on your leisure, but since you have some knowledge already, I wonder, would you feel able, discreetly, of course, to make one or two enquiries?

b. I **hate to ask**.

c. I **hate to be a nuisance** to you.

[5] In the case of the English emotion verbs, used in *politeness formulae*, the verbs have an important pragmatic function in the context of a preparatory strategy. In particular, the English verb *hate* as in *I hate to mention this* (such a politeness strategy is less frequent with the positive emotion verbs such as *I'd like to tell you*) prepares the ground for a negative message and can be paraphrased as 'I will say what I know is not pleasant to you'. By using the verb 'hate' the speaker points to the inevitability of and external responsibility for what is said in the complement clause.

(34)a. If I'm a friend, I'd **hate to see** how you treat your enemies.

b. I **hate to see** a decent man making a mess of his life.

c. I **hate to say it**, but pain may be necessary to art.

d. I **hate to say it**, Uncle Alfred, but some of the things they said were not very nice at all –starving, poison, ambush and attack.

e. I **hate to think** how many women he has assaulted since then.

The verb *to dislike* rarely allows complement clauses and the objects of *to dislike* are most often people, things and ideas.

(35)a. She **disliked the thought**, was surprised at the intensity of that dislike, but knew she must consider the possibility.

b. I asked many Goans if they **disliked the freakish visitors**, and their verdicts were almost unanimous.

c. The other recollection was a speech by Hanif Kureishi, the film-maker, about which I recall only how much I **disliked it**.

d. If he found that the archbishop **disliked a nomination**, he coolly referred it back to Downing Street.

e. In fact she felt that Jennie positively **disliked her**.

f. He **disliked occidental empires** and wished to see them ended as soon as practicable.

The verbs *to hate* and *to dislike* occur with finite *it when* complements, though infrequently:

(36)a. I **hate it when** people cry, cos it makes me want to do the same thing.

b. I **hate it when** they try to add bits, I just like to subtract.

c. I **hate it when** I get like this.

d. Don't you just **hate it when** that happens?

e. It is for this reason that ordinary policemen and women **dislike it when** the typifications become confused, when decent and honest 'victims' of crime, for example, become 'trouble-makers' by taking the law into their own hands.

f. For some reason, he **disliked it when** she behaved badly in front of Marjorie.

In summary, the three Polish verbs expressing HATE occur very rarely with complement clauses. Of all the verbs in (37), only English *to hate* is found in significant numbers in complex sentences, with 12%. This is in a large part due to first person set phrases and polite demurrals. Polish does not employ HATE verbs in politeness routines. In general, DISLIKE/HATE verbs in both languages overwhelmingly prefer nominal objects.

(37)

	Polish			**English**	
	nienawidzić	***nie znosić***	***nie cierpieć***	***hate***	***dislike***
complex sentences	1.6%	6.6%	3.6%	12%	0.3%
że/that clauses	0	0	0	0	0
Infinitives	1%	3.6%	2%	11%	0.1%
(it) when clauses	0.5%	2%	1%	1.6%	0.2%
Gerunds	0.8%	1.8%	1%	0.8%	0.8%

Comparing (37) with (24), we see that the Polish *lubić* and *uwielbiać* and the English *to like* and *to love* really stand out. These four verbs occur with clausal complements with much higher frequency than all the other predicates in the LIKE/LOVE and DISLIKE/HATE fields. Polish *kochać*, *nienawidzić, nie znosić* and *nie cierpieć* and English *to enjoy, to adore, to hate* and *to dislike* tend to refer to concrete objects, people, or ideas, and allow very few complement clauses.

For a final comparison consider the table in (38), which presents similar statistics for 3 Polish intransitive emotion predicates. For all three *że/that* clauses are the most common complement type and only *bać się* allows infinitives. Thus even though verbs in the LIKE/LOVE and DISLIKE/HATE fields mean 'to feel' rather than 'to cause' an emotion, their complementation properties are quite different from intransitive emotion verbs.

(38)

	bać się 'to be afraid'	***martwić się*** 'to be worried'	***cieszyć się*** 'to be glad'
number of examples	1421	338	1304
complex sentences (cs)	580 (40%)	89 (23%)	301 (23%)
że clauses (% of cs)	275 (47% of cs)	46 (52% of cs)	265 (88% of cs)
Infinitives	234 (40% of cs)	0	0
żeby 'lest' clauses	55	4	0
czy 'if' Q-clauses	16	14	0
wh-Q-clauses	0	10	0

In Polish and English similar referent *prototypes* are identified with the LOVE and HATE verbs, even though frequencies of their occurrence in corpus data are different. What is also found is a distinct categorization of the *emotion concepts* as well as their extensions such as the politeness *preparatory* sense, which occurs only in English. The linguistic data we investigated suggest that Poles LOVE and HATE more concretely in the sense that the *objects* of these emotions are more reified in Polish, where higher frequencies of prototypical people and objects have been identified. The objects are also more 'literal' than in English, where more types and tokens of complement constructions appear, with their extension to *politeness* strategies. To what extent extrapolation from the linguistic findings to questions of Polish/English mental setup and cultural preferences is supported by psychological and sociological findings remains to be seen.

4. Conclusions

As a conclusion, we can propose that LIKE/LOVE verbs in English and Polish show a number of similarities, even though frequencies of their occurrence in corpus data are different. In Polish *lubić* and *uwielbiać* and in English *like* and *love* allow infinitival complements and express more abstract things, projected future/hypothetical scenarios and generalized statements. English *like* and Polish *lubić* present a similar range of referents and complement types. Polish *kochać* and English *love* on the other hand show only *partial* equivalence, and like *uwielbiać* and *adore* are semantically close, even though they do not always share the same structural patterns.

Verbs expressing HATE occur with *noun concepts* as the most prototypical objects. However, while Polish does not employ HATE verbs in politeness routines, the English politeness *preparatory* use is quite frequent in the corpus materials and can be considered an extension of the basic pattern, even though the prototypical object will not be a noun but an infinitive in such cases.

REFERENCES

Bednarek, M. & W. Bublitz (2007). "Enjoy!: The (phraseological) culture of having fun". In: P. Skandera (ed.). *Phraseology and Culture in English.* Mouton de Gruyter: 109–136.

Dixon, R. M. W. (2006). "Complement Clauses and Complementation Strategies in Typological Perspective". In: Dixon, R. M. W. and A. Y. Aikhenvald (eds.). *Complementation: A Cross-Linguistic Typology.* Oxford University Press: 1–48.

Dixon, R. M. W. and A. Y. Aikhenvald (eds.) (2006). *Complementation: A Cross-Linguistic Typology.* Oxford University Press.

Dziwirek, K. & B. Lewandowska-Tomaszczyk (forthcoming). *Complex Emotions and Grammatical Mismatches.*

Wierzbicka, A. (1999). *Emotions Across Languages and Cultures: Diversity and Universals.* Cambridge: Cambridge University Press.

Part Five

APPLICATIONS AND IMPLICATIONS

Mikołaj Deckert

University of Łódź

PLEONASMS – FROM COGNITION TO TRANSLATION[1]

Abstract: The paper investigates the mechanics of redundancy in language, paying particular attention to the concept of a "pleonasm." Authentic pleonastic constructions extracted from a corpus of TV news and from the current version of *Narodowy Korpus Języka Polskiego* (The National Corpus of Polish) are analysed with the parameter of "relevance" (Sperber and Wilson 1986) in mind. This is to demonstrate the correlation between communication and pleonasms and to argue that redundancy need not decrease the cost-effectiveness of the former. Based on this, selected translation problems of linguistic and of cultural nature are pointed to and translation implications are suggested.

Keywords: communication, English, French, Polish, redundancy, relevance, translation decisions.

1. Introduction

To scrutinise the target text[2] with a view to finding instances of deviation from what could prescriptively be referred to as linguistic norm is nothing out of the ordinary – it is a crucial component of translation classes and a common practice for translators having the linguistic quality of their work examined by proofreaders or, ultimately, by clients. Whereas formal aspects of the source text[3] are rarely considered.

The present paper focuses on the concept of redundancy. As it occurs on many levels of linguistic organisation, the scope of interest shall here be limited to one of its main types – "pleonasms." The comments are going to be based on examples of pleonastic constructions that come from a demo version of

---

[1] I am indebted to Professor Barbara Lewandowska-Tomaszczyk and Professor Katarzyna Dziwirek for their support and remarks.

[2] Hereinafter abbreviated to "TT."

[3] Hereinafter abbreviated to "ST."

Narodowy Korpus Jezyka Polskiego (The National Corpus of Polish),[4] which currently totals approximately 350 million tokens, and a Polish TV corpus. The data in the latter, amounting to 273 356 tokens, cover broadcast news programmes from two Polish channels – *TVP1* and *Polsat*, a state-owned company and a commercial company respectively.[5] With "relevance" (Sperber and Wilson 1986), or more generally the efficiency of communication, as the major parameter to give an insight into pleonasms, the remarks included hereafter shall predominantly allude to human cognition.

Constructions of pleonastic type have been ubiquitous in language. They can easily be spotted in songs or advertisements but they are also used profusely by sports commentators, TV reporters and presenters, not to mention politicians, viz. individuals whose oratorical skills ought to serve as a model. Pleonasms are also varied – Małocha-Krupa (2003) lists 510 pleonastic items, many of which have several variants or subtypes.

It has to be stressed that deciding whether pleonasms ought to be categorised as linguistic/logical mistakes is not the concern here. The objective is to frame pleonasms as constructs of high linguistic and social significance, and therefore a subject worthy of scrutiny.

2. Redundancy in language

Code redundancy is an inbuilt property of natural language.[6] One instance of such irremovable redundancy are constructions where verbs are obligatorily accompanied by prepositions. In "podejść do" [lit. "to come up to"] the verb would suffice to express the action so the preposition reduplicates the content already included in the syntagm. Obligatory redundancy, for instance on the syntactic level, is at least partially a reaction against the noise that hinders transmission of the linguistic signal and hence such redundancy will be evaluated positively.

---

[4] This version of *NKJP* combines three corpora of Polish: the *IPI PAN* (Institute of Computer Science, Polish Academy of Sciences) corpus, the *PWN* (Polish Scientific Publishers) corpus and the *PELCRA* corpus (built at the University of Łódź).

[5] The corpus was originally collected for the purpose of data analysis in the *Integrated and United? A Quest for Citizenship in an Ever Closer Europe* project realised within the scope of the *6th Framework Programme.*

[6] Though it is a fallacy to categorise as redundant one of the items in sets like "wrócić"–"powrócić" (cf. Janowska 1999: 114) or "głębia"–"głębina" (cf. Małocha-Krupa 2003: 21) since the difference in form is certain to have some semantic import.

Pleonasms and tautologies are, however, instances of pragmatic redundancy – also referred to as "textual" ["tekstowa" (Zydroń 1993)] or "syntagmatic" ["syntagmatyczna" (Buttler 1971)] – which can in most cases be eliminated. Curiously, the distinction between pleonasms and tautologies is often blurred – at times they are seen as overlapping or even as synonymous. This is true for Polish just as well as for English or French, though as Małocha-Krupa (2003: 29) observes, the English linguistic tradition is the least precise and fails to give a single definition that would treat pleonasms and tautologies as discernible concepts. For the purpose of clarity, the distinction proposed by Buttler (1971) shall be used here and pleonasm shall thence be understood as a string of words which determine one another whereby some components are superfluous, whereas tautology shall be seen as a unit whose elements are grammatically homogenous and express similar or identical content.

In her complex classification Małocha-Krupa (2003: 95–104) differentiates between several categories of pleonastic items. The groups, labelled using their flagship members,[7] are:

Table I

English	Polish	French
descend down	zejść na dół	descendere en bas
collaborate together	współpracować razem	collaborer ensemble
final end	ostateczny koniec	le but final
repeat again	powtórzyć jeszcze raz	redemander de nouveau
postpone until later	przełożyć na później	différer à une date ultérieure
walk on foot[8]	iść pieszo[9]	marcher à pied
see with one's own eyes	zobaczyć na własne oczy	voir de mes propres yeux
cold ice	zaspa śnieżna	un dune de sable
foreign imports	importować z zagranicy	importer de l'étranger
more easier	bardziej łatwiejszy	le moindre petit
PIN number	numer PIN	———
exit out[10]	wyjść na zewnątrz	sortir dehors

[7] They are not always literal renditions of one another, e.g. the equivalents of "cold ice" are based on the concept of "snow" in Polish and "sand" in French.

[8] "Go on foot" given by Małocha-Krupa (2003) seems inadequate as "to go" is not limited to covering distance using feet and hence needs specifying.

[9] Many individuals add the preposition "na" [lit. "on"] between the two elements.

[10] This is absent from the classification proposed by Małocha-Krupa (2003). For drawing my attention to the item thanks are due to Professor Michael Halliday.

Presenting pleonasms in such a context-independent fashion can be objected to as certain contextual assumptions might invalidate them; e.g. "zejść na dół" [lit. "to descend to the down"] could be regarded as non-pleonastic if "dół" is understood as a location rather than a direction. This, however, does not undermine the thesis that pleonasms tend to exist universally – across languages and cultures.

3. Pleonasms and communication

The question is how pleonasms actually affect communication. Since many of them[11] are prescriptively termed a type of a grammatical mistake or semantic anomaly (cf. Cruse 2006), one could surmise that their impact on the process of intentional information exchange is negative.

To investigate the issue, I will make use of certain concepts from Relevance Theory (Sperber and Wilson 1986). This framework relies on the claim that traditional "code model" (cf. Shannon and Weaver 1949) fails to account for the mechanisms of communication and needs complementing with the more cognitively-oriented "ostensive-inferential model." The apparatus centres upon the notion of "relevance" whose varied degrees can be retrieved from verbal stimuli by individual comprehenders, and which is primarily the resultant of two factors: "processing effort" and "contextual effects." What is going to be argued for here is that viewed through the prism of relevance, pleonasms turn out not to impair communication.

Take the triplet of utterances:

1. Could you repeat that?
2. Could you repeat that again?
3. Could you say that again?

All three questions/requests have a similar perlocutionary effect upon the addressee – if the interactant is cooperative he or she will probably produce the particular utterance, referred to as "that," once more. But even though the effects brought about by 1, 2 and 3 are ultimately coincident, the effort required from the receptor to process the stimulus is different in each case due to differences in the linguistic form employed to transmit content.

[11] Those with higher incidence become the "usus" – e.g. "miasto Łódź" [lit. "the city of Łódź"] occurring in Polish documents like identity cards or driving licenses where "Prezydent miasta Łodzi" [lit. "President of the city of Łódź"] is given as the "issuing authority." Consequently, it might happen that in certain cases a non-pleonastic variant will be seen as unnatural or "incorrect" by a person who internalises the more popular pleonastic form.

Taking into account the normatively seen ungrammaticality or illogicality, one would conclude that in utterance 2 the adverb "again" is superfluously added to enrich the semantic content of the verb "to repeat" which already denotes recurrence.[12] Utterances 1 and 3 are not pleonastic in this respect – the former does not insert the adverb "again" and the latter employs the verb "to say" which does not entail repetitiveness so the adverb is used soundly there.

With relevance and the effectiveness of communication in mind, however, utterance 2 appears to be no less successful than utterances 1 and 3. The concept of "reproducing" is given twice in this utterance, which does not require the receptor to concentrate on grasping both the constituents, as "missing" a part does not prevent the receptor from deriving the interpretation.[13] Therefore, reduplication of content strengthens the semantic potential of the linguistic signal and protects it against the factors that hamper transmission – by this facilitating comprehension, viz. decreasing the amount of mental energy needed to process it. It could be argued that since the contextual effects derivable from utterance 2 are analogous to those derivable from the two non-pleonastic utterances, it is its pleonasticity that makes the second input the most relevant. But while the argument that pleonasms have a communication-facilitating function has received support, e.g. Małocha-Krupa (2003),[14] the argument that a pleonastic verbal stimulus is more relevant than its non-pleonastic counterpart is still rather tentative and has to be backed up with concrete practical research.

One of the crucial claims to support the line of thought, however, would be that the cutback of processing effort is one reason why language users produce pleonasms. In this vein, the motivation is to ensure successful transmission of information. The means by which the message is to be conveyed are, in most instances subconsciously, intensified by the speaker/writer to safeguard himself or herself against a communication failure. And this again is in keeping with the pragmatic (and relevance-theoretic) postulates – most notably the naive-receptor

[12] Unless what the speaker asks the addressee to repeat has already been repeated.

[13] Yet another property of pleonasms, significant with respect to the parameters of effect and effort, is the surplus of form (addressed also in Section 3.1). The longer the utterance, the larger the space on which attention is to be distributed and the more costly the processing. From this perspective, pleonastic expressions could decrease relevance of an utterance – but the decrease would still be minor because the assumptions included in the additional material overlap with the assumptions of the non-pleonastic material.

[14] She talks of their pragmatically-motivated communicative value which can be: to specify, to strengthen (*intenssiva*) or to explicate.

paradigm whereby sole responsibility for the cost-effectiveness of communication lies with the utterer.[15]

The intention behind using phrases longer than necessary (and hence often pleonastic) is also to pass oneself off as more eloquent or intelligent. Pleonasms of this type occur abundantly. The TV data give the example of the pleonastic noun phrase "dzień dzisiejszy" [lit. "the day of today"] which in different configurations like "dzisiejszy dzień" [lit. "today's day"], "w dniu dzisiejszym" [lit. "on the day of today"], "na dzień dzisiejszy" [lit. "as for the day of today"], "do dnia dzisiejszego," "po dzień dzisiejszy" [lit. "until the day of today"], or "z dniem dzisiejszym" [lit. "with the day of today"] occurs 7 times in the *Polsat* subcorpus and as many times in the *TVP1* subcorpus. *NKJP* gives the following frequencies:[16]

Table 2

combination	frequency
w dniu dzisiejszym	6510
na dzień dzisiejszy	2211
do dnia dzisiejszego	1847
po dzień dzisiejszy	419
z dniem dzisiejszym	85

3.1. Pleonasms and iconicity in language

Within the structuralist paradigm language was a set of signs not motivated by any extralinguistic factors. Arbitrariness, in the de Saussurrean sense whereby "not even purportedly onomatopoeic words are [seen as] directly motivated by the actual sounds found in nature" (Kwiatkowska 1997: 139) spurred a structuralism-driven debate (cf. Chomsky 1968, 1981; Fodor 1983) and it was probably only in the 1960s when it was proposed that "one may entertain the possibility that an inner similarity between the vehicle and referent may occur without this similarity being apparent to an observer (...)" (Werner and Kaplan 1963: 26). Also Jakobson (1971: 700) maintains that iconicity is to be recognised

[15] The use of pleonasms is also motivated by semantic bleaching, viz. gradual erasure of semantic value of a lexical item. When used frequently, words (or combinations of words) lose their effectiveness in eliciting particular cognitive responses and in order to compensate for the loss the semantic content has to be intensified. But this is a vicious circle because the intensified items also start to lose force and as time elapses they need to be strengthened again.

[16] Excluding the alternative word order.

as a language-structuring factor and, therefore, defining "verbal signs as solely conventional, arbitrary symbols proves to be a misleading oversimplification." Among the numerous arguments for the presence of iconicity in language (cf. Kwiatkowska 1997, Fischer 2006) at least one appears applicable to the discussion on pleonasms – it is the MORE OF CONTENT IS MORE OF FORM metaphor.

On a practical level, this dovetails with what has been already hinted at; namely, that in certain contexts reduplicative constructions, and other ploys utilised to add form as an alleged means for adding content, serve to make utterances (and their producers) appear more formal, learned or elegant – Polish instances would be "w miesiącu lipcu" (lit. "in the month of July"), "rzeka Wisła" (lit. "the Vistula river") or "dzień dzisiejszy" (cf. Wilkoń 1987: 72).

4. Pleonasms and translation

The issue of rendering pleonasms across languages and cultures – which is above all whether to remove the pleonasms in translation or come up with analogous items – comprises several facets.

First, there is the parameter of relevance. To polish the ST element so that it cannot be questioned by a prescriptively-oriented grammarian, viz. to efface semantic reduplication, could entail making the utterance more difficult to process and decreasing its relevance. Ultimately, communication could be hampered.

But having left aside the positive communicative value of reduplicative items and deciding that the TT is to be made less redundant, the translator is faced with yet another difficulty, namely whether a relation analogous to that between the ST and its audience (at least with respect to the ST "redundancy saturation") is ideally to be created between the TT and its receptors (cf. Nida 1964, 1964/2004).[17]

The third consideration is more down-to-earth. Idealistically or prescriptively-motivated translational approaches – making an allegedly formally flawed ST an analogously formally flawed TT – might be detrimental to the translator's career. It is a cliché that a TT reader presented with a poorly written piece shall blame the translator even if the poor quality of the TT's form is the reflection of what is found in the original. The translation market and the audience have certain expectations and are subject to norms (cf. Toury 1995, 1998) which the translator can choose to heed or neglect, thus selecting between his or her

[17] Also the later functionally-driven approaches to translation could be applicable here – e.g. Reiss and Vermeer (1984/1991), Holz-Mänttäri (1984), Vermeer (1978, 1996), Nord (1988/1991, 1997), House (1977/1981, 1997).

professional (or financial) well-being and oblivion. Going for the former would probably require the translator to amend the ST.

5. Rendering a pleonasm

Deciding to translate a pleonasm by means of a pleonasm often seems only the beginning of the problem-solving process. Many pleonastic items occur cross-lingually – there are still, however, crucial divergencies in how languages are structured, which will inevitably result in translation hurdles.

One example is the pleonastic cluster produced by Bronisław Komorowski (*Polsat*, *Wydarzenia*, 26.03.2007) to comment on the behaviour of the Polish President during the festivities commemorating the 50th anniversary of the European Union. The passage goes: "takie wyraźne cofnięcie się dwa kroki z powrotem do tyłu nie służy umocnieniu opinii o Polsce jako o kraju który jest liderem postępu procesu integracji europejskiej." [lit. "such a clear reversing two steps back backwards does not serve well to strengthen the opinion about Poland as a country which is the leader of the progress of the process of European integration"]. Here the pleonasm construes Poland physically as moving backwards or, more figuratively, declining and the spatial frame is then again employed when the concept of a "leader" is introduced in the geopolitical context. Interestingly, later on the news item is once more intertwined with the metaphorical thread as Bronisław Geremek declares – "trzeba iść do przodu" [lit. "there is a need to go/walk forward"].

As regards redundancy, the wording used by Komorowski seems to constitute what could be called an *extra-pleonasm* for the semantic content is not only duplicated but trebled; one sees the pleonasticity increase in two stages and the final pleonasm is a combination of two pleonastic items:

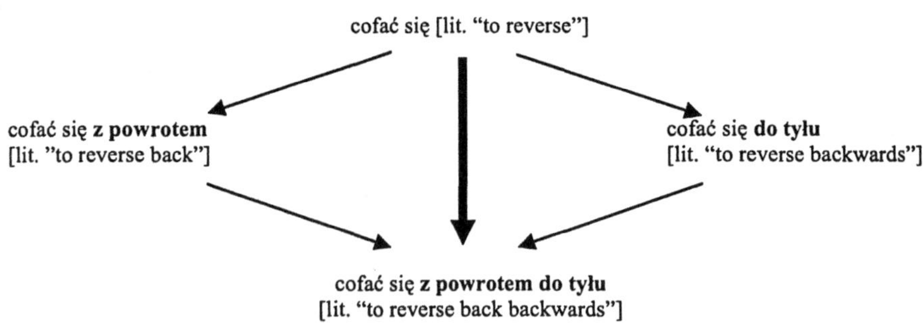

Fig. 1

In this utterance the speaker's linguistic competence is arguably influenced by his emotional attitude towards the addressed matter (the situation of Poland in the political arena of Europe and actions taken by the persona of the President) and the need to state his opinion firmly is mirrored in the form.

Table 3, quoting frequencies from *NKJP*, shows that the components of this pleonastic phrasing and its variants ["cofać" and "cofać się" followed by "wstecz" and "w tył" whose literal renditions into English are invariably "back(wards)"] are strongly represented:

Table 3

combination		frequency		
with the reflexive pronoun "się"	**without the reflexive pronoun "się"**	**with "się"**	**without "się"**	**total**
cof* się wstecz	cof* wstecz	18	10	28
cof* się do tyłu	cof* do tyłu	7	7	14
cof* się z powrotem	cof* z powrotem	7	4	11
cof* się w tył	cof* w tył	9	3	12

Komorowski's pleonasm, with its creativity and complexity, appears to be translationally challenging. The problem lies not in the spatiality or corporality of the scene but in the fact that an item formally equivalent to the Polish *extra-pleonasm* might not sound deft and inconspicuous enough in English.

Also from the perspective of linguistic code, the extensive use of diminutive and augmentative forms in Polish is a hurdle for a translator working in the Polish-English language pair. For instance, "jabłuszko," being the diminutive of "jabłko" [lit. "an apple"] would most probably be translated into English by complementing "apple" by an adjective like "small," "tiny," "miniscule" etc. The structural diversification of languages does not seem cumbersome until one wishes to come up with a translation of a pleonasm like "małe jabłuszko"[18] as the English adjective denoting smallness of the fruit would already have been used to render the non-pleonastic form.

Still, a more complicated problem is when a pleonastic expression becomes strongly embedded in the cultural context of the ST. Polish political discourse offers numerous examples of such obstacles.

[18] Which still need not be a pleonasm if one intends to single out an exceptionally small apple within a set of small apples, or if the purpose of the diminutive is to indicate affection towards the addressee, not size.

One instance is the term "trzeci bliźniak" [lit. "the third twin"] – used to mock the person of Ludwik Dorn[19] (*Polsat*, *Wydarzenia*, 12.02.2007) who showed unanimity with and excessive attachment to the Kaczyński twins (at that time the President and Prime Minister of the Republic of Poland). The concept of "twinness" unequivocally entails the existence of two brothers born from the same mother (and in this instance from one zygote) – a third twin seems to work as a kind of deviation/variation on the topic of the pleonasm "two twins" whereby the number "two" reduplicates the information provided by the noun which follows. The concept of "the third twin" patently violates the logic since the number of twins cannot exceed two. Importantly for the translator, though, the attention-drawing quality of the phrase lies perhaps not as much in its alleged ill-formedness as in its inventiveness and the very idea that someone could be born of the same mother (and at roughly the same time) as the well-known brothers. Essentially, because of the social prominence of Lech Kaczyński and Jarosław Kaczyński, the concept of a "twin," and in particular its plural form ("bliźniacy"), took on a heavy connotational charge which would be (at the minimum partly) lost in cross-cultural transmission.

An even more "famous" and firmly contextualised pleonasm was authored by one of the twins himself.[20] In a radio interview (*Program Pierwszy Polskiego Radia*, *Sygnały Dnia*, 05.06.2007) Jarosław Kaczyński announced – "trzeba pamiętać, że jeśli jakaś osoba nieustannie obraża urzędującą głowę państwa (...) no to nie może liczyć na to, że będzie następnie przyjmowana. To jest chyba oczywista oczywistość." [lit. "one must remember that if some person incessantly offends the incumbent head of state (…) this person cannot count that he or she will then be welcomed. This is perhaps an obvious obviousness."], [One needs to remember that if someone keeps offending the incumbent head of state (…) he or she cannot expect to be then given a warm welcome. It seems to be obvious obviousness.] Substantially, even a person with moderate linguistic awareness can spot the linguistic and logical idiosyncrasy in "obvious obviousness" – it is hence the patent redundancy combined with the eminent persona of speaker that draw attention. The phrase was then extensively discussed and poked fun at,[21] and this created a supplementary set of connotations – connotations which are difficult to transfer into the target language and the target culture. The translation challenge here, just as in the case

[19] *NKJP* provides one instance of "trzeci bliźniak" pointing to Andrzej Lepper and one instance of "czwarty bliźniak" [lit. "the fourth twin"] which, as is suggested in the text, could denote Przemysław Gosiewski, another politician allied with Lech and Jarosław Kaczyński.

[20] *NKJP* has also got one occurrence of the phrase coming from an MP and dated 26.03.2003.

[21] Noticeably, the former president of Poland Aleksander Kwaśniewski did so in the presidential debate with Lech Kaczyński on 01.10.2007.

of "the third twin," is palpably that the pleonastic item is a part of a larger context, of a meaning network. "Obvious obviousness" might be argued to have a metonymic property whereby the person's utterance stands for the person, their way of thinking or behaving, some trait of the utterer's character, or even a particular event. Therefore, once the linguistic barrier has been overcome, the translator still has the cultural hurdle to deal with. Having recourse to a strategy in line with "dynamic equivalence" (Nida 1964, 1964/2004), the "domesticating" method (Venuti 1995) or even "adaptation" (cf. Vinay and Darbelnet 2004) might be a way out.[22]

Another issue is how noticeable the surplus of form in a given component is cross-linguistically and cross-culturally. As English is becoming a *lingua franca* (or a vehicular language) and is frequently used by non-native speakers prone to manipulating it in highly imaginative fashions, a pleonastic unit might, due to its high incidence, pass unnoticed. Native speakers of English have had time to get accustomed to their mother tongue being tampered with. This, in the course of time, enlarged the capacity of the code and increased its flexibility. The formal variations are less detectable in English – at least as compared with the Polish speakers' sensitivity to any type of prescriptively-defined incorrectness. The implication for the translator would then be that the tolerance level for deviation from the norm (fuzzy a concept as it is) is higher in the English-speaking community as compared to the Polish one. Consequently, items that are analogously pleonastic from the point of view of form might be more highly lexicalised in one language than in the other.

6. Redundancy in various types of translation

The different translation circumstances and modes urge the translator to structure the hierarchy of priorities accordingly. One such specific translation type is community interpreting. According to Williamson (1996: 28–30) the major consideration at play there is accuracy, not "elegance." Therefore, "if someone starts to speak, breaks in mid-sentence, continues in a way that makes little sense, uses bad grammar or offensive language, or makes a slip of the tongue the interpreter must reproduce it as accurately as possible." The

[22] This orientation requires the translator to turn to procedures that may raise the issue of translatability, but to conclude whether something can be translated one would first need to give a concise and uncontroversial definition of translation which lies beyond the scope of this study, if it is feasible whatsoever.

interpreter cannot refine the ST stylistically or grammatically as such an intervention might have serious legal consequence.

Still another point is how redundancy functions in specialised languages[23] – for instance the language of the law. Redundant structures, in the form of what legal language theorists refer to as "binomials"[24] (Malkiel 1959, Danet 1980, Gustafsson 1984), "double words," "doublets" (Melinkoff 1963), or more recently as "coupled synonyms" (Šarčević 1997) are an immanent property of this type of discourse. Deciding whether to render "by and between," "fit and proper" or "final and conclusive" as tautological is not up to the translator for these phrases have their fixed equivalents in the target language register.

Similar lexical clusters can be found in general English (e.g. "safe and sound," "nook and cranny"). These items often happen not to have correspondents (form-wise) in the Polish code, which adds yet another argument to confirm the incommensurability of languages (cf. Lakoff 1987, Lewandowska-Tomaszczyk 1992, 1999) and often creates a translational problem.

7. Conclusions

Pleonasms are being utilised widely and creatively. Their impact on communication is not to be underestimated. It is arguably more than a conjecture that language users who insert pleonastic items in their utterances make the stimuli more accessible for their interlocutors by cutting down on the cognitive energy they need to spend on processing a given piece of linguistic evidence. To use the nomenclature devised by Sperber and Wilson (1986), a reduction in processing effort observable in the acquisition procedure of a pleonastic component could boost the relevance of the language sample in which it occurs.

It must be stressed, however, that the cognitive paradigm, in this case Relevance Theory, has its weak points. The reliability of relevance as a tool for analysing the correlation between pleonasms and communication could be questioned because the parameters of effort and effect cannot be calculated more than intuitively and thus approximately. Likewise, particular interlocutors will assess different stimuli as relevant and a different degree of relevance will live

---

[23] Or, as Małocha-Krupa (2003: 117–122) contends, "styles" where a pleonasm might work as the "exponent of style" ["eksponent stylu"]).

[24] Malkiel (1959: 113) defines a binomial as "a sequence of two words pertaining to the same form-class, placed on an identical level of syntactic hierarchy, and ordinarily connected by some kind of lexical link."

up to their expectations. Nonetheless, the dyad of costs and benefits can definitely be utilised in a number of research settings as it underpins all human activity.

With respect to translation, the question how to deal with pleonastic components in most cases boils down to the dilemma whether the TT equivalent of a pleonasm should be analogously redundant.[25] To be borne in mind at this point is that pleonasms are often prescriptively seen as specimens of ungrammaticality, which, juxtaposed with their communication-facilitating capacity contributes to their equivocal status. Additionally, these constructs are often culture-bound, which creates another dilemma – that of the translation strategy selection.

Overall, pleonasms provide a linguist with a vast field or, in fact, a selection of subfields, to be studied. Hence, the objective of this paper is merely to point to the complexity and multidimensionality of these constructions: their omnipresence and, more interestingly from the standpoint of cross-lingual communication, cultural embeddedness, which make pleonasms prominent not only in the *stricte* linguistic but also in the social sense. More generally, the aim here is to raise questions about the feasibility of striking a balance between prescription and description, the feasibility of delimiting the norm in language – however significant its translational ramifications could be. A tentative conclusion could then be that pleonasms, or linguistic redundancy in general, should not be examined with any ossified differentiations in mind but should rather be approached pragmatically, with the efficiency of communication or the relevance criterion as the determinants.

REFERENCES

Buttler, D. (1971). "Źródła „redundancji" leksykalnej." *Prace Filologiczne*, vol. XXI.

Chomsky, N. (1968). *Language and mind.* New York: Harcourt, Brace & World.

Chomsky, N. (1981). "On the representation of form and function." *The Linguistic Review* 1: 3–40.

Cruse, A. (2006). *A Glossary of Semantics and Pragmatics*. Edinburgh: Edinburgh University Press.

Danet, B. (1980). "Language in the legal process." *Law & Society Review* 14: 445–564.

[25] Reversely, the translator might be tempted to insert a pleonasm in the TT where there is no pleonasm in the ST. If this were to function as explicitation, it would reduce the processing effort incurred on the target audience who have no access to certain assumptions (accessible to the source audience) and would ensure communicability – e.g. translating "Wisła" as "the Vistula river."

Fischer, O. (2006). "Dowody na ikoniczność w języku." In: E. Tabakowska (ed.). *Ikoniczność znaku: słowo – przedmiot – obraz – gest*. Kraków: Universitas: 15–45.
Fodor, J. A. (1983). *The Modularity of Mind*. Cambridge Massachusetts: MIT Press.
Gustafsson, M. (1984). "The syntactic features of binomial expressions in legal English." *Text 5/3*: 123–141.
Hejwowski, K. (2007). *Kognitywno-komunikacyjna teoria przekładu*. Warszawa: PWN.
Holz-Mänttäri, J. (1984). *Translatorisches Handeln. Theorie und Methode*. Helsinki: Suomalainen Tiedeacatemia.
House, J. (1977/1981). *A Model for Translation Quality Assessment*. Tübingen: Gunter Narr.
House, J. (1997). *Translation Quality Assessment: A Model Revisited*. Tübingen: Gunter Narr.
Jakobson, R. (1971). *Selected Writings*, vol. II: *Word and Language*. The Hague: Mouton.
Janowska, A. (1999). "Funkcja pleonastyczna i tautologiczna prefiksów." In: A. Janowska (ed.). *Funkcje przestrzenne przedrostków czasownikowych w polszczyźnie*. Katowice.
Kwiatkowska, A. (1997). *The visuo-spatial determinants of natural language*. Łódź: Wydawnictwo Uniwersytetu Łódzkiego.
Lakoff, G. and Johnson, M. (1980). *Metaphors We Live By*. Chicago: The University of Chicago Press.
Lewandowska-Tomaszczyk, B. (1992). "Effability, Expressibility and Translation." In: B. Lewandowska-Tomaszczyk and M. Thelen (eds.). *Translation and Meaning. Part 2, Proceedings of the Łódź Session of the 1990 Maastricht-Łódź Duo Colloquium on 'Translation and Meaning.'* Maastricht: Rijkshogeschool Maastricht: 83–90.
Lewandowska-Tomaszczyk, B. (1999). "A Cognitive-interactional Model of Cross-linguistic analysis: New perspectives on 'tertium comparationis' and the concept of equivalence." In: B. Lewandowska-Tomaszczyk (ed.). *Cognitive Perspectives on Language*. Frankfurt am Main: Peter Lang: 53–76.
Malkiel, Y. (1959). "Studies in irreversible binomials." *Lingua 8*: 113–160.
Melinkoff, D. (1963). *The Language of the Law*. Boston: Little, Brown and Company.
Małocha-Krupa, A. (2003). *Słowa w lustrze. Pleonazm – semantyka – pragmatyka*. Wydawnictwo Uniwersytetu Wrocławskiego: Wrocław.
Nord, Ch. (1988/1991). *Text Analysis in Translation: Theory, Methodology and Didactic (Application of a Model for Translation-Oriented Text*. Heidelberg: J. Groos, Amsterdam: Rodopi.
Nord, Ch. (1997). *Translating as a Purposeful Activity. Functionalist Approaches Explained*. Manchester: St. Jerome.
Nida, E. A. (1964). *Toward a Science of Translating*. Leiden: E. J. Brill.
Nida, E. A. (1964/2004). "Principles of correspondence." In: L. Venuti (ed.). *The Translation Studies Reader*. (2nd edn.). New York and London: Routledge: 153–167.
Reiss, K. and Vermeer, H. J. (1984/1991). *Grundlegung einer allgemeinen Translationstheorie*. Tübingen: Niemeyer.
Shannon, C. and Weaver, W. (1949). *The Mathematical Theory of Communication*. Urbana: University of Illinois Press.

Saussure, F. de (1922/1983). *Course in General Linguistics.* In: Ch. Bally and A. Sechehaye (eds.). Illinois: Open Court.

Sperber, D. and Wilson, D. (1986/1995). *Relevance: Communication and Cognition.* Oxford: Blackwell.

Sperber, D. and Wilson, D. (2004). "Relevance Theory." In: L. R. Horn and G. Ward (eds.). *The Handbook of Pragmatics.* Oxford: Blackwell: 607–632.

Toury, G. (1995). *Descriptive Translation Studies – And Beyond.* Amsterdam and Philadelphia: John Benjamins.

Toury, G. (1998). *A Handful of Paragraphs on 'Translation' and 'Norms,'* http://www.tau.ac.il/~toury/works/gt-tr&no.htm, accessed: 17.04.2008.

Tryuk, M. (2006). *Przekład ustny środowiskowy.* Warszawa: PWN.

Van der Henst, J.-B., Carles, L. and Sperber, D. (2002). "Truthfulness and relevance in telling the time." *Mind and Language,* vol. 17, no. 5: 457–466.

Venuti, L. (1995). *The Translator's Invisibility: A History of Translation,* London and New York: Routledge.

Vermeer, H. J. (1978). "Ein Rahmen für eine allgemeine Translationstheorie." *Lebende Sprachen 23*: 99–102.

Vermeer, H. J. (1996). *A Skopos Theory of Translation. Some Arguments for and against.* Heidelberg: TEXTconTEXT.

Vinay, J.-P. and Darbelnet, J. (1958/2004). "A Methodology for Translation." In: L. Venuti (ed.). *The Translation Studies Reader.* (2nd edn.). New York and London: Routledge.

Williamson, D. (1996). In: *Lingua Legis 3*: 28–30.

Werner, H. and Kaplan, B. (1963). *Symbol Formation.* New York: Wiley.

Wilkoń, A. (1987). *Typologia odmian współczesnej polszczyzny,* Katowice.

Zydroń, J. (1993). "Redundancja językowa w tekstach popularnonaukowych i materiałach glottodydaktycznych." *Przegląd Glottodydaktyczny, XII.*

Hu Ying-Huseh & Ho Yi-Chen

Tamkang University

PREPOSITIONS WE LIVE BY: IMPLICATIONS OF THE POLYSEMY NETWORK IN TEACHING ENGLISH PREPOSITIONS *IN* AND *ON*

Abstract: Spatial particles (SPs), or prepositions, are polysemous items; they have different, but closely related meanings, which can be organized into a network schema (Tyler and Evans 2003). This network is found to have meaningful implications in L2 pedagogical settings (Lam 2003). The present study was inspired by these implications and set out to apply them to teaching two English spatial particles *in* and *on* to learners in a university in northern Taiwan. These two particles were chosen for the inherent difficulties prepositions present to L2 learners. The learners in this study were divided into two groups: PN (polysemy network) and NN (non-polysemy network), according to the approach used in learning the two SPs under investigation. The results of our statistical analyses demonstrate that subjects in the PN group retained the network knowledge longer and better than those in the other group. Most important, the protocol analysis also supports the fact that members of the PN group were using some of the new knowledge they acquired during the 8 hour session. The differences in all tests between these two groups suggest that more culturally specific schemas are harder to acquire when learners are not made aware of the interconnected schemas underlying polysemous words.

Keywords: cultural-specific concepts, image schema, in/on, L2 teaching methodology, learner's strategies, polysemy, polysemy network, spatial particles, universality.

1. Introduction

Image schemas emerge throughout our sensory-motor activities as we manipulate objects, orient ourselves spatially and temporally, and direct our perceptual focus for various purposes (Johnson 1991). Studies in cognitive linguistics suggest that over two dozen different image schemas and several image schema transformations appear regularly in people's everyday thinking, reasoning, and imagination (Johnson 1987, Lakoff 1987). Among these are schematic structures of CONTAINER, BALANCE, SOURCE-PATH-GOAL, PATH, CYCLE, ATTRACTION, CENTRE-PERIPHERY, and LINK. These image schemas cover a wide range of structures that are pervasive in our experiences, have internal structure, and can be metaphorically elaborated to provide for our understanding of more abstract domains.

Gibbs & Colston (1995: 349) propose that image schemas are imaginative and non-propositional in nature, and operate as organising structures of experience at the level of bodily perception and movement. Image schemas exist across all perceptual modalities; therefore, they are at once visual, auditory, kinaesthetic, and tactile. This internal structure is projected onto new domains via metaphor.

Such interactions are incorporated into our language system (Lakoff and Johnson 1980, 1999). One example is the formation of polysemous words. Several linguists have argued in recent years that many polysemous words resist being defined by a general, abstract, core sense, known as "componential analysis" (Brugmen & Lakoff 1988; Fillmore 1982; Geeraerts 1993; Sweetser 1986). Instead, they believe the meanings of polysemous words can be characterised by metaphor, metonymy, and different kinds of image schemas (e.g. Lakoff 1987; Johnson 1987; Dirven 1993; Sweetser 1990). Under this view, the lexical organisation of polysemous words is not a repository of random, idiosyncratic information, but is structured by general cognitive principles that are systematic and recurrent throughout the lexicon. Most important, perhaps, according to Gibbs & Colston (*op. cit.*), is the claim that these principles arise from our phenomenological, embodied experience.

To support this, Gibbs, Beitel, Harrington & Sanders (1994) conducted studies on the English verb 'stand'. Their findings support the claim that the different senses of the polysemous word 'stand' are motivated by various image schemas that arise from our bodily experience of standing. Their meanings understood by the native speakers are not arbitrary but are motivated by people's recurring bodily experiences in the real world.

This conclusion, though it may not explain all phenomena involved in polysemy, suggests that the sense extensions within a polysemous word are not arbitrary, but "are constrained by embodied image-schematic knowledge and by various types of cognitive links relating to different senses, which are, however, not necessarily predictable" (Beitel, Gibbs & Sanders 1997: 243). Many studies of SPs and their polysemy networks (e.g. Tyler and Evans 2003, Evans 2006, Vandeloise 1991, 1994) have provided substantial evidence to support this postulation.

One often cited example in the research on spatial particles and their various senses is the representation of the image schema of *over* (Brugman 1981, 1988).

After several careful studies on its polysemous senses, it is proposed that they are not arbitrarily related but are connected in various degrees through principles of image-schematic transformations, metonymic extensions, and metaphoric instantiations of image schemas in assorted conceptual domains. These senses can be presented in a network model, which captures their inter-connectedness as proposed by Tyler and Evans (2004: 272).

Such networks provide a more systematic and explanatory approach to prepositions and thus can benefit the second language (SL) learner. Tyler and Evans offered some ideas and materials for SL classrooms, which were used in a small scale pilot study (Winke & Kim 2002). Another known study using a similar approach was carried out by Lam (2003) who examined two Spanish prepositions, *para* and *por*. Yet, apart from the above cited literature, research investigating the pedagogical implications of such networks has not been seriously explored thus far.

The present study discusses an experiment that was designed to explore the feasibility of incorporating image schemas and interrelated senses in teaching English to L2 learners in Taiwan. Two groups of lower-intermediate learners were recruited to learn about two English SPs, *in* and *on*, with one group taught with the polysemy network approach (PN), while the other with a more traditional method that is referred to as the non-network approach (NN) in this study. The results of the study show that image schemas, particularly those encoded in a foreign language, can be taught and learned

The following section summarizes the various senses of *in* and *on* and their image schemas as they were used in the experiment as the teaching materials for the PN group. The experimental procedure is explained in section 3, while section 4 presents the results of the study. Limitations and conclusion of the study are discussed in sections 5 and 6.

2. Various senses of *in* and *on*

2.1. Container Schema

In studying SPs two terms are crucial in understanding their underlining schema: Landmark (LM) and Trajectory (TR). In the case of *over* as exemplified in the sentence, *The balloon is flying over the house*, whose prototypical interpretation is illustrated in Figure 1 from Ungerer & Schmid (1996: 161): *tr* (i.e. trajectory) stands for the moving balloon, *lm* (i.e. landmark) stands for the house which is in the static position. *St* (i.e. stage), and 1, 2, 3 stands for the direction of the movement.

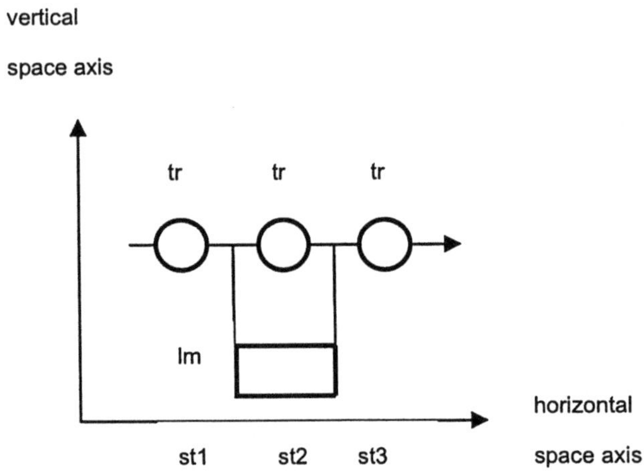

Fig. 1. Representation of the image schema -OVER-

This schema captures the prototypical relation between trajectory (TR) and landmark (LM) of *over*, and from this prototype other variants follow (Tyler and Evans 2004). Tyler and Evans (2003) examined a set of particles such as *in*, *into*, *out of* and *through* and proposed that these words project a bounded landmark (LM) which possesses three properties – an interior, a boundary and an exterior. In line with Lakoff (1987), they termed these properties as the containment schema. Containment itself reveals complex relations. In terms of the container, the bounded LM constrains the movement of TR and in some circumstances, LM provides support to TR because of its constraining properties. Containment can also result in protection since TR is protected by LM.

2.3. The Semantic Network of *in*

Tyler and Evans (2003, 2004), and Evans (2006) proposed a polysemy network of *in* (Figure 2) after having examined and analyzed its various senses. Due Linguistic examples and image schemas that represent the various senses of *in* and schemas are given in Appendix 1A. Together with those representing *on* (see Appendix 1B), they were used as the teaching materials for the PN group.

The teaching materials were organized in the way this network is structured. The network shows that there is the proto-scene of *in* in the center, which is represented by prototypical schemas of **full inclusion, partial inclusion, non-canonical bounded LM,** and **multiplex-mass transformation**. Non-prototypical schemas are further away from the center but are connected to it in a satellite fashion. They are categorized into several clusters, such as **Vantage Point is Exterior, Location, Vantage Point is Interior, Segmentation,** and **Reflexivity.** The schemas that are extended from these clusters are even further away from the center, indicating that the senses they entail are related but have the least connection to the core meanings of *in*. This network was also used as part of the teaching materials in the experiment, so that learners could see the interconnectedness of the various uses of *in*.

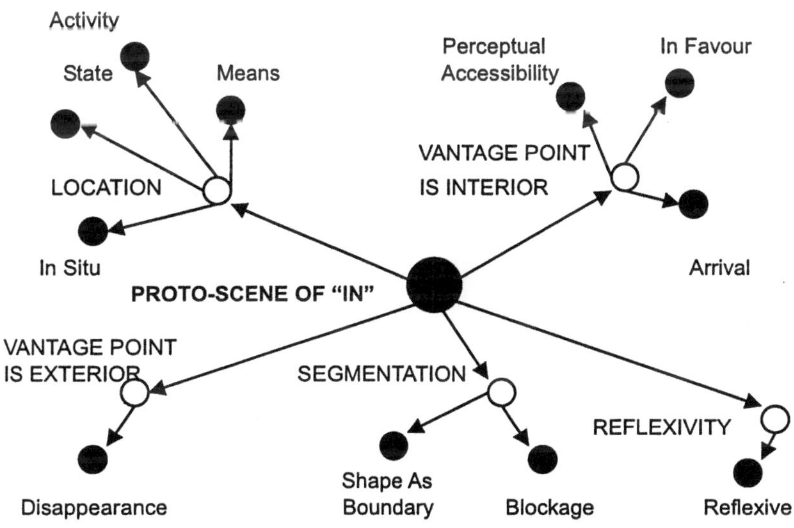

Fig. 2. The lexical network of *In*

2.4. The Semantic Structure of *on*

Unlike the spatial particle *in*, the prototypical meaning of *on* and its meaning extensions have not been widely discussed. The present study combined different viewpoints proposed by various researchers (Beitel *et al.* 1997; Evans 2006; Garrod *et al.* 1999; Lindstromberg 1996, 1998) to present possible schemas for our subjects to learn, based on which a polysemy network was developed.

The network of *on* as shown in Figure 3 can be understood in the same way as that of *in*. The center of the web-like network is the prototypical meaning of *on*, which is when TR is directly in contact with LM. Yet, this contact can vary as the way relating LM to TR changes. These changes do not affect the basic contact between TR and LM, so the senses deriving from these changes are still part of the prototypical schemas of *on*. They are known as the **rotation of the prototype sense** and **TR is in contact at an edge of the LM**. The senses that have been extended from the core are also divided into several clusters, such as **Continuation, State**, and **Support**. Further branching out from these clusters are the least typical senses of *on*.

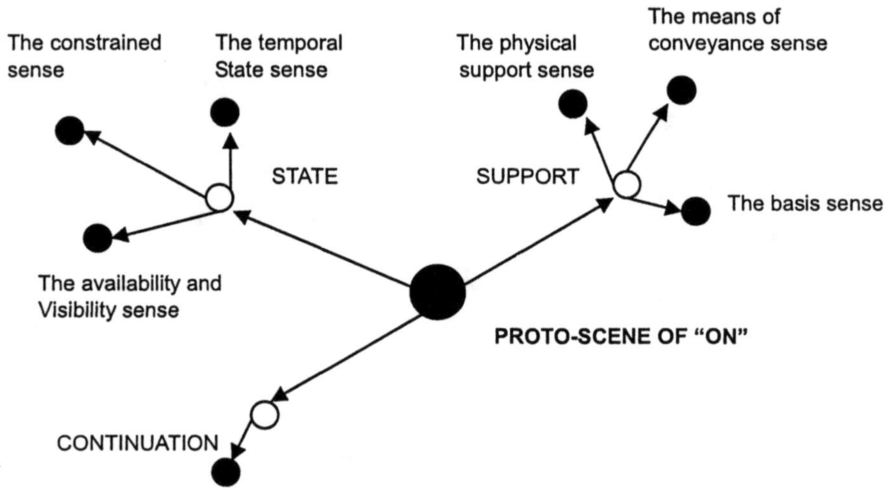

Fig. 3. The Lexical Network of *On*

3. The Experiment

3.1. Participants and Materials

93 of first year college students at Tamkang University were recruited for this experiment, which was conducted from November, 2006 to January, 2007. They were divided into two groups based on their major (all non-English majors),

with one group instructed with the PN approach, the other one with the NN approach. In the PN group (43), images of various sense schemas of the SP in question were shown and explained. Subjects were also asked to act out some of the schemas so as to experience them physically. The interrelated senses were explained and the networks of *in* and *on* were highlighted. The NN group (50) was not presented with image schemas. Instead, they were shown images (see Appendix 2). The interrelated senses were not given, nor were the subjects made aware of any physical connection with the senses. This approach is in line with what most subjects had been familiar with before the experiment, as SPs have been taught in this way in schools throughout Taiwan. Both groups received training from the same teacher who gave them one hour instruction on *in* and *on* each time for 8 consecutive weeks.

3.2. The Pre-test, Immediate Post-test and Delayed Post-test

Two test versions were alternated between the pre-test, post-test and the delayed post-test to examine the development of the two groups after two months (see Appendices 3 and 4). Participants in the two groups were required to take tests before, immediately after, and two weeks after the sessions.

Similar tests were validated on another class who did not participate in the study and had never learned the English spatial particles, *in* and *on*, from the conductor of the experiment. The mean scores of each test version were compared using an independent samples t-test and no significant difference was found ($p = .067 > .05$).

The three tests in the present study are fill-in-the-blank tests using *in* and *on* in fifty sentences. A total of 100 sentences are included in the two versions of the tests; 37 *on* sentences out of 100 were taken from Beitel *et al.* (1997), while 58 *in* sentences out of 100 from Tyler and Evans (2003). The rest of *in* and *on* sentences were selected from the Longman Dictionary. These 100 sentences were randomly and equally arranged into two versions of the tests. Both versions contained senses of *in* and *on* from the prototypical to the extended meanings. None of the sentences used in the tests had been taught in the lessons to see whether participants could extend the newly acquired knowledge in new contexts.

In addition to selecting the right answer, participants were also required to evaluate how certain they were when answering each question on a seven-point Likert scale as in Lam (2003). This metric provided the additional data to differentiate between the two treatments in the current study.

3.3. The Interviews

Interviews were separately carried out with five volunteers from each group and their responses tape-recorded. The interview questions were adopted from Lam (2003) with some minor modifications to comply with the situation in the present study. These questions (see Appendix 6) were administered in Chinese and should provide insight into the subjects' receptiveness of learning *in* and *on* with different approaches.

3.4. The Verbal Protocol Analysis

A verbal protocol adopted from the Think-Aloud Protocol Approach (Patton 2002) was administered after a four-month lapse to support the quantity findings elicited from the tests and to establish which treatment would lead to more long-termed retention and whether participants could use the freshly acquired concepts and rules in new contexts. Twenty sentences selected from the previous two test versions (ten sentences for *in*, and ten for *on*, respectively) were used.

Twenty participants in each group were randomly selected to participate in this task (see Appendix 5). The task for each group took place separately. In addition to selecting the best answer, the subjects were required to give written verbal explanations on their choice, such as which concept or rule they used to arrive at their decision. The data from the verbal protocol analysis should also help determine whether schematic concepts can be learned or not, particularly those that are encoded in the extended meanings of SPs, which are presumably more culturally specific.

3.5. The Analysis of the Data

The mean scores from the pre-test of the two groups were compared by an independent samples t-test to ensure that there was no significant difference between them. The mean of the three tests scores of the PN and NN groups were also compared using an independent samples t-test. Within each group, a paired-sample t-test was administered to determine how much performance differed before and after the treatments.

With regard to the levels of certainty between groups, the mean for how certain they were on responses in the three tests were analyzed by an independent samples t-test. Within groups, a paired-sample t-test was also used to see whether certainty was at a significant level. Further examination of the learning of extended meanings was also carried out. An independent samples t-test was used to analyze the performance between groups, while a paired-sample t-test was used to gauge performance in each group.

4. Discussion of Results

4.1. Overall Scoring

Our statistical analysis on pre-test and post-test results reveal that subjects in both groups progressed after 8 hours of instruction, with the PN group not significantly better than the NN group (P-value = .344 > .05). Members of the PN group scored significantly better on the pre-test (P-value = .024 < .05), than the NN group (P-value = .278 > .05). The analysis on the delayed post-test shows regression in both groups (PN group: P-value = .111 > .05), with the NN group significantly so (P-value = .000 < .05), even though the difference between these two groups is not statistically significant (P-value = .092 > .05), suggesting that subjects in the PN group retained their learning better in the long-term memory.

4.2. Prototypical Meanings

The comparisons of the overall performance in the post-test and delayed post-test did not indicate striking differences between these two groups. Further analysis on our data provides a more detailed picture. First, in terms of prototypical *in* the independent t-test reveals that there was no significant difference between the groups (p-value = .397 > .05). However, the mean score was 7.429% for the PN and 4.319% for the NN. There was 1.37 times difference after the treatment. The statistically indiscernible difference yielded by the t-test might have resulted from prototypical meanings being more salient since they were presumably acquired early in the evolution of human cognitive function (Clark 1973), although the mean scores in this case arguably suggest that participants receiving the embodied instructions (i.e. the PN group), generally performed better in learning the prototypical meanings. Nonetheless, when we break down the results for each tested items in terms of various senses, we see a different picture. In learning the extended senses of the SP in question, some variations appear.

Table 1. Independent Samples T-Test in Each Category between the PN Group and NN Group after the Treatments: *IN* *p < .05

Group	N	Mean (%)	Std. Deviation	T	P-value Sig. (2-tailed)
Prototype *IN*					
PN	50	7.429	.185	-.851	.397
NN	43	4.319	.163		
Extension *IN*					
Location Category					
PN	50	5.333	.200	-1.077	.285
NN	43	0.387	.242		
Vantage point is interior category					
PN	50	5.333	.294	-0.635	.527
NN	43	1.55	.276		
Vantage point is exterior category					
PN	50	-4	.532	1.257	.212
NN	43	9.302	.478		
Segmentation category					
PN	50	10	.335	-2.068	.042*
NN	43	-4.07	.317		
Reflexivity category					
PN	50	28		-2.120	.037*
NN	43	-2.33			

4.3. Extended Meanings

No significant difference was found between the two groups, in the *Location* category, *Vantage point is interior* category, and the *Vantage point is exterior* category. Although their results were not significant, the PN still performed 13.7 times better when looking at just the mean than the NN in the category of *Location*. Similarly, the PN performed 3.4 times better than the NN in the category of *Vantage point is interior*, with values of 5.333% and 1.55%, respectively.

As illustrated in Table 1, in the category of *Vantage point is exterior*, the PN group shows a serious regression (mean score = –4%), whereas the NN group shows a better performance (mean score = 9.302%). This result is not consistent with the general hypothesis that polysemy-network instruction is better. There might have been a misunderstanding of this particular concept deriving either from the confusion of perspective or L1 transfer. According to the interviews, participants from the PN group mentioned that the disappearance sense was not consistent with the spatial-geometric account of *in* when they read examples such as *The wine quickly soaked in* and *Millie rubbed in the lotion*, since, to them, the experiencer still could access the TR at the beginning of the action and TR only disappeared toward the end. Presumably, from this perspective they conceptualized the experiencer in each case as a human being, the wine and the lotion appeared to have been put "on" other substances by someone. Thus, this confusion made it difficult to conceptualize that there is a boundary, an interior and an exterior when the perspective is focused on the wine and the lotion.

Alternatively, this misunderstanding could have resulted from a lack of correspondence between L1 and the target language (Taylor 1988). Participants in the PN group could have been confused by the newly acquired *Vantage point is exterior* category; as a result, they might have turned to a "semantic equivalence hypothesis" for interpretation, because learners tend to map conceptual and semantic criteria in L1 to those in L2 (Ijaz 1986). In Chinese, people say *Millie rubbed the lotion* ***on*** *(her skin)* rather than *Millie rubbed* ***in*** *the lotion* as a result of different construction deriving from a dissimilar perspective. Thus, the potential cross-linguistic differences in the construction of image schema can be responsible for this phenomenon. However, such confusion is not detrimental to the effectiveness of the PN methodology; on the contrary, it suggests that participants, after receiving PN treatment, started to actively apply the knowledge they acquired during the learning session.

On the other hand, the better performance by participants in the NN, in this *Vantage point is exterior* category, may have resulted from their fresh memory. It is assumed here, as supported by the result of the interview and protocol, that those participants relied mainly on memorizing the meaning of the spatial particles rather than understanding the interrelatedness among senses through embodied experience. Recalling was easier for them as they were not confused by the discrepancy in image schemas.

In other categories, the differences between the two groups are less complicated. The independent samples t-test shows that in the category of *Segmentation*, the PN group outperformed the NN group (p-value = .042* < .05), with a 10% increase in the correct responses for the PN and a –4.07% regression for the NN. Also, in the category of *Reflexivity*, the data show that the PN group performed significantly better than the NN group (p-value = .037* < .05), with a 28% increase in the correct responses for the PN and a –2.33% regression for the NN. The results of the two categories support the hypothesis that embodied experiences and conveying interrelatedness can result in a better performance.

On the other hand, the statistical analysis of *on*, in the immediate post-test as shown in Table 2, reveals that the NN group did slightly better in prototypical senses, though not significantly. Surprisingly, it performed far better than the PN group in the State sense. As this is an exception, it might have been caused by an incomplete explanation by the instructor or the inherent fuzziness these two senses share. When the PN learners had to struggle making sense of what they learned, the NN group did not have such a dilemma as they only had to fall back on their memory, which was still fairly fresh two weeks after the instruction. This speculation can be substantiated by the result of the protocol analysis that was taken four months after the treatment. The advantage of the NN group in this regard disappeared, when the time lapse was even longer.

Table 2. Independent Sample T-Test in Each Category between the PN Group and NN Group after the Treatments: *ON* *p < .05

Group	N	Mean (%)	Std. Deviation	T	P-value Sig (2 tailed)
Prototype *ON*					
PN	50	.285	.185	-.851	.397
NN	43	.000	.163		
Extension *ON*					
State sense category					
PN	50	-4.73	2.215	2.680	.009*
NN	43	6.554	.185		
Support category					
PN	50	-3	.301	-.778	.438
NN	43	-8.14	.335		
Continuation category					
PN	50	1	.422	-.248	.805
NN	43	-1.16	.415		

4.4. Efficacy in the Long-term Memory

To test the effect of the PN approach, and to uncover the strategies learners used after a long lapse, a verbal protocol analysis was conducted. There were twenty fill-in-the-blank tasks, 10 for *in* and 10 for *on*. An independent samples t-test was applied to see whether there was any significant difference between these two groups after a four-month lapse. The results reveal that the PN group performed significantly better than the NN in the protocol (p-value = 0.026* < 0.05).

4.5. Discrepancy in Schema Construction – What Interviews and Protocols Reveal

The protocol analysis (Tables 3–6) indicates that subjects in the PN group were able to remember and even construct extended meanings of *in* and *on*, whereas those in NN group could not apply what they knew about the prototypical meaning to extended meanings. Even though the results of the interview (from a small sample) stated clearly that the NN group considered their approach (using pictures) very effective, the protocol analysis does not support this observation. Some subjects in this group either relied on memory, which was no longer accurate at the point of the test, or some inherent schemas that are presumably universal. For example, most subjects demonstrated an awareness of CONTAINER, CONTACT, or SUPPORT, but could not verbalize other extended senses.

Table 3. The Percentage of Each Category Interpreted by the PN Group in the Protocol: *IN*

Category	Percentage
Prototype IN	
Interior	90%
Exterior	5%
Boundary	80%
Extensions *IN*	
Location category:	
In Situ sense	5%
State sense	80%
Activity sense	15%
Means sense	10%
Vantage point is interior category:	
Perceptual accessibility sense	55%
In favor sense	5%
Arrival sense	5%
Vantage point is exterior category:	
Disappearance sense	5%
Segmentation category:	
Shape as boundary sense	0%
Blockage sense	15%
Reflexivity category:	
Reflexivity	5%

Table 4. The Percentage of Each Category Interpreted by the PN Group in the Protocol: *ON*

Category	Percentage
Prototype ON	
Contact	75%
Support	100%
Extensions *ON*	
State category:	
Temporal sense	40%
Constrained sense	5%
Availability/Visibility sense	15%
Support category:	
Means of conveyance sense	0%
Basis sense	55%
Continuation category:	
Continuation sense	25%

Table 5. The Percentage of Each Category Interpreted by the NN Group in the Protocol: *IN*

Category	Percentage
Prototype IN	
Interior	100%
Exterior	25%
Boundary	20%
Extensions *IN*	
Location category:	
In Situ sense	0%
State sense	10%
Activity sense	20%
Means sense	0%
Vantage point is interior category:	
Perceptual accessibility sense	5%
In favor sense	0%
Arrival sense	20%
Vantage point is exterior category:	
Disappearance sense	5%
Segmentation category:	
Shape as boundary sense	0%
Blockage sense	0%
Reflexivity category:	
Reflexivity	0%

Table 6. The Percentage of Each Category Interpreted by the NN Group in the Protocol: *ON*

Category	Percentage
Prototype ON	
Contact	0%
Support	95%
Extensions *ON*	
State category:	
Temporal sense	5%
Constrained sense	0%
Availability/Visibility sense	5%
Support category:	
Means of conveyance sense	0%
Basic sense	55%
Continuation category:	
Continuation sense	5%

As discussed in Section 4.3, it seems the mistakes most learners made, including those in the PN group, were the result of a wrong construction of schema or perspective, and this occurred when the schema or a concept encoded in the sentences was very different from the learners' native language. Nonetheless, as the PN group had been instructed to see the extended senses from the perspective of the target language, the subjects in this group could predict better. Such an awareness and ability was not available to the NN group. Furthermore, several people in the PN group expressed both in the interview and protocol task that the bodily experiences helped them understand the senses of SPs fairly effectively.

4.6. Summary

The overall results of the post-test and the delayed post-test did not entirely support the efficacy of the PN approach in comparison with the NN approach. More detailed analyses suggest that the NN group did not have difficulty in acquiring the more prototypical senses of the SP in question, nor those extended meanings that rely on schemas both languages share. In the protocol task, after four months of the initial treatment, the PN group outperformed the NN group significantly, and their verbal think aloud protocols show that they were still capable of applying the knowledge of image schema, including culturally specific ones to predict usages. The NN group was less capable of doing so.

5. Limitations of the Study

Arguably, such an experiment can benefit when the instruction time, design of the tests and perhaps the competence of the instructor are better controlled. It seems that the most important limitation in teaching or learning image schemas is the teachability of image schemas in the target language, as some of the learners' confusion was not the result of ineffective teaching or poor learning.

Some senses of SPs are not transparently clear-cut, as Gibbs and Matlock (1997) and Tyler and Evans' experiments (2003), in which native speakers of English had to rate these senses, demonstrate. In the rating, many senses run on a continuum, meaning that senses do overlap. Therefore, confusion of the senses for L2 learners is only natural. This, in turn, leads to the question of whether such network models can always work due to this inherent fuzziness. This issue should be further explored in future studies.

Our experiment also indicates that some senses were easier to comprehend than others. This can be attributed to culture or, more likely, the nature of language. It seems that when people learn a foreign language, the desire for certainty is enhanced, perhaps through learning anxiety. Learners yearn for one to one linguistic matching, which is not always possible, rather than for concept matching. Unfortunately, our experimental results could not clearly differentiate psychological factors from cultural or linguistic ones.

6. Conclusion

The efficacy of the PN approach has been established in our study. This is not to say that the NN approach should be replaced or discarded. The experiment indicates that the latter is quite effective for prototypical, culturally shared, or universal concepts. It even helps learners' short-term performance. However, if learning is about long-term effects, and understanding the concepts encoded in the target language, the PN approach offers a better chance. It promises a long-term, but rewarding route to foreign language learning. Our study indicates that given time, interrelated schemas can be taught and can be learnt.

REFERENCES

Beitel, D. A., Gibbs, R. W. & P. Sanders (1997). "The embodied approach to the polysemy of the spatial preposition *on*". In: H. Cuyckens & B. Zawada (eds.). *Polysemy in cognitive linguistics: selected papers from fifth international cognitive linguistics conference.* Amsterdam: John Benjamins: 241–260.

Brugman, C. (1981). *The story of over,* Trier: LAUT.

Brugman, C. (1988). *The story of over: Polysemy, semantics, and the structure of the lexicon.* New York, London: Garland.

Brugman, C. & G. Lakoff (1988). "Cognitive topology and lexical networks". In: S. Small, G. Cottrell & M. Tannenhaus (eds.). *Lexical Ambiguity Resolution.* San Mateo, CA: Morgan Kaufman: 477–507.

Clark, E. V. (1973). "Non-linguistic strategies and the acquisition of word meaning". *Cognition*, 2: 161–182.

Divern, R. (1993). "Metonymy and Metaphor: Different mental strategies of conceptualization". *Leuvense Bijdragen*, 82: 1–28.

Evans, V. (2006). "A lexical concepts and cognitive models approach to spatial semantics: the "state" sense of English prepositions". In: V. Evans & P. Chilton (eds.). *Language, cognition and space.* Unpublished manuscript. London: Equinox Publishing.

Fillmore, J. (1982). "Towards a descriptive framework for spatial deixis". In: R. J. Jarvella & W. Klein (eds.). *Speech, place and Action.* New York: Wiley and Sons: 31–59.

Garrod, S. C., Ferrier, G. & S. Campell (1999). "In and on: Investigating the functional geometry of spatial preposition". *Cognition*, 72(2): 167–189.

Geeraerts, D. (1993). "Vagueness's puzzles, polysemy's vagaries". *Cognitive Lingusitics*, 4: 223–72.

Gibbs, R. W. & H. L. Colston (1995). "The cognitive psychological reality of image schemas and their transformation". *Cognitive Lingusitics*, 6: 347–78.

Gibbs, R.W & T. Matlock (1997). "Psychological perspective on polysemy". In: H. Cuyckens & B. Zawada (eds.). *Polysemy in cognitive linguistics: selected papers from fifth international cognitive linguistics conference.* Amsterdam: John Benjamins: 213–239.

Gibbs, R. W., Beitel, D. A., Harrington, M. & P. Sanders (1994). "Taking a stand on the meanings of *stand*: bodily experience as motivation for polysemy". *Journal of Semanitcs*, 11: 231–251.

Gibb, R. W. (1997). "Taking metaphor out of our heads and putting it into cultural world". In: R. W. Gibbs Jr. & G. J. Steen (eds.). *Metaphors in cognitive linguistics: selected papers from the fifth international cognitive linguistics conference.* Amsterdam: John Benjamin Publishing Company. 175: 145–165.

Ijaz, I. H. (1986). "Linguistic and Cognitive determinants of lexical acquisition in a second language". *Language Learning*, 36(4): 401–451.

Johnson, M. (1987). *Body in the mind.* Chicago: University of Chicago Press.

Johnson, M. (1991). "Knowing through the body". *Philosophical Psychology*, 4: 3–18.

Lakoff, G. (1987). *Women, Fire and Dangerous things: What Categories Reveal about the Mind.* Chicago: University of Chicago Press.

Lakoff, G. & M. Johnson (1980). *Metaphors We Live by.* Chicago: University of Chicago Press.

Lam, Y. Y. (2003). *Challenging prepositions: the effectiveness of interrelating rules for teaching POR and PARA in Spanish as a second language* (Doctoral dissertation, University of Toronto, 2003).

Lindstromberg, S. (1996). "Prepositions: meaning and method". ELT Journal, 50: 225–236.

Linstromberg, S. (1998). *English Prepositions Explained.* Amsterdam: John Benjamins.

Patton, M. Q. (2002). *Qualitative Research & Evaluation Methods* (3rd ed.). California: Sage Publiications.

Sweetser, E. E. (1986). "Polysemy vs. abstraction: Mutually exclusive or complementary?" In: K. Nikikoridou, M. Varclay, M. Niepokuk & D. Feder (eds.). *Proceedings of the 12th annual meeting of the Berkeley Linguistic Society.* Berkeley: Berkeley Linguistic Society: 528–538.

Sweetser, E. E. (1990). *From Etymology to Pragmatics: Metaphorical and Cultural Aspects of Semantics Structure.* Cambridge: Cambridge University Press.

Tyler, A. & V. Evans (2003). *The Semantics of English Prepositions: Spatial Senses, Embodied Meaning and Cognition.* Cambridge: Cambridge Press.

Tyler, A. & V. Evans (2004). "Spatial experience, lexical structure and motivation: the case of in". In: G. Rudden & K. Panther (eds.). *Studies in Linguistic Motivation*: 157–192. Berlin: Mouton de Gruyter.

Ungerer, F. & H. J. Schmid (1996). *An Introduction to Cognitive Linguistics.* London: Longman.

Vandeloise, C. (1991). *Spatial prepositions: A case study in French.* Chicago: The University of Chicago Press.

Vandeloise, C. (1994). "Methodology and analyses of the preposition in". *Cognitive Linguistics*, 2: 157–184.

Winke, P. & Y. Y. Kim (2002). Poster presented at Second Language Research Forum. Toronto, Canada (October 2002).

Appendix 1/ A

Material for *in* for the PN group

1. The prototypical meaning of *in*

1.1. Full Inclusion

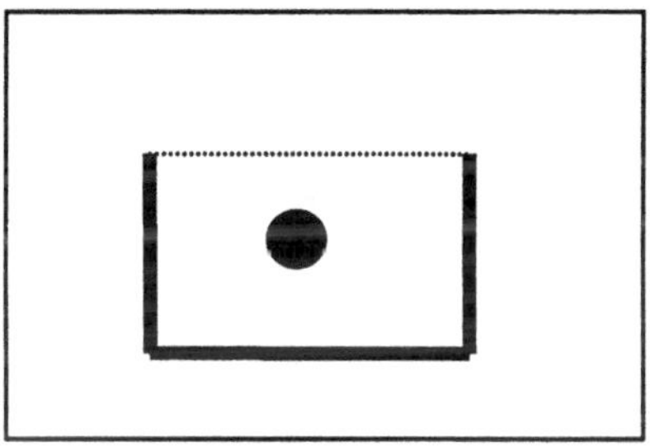

Proto-scene for *in*

(a) Pencils and the eraser are in the pencil box.
(b) The sweater was in the beautifully wrapped box.

1.2. Partial Inclusion

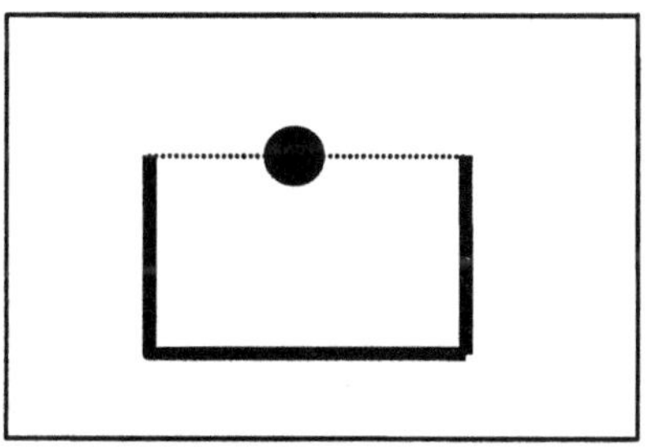

Proto-scene for *in* (partial inclusion)

(a) The flower is in the vase.
(b) The rock singer in the tight leather pants.

1.3. Non-canonical Bounded LM

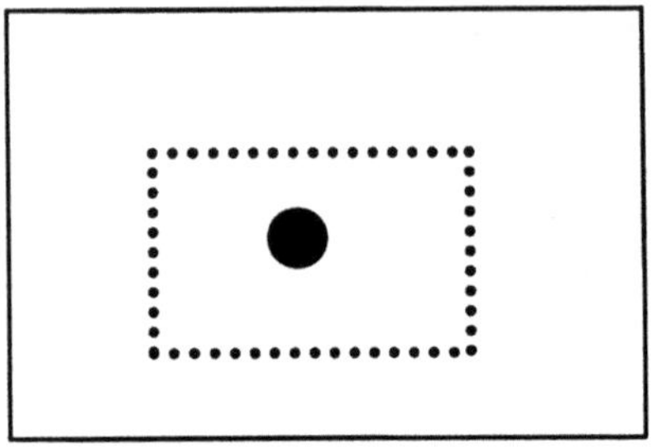

Proto-scene for *in* (The mo

The movement of the object is constrained by the boundary. The boundary may be physical or non-physical.

(a) The rabbits are hopping around in the field.
(b) My parents live in China, but I live in Taiwan.

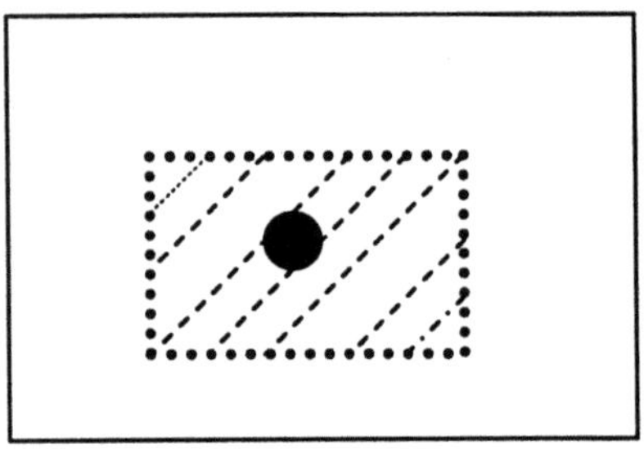

Proto-scene for *in*
(the atmospheric condition)

(a) We were walking in the rain.
(b) The newborn baby was found in the snow.

1.4. Multiplex-mass Transformation for Proto-scene of *in*

A single mass is conceptualized as an entity with an interior, a boundary and an exterior.

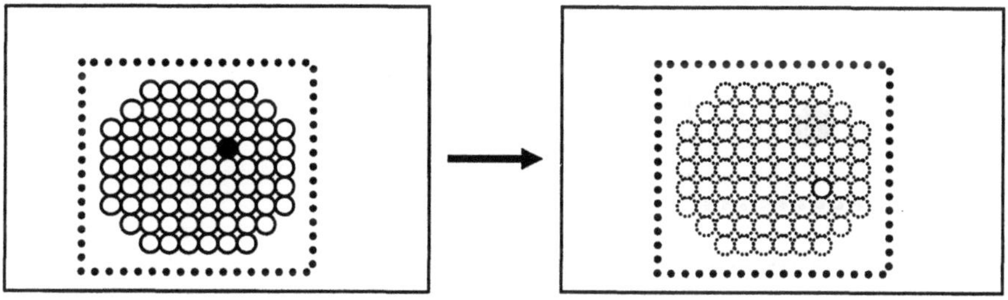

Proto-scene for *in*

(a) The house is built in the forest.
(b) When the singer was singing, someone in the audience booed.

2. Beyond the proto-scene

2.1. The Location Cluster

2.1.1. The In Situ Sense

The object is located in the container for an extended period of time with an intended purpose.

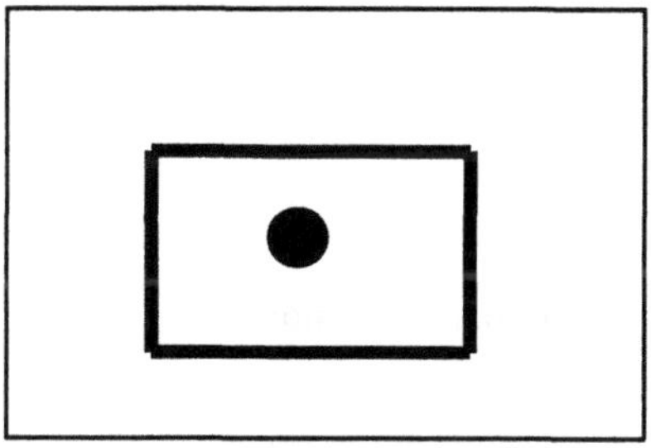

The In Situ Sense

(a) John prayed in church.
(b) My sister was in the hospital.

2.1.2. The State Sense

The experiencer has an experience in a particular situation.

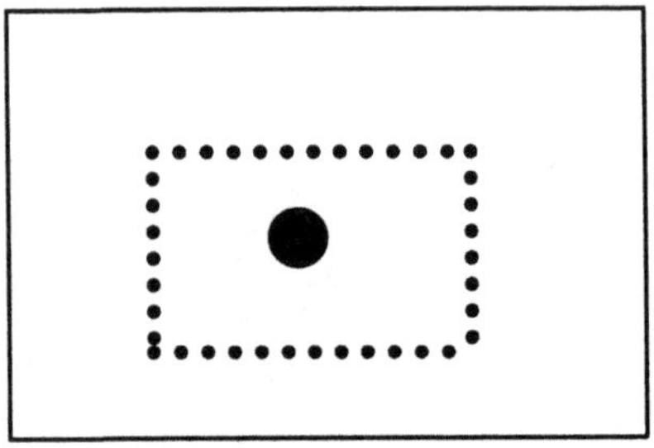

The State Sense

(a) My grandma was in a bad mood.
(b) Because of losing all the money, they are in trouble.

2.1.3. The Activity Sense

The activity happens in a particular place.

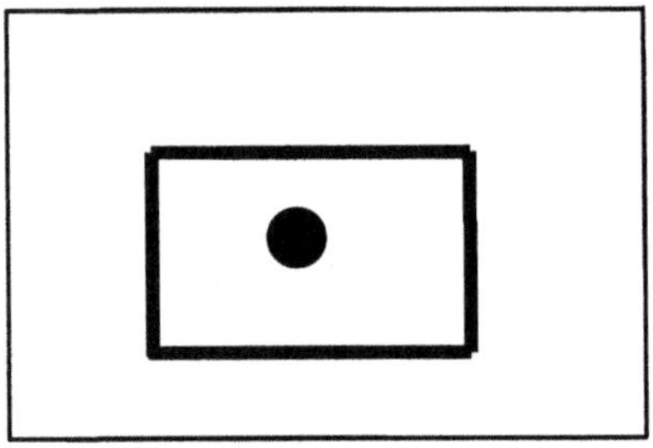

The Activity Sense

(a) My mom used to be a teacher, but she is in marketing now.
(b) Mary has worked in business for 10 years.

2.1.4. The Means Sense-

The activity can be done by the means. The means is influencing or constraining the activity.

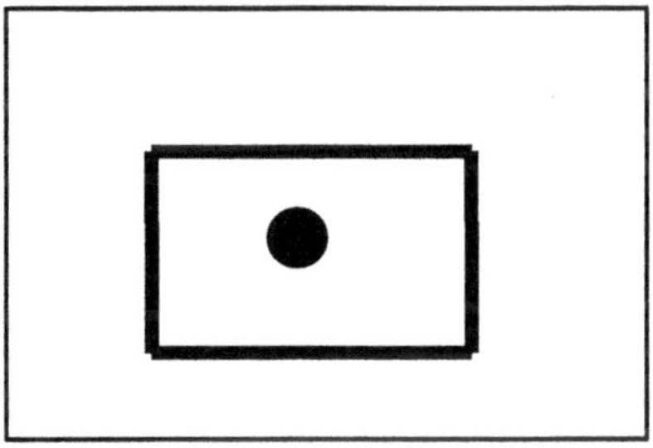

The Means Sense

(a) Students are not allowed to scribble in pencil.
(b) She called out in a loud voice.

2.2. The Vantage Point is Interior Cluster

2.2.1. The Perceptual Accessibility Sense

The experiencer can see, touch, or smell the object or the activity in the same place/situation.

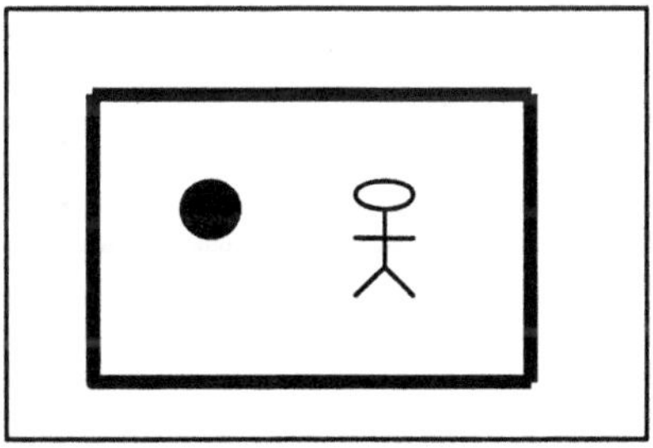

The Perceptual Accessibility Sense

(a) The mother always kept her baby in sight.
(b) The animal is still in range of my gunshot.

2.2.2. The In Favor Sense

The experiencer gains access to a favorable and privileged place.

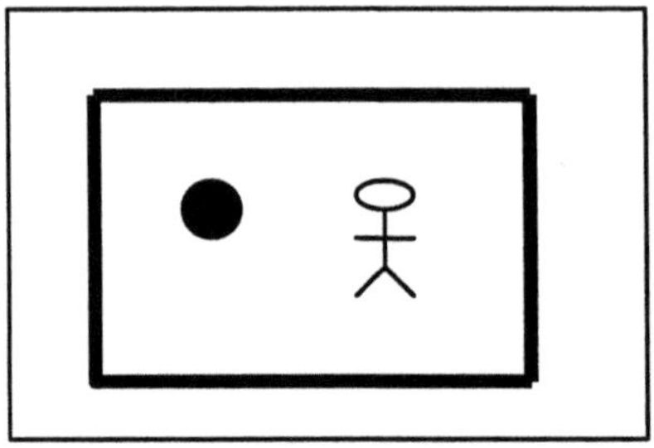

The In Favor Sense

(a) Carrying a small bag is in fashion right now.
(b) This restaurant is the in place to go right now.

2.2.3. The Arrival Sense

The object is approaching the experiencer and eventually they are in the same place.

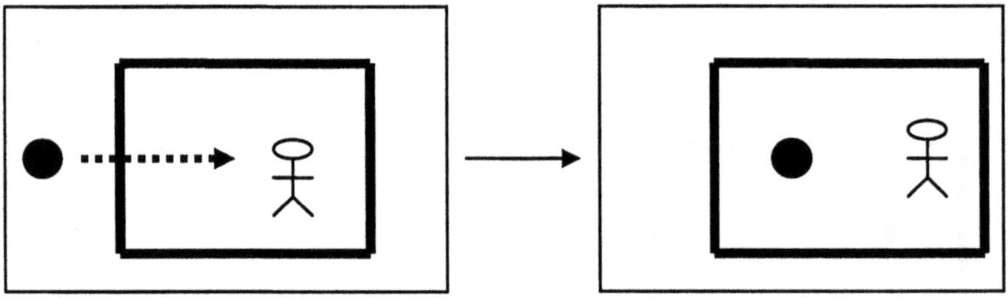

The Arrival Sense

(a) The train is not in yet.
(b) The bus is in already and it will leave in ten minutes.

2.3. The Vantage Point is Exterior Cluster

2.3.1. The Disappearance Sense

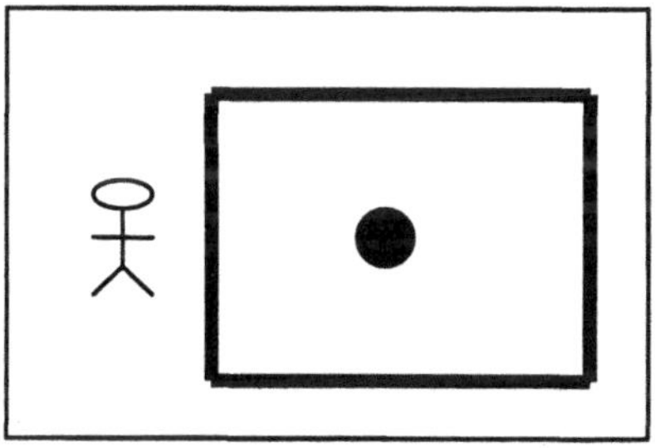

The Disappearance Sense

(a) The water is absorbed in.
(b) One way to give your leather bag a good shine is to rub Vaseline in.

2.4. The Segmentation Cluster

2.4.1. The Shape as Boundary Sense

The shape of the object(s) or experiencer(s) is the boundary

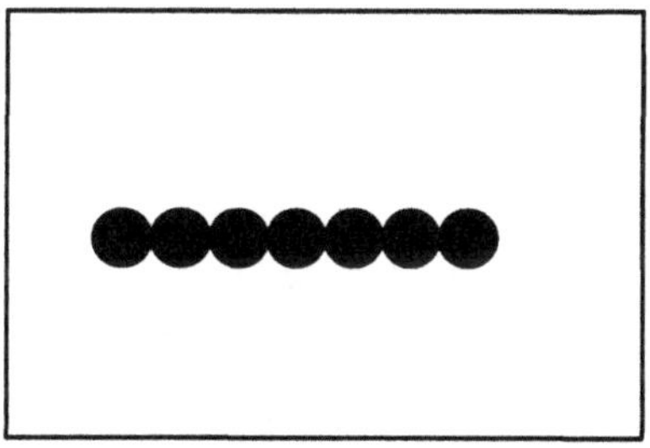

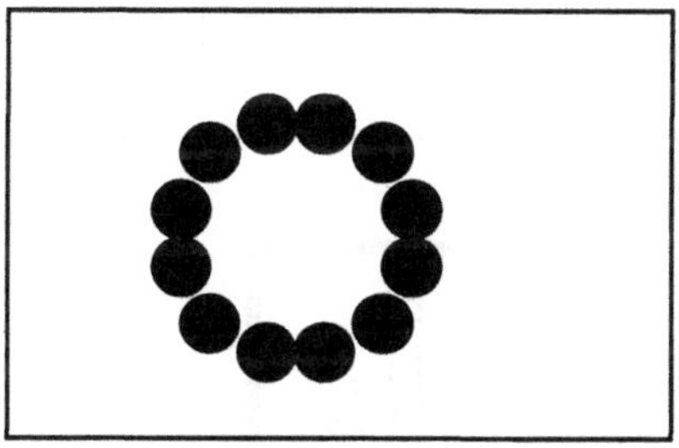

The Shape as Boundary Sense

(a) The cat slept curling up in the ball.
(b) Please put the files in alphabetical order.

2.4.2. The Blockage Sense

The boundary of the place prevents the object/experiencer from moving in that place.

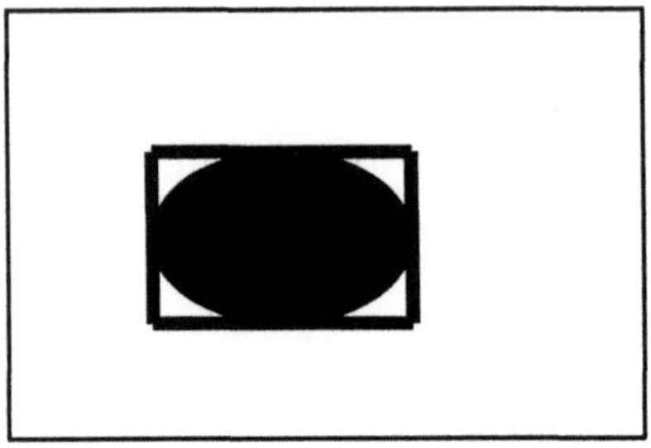

The Blockage Sense

(a) After the typhoon, the traffic light fell in the roadway.
(b) I got something caught in my ear.

2.5. Reflexivity

2.5.1. The Reflexivity Sense

The object/place loses its shape so interior space no longer exists.

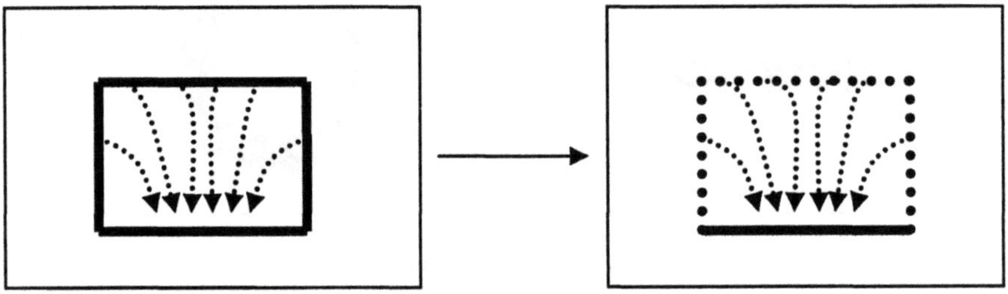

The Reflexivity Sense

(a) The cover of the book curves in at one corner.
(b) The map had started to curl in at the edges.

Appendix 1/B

Material of *on* for the PN group

1. The prototypical meaning of *on*

1.1. Direct Contact

1.1.1. Direct Contact

The subject is in contact with a line or surface. In turn, the line or the surface provides support to the subject.

The proto-scene for on

(a) The apple is on the table.
(b) The pencil is on the book.

1.1.2. Rotation of the Prototype

Rotation of the prototypical meaning of *on*

The subject's contact with a line or surface can vary. But the line and surface still provide the support to the subject.

(a) The butterfly is on the ceiling.
(b) The painting is on the wall.
(c) The map is on the floor.

1.1.3. The TR is in contact at an edge of the LM:
The subject is in contact at an edge of a line or surface.

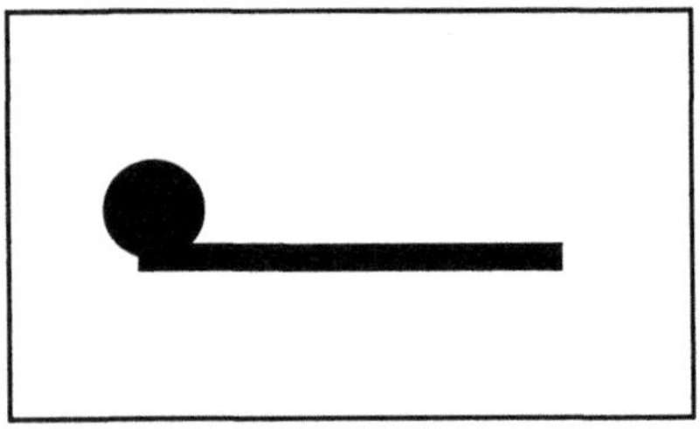

The proto-scene for on (contact at the edge)

(a) I have a house on the lake.
(b) You walk down First Street and you will see the building on your left side.

2. Beyond the proto-scene

2.1. The Support Cluster
2.1.1. The Physical Support Sense

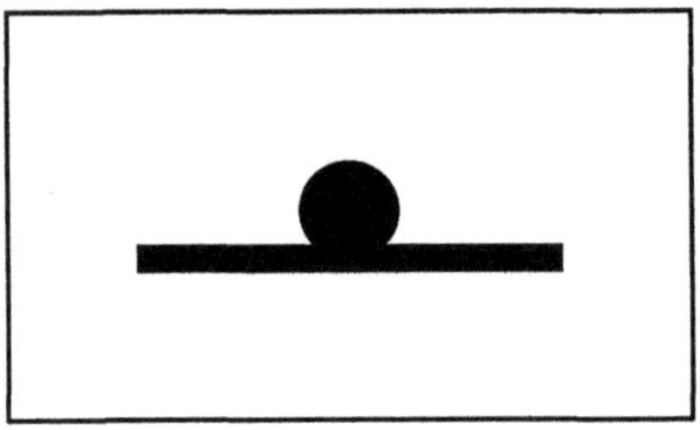

The Physical Support Sense

(a) The little boy passed by on tiptoe to avoid making any sound.
(b) She was on her knees weeding the garden.

2.1.2. The Means of Conveyance Sense

The vehicle provides the support to the subject as a means in order to get to some place.

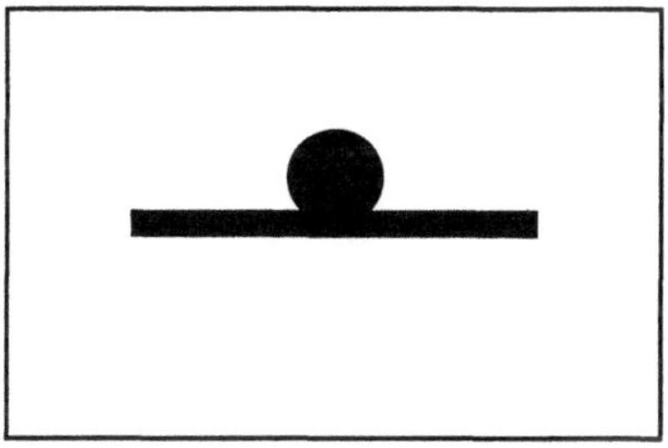

The Means of Conveyance Sense

(a) We are going on foot, not by car.
(b) Children are on the bus.

2.1.3. The Basis Sense

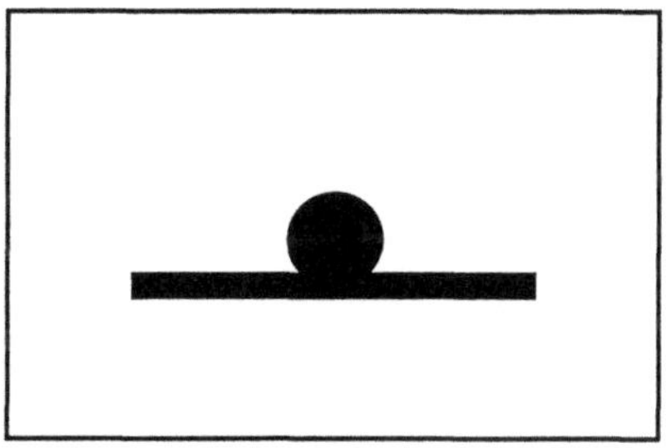

The Basis Sense

(a) The statue is on a broad plinth.
(b) The movie is based on a true story.

2.2. The State Cluster

2.2.1. The Temporal State Sense

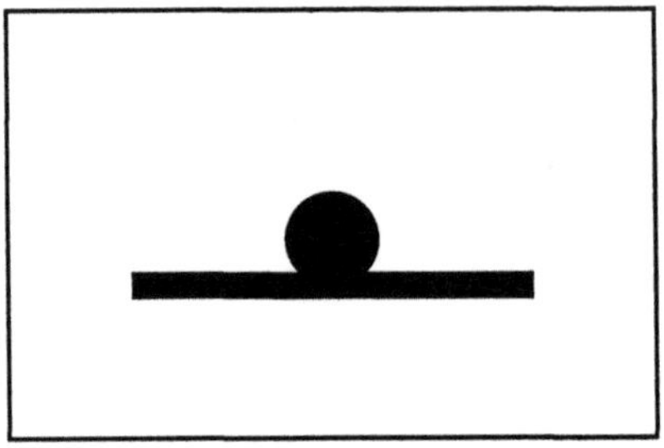

The Temporal State Sense

(a) The DVD is on pause.
(b) The book I wanted was out on loan.

2.2.2. The Constrained Sense

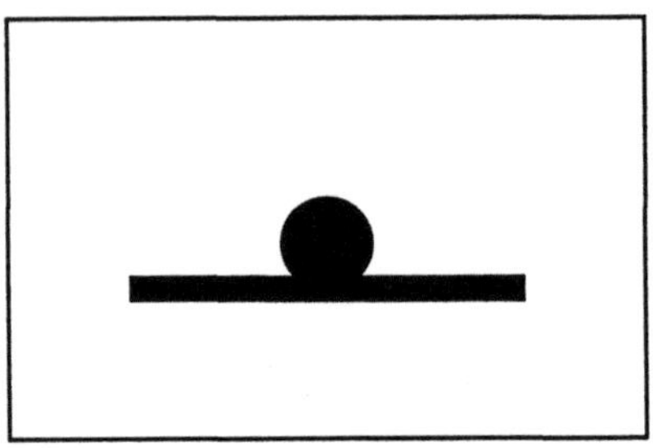

The Constrained Sense

(a) The baseball game has a great influence on young people's lives.
(b) There will be new restrictions on the sale of weapons.

2.2.3. The Availability and Visibility Sense

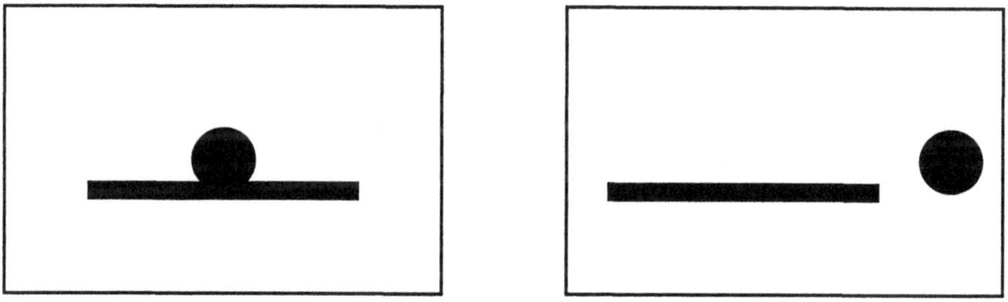

The Availability and Visibility Sense (on & off)

(a) The party/meeting/conference is on.
(b) The show "Friends" is on TV.

2.3. The Continuation Cluster

2.3.1. The Continuation Sense

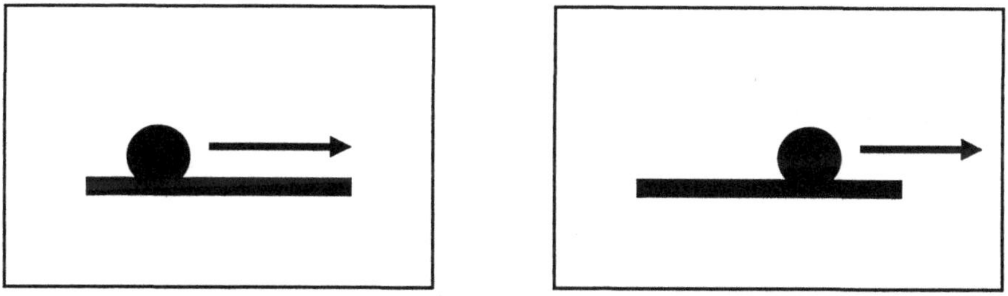

The Continuation Sense

(a) Come on! (When directing a driver into a parking space)
(b) Please don't stop, keep on talking.

Appendix 2

Examples of Material of *in* For the NN Group

1. The meaning of ***In***: ______________________
1.1. Pencils and the eraser are ***in*** the pencil box.

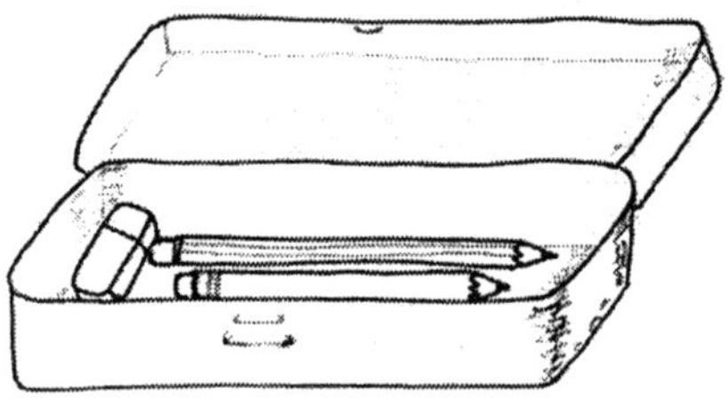

2. The meaning of ***In***: ______________________
2.1. The flower is ***in*** the vase.

Appendix 3

Examples of The Pretest and the Post-test

Name: __________ Class: __________ Date: __________

1. They hung a picture **on/in** the wall.
   very uncertain 1 2 3 4 5 6 7 very certain
2. John is **on/in** the house.
   very uncertain 1 2 3 4 5 6 7 very certain
3. The bulb is **on/in** the socket.
   very uncertain 1 2 3 4 5 6 7 very certain
4. China is **on/in** Asia.
   very uncertain 1 2 3 4 5 6 7 very certain
5. All books are **on/in** sale.
   very uncertain 1 2 3 4 5 6 7 very certain
6. She has a beautiful ring **on/in** her finger.
   very uncertain 1 2 3 4 5 6 7 very certain
7. He resides **on/in** the continent.
   very uncertain 1 2 3 4 5 6 7 very certain
8. The flag flapped **on/in** the wind.
   very uncertain 1 2 3 4 5 6 7 very certain
9. The child couldn't be seen **on/in** the crowd.
   very uncertain 1 2 3 4 5 6 7 very certain
10. The cow munched grass **on/in** the field.
    very uncertain 1 2 3 4 5 6 7 very certain

Appendix 4

Examples of The Delayed Post-test

Name: _________ Class: ________ Date: _________ No: ________

1. My mother was **on/in** the kitchen.
   very uncertain 1 2 3 4 5 6 7 very certain
2. The fly is **on/in** the ceiling.
   very uncertain 1 2 3 4 5 6 7 very certain
3. London is the largest city **on/in** the United Kingdom.
   very uncertain 1 2 3 4 5 6 7 very certain
4. The case is **on/in** the table.
   very uncertain 1 2 3 4 5 6 7 very certain
5. The actor is **on/in** stage.
   very uncertain 1 2 3 4 5 6 7 very certain
6. The child shivered **on/in** the cold.
   very uncertain 1 2 3 4 5 6 7 very certain
7. He pulled a gun **on/in** me.
   very uncertain 1 2 3 4 5 6 7 very certain
8. The city hall is **on/in** Main Street.
   very uncertain 1 2 3 4 5 6 7 very certain
9. The old cottage was located **on/in** the wood.
   very uncertain 1 2 3 4 5 6 7 very certain
10. The tiny oasis flourished **on/in** the desert.
    very uncertain 1 2 3 4 5 6 7 very certain

Appendix 5

Examples of the Verbal Protocol Test
Please choose the correct spatial particle (*in* or *on*) and write down each sense/meaning match to the answer you choose

1. China is **on/in** Asia.

____

2. The child couldn't be seen **on/in** the crowd.

____

3. He stayed **on/in** for the evening.

____

4. Jane is **on/in** <u>awe</u>(敬畏).

____

5. He works **on/in** <u>stocks and shares</u>(股票市場)

____

6. I stayed (with) **on/in** earshot of baby Max's cry.

____

7. That's the **on/in**-joke this week.

____

Appendix 6

Interview Questions

1. What did you like about the lesson? What did you not like about the lesson? Explain.
2. Did you find it easy to understand *in* and *on* with this teaching methodology? Why?
3. Was the treatment carried out in your class the same as or different from your previous English-learning experiences? Which way is more helpful to you?
4. What impressed you the most in this treatment?
5. If you have the chance to teach *in* and *on* to the person who has never learned them before, how would you do it?

Anna Turula

The English Department
University of Bielsko-Biała

EXTENSIVE STUDY OF AN ANGLOPHONE FILM CORPUS AS A WAY OF IMPLICIT LEARNING COMPLEX FL GRAMMAR

Abstract: Learning the grammar of a foreign language posits problems for every learner. For beginning and intermediate students, the emphasis is, first and foremost, on communicative competence, grammar is treated functionally, and its pedagogy aims – with considerable effort– at automatization of the learned structures in order to take the cognitive load off line. This, at least in Polish schools, involves grammar training which is a combination of the explicit presentation of rules and ample *drill-it-in-communicative-context* practice. If, at this level, learners notice the gap between themselves, non-native speakers (NNS), and the native speakers (NS) of the target language, it is in the area of formal accuracy with which the structure is put together and/or the compliance with rules determining which structure is suitable for a given, usually one-sentence, context. On the advanced level, however, the character of grammar-related pedagogy changes. With structures usually sufficiently entrenched and ready for on-line use, and with the knowledge of rules enabling almost instantaneous retrieval of a required learned response, the gap is usually of a conceptual nature and can be described by a question often asked: "*why is my choice – and, consequently, understanding – of grammatical structures usually different from that of a native speaker?*" and "*why is it that so often the rules I know are violated in the NS discourse?*".

In the present article, we concentrate exclusively on the reparatory measures to reduce the NS/NNS gap on the advanced level. A pedagogical proposal called *organic approach deductivised* (Turula 2006) together with the results of its implementation will be briefly presented in Section 1. The presentation will include the description of the training in form-meaning mappings – in the area of English tense and aspect – undertaken as part of the experiment as well as the quantitative and qualitative results of such a treatment. As the pedagogical proposal with the rationale for its deductive procedures as well as the results of the experiment have already been described in Turula (2006); Turula (2007a) and Turula (2007c), the present article is going to concentrate on how the organic (= implicit) part of the remedial measures contributed to the changes in the NNS conceptualizations of tense and aspect.

For this purpose, the article will, first of all, discuss implicit learning paradigms (Section 2), with special regard to the control of complex systems (Berry and Dienes 1993; Dienes and Berry 1997), resulting from the assumption that learning an FL grammar is a multi-faceted, dynamic task. Section 3 will show how the implicit knowledge might have contributed to the emergence of the explicit know-how using the Adaptive Control of Thought (ACT-R) model as a point of departure.

Keywords: ACT-R, FL grammar pedagogy, implicit learning of complex systems, neuronal networks.

1. Organic approach deductivised – the procedure and results

The *organic approach deductivised*[1] was a pedagogic treatment undertaken as a means of leveling the NS/NNS conceptual gap in the use of tense and aspect. The underlying assumption was that the NNS semantic frames for target language structures are conceptually warped, the FL grammar semantics being almost entirely obscured by the rule-oriented pedagogical treatment applied on lower levels. The semantic deficiency, however, cannot be sufficiently compensated for by organic exposure to language – already considerable in advanced learners – because the default assignments indispensible for a proper delineation of a semantic frame are often already filled in a way that demonstrates conceptual L1→FL transfer (cf. Leńko-Szymańska 2004). Consequently, the remedial measures taken in the treatment had to consist in a number of interactive steps. First of all, the gap had to be noticed, for which purpose language awareness activities were devised. Students taking part in the experiment were asked to watch Anglophone films, each time paying attention to a different tense/aspect, with particular attention to the use of the structure which deviated from their rule-based grammatical knowledge. As the film corpus contained a hundred plus films, the task was devised as collaborative: individual students' contributions – selected scenes containing tense/aspect – were compiled and e-mailed to every participant of the experiment. Secondly, as the rules-first pedagogical procedures had to be overridden, the semantics-first instruction was offered. The subjects were given the primary semantic characteristics of each structure under investigation (Lewis 1986; Mindt 2004). Finally, in order to reconstruct the semantic frame of a structure, the default assignments – the rationale behind the NS choice of a given tense/aspect – were reconstructed for every context. This happened as a result of a detailed

[1] For a detailed description of the treatment – see Appendix 1.

analysis of every event, which was based on the primary semantic characteristics on the one hand and broadly understood contextual clues on the other (cf. Turula 2006 and 2007c).

The study was carried out in 2005–2007 as a classical experiment, so the above-described treatment was preceded by a pre-test[2] examining the tendencies in the participants' choices of English tense and aspect. A similar post-test and a delayed post-test were carried out, respectively, on the completion of the experiment and a year later. The same tests were carried out in 2 control groups – a native speaker group (NS) and non-native (NNS) controls.

The NNS subjects – both the experimental and the control groups – were second year students of English Philology at the University of Bielsko-Biała; the NS controls were second-year English majors from Transylvania University, KY and Asbury College, KY in the USA. As the main focus of the study was the possibility of diminishing the distance between NS and NNS users of the target language, the results of all tests were not subject to statistical analysis; instead, the interpretation was based on a mathematical method known as distance calculation in multidimensional spaces (Steinhaus 1960). Each test unit (26 for pre-test and delayed post-test; 23 for post-test) was treated as one dimension in the multidimensional test space. The results are presented in tables 1–3.

Table 1. Distance on pre-test

US/ATHe	US/ATHc	ATHe/ATHc
2,776761	2,3937	1,72563

Table 2. Distance on post-test

US/ATHe	US/ATHc	ATHe/ATHc
2,471093	2,61226	1,15646

Table 3. Distance on pre-test and delayed post-test; the long-term change

US/ATHe	US/ATHe[d]	US/ATHc	US/ ATHc[d]	ATHe/ ATHc	ATHe[d]/ ATHc [d]	ATHe/ ATHe [d]	ATHc/ ATHc
2,776761	**2,306014**	2,391192	2,222814	1,717323	1,605833	**1,507083**	1,259484

US – NS controls; ATHe – the experimental group; ATHc – NNS controls; [d] – on delayed post-test

As can be seen in the tables, the distance between NS and the experimental NNS group diminished as a result of the treatment (from 2.776761 on pre-test to 2. 471073 on post-test), and the change turned out to be time-resistant (2.306014 on delayed post-test). As for the NNS control group, it can be said that in spite of their initial result (2.3937 on pre-test compared to 2.776761 by ATHe), they

[2] For pre-test and post-test sample – see Appendix 2.

were outperformed by the experimental group on post-test (2.61226 compared to 2.306014 by ATHe). Besides, the long-term change in the case of the control NNS group is nowhere near the result of the experimental group (from 2.3937 on pre-test to 2.222814 on post-test).

The study was replicated a year later (2006–2008) with similar results. This time, however, the quantitative investigation was enriched by a qualitative analysis of the rationale behind the choices made by the experimental group. A sample of 10 was randomly singled out from the experimental group. These testees were asked to give rationale for their grammatical choices in verbal reports which were recorded and analysed. These NNS interpretations were later compared with data from an earlier study (Turula 2007b) of 4 native speakers of English, 2 BE users and 2 AE users. The justifications both NS and NNS offered were assigned to a number of categories (see Figure 2 for the explication of category coding). Before the final analysis, the number of answers in each category for NS and NNS groups on both tests was totaled and averaged. Subsequently, each mean score was treated as one dimension in the multidimensional test space (26-D for pre-test and 23-D for post-test). The distance between groups was established by means of the already-mentioned mathematical method of distance calculation in multidimensional spaces. The results are diagrammed in Figure 1.

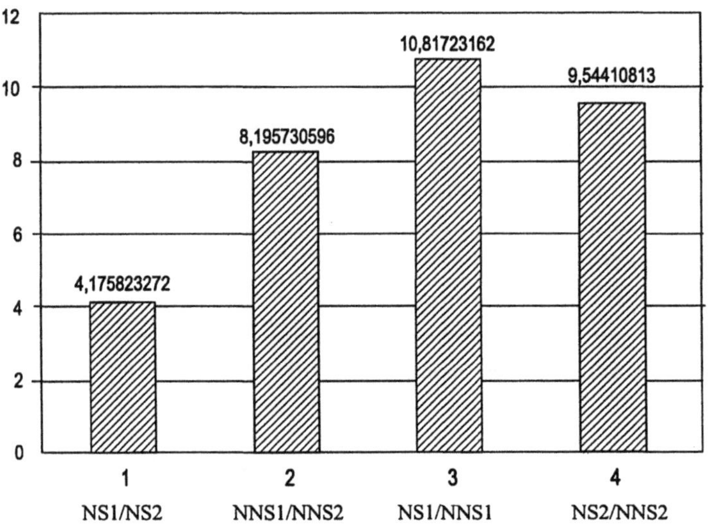

Fig. 1. Distance between groups

NS1 – native speakers on pre-test; NS2 – native speakers on post-test; NNS1 – non-native speakers on pre-test; NNS2 – native speakers on post-test

When it comes to detailed results – group profiles, the categorical differences between groups as well as changes resulting from treatment – they are presented in Figure 2:

	R	R[A]	S(i)	S(t)	S(i) [A]	S(t) [A]	SG (kw)	SG (f)	SG (tx)	SG (e)	SG (i)	TT
ns1	3,25	0	8	0,25	0	0	0,25	3,25	0,25	0	12,5	0
ns2	2	0	10	0	0	0	0,25	2,75	0,25	1	9,25	0
nns1	**9,9**	0,3	**4,2**	**1,4**	**2,6**	0,5	1	**1,5**	0,7	**1,1**	**5,8**	0
nns2	**4,8**	0	**8,8**	**2,5**	**3,8**	0,4	1,5	**0,3**	1,9	**0,1**	**2,2**	0,4

Fig. 2. Group profiles – category analysis

Coding: R – rules (which, in fact stand for the clichés repeated after pedagogical grammars currently in use); S – semantics: (i) – interpretation (efforts aimed at determining the rationale behind the speaker's choice of this particular, and nor any other, grammatical form); (t) – translation (translating the grammar form into its L1 equivalent); [A] – attempt (unsuccessful, at rules or sematic interpretation); SG – sounds good because of: (kw) – key word(s), (f) – it is part of a formula/lexical chunk, (tx) – as part of the text, (e) – it fits into the event schema or (i) – intuition (no justification is offered); TT – (overt) transfer of training (the justifications offered by the NNS on post-test which directly refer to class discussions of form-meaning mappings); NS1 – native speakers on pre-test; NS2 – native speakers on post-test; NNS1 – non-native speakers on pre-test; NNS2 – native speakers on post-test

As can be seen in Figure 1, the distance between NS and NNS decreased as a result of treatment from 10.81723162 to 9.54410813. As for categorical changes (Figure 2), certain gains (+) and trade off effects (–) can be observed:

(+) there is a considerable increase in the number of semantic interpretations and translations (from 4.2 out of 26 to 8.8 out of 23 for S(i) and from 1.4/26 to 2.5/23 for S(t)) with a simultaneous decrease in the use of traditional grammar rules as a justification of one's grammatical choice (from 9.9/26 to 4.8/23);

(–) there are much more semantic attempts (increase from 2.6/26 to 3.8/23); there is also a considerable decrease in SG (sounds good) answers based on the knowledge of lexical chunks and on intuition.

What these results show is that the *organic approach deductivised* treatment has the potential of diminishing the NS/NNS gap in the area of grammar conceptualization and that it is effective in terms of both immediate and long-term outcomes. It is also important to point out that the Polish control group (NNS), in whose case sheer exposure to language was the major development-triggering factor, does not seem to have undergone a comparable change.

What cannot pass unnoticed, though, is that the change, if analysed qualitatively, is obviously the result of the deductive part of the experiment. The gains in competence are explicit in nature: the metaknowledge of rules was replaced by another type of awareness – of grammar semantics. What is more, the newly acquired knowledge might have been partly stored as goal strategies – conceptual scenarios, algorithmic in nature (if you see X, use semantic explication Y) to be applied in grammar decision making. The last hypothesis may be, at least partly, proved by the number of semantic attempts, unsuccessful – sometimes even nonsensical – interpretations of the given structure in context. The final factor proving the explicitness of the knowledge is the decrease in intuitive choices. This change – seen as a trade-off effect – may be the result of two processes: – declarativisation of the previously procedural (=implicit) knowledge which resulted from the fact that the treatment offered ample language awareness raising; or the fact that explicit instruction prior to the task and the resulting use of declarative knowledge negatively affect implicit learning, as noticed by Berry and Dienes (1993).

On the other hand, however, the *organic approach deductivised*, with its extensive study of the Anglophone film corpus, was devised in such a way as to cater to both the declarative element of the treatment as well as ample exposure to contexts which were in fact conceptual gestalts: scenes and episodes. The rationale behind the pedagogic decision about relating the deductive element to event-based learning was multi-faceted. First of all, it was based on the knowledge of the declarative memory system as composed of two subsystems – the semantic and the episodic, the former being the memory of meanings, understandings, and other concept based knowledge unrelated to specific experiences, the latter – the memory of events, times, places, associated emotions, and other conception based knowledge in relation to an experience. Second, the idea of combining the focus on primary semantic characteristics with organic learning was rooted in the belief that human attention is not an exclusively conscious phenomenon. As pointed out by Truscott (1998), attention is too complicated a phenomenon to make any final judgments about what it is and "when it is or it is not allocated to a given task" (105). Truscott suggests that, in fact, attention may be a combination of "a number of separate pools of resources which can be allocated to tasks more or less independently (1998:

105), some of which are focal in nature and some global. Consequently, we can say that in order for any pedagogical intervention to be genuinely conducive to learning, it has to rely on both conscious and global attention. Finally, as will be shown in the section describing the ACT-R model, complex tasks actually benefit from an interaction between implicit and explicit learning modes. The fact that the gap between the experimental NNS and NS was leveled to a greater degree that the one between the native speakers and the NNS controls is a success which is unlikely to be the outcome of the deductive part of the treatment alone, especially as the effects proved to be lasting and, as demonstrated by Dienes and Berry (1997), it is the implicit – and not the explicit – knowledge that is known for its robustness and imperviousness to time.

The following sections show in what way the extensive study of the Anglophone film corpus could have led to the implicit grammar knowledge in the experimental group. First of all, however, implicit learning will be defined together with a presentation of the main implicit learning paradigms and relevant research results. It will also be discussed, on the basis of the ACT-R model, in what way the implicit knowledge might have contributed to the formation of the metaknowledge which emerged in the experimental group, as demonstrated by the qualitative analysis of the change (cf. Figure 2).

2. Implicit learning. The paradigms

When approaching certain tasks on a day-to-day basis, we very often respond according to certain pre-learned criteria: we have an algorithm specifying which steps need to be taken in a particular situation. When asked to give a rationale for our actions, we are usually able to describe the rules – social, institutional, scientific – that we have followed. However, at times, when acting in some rule-governed way we are unable to explicate these rules. This is because, according to Dienes and Berry (1997: 3), we "typically learn about the structure of a fairly complex stimulus environment, without necessarily intending to do so, and in such a way that the resulting knowledge is difficult to express. This is what we mean by implicit learning".

The criteria for implicitness, far from clear-cut, have been subject to debate for some time. The major question is whether, to be implicit, the knowledge has to be unconscious. Diennes and Berry (1997) claim that, the notion of consciousness being far from transparent itself, it might be better to consider implicitness in terms of inaccessibility of what the learner knows, which may be manifested by the lack of metaknowledge in the following representations

(Dienes and Perner 1996): content explicitness and attitude explicitness. These two will, respectively, be, using Reber's (1993) explication, knowing something and knowing that one knows it and is not just guessing. The latter dimension – the attitude implicitness – is, according to Diennes and Berry (1997), close to the below-the-subjective-threshold[3] criterion, which they see as a promising interpretation of implicitness. They claim that the implicit learning that takes place below the subjective threshold demonstrates the following characteristics:

➔ it is not subject to transfer of learning
➔ the learning focus is on particular items rather than underlying rules
➔ the resulting knowledge is durable, more intact than the explicit knowledge

Implicit learning research to date have been carried out within a number of experimental paradigms (see Diennes and Berry 1997 for a detailed overview), out of which three have seen the greatest interest: artificial grammar learning; sequence learning; and control of complex systems (also called complex problem solving [CPS] or complex dynamic control [CDC] tasks). In artificial grammar learning (AGL; Reber 1967) research, subjects are asked to memorize strings of letters generated by a finite-state grammar. They are later informed that there are certain word(=letter) order rules in this system and asked to classify new strings as grammatical or ungrammatical (complying or not with these rules). Sequence learning, in turn, can be subdivided into two experimental domains: one in which facilitated processing of sequences is studied; and one in which the next element in a sequence has to be predicted. The first subparadigm is represented, among others, by the study of Nissen and Bullemer (1987), in which lights appearing on the computer screen followed either the repeating sequence condition or the random condition. Nissen and Bullemer found out that reaction time decreased for the former while remaining stable for the latter condition. The sequence prediction task (Kushner *et al.* 1991) consisted of a successive presentation of 5 different stimuli. The participants were supposed to foresee the place where the sixth stimulus was going to be located. Finally, in the control of complex systems (Berry and Broadbent 1984), the subjects, by making certain decisions about input variables, are supposed to control output variables. An additional element is the constant feedback they receive on the output they generate. The best-known dynamic control task is the SUGARFACTORY experiment (Berry and Broadbent 1984). In the task, the testees are asked to play the role of the

[3] The terms 'objective threshold' and 'subjective threshold' were originally used in the subliminal perception literature (Cheesman and Merikle 1984). In a typical subliminal perception experiment, subjects are given a sequence of trials in which a stimulus is either presented or not. The subjective threshold is the point at which subjects do not know that they know that a stimulus was presented; the objective threshold is the point at which subjects do not know that a stimulus was presented. (Dienes and Berry 1997: 3).

manager in a small sugar producing factory. Their task is to reach and maintain a certain product output by manipulating the number of employees.

In their comparison of the three paradigms, Dienes and Berry (1997) notice that there indeed was learning in all of the experiments, as the participants' scores on subsequent tests were above chance. At the same time, the learning was definitely implicit as the testees were "able to choose the correct reaction while in a task, but [were] later unable to recall the key characteristics that controlled the behaviour (Broadbent 1991: 128)". In terms of thresholds, in all three types of experiments the resulting knowledge was below the subjective level: in the AGL tasks subjects concentrated on individual items within the letter strings rather than on rules motivating the accuracy of a given "word order" and their level of metaknowledge, as shown on a subsequent test, was low; in sequence learning tasks subjects were surprised when informed that there actually was some regularity behind the stimuli; in the SUGARFACTORY experiment, the testees, unable to specify how they exercised control over the system, claimed they were guessing. Furthermore, it is important to point out that the knowledge that resulted from the three types of experiments was far from flexible – it was not transferable to new tasks – and proved to be robust. In conclusion, as Dienes and Berry (1997: 18) put it, the studies "all provided evidence that subjects could learn to perform well in a task without being able to freely report what they had learned or why they had made the right decision".

If considered against the above-mentioned paradigms, the extensive study of the Anglophone film corpus seems to be the closest to the control of complex systems. These systems, as described by Quesada *et al.* (2004: 6; following Frensch and Funke 1995) are:

- ➔ dynamic, because early actions determine the environment in which subsequent decisions must be made, and features of the task environment may change independently of the solver's actions;
- ➔ time-dependent, because decisions must be made at the correct moment in relation to environmental demands;
- ➔ and complex, in the sense that most variables are not related to each other in a one-to-one manner.

Similarly, the *organic approach deductivised* pedagogic intervention presented in this article is:

- ➔ dynamic, as the dynamics of the students' grammatical choices were influenced by teacher feedback: the speculations the testees offered about why the speaker in the selected scene chose a particular tense/aspect were commented on in one-to-one e-mail exchanges between these testees and their tutors. This feedback, primarily aimed at adjusting the students' explicit knowledge, had the potential, as indicated by the

SUGARFACTORY experiment procedures as well as by Dale and Christiansen (2004), to influence implicit learning as well. It was possible in a way similar to the operation of an artificial neural network (NN), in which the learning – implicit, as carried out in an inaccessible layer called "hidden" – takes place as result of the adjustment of output values. In such a network (Bartkowski 2001), neurons are grouped into three main types of layers: input, the hidden, and output. The input layer receives input data from the external environment, and passes it to the hidden layer(s). The hidden layer neurons are where the information is processed and sent to the output layer, where the output is compared with the required output and the network error is computed. Typically, the information about the error flows backward through the network and the values of connection weights between the neurons are adjusted using the error term (=information how much the actual result differed from what had been expected). The process is repeated in the network for a number of times that is necessary to achieve the output closest to the desired (actual) one. Finally, the network output is presented to the user. Neuronal network *learning* is basically the process by which the system arrives at the values of connection weights between neurons. It is highly probable that a similar process, consisting of tiny gradual adjustments, may happen when human beings are acquiring their implicit knowledge of a complex phenomenon.

➔ time dependent, as the data processing takes place on-line, while watching a film, as well as immediately upon evoking a certain semantic frame necessary for the interpretation of grammar semantics of a given structure.

➔ complex in the sense that it requires simultaneous management of different facets of every tense/aspect related task: the focus is on grammar semantics, the context, possible default assignments of the speaker(s) in the analysed scenes, the effect their words have on the interlocutor(s) on the one hand, and a number of potentially relevant items within the studied frame on the other. If we assume that elements from the first group are salient and the "potentially relevant items" – rather opaque, we can say, following Berry and Broadbent (1987, 1988), that while the former have a chance to be learned explicitly (and they were, as demonstrated by the qualitative results of the study; see Figure 2), the latter are good candidates for implicit learning. The knowledge acquired in this way, like in every CPS task (Dienes and Fahey 1995), will be based on implicit memory for specific instances. Such instances, in the light of instance-based learning theories (Logan 1988, 1990; cited in Lebiere *et al.* 1998), differ from rule-based approaches in their understanding of skill formation: they see it as storage and deployment of particular episodes and instances rather than learning of abstract rules. Considering the fact that *organic approach deductivised* was a pedagogic treatment based on an extensive study of a corpus containing Anglophone films, it can be said that the accumulation of episode-based knowledge was far from difficult.

The question that arises at this point is: if we are to consider the role of implicit knowledge in the learning of grammar semantics, we have to examine the character of the interplay between this knowledge and the explicit store. In other words, in what way is the latter reinforced by the former?

The answer offered by Białystok's (1978) model, in which implicit knowledge leads to explicit knowledge through inferencing is only partly adequate. According to Dienes and Berry (1997), implicit learning is associated with observation and memorization and not with hypothesis testing. This is confirmed by the results of the experiments carried out in all three implicit learning paradigms. It is possible for the implicit knowledge to become explicit, but it is quite rare. As demonstrated, among others, by Reber's (1989) study, explicit knowledge was gained by 16.67% of the subjects, which is not a particularly impressive percentage. This, as suggested by Lebiere *et al.* (1998) can be best understood if we use the concept of a mental model (Johnson-Laird 1983). If a particular chunk of implicit knowledge is seen as such a mental model, the transition form it to a production rule is possible only if the mental model is sufficiently simple to enable such conversion. With *organic approach deductivised*, the models created in the extensive study of the film corpus were too complex and too opaque to be easily converted.

An alternative view, presented in Lebiere *et al.* (1998) is that implicit – or as they call it – subsymbolic knowledge does not lead directly to new conscious knowledge, but, instead, makes the existing symbolic knowledge more available. This hypothesis, as well as other ways in which implicit knowledge may interact with what is known explicitly will be discussed in the next section, in relation to the ACT-R model.

3. The Adaptive Control of Though model

ACT (Anderson 1987) and its later ACT-R version (Anderson 1993; Anderson *et al.* 1997) is "a general system modeling a wide range of higher level cognitive processes" (1997: 439). It is a model of human memory and an insight into learning. In the model, there are two types of knowledge: declarative, relating to things we are aware we know; and procedural, displayed by behaviours but unconscious. The latter is the implicit knowledge which is of interest to the present article. "Procedural knowledge," as Anderson *et al.* (1997: 441) put it, "specifies how to bring declarative knowledge to bear on solving problems". The operation of the ACT model is diagrammed in Figure 3.

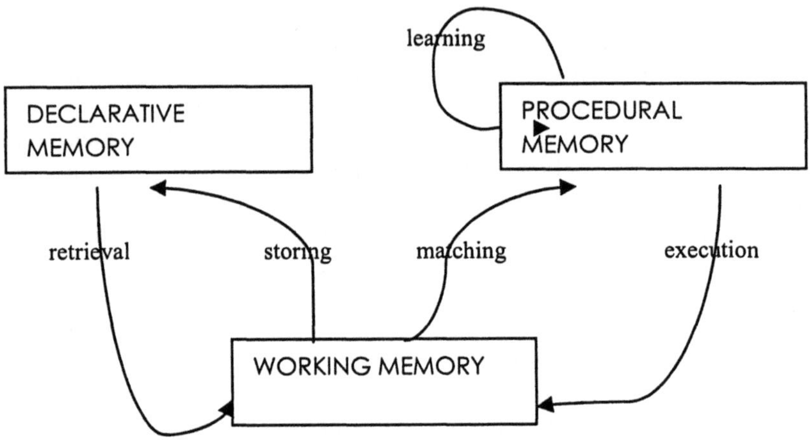

Fig. 3. The ACT model (Anderson 1987: 471)[4]

The arrows in the diagram show the information flow in the system. When a certain task enters the working memory, declarative knowledge chunks that are suitable for this particular problem solving are retrieved from the declarative memory. These chunks may include explicitly remembered knowledge as well as past procedures used in dealing with similar tasks. These declarative chunks are matched with the task requirement and, if they are suitable, the task is executed. During this execution learning takes place, procedure-execution chunks are adjusted and the new, improved/enriched pattern is stored in the declarative memory.

According to Lebiere *at al.* (1998), who investigated the possible application of ACT-R to complex problem solving adapting it for the SUGARFACTORY experiment, the model operates on two levels: symbolic and subsymbolic. While, at the symbolic level, the undertaken steps are discrete and algorithm-governed, the subsymbolic domain is characterized by continuity and randomness. The interaction of the two systems is necessary when more than one chunk is

[4] The figure presents the cognition layer alone as the perceptual layer is irrelevant to the present line of reasoning.

activated in the declarative retrieval. In such a case chunk selection is based on the strength of activation which is "the sum of a base-level activation and an associative activation" (Lebiere *et al.* 1998: 1). This associative activation is where the randomness occurs. It is possible that in the retrieval-matching phase there is an interplay of chunks of explicit knowledge recovered from the semantic subsystem of the declarative store and the instance chunks supplied by the episodic subsystem. Here again, the episode-based chunks may compete for priority in this matching process. Which one is selected is determined by a number of factors: how strongly they are activated; how often particular semantic and episodic chunks have appeared together; the family resemblance between the chunk and another chunk used with the already-activated declarative chunk; and last but not least, guessing, as, according to Klarreich (2001), the randomness and unpredictability are an integral part of human cognitive activity. This will happen especially if the semantic chunks contain information that is too general and the episodic chunks are too scarce or poorly entrenched.

Considering all this, and relating it to *organic approach deductivised* and its film corpus study, it can be said that the retrieval-matching phase is when the implicit knowledge in the form of instance chunks is used. Every task consisting of semantic interpretation of tense/aspect activates the explicitly learned primary semantic characteristics and all the remembered watched episodes that contain the studied structure. While the declarative knowledge chunks are matched to the task, the implicit knowledge instance chunks, with all their default assignments normally inaccessible for processing compete to endorse the declarative choice, as if paving the cognitive way for it. In this way, as declared by Lebiere *et al.* (1998), the subsymbolic knowledge makes the symbolic knowledge more available.

Summing up, it can be said that although the qualitative analysis of the results *organic approach deductivised* experiment indicates a considerable primacy of the declarative, explicit knowledge over the implicit, intuitive knowledge, the robustness of the effects of the treatment – as demonstrated by the result on a delayed post-test (table 3) – proves the presence and intervention of implicit knowledge.

REFERENCES

Anderson, J. R. (1993). *Rules of the Mind.* Hillsdale, NJ: Erlbaum.

Anderson, J. R., Matessa, M. and C. Lebiere (1997). „ACT-R: A theory of higher level cognition and its relation to visual attention". *Human Computer Interaction*, 12(4): 439–462.

Bartkowski, B. (2001). Sieci jednokierunkowe http://www.neuron.chost.pl/pliki/start.html

Berry, D. C. & D. E. Broadbent (1984). "On the relationship between task performance and associated verbalizable knowledge". *Quarterly Journal of Experimental Psychology*, 36: 209–231.

Berry, D. C. and D. E. Broadbent (1987). "The combination of explicit and implicit learning processes". *Quarterly Journal of Experimental Psychology*, 39: 585–609.

Berry, D. C. & D. E. Broadbent (1988). "Interactive tasks and the implicit-explicit distinction". *British Journal of Psychology*, 79: 251–272.

Berry, D. C. and Z. Dienes (1993). *Implicit learning: Theoretical and Empirical Issues.* Hove: Lawrence Erlbaum.

Bialystok, E. (1978). "A theoretical model of second language learning". *Language Learning* 28: 69–84.

Broadbent, D. E. (1991). "Recall, recognition, and implicit knowledge". In: W. Kessen, A. Ortony, & F. I. M. Craik (eds.). *Essays in Honour of George Mandler*. Hillsdale, NJ: Erlbaum: 125–134.

Cheesman, J. and P. M. Merikle (1984). "Priming with and without awareness". *Perception and Psychophysics*, 36: 387–395.

Dienes, Z. and D. Berry (1997). "Implicit learning: below the subjective threshold". *Psychonomic Bulletin and Review*, 4: 3–23.

Dale, R and M. H. Christiansen (2004). "Active and passive statistical learning: Exploring the role of feedback in artificial grammar learning and language". *Proceedings of the 26th Annual Conference of the Cognitive Science Society* Mahwah, NJ: Lawrence Erlbaum: 262–267 http://cnl.psych.cornell.edu/papers/DC-cogsci04.pdf

Dienes, Z. and R. Fahey (1995). "Role of specific instances in controlling a dynamic system". *Journal of Experimental Psychology: Learning, Memory, and Cognition*, 21(4): 848–862.

Dienes, Z. and J. Perner (1996). "Implicit knowledge in people and connectionist networks". In: G. Underwood (ed.). *Implicit Cognition.* Oxford University Press: 227–256.

Frensch, P. and J. Funke (1995). "Definitions, Traditions and a General Framework for Understanding Complex Problem Solving". In: P. A. Frensch and J. Funke (eds.). *Complex Problem Solving: The European Perspective*. Hillsdale, NJ: Lawrence Erlbaum: 3–25.

Johnson-Laird, P. N. (1983). *Mental Models: Towards a Cognitive Science of Language, Inference, and Consciousness*. Cambridge, MA: Harvard University Press.

Klarreich, E. (2001). Do minds play dice? Published online: 10 September 2001; doi:10.1038/news010913-7

Kushner, M., A. Cleeremans and A. Reber (1991). "Implicit detection of event interdependencies and a PDP model of the process". *Proceedings of the Thirteenth Annual Conference of the Cognitive Science Society*, Hillsdale, NJ: Erlbaum: 215–220

Langacker, R. W. (2000). *Grammar and Conceptualisation*. Berlin, New York: Mouton de Gruyter.

Lebiere, Ch., D. Wallach and N. Taatgen (1998). "Implicit and explicit learning in ACT-R". In: F. Ritter and R. Young (eds.). *Proceedings of the Second European Conference on Cognitive Modelling.* Nottingham, UK: Nottingham University Press.http://www.ai.rug.nl/~niels/publications/ECCM97.pdf

Leńko-Szymańska, A. (2004). Past Progressive or Simple Past? The acquisition of the progressive aspect by Polish advanced learners of English. Article presented at the 7th Congress of international Society of Applied Psycholinguistics. Cieszyn, Poland

Lewis, M. (1986). *The English Verb.* Hove: Language Teaching publications.

Logan, G. D. (1988). "Toward an instance theory of automatization". *Psychological Review*, 95: 492–528.

Logan, G. D. (1990). "Repetition priming and automaticity: Common underlying mechanisms?" *Cognitive Psychology*, 22: 1–35.

Mindt, D. (2000). *An Empirical Grammar of the English Verb System.* Berlin: Cornelsen

Nissen, M. J. and P.Bullemer (1987). "Attentional requirements of learning: evidence from performance measures". *Cognitive Psychology*, 19: 1–32.

Quesada, J., W. Kintsch and E. Gomez (2005). "Complex Problem Solving: A field in search for a definition?" *Theoretical Issues in Ergonomic Science*, 6 (1): 5–33.

Reber, A. S. (1967). "Implicit learning of artificial grammars". *Journal of Verbal Learning and Verbal Behaviour*, 6: 855–863.

Reber, A. S. (1989). "Implicit learning and tactic knowledge". *Journal of Experimental Psychology: General*, 118: 219–235.

Reber, A. S. (1993). *Implicit Learning and Tacit Knowledge: An Essay on the Cognitive Unconscious.* New York: Oxford University Press.

Steinhaus, H. (1960). *Mathematical Snapshots. New edition, revised and enlarged.* New York: Oxford University Press

Truscott, J. (1998). "Noticing in Second Language Acquisition: a Critical Review". *Second Language Research* 14, 2: 103–135

Turula, A. (2006 in press). "The Semantics of Grammar: organic approach deductivised. Some conclusions based on a grammar test analysis". Paper read at XVIIIth ICFSLA; Szczyrk, Poland

Turula, A. (2007a). „Rola pamięci epizodycznej w dydaktyce gramatyki języków obcych". In: S. Wróbel (red). *Iluzje pamięci.* Poznań–Kalisz: Wydawnictwo UAM: 257–272.

Turula, A. (2007b). "Focus on form and its meaning – Conceptual Integration Theory and its implications for teaching grammar to advanced FL learners". In: J. Arabski, D. Gabryś-Barker, A. Łyda (eds.). *PASE Papers 2007. Studies in Language and Methodology of Teaching Foreign Languages.* Vol. 1. Katowice: PARA: 351–366.

Turula, A. (2007c). „Studia nad semantyką czasu i aspektu jako forma pracy nad i-językiem na poziomie neofilologii". In: J. Majer i J. Nijakowska (eds.). *Język – poznanie – zachowanie: Studia nad psycholingwistycznymi aspektami przyswajania języka.* Łódz: Wydawnictwo Uniwersytetu Łódzkiego: 89–108.

Appendix 1

The proposed *organic approach deductivised* is a combination of three components:

- exposure to language forms in context
- the analysis of every form in question and the meaning it carries on the background of the context it belongs to and the primary semantic characteristics of the form as proposed by Lewis (1986) and Mindt (2004)
- hypothesising – on the bases of both the primary and the contextual meaning – the possible default assignments of the speaker who chooses a particular form to carry their intended meaning ; teacher feedback is offered at this stage

For example, if the tense used in a certain context is the *present simple*, the participants of the treatment will be given the primary semantic characteristics of this tense – "single, simple entities, unities, totalities" (Lewis 1986: 66) – and will try, during the exposure stage, to speculate what contextual meaning is arrived at as a result of using a tense with such primary semantics in a given situation. In addition to this, students would speculate what in the broadly understood context (the episode as seen as part of the whole film) particularly endorses such an interpretation.

The procedure

During the experiment, which started in October 2005 and finished in January 2006, the ATH (E) group underwent 8 *organic approach deductivised* sessions. Each session consisted of 3 parts:

- classwork – during which primary semantic characteristics of a given grammatical form were presented and discussed on the basis of selected film extracts;
- homework – when all students watched films of their choice and noticed form-meaning mappings (every participant watched a different film; the uniting factor was the form currently under inspection); the results of these individual studies of tense and aspect – in the form of the students' interpretations and speculations – where then subject to one-to-one e-mail exchanges between the contributors and the tutor during which teacher feedback was offered; at the end of this stage, a collection of all student contributions was compiled and e-mailed to every participant for further analysis;

- classwork – during which all students examined the form-meaning mappings from the above-mentioned collection with special attention to the mappings they considered "untypical" judging on the basis of their pedagogical grammar knowledge. After the presentation, the group considered selected form-meaning mappings and collaboratively deliberated why a certain grammatical form was used in the particular context.

Additionally, it is important to point out that during the experiment students wrote 4 tests, in which they had to decide which tense/aspect is best for a given context and they were asked to offer the rationale for their choices. The tests were graded.

As the treatment was planned as a classic experiment, the participants were pre-tested in October 2005, post-tested in January 2006 (upon the completion of the treatment) and wrote a delayed post-test in January 2007.

The study was replicated in the years 2006–2008.

Appendix 2

The test format

Both the pre- and the post-test were grammar tests based on extracts from British and American films. A sample question is presented below.

Pre/post-test; a sample episode

> *A woman who has long refused to marry the commodore is trying to win a favour with him. That is why she says:*
>
> 'Commodore, I [1] ______________(beg) you please, do this for me as a wedding gift.'
>
> *The woman's father, who's listening to the conversation and is very much in favour of the marriage, asks (hopefully)*
>
> 'Elisabeth, [2] __________________________ (accept) the commodore's proposal?

An extract, like the one quoted above was treated as one testing episode. The number of blanks in each episode was between 1 and 5 and each blank was treated as one test unit. The pre-test consisted of 26 such units; the post-test was a 23-unit test.

Irena Czwenar

University of Humanities and Natural Sciences, Piotrków Trybunalski

THE GROWTH OF GRAMMATICAL COMPLEXITY IN THE SPOKEN LANGUAGE OF ADULT LEARNERS OF ENGLISH

Abstract: The article reports on the results of a study of developmental aspects of grammatical complexity in L2 at the upper-intermediate and advanced levels. The aim of the study was to investigate the development of spoken English proficiency in terms of grammatical complexity, linguistic accuracy and fluency. The database for the study was collected over a period of three years by interviewing students of English philology in Poland. The analysis of the data was conducted by means of corpus tools. The paper examines the most salient features of spoken English, provides the details of the study and describes the quantitative and qualitative changes in the syntactic complexity of the students' interlanguage. The findings are given a cognitive linguistic interpretation.

Keywords: spoken English, grammatical complexity, longitudinal study, entrenchment, semantic complexity, iconicity.

1. Introduction

The cognitive view of language has changed our understanding of the role of grammatical structures. Like words and morphemes, syntactic structures function as symbolic assemblies of form and meaning. In other words, they are meaningful units of language rather than empty structural frames with slots to be filled in with lexical items. This view of syntax has important implications for our understanding of the processes involved in second language acquisition.

The study of second language acquisition is accompanied by growing interest in real-world linguistic data since the empiricist approaches to the study of language view such data as an invaluable source of information on which to build theoretical models of language and language development. Cognitive, empirically-driven usage-based linguistic models have been greatly aided by dynamic progress in computer technology. The development of language corpora has moved the study of natural languages forward and enhanced our knowledge of what language patterns *actually* occur in speech and writing and how they are used for communication.

This paper presents a small fraction of the findings of a longitudinal study of spoken English proficiency development in adult learners. The study combines an empiricist approach to data collection with corpus-based methods of analysis. The ultimate goal is to develop a cognitive interpretation of the linguistic phenomena documented in the study. The results of analyses illustrate a diversity of individual paths of development and the nature of quantitative and qualitative growth of the learners' inventories of grammatical patterns emerging as a result of learning.

2. Characteristics of the spoken language

Spontaneously produced speech has unique linguistic features which are determined by a number of social, psychological and physical factors underlying the realization of specific communicative goals and social functions (Biber *et al.* 1999: 1041). To begin with, spoken language is typically dynamic and interactive; discourse develops as a result of interaction between the speakers, and between the speakers and the context. Furthermore, speech is delivered via the oral/auditory channel, which means that it is produced by interlocutors talking face-to-face in a particular context. This inevitably affects the way in which speakers 'package' information and the language choices they make. Lastly, most speech is produced spontaneously, with no possibility of planning or rehearsing in advance. The real-time, 'online' processing makes it subject to the constraints of short-term memory.

The above properties have profound implications for the organisation and quality of the grammar and lexicon of the spoken language. In most general terms, the syntax of the spoken language tends to be fragmented and relatively simple; phrasal and clausal structures are less elaborated than those typical of the written genres. A similar lack of elaboration characterises the spoken vocabulary, which has a narrower range and is more repetitive than the vocabulary used in the written language. However, the inadequacy of the claim that the spoken language is disorganised, fragmentary and simple has long been recognised. In his discussion of the distinctive features of speech, Halliday (1989) observes that:

> The spoken language is [...] as highly organised as the written, and is capable of just as great a degree of complexity. Only, it is complex in a different way. (Halliday 1989: 86)

The spoken language has its own grammar and lexicon. Although most grammatical features found in speech are shared by the written language, there are significant differences between the two modes, in particular, in those areas which correspond to the goals and relationships among participants in specific contexts. As a matter of fact, there is no clear-cut boundary dividing the written and spoken language; both modes exist on a continuum (Carter & McCarthy 2006). This observation is substantiated by language corpus research, which has shown that the same set of descriptive linguistic categories can be effectively applied to both written and spoken language. Various grammatical and lexical features are represented in both modes, the main difference being the frequency with which a particular feature occurs in either mode.

What is traditionally recognised as the fundamental structural unit of grammar – *the sentence* – does not really exist in the spoken language because the 'building blocks' of speech cannot be defined as sentences in terms of the syntactic form or semantic content. Hence, depending on the type of approach adopted, it is possible to identify a great variety of structural units of the spoken language. In grammar-oriented approaches, the organisation of speech can be analysed in terms of *clausal* or *non-clausal units* (Biber *et al.* 1999: 1039). A clausal unit is an entity of a definable structure whose core element is the verb phrase. Non-clausal units are typically represented by single words or phrases which do not act as parts of neighbouring clauses and whose internal structure cannot be analysed in terms of clause constituents. Like full clauses, non-clausal units can express various speech functions, such as questions or commands, as well as a range of communicative functions.

The organisation of clauses on the discourse level is characterised by lower frequency of subordination and embedding than in the written mode. The most common pattern of clause combination in the spoken language is that of linking a number of clauses in a sequential way, with clauses being added one after another. This is obviously a result of real-time processing, when speakers have no time to work out complex patterns of the main and subordinate clauses. Thus, clause subordination is relatively rare in informal spoken English; the prevailing clause-linking device is coordination, with conjunctions such as *and*, *but*, *or*. There are examples of clause subordination by means of *because* and *so*, but these often act more like coordinating than subordinating conjunctions. Subordinate clauses often occupy complete speaker turns, in which case they do not appear to be overtly connected to any specific main clause. Very often, they refer to and complement the other speaker's turn. Clausal blends, i.e. syntactic structures which are completed differently from the way in which they were begun, are also typical in spoken English (cf. Carter & McCarthy 2006).

The use of syntax in spontaneous spoken interaction is thus characterised by reliance on economical and efficient means of expression as a result of real-time processing on the one hand, and availability of contextual clues on the other. Most clauses tend to be short and arranged in discourse in a linear fashion. Non-clausal units, which often result from ellipsis used in communicative contexts where certain meanings are understood without verbalisation, are also important structural characteristics of speech. The fact that it is natural even for native speakers to avoid syntactic elaboration inevitably poses the problem of having to decide how to evaluate spoken language complexity in the foreign language learning context. The study reported below is an example of how this problem was approached in the context of tertiary education in Poland.

3. Description of the study

This section reports the details of the empirical study undertaken by the author in order to examine the emergence of fluency, accuracy and complexity of the spoken language of upper-intermediate and advanced students of English. The study was conducted at the English Philology department at Piotrków College on nine students attending a three-year bachelor degree programme in English. Its ultimate aim was to develop a structured way of evaluating the development of oral proficiency in upper-intermediate and advanced students of English. Owing to the lack of a general index of foreign language acquisition (Ellis 1994) and to the complexity of language, it is impossible to capture the sense of progress by examining improvement in a single component of proficiency (Skehan & Foster 1997). Therefore, the specific aims of the study were to investigate the gains in oral fluency, accuracy and complexity of the spoken language production by the students.

The research design represents *a longitudinal group study*. The data were collected and recorded at periodic intervals over the time of three years. The instrument used for data collection was a structured interview conducted by the author on a one-to-one basis. The initial interview was conducted at the very beginning of the first academic year (referred to as *Year 0*); the remaining three followed each academic year. The open-ended questions which were used in the interview were predetermined. No time was allowed for the planning of utterances. The purpose of designing the research instrument in this way was to enforce on-line production of speech and obtain a substantial amount of 'natural-sounding' spoken English data.

The questions were grouped around three tasks, in which the interview format resembled the procedure formerly used in CFC[1] examinations. The tasks elicited transactional language in the form of long-turns. The same tasks were repeated on every application of the interview. The following tasks were used:

- Answering a sequence of questions about one's home town, family, interests and future plans.
- Comparing and contrasting two situations on the basis of a visual prompt, followed by personal reflections on the problem suggested by the visuals.
- The interviewee's opinion on the issue of successful language learning.

Each of the interviews was tape-recorded and transcribed for later analysis. The transcripts were saved in an electronic form, thus yielding a mini-corpus of learner language containing 24, 500 words. They were subsequently coded for fluency, accuracy and complexity.

4. Results and discussion

Grammatical complexity was described in terms of syntactic sophistication. Two measures were adopted to this end, namely, the amount of clause subordination and the degree of syntactic elaboration on the phrase level. A taxonomy of linguistic units was drawn up, adapted from the wide range of descriptive categories provided by Miller and Weinert (1998) and Biber *et al.* (1999). The relevant syntactic units were totaled separately for dependent (subordinate) clauses and phrases. The ultimate measures of clausal and phrasal complexity were arrived at by calculating the number of clauses and phrases per 100 words, respectively. As regards the treatment of units containing errors, if an error affected the verb phrase or word order in a clause, the clause was excluded from the count. Clauses were identified as types, rather than tokens. For each set of results, *the mean score (M)* was calculated to show the central tendency in the data and to illustrate the group's average on the given parameter in successive years. The present paper focuses on the results obtained for grammatical complexity on the clause level. The results are shown in Table 1 and Figure 1.

---

[1] Cambridge First Certificate: a proficiency examination administered by the University of Cambridge Local Examinations Syndicate.

Table 1. The degree of subordination measured as the number of dependent clauses (finite and non-finite) produced by each student per 100 words of discourse

Student	*Year 0*	*Year 1*	*Year 2*	*Year 3*
A	3,27	5,49	5,63	5,21
B	4,74	5,20	5,46	5,73
C	4,14	5,22	6,41	5,81
D	4,32	4,57	4,29	4,81
E	3,23	4,02	3,54	4,97
F	3,36	4,67	4,86	5,68
G	2,32	-	3,68	5,35
H	2,79	4,25	3,83	4,37
I	3,54	3,69	4,51	4,99
The mean	**3,52**	**4,64**	**4,69**	**5,21**
SD	**0,67**	**0,60**	**0,97**	**0,43**

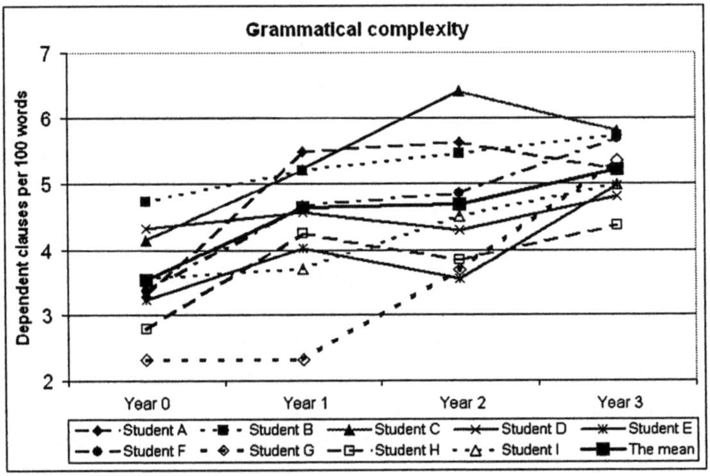

Fig. 1. Comparison of individual paths of grammatical complexity growth

As can be inferred from the ascending trend in the figures marking each point of measurement, all the students improved their performance in the use of clausal subordination, and most of the students improved consistently throughout the years. Even though in some cases there was a falling trend in the final year

(Students A and C), the end results were markedly better than at the initial stage. We can observe a gradual rise in the value of the mean score obtained in the consecutive years of the study. The standard deviation (SD) index reached its lowest value in Year 3, which indicates less variation in the grammatical complexity of performance by the group as a whole at the final stage of college instruction.

Quantitative data reveal highly generalised characteristics of the students' interlanguage. In order to obtain more detailed information about the students' use of subordination, qualitative analyses of the corpus were conducted. The graph below (Figure 2) shows the results of analyses of the types of finite dependent clauses used by *all* the students. For the sake of transparency, only the initial and final measurements have been taken into consideration.

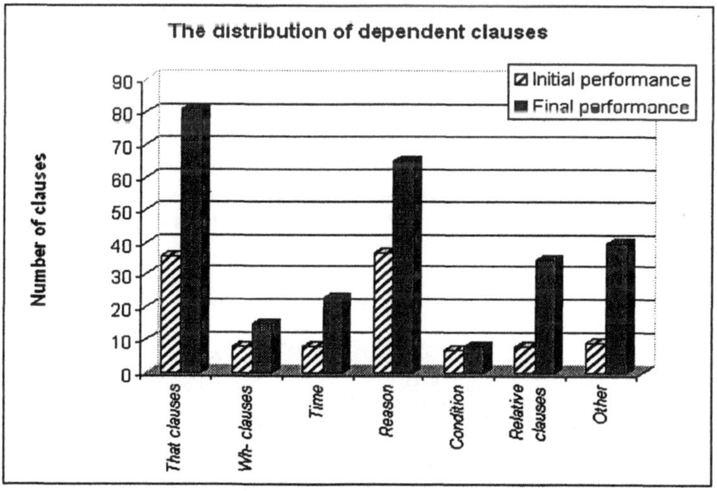

Fig. 2. The distribution of finite dependent clauses in the student corpus (in raw scores)

The raw scores calculated for the frequency of use of various types of dependent clauses indicate a clear predominance of complement *that* clauses and adverbial clauses of reason over the remaining clause types. The same results, converted into percentages, are shown as pie-charts in Figure 3.

The scores as percentages do not show substantial differences in the distribution of the different types of dependent clauses in the student output produced during the first and the last interview (initial and final performance, respectively). What is more, they confirm an overwhelmingly high frequency of complement *that* clauses and clauses of reason in the corpus, previously illustrated by the raw scores. The comparison of the two types of scores strongly suggests a *quantitative* change in the grammatical complexity of the students' production, but not necessarily a *qualitative* change.

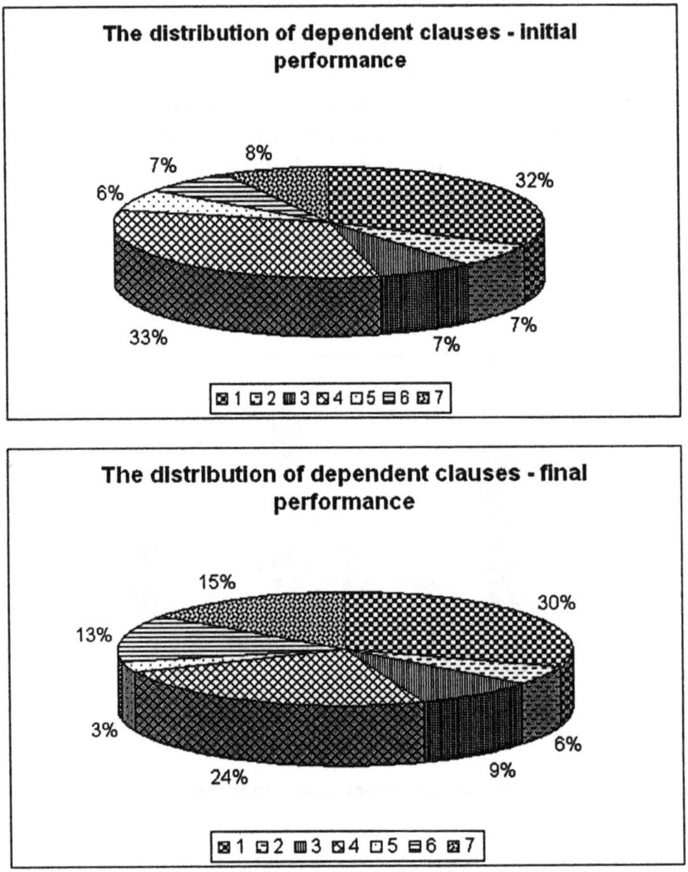

Fig. 3. Dependent clauses in the learner corpus. The key to sections of the graphs:
1 – complement *that* clauses; 2 – complement *wh-* clauses; 3 – adverbial clauses of time; 4 – adverbial clauses of reason; 5 – adverbial clauses of condition; 6 – relative clauses; 7 – other

Focusing on the most frequently represented types of clauses, we get insight into the lexico-grammatical patterns which the students tend to use, or perhaps overuse. The samples below come from the sub-corpus based on the final interviews and illustrate the types of clause patterns used in complement *that*-clauses (the samples have been coded for pauses and errors[2]):

1) [subject] + [verb phrase (intransitive)] + [optional adverbial]
a. I **think** now she is going to get married
b. I just **noticed that** (.) it just EG *improved*
c. I **assume that** er (1.6) er (.) they are parting for some time

(2) [subject] + [verb phrase (intransitive)] + [obligatory adverbial]
a. **I'm er pleased that** I've lived here

(3) [subject] + [verb phrase] + [subject predicative]
a. I **think that** it was the most beautiful period of my life
b. I **feel that's** (.) that's the point

(4) [subject] + [verb phrase] + [direct object] + [optional adverbial]
a. I must **say that** during these years I: (.) er (.) I was having fun all the time
b. I **know that** soon I will have to leave it
c. **it's true that** we should er (.) we should: (.) have materials

(5) [there] + [be] + [indefinite noun phrase] + [time or place adverbial]
a. from my experience **I will say** (.) **that** (.) there is a problem of: being er (1.0) self (2.5) of being responsible for all the duties

Discourse functions which complement *that*-clauses serve in the above samples include reporting thoughts, feelings and observations. The frequency with which the students use the verb *think* is not surprising, since this is by far the most common verb controlling *that* clauses in spoken and written registers (cf. Biber 1999: 668). What is surprising, however, is the limited range of other *mental* verbs (expressing the speaker's stance) found in the corpus, despite the fact that many of the questions asked in the interview invited the interviewee's personal reflections on the given subject. A similar limitation in the use of lexico-grammatical patterns characterises the remaining types of clauses.

It is worth emphasising at this point that the notion of complexity as applied in this study is intended to reflect the standards defined for spoken English. The specificity of spoken English syntax – by contrast to the written modality – lies

---

[2] The following symbols are used in the samples: (.) – a pause of less than a second; (1.6) – a pause of exactly 1.6 seconds; EG – a grammatical error.

in the absence of clear-cut boundaries for sentences. Since sentence boundaries are difficult, if not impossible, to delineate, it seems reasonable to describe grammatical complexity in terms of the degree of clause subordination and embedding. We might thus assume that the higher the index of subordination in a text, the more complex the language it contains.

Viewed in this way, the spoken texts produced by the student participants in the study are indicative of language improvement. However, the inevitable question to ask is whether the observed markers of complexity actually account for success in language learning perceived in terms of approximation to the native speaker's norm.

Spoken English, as used by its native speakers, relies to a great extent on stereotyped, prefabricated lexico-grammatical chunks. Such multi-word sequences, often idiomatic, are remembered and produced as unanalysed wholes. Efficient storage and production contribute to greater fluency and naturalness of the user's language (cf. Pawley and Syder 1983). Near-nativeness – presumably the ultimate goal of the students participating in the study – can only be achieved if such expressions become part of the language learner's productive repertoire.

On closer examination of the learner corpus in question, we find a striking absence of fixed lexico-grammatical patterns, be it phrasal verbs, collocations, or idiomatic phrases. The implication of this finding is that the students have not yet achieved that kind of complexity, which is accounted for by *the idiom principle* (cf. Sinclair 1991), and which communicates meanings that are both structurally concise and semantically complex. It seems that the steady growth of grammatical complexity characterising the students' interlanguage is counterbalanced by their inability to use native-like, stereotyped lexico-grammatical patterns.

5. Cognitive linguistic implications

The corpus of data collected for the purpose of the study offers further possibilities of multi-strand analyses. The ultimate goal is to relate the above findings to the cognitive models of foreign language acquisition. The data, of which a small sample has been presented above, are corpus-based, and, as such, constitute a point of departure for cognitive analyses of the emergence of a complex language system.

It seems that the data obtained in the study allow to formulate some generalizations concerning interlanguage development with reference to *entrenchment*, one of the fundamental concepts of usage-based approaches to grammar and language acquisition. The degree of entrenchment of a particular linguistic unit defines its status in a given language. Morphological and syntactic units become entrenched as a result of frequency of use. Token frequency results in the entrenchment of instances, while type frequency leads to the entrenchment of more general schemas (Croft 2004). Since the main factor here is the frequency of use, those units which are highly entrenched comprise the core repertoire of conventionalized expressions in a language.

The cognitive interpretation of the above data allows to characterize the interlanguage systems of the subjects in terms of their familiarity with the linguistic convention. The subjects show preference for using those patterns of English which represent highly conventionalized abstract schemas, which is to say that they are more familiar with the patterns that are highly entrenched in the system of English. Consequently, those patterns of English which are likely to be less entrenched or entrenched as instances are rarely used.

When interpreted in cognitive terms, a syntactic unit – a clause or a phrase – constitutes a symbolic pairing of form and meaning (Langacker 1987, 1991). The meaning of a clause as a whole is conveyed not only by the meanings of its lexical components, but also by the type and arrangement of its syntactic constituents. This implies that a wide and varied repertoire of syntactic units available to the speaker allows him/her to express a correspondingly wider range of meanings. This view of the role of syntax has important consequences for second language learners. If interlanguage development consists in achieving higher levels of communicative efficiency, then the growth of syntactic complexity in terms of a number of patterns the learner is able to produce is inextricably linked with it.

This interpretation of progress in language acquisition applies to the notion of grammatical complexity growth both along the quantitative and qualitative dimensions. In accordance with a cognitive linguistic principle of *iconicity*, a form which is formally complex is conceptually complex as well. Various syntactic schemas used in language production show the varying perspectives which the learners use to view and construe scenes / situations. The reason why the growth of syntactic complexity can be viewed as an important index of progress in foreign language acquisition is that it parallels semantic complexity and, consequently, enables the language user to communicate meanings in ways which are more complex, more precise and which mirror the wealth of his/her experience more adequately.

The relatively low degree of internal clause complexity combined with the subjects' preference for high-frequency linguistic items suggests that the students participating in the study have not fully succeeded in achieving the levels of competence which characterize proficient users of English. It is possible that other foreign language learners in similar educational contexts experience the same problems. Our role as language teaching experts is to help them to succeed by pointing the right direction. The history of foreign language teaching provides examples of approaches which emphasized either the linguistic form (e.g. the Audio-Lingual method) or the linguistic meaning (e.g. the Communicative Language Teaching approach), but rarely integrated the focus on meaning with the focus on form. It is argued that when such integration is achieved, it will allow foreign language learners to gain awareness of the interdependence of the semantic and syntactic layers of language, and, consequently, enable them to achieve high levels of proficiency in the foreign language.

REFERENCES

Biber, J., Johansson, S. and Leech, G. (1999). *Longman Grammar of Spoken and Written English.* Harlow: Longman.

Carter, R. and McCarthy, M. (2006). *Cambridge Grammar of English: a Comprehensive Guide. Spoken and Written English. Grammar and Usage.* Cambridge: Cambridge University Press.

Croft, W. and Cruse, A. P. (2004). *Cognitive Linguistics.* Cambridge: Cambridge University Press.

Ellis, R. (1994). *The Study of Second Language Acquisition.* Oxford: Oxford University Press.

Halliday, M. A. K. (1989). *Spoken and Written Language.* Oxford: Oxford University Press.

Langacker, R. W. (1987). *Foundations of Cognitive Grammar.* Vol. 1. *Theoretical Prerequisites.* Stanford, Ca.: Stanford University Press.

Langacker, R. W. (1991). *Foundations of Cognitive Grammar.* Vol. 2. *Descriptive Application.* Stanford, Ca.: Stanford University Press.

Miller, J. and Weinert, R. (1998). *Spontaneous Spoken Language. Syntax and Discourse.* Oxford: Clarendon Press.

Pawley, A. and Syder, F. H. (1983). "Two puzzles for linguistic theory: nativelike selection and nativelike fluency". In: Richards, J. R. and Schmidt, R. W. (eds.). *Language and Communication.* London: Longman: 191–225.

Sinclair, J. (1991). *Corpus, Concordance, Collocation.* Oxford: Oxford University Press.

Skehan, P. and Foster, P. (1997). "Task type and task processing conditions as influences on foreign language performance". *Language Teaching Research*, 1 (3): 185–211.

INDEX OF TERMS

ŁÓDŹ
Studies in Language

Edited by
Barbara Lewandowska-Tomaszczyk

Vol. 1 Barbara Lewandowska-Tomaszczyk / Patrick James Melia (eds.): PALC'99: Practical Applications in Language Corpora. Papers from the International Conference at the Universtiy of Łódź, 15-18 April 1999. 2000.

Vol. 2 Lou Burnard / Tony McEnery (eds.): Rethinking Language Pedagogy from a Corpus Perspective. Papers from the third international conference on Teaching and Language Corpora. 2000.

Vol. 3 Barbara Lewandowska-Tomaszczyk / John Osborne / Frits Schulte: Foreign Language Teaching and Information and Communication Technology. 2001.

Vol. 4 Piotr Cap: Explorations in Political Discourse. Methodological and Critical Perspectives. 2002.

Vol. 5 Ewa Waniek-Klimczak / Patrick James Melia (eds.): Accents and Speech in Teaching English Phonetics and Phonology. EFL perspective. 2002.

Vol. 6 Barbara Lewandowska-Tomaszczyk / Kamila Turewicz (eds.): Cognitive Linguistics Today. 2002.

Vol. 7 Barbara Lewandowska-Tomaszczyk (ed.): PALC 2001: Practical Applications in Language Corpora. 2003.

Vol. 8 Corpus Linguistics by the Lune. A Festschrift for Geoffrey Leech. Edited by Andrew Wilson, Paul Rayson and Tony McEnery. 2003.

Vol. 9 Barbara Lewandowska-Tomaszczyk (ed.): Practical Applications in Language and Computers. PALC 2003. 2004.

Vol. 10 Imagery in Language. Festschrift in Honour of Professor Ronald W. Langacker. Edited by Barbara Lewandowska-Tomaszczyk and Alina Kwiatkowska. 2004.

Vol. 11 Seana Coulson / Barbara Lewandowska-Tomaszczyk (eds.): The Literal and Nonliteral in Language and Thought. 2005.

Vol. 12 Piotr Cap (ed.): Pragmatics Today. 2005.

Vol. 13 Jacek Waliński / Krzysztof Kredens / Stanisław Goźdź-Roszkowski (eds.): Corpora and ICT in Language Studies. PALC 2005. 2007.

Vol 14 Krzysztof Kosecki (ed.): Perspectives on Metonymy. Proceedings of the International Conference "Perspectives on Metonymy", held in Łódź, Poland, May 6–7, 2005. 2007.

Vol. 15 Barbara Lewandowska-Tomaszczyk / Tomasz Płudowski / Dolores Valencia Tanno (eds.): The Media and International Communication. 2007.

Vol. 16 Krzysztof Kredens / Stanisław Goźdź-Roszkowski (eds.): Language and the Law: International Outlooks. 2007.

Vol. 17 Barbara Lewandowska-Tomaszczyk (ed.): Corpus Linguistics, Computer Tools, and Applications – State of the Art. PALC 2007. 2008.

Vol. 18 Barbara Lewandowska-Tomaszczyk / Katarzyna Dziwirek (eds.): Studies in Cognitive Corpus Linguistics. 2009.

www.peterlang.de